The POWER of SCALE

Kevin Reilly, Series Editor

THE ALCHEMY OF HAPPINESS
Abu Hamid Muhammad al-Ghazzali
Translated by Claud Field, revised and
annotated by Elton L. Daniel

NATIVE AMERICANS BEFORE 1492
*The Moundbuilding Centers of the
Eastern Woodlands*
Lynda Norene Shaffer

GERMS, SEEDS, AND ANIMALS
Studies in Ecological History
Alfred W. Crosby

BALKAN WORLDS
The First and Last Europe
Traian Stoianovich

AN ATLAS AND SURVEY OF SOUTH ASIAN HISTORY
Karl J. Schmidt

THE GOGO
History, Customs, and Traditions
Mathias E. Mnyampala
Translated, introduced, and edited by
Gregory H. Maddox

WOMEN IN WORLD HISTORY:
Volume 1—Readings from Prehistory to 1500
Volume 2—Readings from 1500 to the Present
Edited by Sarah Shaver Hughes and Brady Hughes

MARITIME SOUTHEAST ASIA TO 1500
Lynda Norene Shaffer

THE COURSE OF HUMAN HISTORY
Economic Growth, Social Process, and Civilization
Johan Goudsblom, Eric Jones, and Stephen Mennell

ON WORLD HISTORY
An Anthology
Johann Gottfried Herder
Translated by Ernest A. Menze with
Michael Palma
Edited by Hans Adler and Ernest A. Menze

TEACHING WORLD HISTORY
A Resource Book
Edited by Heidi Roupp

THE WORLD AND A VERY SMALL PLACE IN AFRICA
Donald R. Wright

DOUBLE GHOSTS
Oceanian Voyages on Euroamerican Ships
David A. Chappell

SHAPING WORLD HISTORY
Breakthroughs in Ecology, Technology, Science, and Politics
Mary Kilbourne Matossian

TRADITION AND DIVERSITY
Christianity in a World Context to 1500
Karen Louise Jolly

LIFELINES FROM OUR PAST
A New World History
Revised Edition
L.S. Stavrianos

THE FACE OF THE EARTH
Environment and World History
Edited by J. Donald Hughes

THE WORLD THAT TRADE CREATED
Society, Culture, and the World Economy, 1400 to the Present
Kenneth Pomeranz and Steven Topik

COLONIALISM AND THE MODERN WORLD
Selected Studies
Edited by Gregory Blue, Martin Bunton, and Ralph Croizier

THE POWER OF SCALE
A Global History Approach
John H. Bodley

The POWER of SCALE

A Global History Approach

John H. Bodley

M.E. Sharpe
Armonk, New York
London, England

Copyright © 2003 by M. E. Sharpe, Inc.

All rights reserved. No part of this book may be reproduced in any form
without written permission from the publisher, M. E. Sharpe, Inc.,
80 Business Park Drive, Armonk, New York 10504.

Library of Congress Cataloging-in-Publication Data

Bodley, John H.
    The power of scale : a global history approach / John H. Bodley.
      p. cm. — (Sources and studies in world history)
    Includes bibliographical references and index.
    ISBN 0-7656-0984-3 (hc : alk. paper) ISBN 0-7656-0985-1 (pbk : alk. paper)
     1. World History. 2. History, Modern. 3. Civilization, Modern. 4. Imperialism—
History. 5. Capitalism—History. 6. Geopolitics—History. I. Title. II. Series.

D208.B58 2003
909—dc21

                                                                     2002066806

Printed in the United States of America

The paper used in this publication meets the minimum requirements of
American National Standard for Information Sciences
Permanence of Paper for Printed Library Materials,
ANSI Z 39.48-1984.

BM (c)   10   9   8   7   6   5   4   3   2   1
BM (p)   10   9   8   7   6   5   4   3   2

Contents

List of Tables and Figures	ix
Foreword by Kevin Reilly	xi
Preface	xv
Acknowledgments	xvii

1. Introduction: Imperia and the Power of Scale	3
Imperia, Social Power, and Scale	4
Three Cultural Worlds: Tribal, Imperial, and Commercial	6
Great Cultural Transformations	8
Quality of Life in the Tribal World	13
The Irreducible Minimum in the Tribal World	15
Political Imperia and Conditional Rights in the Imperial World	18
The Commercial World and Capitalism	22
2. Imperia in Three Worlds	28
Domestic Imperia in the Amazon Rain Forest: The Ashaninka	28
Circles of Kings: Political Imperia in Southeast Asian Kingdoms	33
The Thai Kingdom, 1782–1932	37
Modern Thai and Balinese Imperia	44
Commercial Imperia: The United States, 1998	45
3. Why Scale Matters	54
Power Laws, Energy, and the Disproportions of Scale	55
The Illusion of Evolutionary Progress	61

Culture, Biology, and the Problem of Size	64
Human Community, Society, and Scale	66
Scale Limits in the Tribal World: Australian Bands	67
Scale Limits to Power in the Tribal World: The Ashaninka	70
The Power of Scale in the Urbanization Process	71
Bureaucracy and Domination	74
Scale, Imperia, and Growth Trajectories	76
4. The Political Elite Take Power	**79**
Crossing the Great Divide from Tribal to Imperial Worlds	81
Village Headman to Divine King in Southeast Asia	84
Beyond 500: Scalar Stress and Urban Growth	87
Elite Payoff: Mates, Servants, and Palaces	91
Strategies of Domination in the Ancient Imperial World	96
The Romans: Conquerors and Slaves in a Legionary Economy	101
5. The Rise of European Commercial Elites	**104**
Urban Growth and the Origins of Capitalism, 1100–1600	105
Medieval City-States and the Medici Imperium	108
Crisis as Opportunity: England, 1500–1688	110
Landed and Monied Interests in the London Financial Revolution, 1600–1900	115
British Colonialism: Merchant Capitalists Transform the World	117
The Business of Government in the Fiscal-Military State	123
Capitalist Manufacturers: Canals, Pots, Guns, and Lobbies	125
The Power of Scale in Britain, A.D. 1066–2000	127
A Tale of Three Families: Grosvenors, Rothschilds, and Bonapartes	131
Commercial Elites in Control: Summary and Assessment	135
6. The Power Elite in Action: America's Commercial Revolution, 1787–1945	**137**
Founding Fathers and the Constitution	138
The Rise of Big Business	143
Urban Elites and American Inequality: Boston, New York, and Philadelphia	148
J.J. Astor, Real Estate, and the Fur Empire	150
The Rail Empires, 1840–1870	152
American Financial Imperia	155
Rockefeller Imperium and the Fossil Fuel Revolution	157
Factory Farms and the American Food System	158

The Triumph of Cars over Rails	160
The Millionaire Imperia: Super-Elite Lifestyles	164

7. Counter-Imperia: Imagining Alternative Worlds — 170

Tribals Against the State	171
Plato's Republic and Medieval Utopias	174
The English Revolution: Regicides, Levelers, and Luddites	178
Thomas Paine and the Rights of Man	182
Anarchists, Owenites, and Fourerists	185
Did Early Industrial Growth Benefit the English Poor?	188
Marxists and Totalitarianists	192
American Populists and Progressives Challenge Big Business	194

8. Utopian Capitalists: Constructing and Reconstructing the World Order, 1945–2000 — 199

Constructing Progressivist Global Institutions: The UN, IMF, and World Bank	201
Prospects for America: The Rockefeller Panel Reports	204
Ending Poverty Through Globalization	208
Feeding the Commercial World	218
The Triumph of Neoliberal Economic Theory: Wealth = Growth = Wealth	221
Elite Power in the Global Market Society	229
Wriston, Citicorp, and the Globalization of Finance Capital	232

9. Beyond 2000: An Optimal-Scale Commercial World — 235

Scale Thresholds and the Good Life	236
Small Scale in Colonial New England	241
The Growth-Maximizing Nation: How America Overshot the Optimum	242
Imperia and the Scale of Business: When Is Big Too Big?	244
Market Scale and Social Power in American Urban Places	252
The Indigenous People Challenge	258
Conclusion	262

References	263
Index	283

List of Tables and Figures

Tables

1.1 Cultural Worlds, Scale, and Cultural Process	11
2.1 Thai Households by Class, Rank, Title, and Imperia, During the Chakri Dynasty, 1782–1932	42
2.2 American Imperia, 1998	48
4.1 Major Settlement Size Increases (hectares)	91
4.2 Roman Imperia by Wealth, Income, and Social Class, A.D.100	94
4.3 Norman England Imperia by Wealth, Income, and Social Class, A.D.1086	98
5.1 Florentine Imperia by Tax Rate, Wealth, and Income, A.D.1457	114
5.2 Stuart England Imperia by Income and Social Class, A.D.1688	128
5.3 Georgian Great Britain and Ireland, Imperia by Income and Social Class, 1812	129
6.1 U.S. Property Wealth Distribution by Households, 1850	149
8.1 Distribution of Global Income and Wealth by Household Imperia, 1999	218
9.1 Social Scale and the *Summum Bonum*	237

Figures

1.1 Great Cultural Transformations	10
1.2 Global Population Scale by Cultural World	12
3.1 Social System Scale Thresholds	56

3.2 American Taxpayers by Size of Income, 1995	59
3.3 American Business Corporations by Size of Revenue, 1994	60
3.4 The Distribution of Urban Places by Size of Market Area, Germany, 1930	72
4.1 The Scale of Residential Space in the Imperial World	97
5.1 The Medici Imperia: Locations of Offices of the Medici Bank, 1451	112
5.2 The Medici Imperia: Organizational Structure of the Medici Bank, 1451	113
5.3 Agents in Richard Oswald's Personal Imperia, 1735–1785	121
8.1 Distribution of Global Household Imperia Rankings, 1965 and 1999, in Constant 1995 Dollars	213
8.2 Average Income of Global Households by Imperia Rankings, 1965 and 1999	215
8.3 Percentage Distribution of Global Income by Imperia Rankings, 1965 and 1999	217
8.4 Percentage Distribution of U.S. Income by Imperia Rankings, 1929–1998	227
9.1 Outcomes of American Growth Options, 1790–1990	243
9.2 Correlates of Market Power in Sample American Business Centers, 2000	254
9.3 Median Income and Market Power in Principle American Business Centers, 2000	255
9.4 Market Power and Net Worth of the Wealthiest Person in Principle Market Centers, 2000	256

Foreword

More than a hundred years ago, the emerging discipline of anthropology charted a broad and well marked road toward an understanding of world history. From the mid-nineteenth to mid-twentieth century, the leading founders of anthropology offered interpretations of the global past that contrasted the "primitive," pre-literate, tribal, or "traditional" society with "the modern" in highly suggestive polar categories. Among the more memorable were Ferdinand Tonnies' "community" and "society," Sir Henry Maine's "status" and "contract," Emile Durkheim's "mechanical" and "organic solidarity," and Robert Redfields' "folk" and "urban" societies. Even more famously, Edmund B. Tylor and Lewis Henry Morgan, the preeminent founders of anthropology, posited a three-stage evolutionary development from "savagery" to "barbarism" to "civilization" that influenced the historical writing of Karl Marx, Max Weber, and generations of social scientists.

Over the last fifty years, the simplifications and European biases of grand evolutionary anthropology have been unmasked. New generations of ethnographers and historians have revealed histories of more than half the world's people that can no longer be subsumed under neat categories of "traditional" and "modern," much less "savage" and "barbarian." The academic study of world history emerged in this period as a departure from, and correction of, these stage theories of human development. Instead of a broad highway that climbed majestically to the high plain of Western Civilization, world historians, along with most other specialists in history and anthropology, described the myriad paths, byways, detours, and meandering alternatives. But the idea of stages of development did not completely disappear from the literature. Many archaeologists still organized pre-history in terms of the progressive series: band, tribe, chiefdom, kingdom, state. The world historian, Leften Stavrianos, contributed a volume to this series, *Lifelines from the Past*, organized in terms of kinship, tributary, and capitalist stages. Nevertheless, few current models of world history take their inspiration or methodology from evolutionary anthropology.

John Bodley shows why this is unfortunate. In this volume, he revives the best aspects of evolutionary anthropology's road to world history. Like his illustrious predecessors in this tradition, he demonstrates how the idea of distinct stages of history gives coherence and narrative power–a driving sense of direction and meaning—to world history. He takes us firmly in hand through three distinct forms of human society, choosing to represent each type with well chosen case studies he knows intimately. The advantage of this approach is that the reader is immersed in particular worlds on the way to understanding the human journey. Our first stop is with the Ashaninka people of the Peruvian Amazon, with whom Bodley has frequently stayed. They represent the "tribal" society that precedes the "imperial" world, represented by the nineteenth-century Thai kingdom, followed by modern "commercial" society, represented by the United States. Unlike earlier anthropologists, Bodley does not suggest that this is a moral progression from tribe to civilization. In fact, Bodley argues, the history of human well-being has been largely frustrated since the tribal stage. The belief that historical evolution has been more regressive than progressive is, of course, not new to Bodley, but he presents this idea with an unusual array of mathematical modeling and theoretical support.

Like many of the earlier generation of historical anthropologists, Bodley offers something that most historians despair of ever providing: a theory of change. He argues that the actual process of growth–physical, demographic, and economic–plays a major role in determining the quality of life. As societies have grown from the optimum sizes of most indigenous tribal communities, where all of about 500 members could be known personally, they have become increasingly stratified, unequal, and subject to the rule of power elites. In early state societies (medieval England or nineteenth-century Siam), royalty and nobility had inordinate power over subjects, but they were restrained by feudal politics and constrained by a limited scale of transportation and communication networks. With the rise of commercial empires (notably, the United States), populations increased from the scale of hundreds of thousands or millions to hundreds of millions and billions. The "power of scale" increased the gap between the powerful and the weak with each increase in size. In the last half of the book, Bodley details the growth of power elites in the United States. In some of the most interesting sections he shows how particular individuals have continually managed to turn public resources into personal and family wealth. He tells even familiar stories, like the conversion of efficient public transportation facilities into the world of the private automobile, the influence of the Rockefeller family, and the systematic scuttling of the welfare state, with fresh detail and compelling effect.

This is a remarkably thought-provoking volume. Whether or not the reader ultimately finds Bodley persuasive, *The Power of Scale* offers a vastly expanded sense of the possibilities inherent in studying world history. It should broaden the field as it deepens our understanding.

Kevin Reilly
Series Editor

Preface

This book demonstrates that throughout world history particular individuals, driven by the natural human desire to accumulate social power, have promoted growth, or scale increases, that amplified many human problems by socializing the costs of development and disproportionately concentrating the benefits. The implication of this perspective is that many of the most serious global problems such as war, environmental deterioration, poverty, and human rights abuses are really problems of scale and power. They are not inevitable, but they will be further amplified if strictly technological solutions that promote further growth in scale are unilaterally pursued. The power and scale approach to global history and global problems draws on history, cultural anthropology, archaeology, sociology, economics, and biocultural evolutionary theory. This book can serve as a thought-provoking supplemental text for college-level world civilization courses that take a critical, theoretical perspective. It will also appeal to a broad readership interested in contemporary public policy issues, human rights, and history, as well as disciplinary generalists in the social sciences. It seeks to bridge the impasse between social science theorists who favor interpretive, symbolic, or postmodern perspectives, and those who favor materialist, political-economic, or practice approaches. Power and scale theory introduces the *imperium*, a household-based personal power network, as a primary unit of analysis, and sees power-seeking individuals as the agents of cultural development. It treats ideology, social institutions, personal networks, energy, materials, and technologies all as tools that individuals use for their own purposes. This book is an ambitious project, but it builds on a few very simple ideas and samples a very rich, cross-cultural database to make a few strong arguments about very important human issues.

The present work builds directly on my previous books on indigenous peoples and development issues (Bodley 1988, 1999a), on general cultural anthropology (2000), and on anthropology and contemporary global problems (2001a), and my other recent articles on scale (1994, 1995, 1999b, 2001b). All of these works develop a consistent theoretical perspective on scale and power in relation to development issues beginning with my initial research with the Ashaninka in the Peruvian Amazon in 1966–69. I approach world history as an anthropologist, but I agree with pioneer American anthropologist Alfred Kroeber (1915), who in his famous "Eighteen Professions" proclaimed that anthropology is history.

Acknowledgments

My most recent research that led to this book was supported by a sabbatical leave from Washington State University during the 1998–99 academic year, and by two research grants from the Edward R. Meyer Fund at Washington State University in 1996–97 and 1998–99. Since 2001 my research and writing has also been supported by funds generously provided through an Edward R. Meyer Distinguished Professorship in Anthropology. My interest in teaching and writing on world history and world civilizations was stimulated by my participation in the early planning for Washington State University's world civilization component of the general education core curriculum, directed by Richard Law. I would also like to thank my former professors at the University of Oregon, whose ideas continue to influence my thinking, but especially anthropologists David Aberle and Joseph Jorgenson. I also benefited greatly from the encouragement of Gerald Berreman at University of California, Berkeley, and Helge Kleivan, former director of the International Work Group for Indigenous Affairs in Copenhagen. Robert Gordon invited me to teach a summer course at the University of Vermont in 2000, allowing me to test out many of my theories of scale and power in a small state. Many others offered critical reviews of earlier works related to the present book, or they provided materials, or simply listened to my ideas; they include: Richard N. Adams, Jim Bodley, Tom Bodley, Elizabeth DeMarrais, Robert Dirks, Richard G. Fox, Patrick Green, Chris Harris, Chaia Heller, Barry Hewlett, Barry Hicks, David Hyndman, Ken Kardong, Tim Kohler, Bill Lipe, James H. McDonald, Barv Menay, Steve Mikesell, Gary Mills, Robert Gordon, John Prater, William Willard, as well as numerous students in my anthropology classes at Washington State University. I also want to thank M.E. Sharpe's series editor Kevin Reilly, and former editor Peter Labella, for their early interest and encouragement. Special thanks to Susanna Sharpe for finding errors and omissions. The ones that remain are all mine. Last, and most important, my wife Kathleen was a major part of our field research with the Ashaninka and in many ways shaped the present project. I tried hard to follow her advice; however, I disregarded her recommendation that the three cultural worlds be called tribal, political, and commercial, going instead with tribal, imperial, and commercial. She is right that it is confusing to speak of a particular imperial world and the personal imperium that can be found everywhere, but I like the sound of "imperial world."

The POWER of SCALE

1

Introduction: Imperia and the Power of Scale

This book introduces a scale and power perspective on human development from the dawn of culture to the present and identifies the crucial transformations, the decision makers, and the cultural processes that have produced our present world. Imperia and the power of scale shed light on such contemporary global problems as war, environmental deterioration, poverty, and human rights abuses. From this new perspective these problems are seen as unintended consequences of the operation of personal power networks that have become too big and too dangerous to be safely controlled. Identifying imperia and scale as problems in themselves means that the most intractable human problems are not a result of human greed, Malthusian overpopulation, or technological backwardness. They are problems of the power of scale, and they have been with us for a very long time. Developing a better understanding of how social power is distributed and how it is used is an important and long-overdue step toward solving global problems. The unique convergence of democracy, mass production, and information technology at the dawn of the new millennium is a unique opportunity for humanity to improve the overall conditions of life if social power can be safely controlled and distributed. <u>For the first time in human history we can create a truly democratic world, but we need to create optimum scale societies, with optimal distributions of social power.</u>

Imperia, Social Power, and Scale

Imperia are important keys to understanding past, present, and future cultural development. Imperia is the plural of *imperium*, the Latin word for command over others, rule by an individual, or rule by an elite few. It is a conceptual tool to examine the role of individuals in directing cultural development. As a multidimensional concept, imperium is shorthand for any personal power network and elite organizational structure; it can be applied to households and to many kinds of corporate groups, including businesses and governments, where human decision makers have a prominent role. Imperium also means *empire*, and refers to absolute power or domination by a ruler, or an elite few, in any power domain—political, economic, ideological, or military—following Mann's (1986) analysis of social power. Imperia include antidemocratic command structures. Imperia exist wherever control is permanently exercised by an individual or an elite minority who are fewer than half of the members of any social group. Clans and lineages can be organized as imperia. A business corporation is an imperium, although its directors may be virtually anonymous in society at large. The household controlled by its adult members is a universal imperium in all human societies, but there are many other imperia or empires in the world today, and they exist at all levels of society from local to global.

Power in this context refers to *social power*, the ability of individuals to influence other people and events in order to maintain or improve their own and their children's material opportunities, or life chances. The ability to make strategic decisions that transform or "develop" entire societies and cultures to suit one's purpose is the apex of social power. The effectiveness of one's imperium can be measured by the degree to which one's household enjoys a higher than average level of material well-being and the ability to transmit these advantages to the next generation. In societies where social power is differentially distributed, the superior life chances of the more powerful are likely to be reflected in their larger, more comfortable households, superior health, life expectancy, nutrition, greater esteem, privilege, and overall security. This kind of power may be demonstrated by victory in competitive struggles with other households, but social power fundamentally means the ability to have one's needs met, regardless of opposition or adverse circumstances. Where there are cultural opportunities for elites to construct large imperia, and effective limits on power are absent, power elites may become a privileged minority who are able to impose their will on the majority. Very powerful elites may succeed in rising to the top in multiple-power domains, and they may dominate an entire society or multiple societies. It is also possible that multiple hierarchies and mobilized majorities may constitute countervailing forces that prevent growth from becoming an opportunity for unlimited power seeking.

Scale refers to the absolute size of populations, economic enterprises, markets, armies, cities, or anything that affects the well-being of people. Scale calls attention to growth thresholds, order-of-magnitude increases in the size of societies, and the new cultural features that are required to sustain larger systems. Scale is about growth and power. As societies grow larger, it is likely that the organization of social power will need to change. A principal assumption of this book is that growth is an elite-directed process that concentrates power in the form of ever-expanding imperia. The power of scale is the reality that scale increases can be expected to mathematically produce disproportionate concentrations of power for those at the very top of any hierarchy in any power domain, while the costs of growth are likely to be socialized or borne by society at large. This explains why some people invariably promote growth and attempt to persuade everyone that growth is universally beneficial, even as growth changes the distribution of opportunities in ways that may disadvantage many others.

Everyone opportunistically seeks to build imperia because people naturally need physical and emotional security for themselves and their families and personal control over the conditions of their daily life. Just as the universal incest taboo restrains and regulates human sexual drives, the majority construct cultural and social institutions to restrain the natural drive for personal power and domination within socially beneficial limits because when individuals are allowed to create ever larger imperia, the well-being and basic human rights of others may be threatened. An imperium can benefit society at large, but unlimited power is always potentially dangerous. Power elites are different from the majority because they are in a position to concentrate greater than average power in personal imperia by manipulating personal networks of kin, allies, and associates scattered throughout society, many of whom may themselves have more than average power. Elites also control and manipulate a variety of corporate groups and institutions. Elites can use their more powerful imperia to transform culture for their own benefit. Elites gain their added power from increases in the size or scale of societies, polities, and economic enterprises. Elites may be well-intended people, but they have human weaknesses and can make mistakes, and the potential for abuse of imperial power, intentional or not, increases as imperia grow. The inequities, injustices, and maladaptations of the past and present are by-products of empire building, competition between elites, countervailing social movements, and the power imbalances that imperia create.

The imperia and scale approach explicitly rejects prevailing neoclassical economic models that present global capitalism as a benevolent, self-organized system and an irresistible force. Rather, unfettered global capitalism may amplify the problems of scale and power, and may not be the best way to enhance human freedom and well-being. Although elite power in the form of imperia is a central theme of this book, it is not another Marxist version of class struggle theory. The focus on imperia highlights the role of individuals rather than social classes and emphasizes the diverse pathways to power, multiple-power domains, hierarchies, and networks. This is not to ignore the importance of organized groups as power blocks, but these will be treated as sources of individual power. Imperia and scale draw attention to the often wide divergence between formal social structures and cultural ideals and human realities in practice, especially as these are expressed in public discourse. Throughout this book I will avoid personifying such cultural constructions as the state and corporations and will resist appealing to such impersonal forces as markets as inevitable and irresistible determinants of our future. I will look instead at how people use these artificial entities and processes in ways that create unequal opportunities. In scale theory no single driving force behind cultural development exists other than opportunistic individuals and the contingencies of culture, nature, and history. In this analysis growth in scale itself is the central problem, and the objective is to explain why perpetual growth occurs, to understand its human consequences, and to consider the alternatives. Throughout history people repeatedly resisted the negative consequences of misguided imperia and developed many imaginative proposals for more humane, democratic, and sustainable worlds. Counter-imperia social movements have been crucial sources of cultural development. Democracy itself was a product of fierce popular resistance to tyrannical imperia. A world composed of optimal-scale societies would make the problem of power imbalances much easier to solve.

Three Cultural Worlds: Tribal, Imperial, and Commercial

The 5,000 or so distinct ethnolinguistic groups that anthropologists have described ethnographically are only a fraction of the tremendous cultural diversity created over the past 200,000 years of cultural development. However, the organization of social power is such an important determinant of the conditions of human life and well-being that all cultures can be sorted by their dominant forms of imperia into just three distinct cultural worlds: tribal, imperial, and commercial. Each world is dominated respectively by households, political rulers, or economic elites. It may seem overly simplistic and even trivial to reduce all of cultural evolution and diversity to such a sweeping generalization, but this is not a banal exercise. Imperia seem so familiar that it is difficult to grasp their real significance. Imperia are so close, sometimes so large, and so pervasive that they become invisible, but it would be a mistake to disregard them. Imperia not only determine human well-being, but they determine how cultures develop and grow, how and why growth occurs, how growth is regulated, and when it stops. Imperia focus our attention on who controls and directs culture, and for what purposes.

Cultural worlds are the most extensive social environments where people routinely interact to secure their existence, and where in spite of linguistic or ethnic differences, people share understandings about the nature of the world, and about common human rights and obligations. The operation of distinctive dominant imperia in each world can create extreme differences in levels of economic productivity, standard of living, and overall well-being of households that are related to differences in the scale of settlements, societies, and regional and global populations. The most striking aspect of the three worlds is the scale and scope of human activities that each permits, and the distinctive ways imperia are constructed in each, and how social power is organized and distributed. The present chapter looks closely at the basic design and function of imperia in these three worlds and their human consequences, and examines the major transformations that created them. Chapter 2 will examine representative cultures from each world, and Chapter 3 will show how natural scale laws amplify the power of imperia and promote further growth.

The human consequences of life in each world are profound and largely the result of the different ways imperia operate in combination with scale differences. In the tribal world each household had direct access to the material resources needed for survival, and everyone lived in politically autonomous bands and villages. The household was the most permanent and the only dominant imperium. This was possible because societies were kept small and resources remained abundant. The tribe was an inclusive interest group, but did not operate as an imperium because no single person or dominant minority could direct it by gaining permanent control over the entire tribal society. Tribal leadership was temporary, and anyone with the personal qualifications could be a leader. All tribal members belonged to smaller, community-level groups controlling their own resources, but every household was incorporated within these groups, and everyone and every household could participate in decision making to the limits of their natural abilities. Under these conditions, competition between households was minimized, there was little capital accumulation, and the material level remained very low, but basic human needs were easily satisfied. Everyone was comfortable, within the cultural definition of comfort.

In the imperial world, where societies were much larger, strategic resources were controlled by dominant political imperia and societies were divided into hierarchical interest groups, or social classes, that systematically excluded and disadvantaged lower-ranked households. The term "imperial" is applied to this world to evoke the common meaning of empire with reference to a territorially based, politically centralized society controlled by a political elite. Even though money, trade, and markets were often essential in the ancient imperial world, those who made their living in these areas were often distrusted and despised, and were relegated to the social background. The rulers and priests occupied the power center of the imperial world, and the military, tribute, and religion were the principle means used by the elite to mobilize social power from the subordinate masses. People gained access to resources only at the will of rulers and landlords, and by manipulating patron–client relationships. Local communities were politically dependent on urban-based centers of power, and most households were socially and economically dependent. The political elite formed an exclusive, privileged subset of society, enjoying superior power and superior life chances, while many nonelites experienced drastically reduced life chances. There was a striking increase in wealth accumulation, but it was largely directed and controlled by the political elites for their personal benefit. This is the human problem of political tyranny and exploitation.

In the commercial world material well-being depends on access to capital, markets, and employment, all of which are controlled by imperia organized by economic elites and the political rulers who support them. Economic power and economic elites are supreme in the commercial world, such that both local communities and governments are subservient to commercial interests, enterprises, and institutions. Risks are widely shared throughout commercial societies, but rewards are highly concentrated. The crucial reality of life in the commercial world is that because there are more total people than ever before, there are also vastly more people with less social power than others, and most people may have less control over the conditions of daily life than in any previous cultural world. This is the problem of economic tyranny and exploitation, added to the problem of political tyranny. The most important question is whether there are reasonable alternatives to these forms of tyranny, but first we need to understand the basic cultural features of each world, and briefly consider the transformations required to create each world.

Great Cultural Transformations

No culture is static. They all change, but change occurs for different reasons and has different human consequences. The three cultural worlds—tribal, imperial, and commercial—were produced and shaped by a sequence of eight great cultural transformations that changed how people lived, raised global population levels, and eventually increased the scale and form of societies and cultures over many thousands of years (Figure 1.1). All people participated in and shared in the benefits of the first three great transformations that produced the tribal world:

1. Hominids became physically modern humans (by 100,000 B.P.*, or earlier);
2. Humans created effective foraging cultures (by 50,000 B.P., or earlier); and
3. Foragers became effective village farmers (by 10,000 B.P.).

These transformations were democratically directed by all households, or domestic imperia, and were all part of the biocultural evolutionary process that made people human. All the transformations that followed can be regarded as dehumanizing, because their human benefits were narrowly distributed such that they left whole groups of people relatively disempowered, and because they subordinated the humanization process—which is the production and maintenance of human beings—to the politicization and commercialization processes, which are the production and maintenance of governments and businesses respectively. All of these processes and their various subprocesses are listed by cultural scale and the three cultural worlds in Table 1.1 and will be discussed in more detail in the following chapters.

After the tribal world, each transformation wave was for the first time directed by a self-selected subset of people who were uniquely situated to take advantage of the special opportunities opened to them by the changes they introduced. The next two great transformations:

4. Chiefs began to gain control over independent villages (by 8,000 B.P.); and
5. Chiefdoms became agrarian civilizations (by 6,000 B.P.), produced the imperial world, and were directed by the leaders of political imperia.

The three most recent transformations created the commercial world, and reflect the progressive dominance of the leaders of:

6. Mercantile imperia (by A.D. 1450);
7. Industrial imperia (by A.D. 1800); and
8. Financial imperia (by A.D. 1900).

---

*B.P. means "before present" and is widely used in archeology with "present" set by convention at A.D. 1950.

Figure 1.1 **Great Cultural Transformations**

1. Hominids > Humans, 100,000 BP (Culture Capacity)
THE TRIBAL WORLD
2. Humans > Forager Cultures, 50,000 BP (Speech, Kinship, Ritual)
3. Foragers > Village Farmers, 10,000 BP (Domestication)
THE IMPERIAL WORLD
4. Villages > Chiefdoms, 8,000 BP (Imperial Organization)
5. Chiefdoms > Agrarian Civilizations, 6,000 BP (Urbanization, Agriculture)
THE COMMERCIAL WORLD
6. Agrarian Civilizations > Mercantile Capitalism, 1450 AD
7. Mercantile Capitalism > Industrial Capitalism, 1800 AD
8. Industrial Capitalism > Financial Capitalism, 1900 AD

These last three rapid waves of change were all produced by different types of commercial imperia, often closely intermeshed with and supported by political imperia. It is not yet clear what kind of world will be created by the leaders of the new imperia who are now directing the present rapid expansion of information and communication technologies.

The first great wave involved the biological transformation of our hominoid ancestors into physically modern humans who were capable of creating culture by at least 100,000 years ago, perhaps much earlier. The second great transformation from this human base was the development of human speech and the relatively rapid proliferation of kinship systems, ritual, and the technologies that sustained small, nomadic foraging bands organized in decentralized tribal societies. People carrying forager technology quickly settled the entire world, raising global population by an order of magnitude, or ten times greater, from perhaps 1 million to 10 million. In the third transformation people in many parts of the world shifted from mobile bands into small, relatively permanent villages, and changed their subsistence technologies from foraging to gardening and herding. The fourth transformation was the change from autonomous tribal villages to politically organized chiefdoms. This meant crossing the great divide from the tribal world into the imperial world. Initially this was an organizational change that did not immediately require new subsistence technologies, but it led to order-of-magnitude increases in the scale of society and soon produced the next wave of change. The fifth transformation was a further intensification involving the emergence of cities, government, and intensive agriculture, again leading to order-of-magnitude increases in social scale and global population. The fourth and fifth transformations are the subject of Chapter 4.

In this succession of worlds there is an obvious trend for population to increase, economic production to intensify, and for power to become increasingly concentrated, all by orders of magnitude. Eight thousand years ago, when the entire world was tribal, the global population numbered no

Table 1.1

Cultural Worlds, Scale, and Cultural Process

I. Tribal world, domestic-scale culture humanization: producing and maintaining human beings, societies, and cultures.
    Conceptualization: producing abstract concepts and symbols
    Materialization: giving physical form to concepts
    Verbalization: producing human speech
    Enculturation: reproducing culture
    Intensification: producing more food/km^2
    Sedentization: settled village life

II. Imperial world, political-scale culture politicization: concentrating social power by coopting the humanization process to produce and maintain political institutions.
    Taxation: extracting surplus production to support government
    Specialization: government employment
    Militarization: use of organized violence
    Urbanization: development of cities

III. Commercial world, global-scale culture commercialization: concentrating social power by coopting the humanization and politicization processes to produce and maintain for-profit business enterprises.
    Industrialization: mass production and distribution of commodities
    Commodification: markets for land, labor, money, and everything else
    Capitalism: control of capital separated from producer-consumers
    Externalization: costs of business enterprise socialized
    Corporatization: business enterprise becomes suprahuman
    Elitization: elites physically detached from larger community
    Supralocalization: business enterprise detached from community
    Financialization: investment detached from industry

more than perhaps 85 million people living in some 200,000 tiny independent villages and mobile bands. By A.D. 1200 the globe had become divided into two worlds. Half of the globe continued to be a tribal world occupied by some 60 million people in 150,000 politically autonomous settlements, and the other half was an imperial world of 300 million people controlled by political imperia centered in a few hundred chiefdoms, city-states, kingdoms, and empires (Figure 1.2). By A.D. 2000 the globe had become one commercially organized world of nation-states; only a few thousand people still lived independently in a tribal world. Virtually all former political powers were subordinated by the economic leaders and business corporations of the commercial world. Six billion people lived under the nominal political control of 191 national governments, but the practical power of political rulers was increasingly overshadowed by the economic power held by the directors of a relative handful of giant commercial imperia.

    In the tribal world everyone lived at approximately the same material

12

Figure 1.2 Global Population Scale by Cultural World

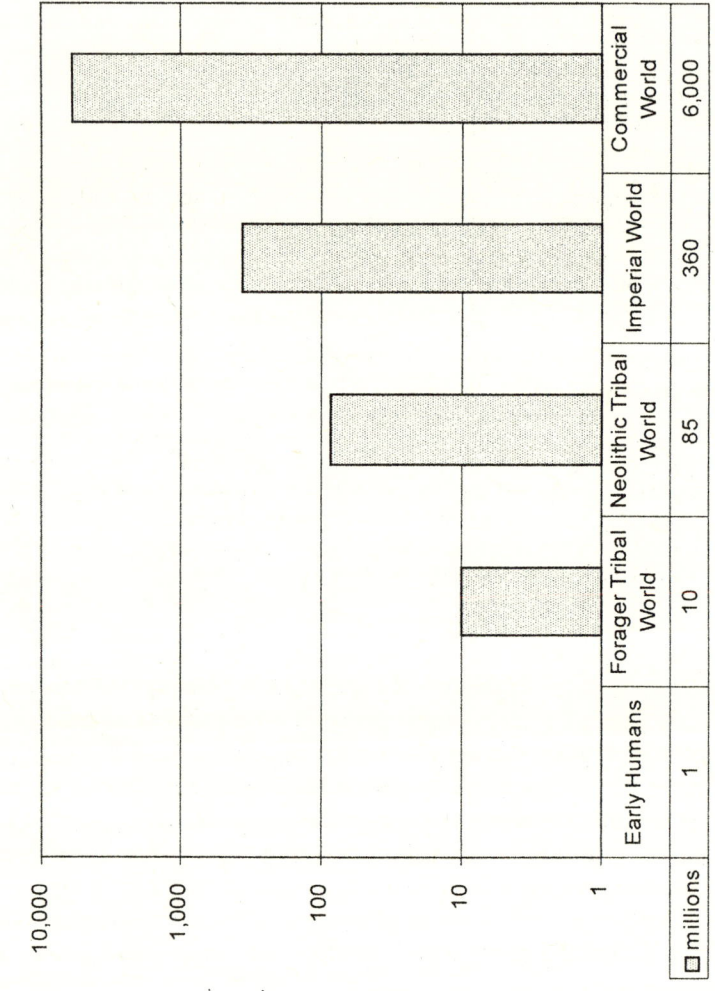

level, such that everyone's basic needs were met and all households enjoyed roughly equal chances to maintain themselves and reproduce the next generation. The scale of human activities remained small, and adaptive adjustments to the natural and human environment were managed by every household and by small groups acting by consensus. As power shifted into disproportionately fewer hands with the creation of the imperial world, households began to differentiate materially and crucial decisions about cultural development were made by fewer people. Many people experienced declining material levels and were unable to form stable households; others maintained themselves at marginal subsistence levels, while a few were able to accumulate surpluses and enlarge their households with dependents and servants. As new imperia were created and power became more concentrated, the scale and scope of economic activities and conflicts intensified, and entire civilizations began to rise and collapse. In the commercial world these destabilizing trends have become more extreme, and material inequities have increased dramatically. Political and commercial volatility and instability have raised costs and increased risks for millions, but they have also created enormous opportunities for a few. By the year 2000 the wealthiest 7 million individuals in the world, less than 0.1 percent of global population, had accumulated more than $27 trillion in investable assets (Gemini 2001), which represented more than half of global GDP, yet according to UN estimates, more people lived in absolute hunger than the entire population of the world (720 million) in 1750!

Quality of Life in the Tribal World

The most distinctive feature of the tribal world was that the dominant tribal imperia were domestic imperia, and they were focused exclusively on the production and maintenance of human beings, human society, and culture. Members of the contemporary commercial world are likely to deprecate life in the tribal world as "subsistence-level," because tribals accumulated little surplus beyond daily consumption needs, but this is a matter of optimizing means for a particular end. Tribal people selected the simplest, most efficient, and thus *best* means to their primary objective of producing and maintaining people. As long as humanization remained the dominant goal for everyone, government and commerce were not needed. In technical terms, the tribal world was characterized by *anarchy* (absence of government) and *autarky* (self-subsisting), but this does not mean disorder or poor quality of life. Accurate comparisons are difficult because we have few eyewitness accounts of daily life in the independent tribal world, apart from observers from the imperial and commercial worlds in chaotic frontier settings. Based on fragmentary archaeological evidence and carefully selected modern ethnographic observations, it appears that life expectancy was generally lower and infant mortality higher in the tribal world than under modern conditions. However, tribals apparently lived at least as long as people in the ancient imperial world and the early stages of the commercial world, and were probably healthier overall. It is known that some Australian aboriginals and Arctic peoples lived longer than the English during the 1300s. The average life expectancy at birth was only about thirty-five years for most of humanity until about 1840, less than half of the average for much of the world in the year 2000. Significant improvements in life expectancy for any peoples have been extremely recent products of vigorous public health measures, immunizations, and antibiotics.

Life may have been relatively short for tribals, but quality of life was high for those who survived infancy. The advantage of high infant mortality rates and the absence of antiseptics and antibiotics is that tribal people developed strong natural immunities. At the same time, they lived active lives in healthful environments. Tribal culture promoted public health. Low-density mobile populations had little difficulty maintaining sanitary settlements and finding pure water. With food chains short, all food on hand was consumed fresh daily, and food quality was equal or superior to their commercial counterparts. Where medical teams were able to conduct health surveys on tribal groups living in remote areas in the twentieth century they consistently found them to be vigorous and free of debilitating disease. Independent tribals were typically well nourished and showed healthy teeth and an absence of the obesity, heart disease, digestive problems, and degenerative diseases that plague commercialized populations. Some of this can be attributed to low-fat, low-sodium, high-fiber, high-carbohydrate tribal diets, and their consumption of low-cholesterol wild fish and game. Plenty of varied outdoor exercise, and walking everywhere, must have also been beneficial.

It is not surprising that the first Europeans to encounter tribal peoples in North and South America invented the myth of the "noble savage," because they were so impressed with their superior physical condition. The native Americans were often taller, stronger, cleaner, healthier, and more self-confident than the Europeans who met them. Tribals continue to stand up well in comparison with impoverished people in many less developed countries. For example, doctors have found the children of independent forager groups to be healthier than the children of the urban poor in some countries.

The conclusion that independent tribals were basically healthy is further supported by the striking physical deterioration that has typically accompanied their adoption of commercial lifestyles. Whenever commercial clothing, foods, and housing replaced tribal patterns, infectious disease rates increased, along with degenerative diseases, malnutrition, dental problems, alcoholism, family disintegration, and suicide. Many of these problems were obvious results of lifestyle changes, but they were not always voluntary choices, and they were often diseases of poverty. This is significant because poverty was not part of the tribal world. These new health and social problems were compounded by the inability of many impoverished tribals to secure healthcare or any form of public assistance. Given our definition of social power as the ability to influence events and maintain or improve one's life chances, tribals became impoverished and disempowered when they were incorporated into the imperial and commercial worlds.

The Irreducible Minimum in the Tribal World

Each cultural world is based on a particular view of how that world is naturally constituted, and the place of individuals in that world. In the tribal world each individual was assumed to be equally human, and the name of the tribe, the largest society, typically meant "the people," or "human beings." Social categories, such as male and female, young and old, were naturally defined in reference to human biology and the life cycle, and kinship categories, such as father, mother, son, daughter, brother, sister, husband, and wife, derived from marriage and the family. In the tribal world every member of the tribe was born with a "natural" entitlement guaranteeing the opportunity to enjoy a full life. Everyone had an estate to pass on to their children. Anthropologist Paul Radin (1971) called this human entitlement the "irreducible minimum," and argued that it was a unique characteristic of the tribal world. In a sense the irreducible minimum is what makes people human and could be considered the most fundamental of human rights. It is what social power is all about. This human entitlement is the natural right that empowers people to make a living, marry, form a household, and raise children, simply because they are human beings, although in detail it is allocated to individuals through the human universals of kinship, age, and gender categories.

The essential spirit of an irreducible human minimum is incorporated in the United Nations 1948 Universal Declaration of Human Rights, which states, for example, that:

- "All human beings are born free and equal in dignity and rights" (Article 1);
- "Everyone has the right to life, liberty and security of person" (Article 3);
- "Men and women . . . have the right to marry and found a family" (Article 16);
- "Everyone, as a member of society, has the right to social security and

is entitled to realization . . . of the economic, social and cultural rights indispensable for his dignity and the free development of his personality" (Article 22);
- "Everyone has the right to a standard of living adequate for the health and well-being of himself and of his family, including food, clothing, housing and medical care and necessary social services . . ." (Article 25); and
- "Everyone has the right freely to participate in the cultural life of the community . . ." (Article 27).

These humane ideals were conspicuously absent from the legal codes of the ancient imperial world, and were often explicitly denied. They may be formally recognized as human rights by some countries in the contemporary commercial world, but they are often disregarded or are treated as inferior to civil and political rights. The concept of any absolute human "entitlement" is often viewed with suspicion as being somehow illegitimate.

In the tribal world the irreducible minimum entitlement was constituted as a material and cultural estate that was automatically transmitted to everyone at birth. Materially the estate consisted of permanent rights to use portions of the tribal domain and all of its natural resources to secure a living. Everyone was a shareholder in a joint patrimony. Everyone was also entitled to full access to all cultural information required for human success or household well-being. An individual's complete estate thus included a bundle of rights that each person enjoyed as a human being, specific rights he/she held as a particular biological and cultural individual. This estate included access to real property in the form of territory and its natural resources, and cultural property in the form of information. At the time of marriage every individual was fully equipped to succeed in life, and was dependent only on other family members. In this sense, everyone enjoyed equal life chances, although the final outcome depended on individual personality, skill, and ambition. The household, the extended family, more distant kin, and the tribe as a whole provided everyone with a social support system that smoothed out the inequities of fortune, gender, and the life cycle.

Closely connected with the concept of an estate was the corporate group. In the tribal world a corporation was any, usually named, social group that had a recognized existence apart from the life of any individual member. A household, descent groups such as lineages and clans, residential groups such as bands and villages, regional associations such as moieties, and tribes were all corporate groups. Corporate groups owned and managed natural and cultural resources as estates, and tribal people gained access to these corporate estate properties through their membership in corporate groups. The important feature of tribal corporations in contrast to corporations in the imperial and commercial worlds is that tribal corporations were inclusive groups that incorporated everyone on equal terms, excluding no one.

The key features of interpersonal and intergroup relations in the tribal world were cooperation, reciprocity, complementary opposition, and overlapping networks. People performed most daily domestic routines as cooperative tasks within corporate groups. Economic activities were shared and products were distributed on the basis of reciprocity between individuals and households, on the assumption that this would be fair because effort and returns would balance out over the long run. The assumption of fairness was realistic in these small societies where everyone knew everyone else, and everyone's possessions and activities were on constant public display. Social categories such as male and female, or group A and group B, were treated as connected sets, and the different parts were culturally understood to be two interdependent complementary halves of a larger whole, such that one half could not exist without the other. Membership in social groups also frequently overlapped, forming cross-cutting networks that made it difficult for aspiring leaders to organize competing alliances.

This combination of a universal human rights entitlement, supported by an emphasis on economic cooperation and equity together with specific social features that reduce conflict, all worked together to reduce the natural incentive for rivalry between groups of individuals. Ideally, there was no cultural incentive for households to produce more than their immediate material needs. Instead, people were free to focus on minimizing energy expenditures and risk, and maximizing household security and well-being. There was also no incentive for either economic growth, or population growth. Even more remarkable, in this kind of world there was no economic scarcity because everyone's material needs could be readily satisfied. There was social power in the form of property, income, and wealth, but people worked relentlessly to level differences and redistribute benefits. Equity and universal entitlement meant that economic advantage did not easily become the basis for competitive emulation.

The problem with the tribal world was that its human benefits applied only within the tribe itself and were most secure only within the band or village. Vengeance, raiding, and intergroup violence were chronic problems. Nontribal members were potential enemies and were not always considered human. Over the very long term, the real problem of tribal culture was that it was not always able to prevent assertive individuals from expanding their personal imperia and promoting scale increases. The organization of power in the tribal world is illustrated in Chapter 2 by the example of the Ashaninka, foragers and shifting cultivators in the Amazon.

Political Imperia and Conditional Rights in the Imperial World

Beyond all their obvious differences of language, religion, and details of culture, the ancient world's politically organized great agrarian civilizations—such as ancient Greece, imperial Rome, China, the Hindu and Buddhist kingdoms, the Maya, the Aztecs, and the Inca—all share important features that set them apart from cultures of both the tribal and commercial worlds. The dominant cultural process in all of these civilizations can be called *politicization*—the production and maintenance of governments. Elites used the politicization process to coopt the humanization process, and they developed new subprocesses such as taxation, occupational specialization, militarism, and urbanization. In contrast with the tribal world, both the ancient imperial world and the modern commercial world are characterized by the conspicuous presence of a bewildering array of imperia that organize social inequality in ways that give some families exclusive advantages over others. Politicization can be said to coopt the humanization process because it is the means by which elites appropriate resources that others require for their own maintenance and reproduction. These imperia are constructed from multiple status hierarchies in different power domains that exaggerate the personal differences between individuals. Ranked status positions are frequently inherited, and in the ancient world multiple imperia were often consolidated under the control of a single political ruler, his extended kin, and personal allies to create a dominant, highly personalized power network taking the form of a political economy and a political ideology with military support. All of this would appear bizarre, if not actually inhuman, to a visitor from the tribal world.

These are not new observations about political power, but they are seldom acknowledged in idealized histories that focus on the cultural achievements of "great" civilizations and treat progress as both inevitable and universally beneficial. In contrast, the ancient Chinese philosopher Mencius (371–289 B.C.) was sharply critical of the inhumanity of Chinese civilization. He deplored the historical reality that rulers and their officials routinely used war to expand their powers and sought personal profit from their domains, calling such inhumane rulers "plunderers of the people." This, of course, was in opposition to his utopian ideal of the good king who enjoyed the "mandate of heaven" because he displayed humanity and justice to his subjects. Mencius's concept of justice (*yi*) approximates the tribal irreducible minimum, and explicitly recognizes the right of common people to a standard of living that would allow them to maintain their elderly in comfort.

The imperial world is distinguished from the commercial world by the subordinate position occupied by traders and merchants in the former, and their dominant, even exalted role in the latter, as well as by the position of the economy as a whole. This is clear in the origin myth that Plato created to distinguish the principal social classes in his ideal Republic, where he called the political elite "golden," and their assistants "silver," but farmers were iron, and craftsmen were the inferior brass. Slaves were not citizens. The Greeks regarded production and exchange as necessary evils, not really suitable activities for the nobility. Gold and silver had a dual significance for Plato because he would not allow his ruling class to even touch these metals, or money. This cultural attitude resembles the Hindu origin myth, which ranked in descending order the separate occupational castes sprung respectively from the mouth, arms, thigh, and feet of the creator god Brahma: (1) priests, (2) ruler-warriors, (3) herders, farmers, and traders, and (4) servants.

In Plato's ideal state the elite could not own private property, land, or houses, nor accumulate wealth, because these would be corrupting influences. Plato's *Republic*, as well as Aristotle's writings on the ethics of exchange, reflected the ideal of the Greek *polis* (city-state), which assumed a community of relatively equal citizens who would subordinate personal gain for the interests of the commonwealth; it stigmatized commercial exchanges that were presumed to generate an unjust profit and undesirable inequalities (see Chapter 7). Wealth was always suspect in classical Greece because it could lead to luxury and impropriety. It was expected that personal wealth would be generously directed toward the public good, and it was not to be endlessly reinvested. In the ancient world wealth was important largely as a status marker, as a reward for loyal allies, and for conspicuous display. This explains why treasures were often buried in royal tombs, or incorporated in mummy cults, rather than used to produce more wealth.

Following the insights of Karl Polanyi (1968), it is reasonable to characterize the economy of the ancient world as "embedded" in the culture as a whole. It was not thought of as having a separate existence. This is reflected in the Greek invidious distinction between a respectable economy (*oikonomia*), such as household management or domestic economy, and a disreputable economy directed toward money making (*chrēmatistikē*). The household economy was superior to the money-making economy for the household was the focus of economic activity. This antieconomic growth attitude, and the accompanying general suspicion of money handlers, is also represented in the negative view of usury in the canon law of the Roman Catholic Church and in the Islamic prohibition of usury. This general antimerchant picture seems to have been true of the entire ancient world, and helps explain why economic growth was not an important goal, although imperial expansion and military conquest were prominent and honorable activities.

The technology of production in the imperial world was more intensive and dynamic than in the tribal world, because imperial political leaders had such a strong incentive to increase the density of the societies they controlled. Tribal members could comfortably meet their material needs with land-extensive, low-energy production systems such as foraging, gardening, and herding because they did not need to produce a surplus beyond the nutritional needs of their households. Rulers, as "plunderers of the people," extracted food as rent, taxes, or tribute, and promoted expensive and vulnerable irrigation and intensive plow agriculture in combination with draft animals and metallurgy in order to raise carrying capacity in the most productive zones.

Throughout the imperial world empires were headed by ranked patriarchal households. Political imperia in the ancient agrarian civilizations were ego-driven power hierarchies directed at the top by a single, usually male, head. Emperors became the heads of great families, whose members attempted to construct kin-based patrilines, or dynasties, to perpetuate the core leadership structure of their personal imperia. Descent groups are cultural constructions modeled after biological facts, but they often consist of fictitious personal histories that can be manipulated for power purposes. In order to prevent political power from being diffused, rulers often selected their successors on the basis of primogeniture in the male line. Secondary sons received empty titles and had to create their own power bases, or were given control of religious imperia. The heads of political imperia were inherently driven to perpetual growth, because ego gratification knows no natural limits, and because emperors and empires were likely to have competitors. However, imperial overextension was a recurrent problem because physically, growing empires do reach natural limits. Empires either grow until they collapse or the leader finds a way to overcome the growth threshold and grows a larger empire until a new threshold is reached.

In the imperial world all human rights were naturally conditional and ranked, depending on one's relation to god or the temporal or spiritual lords, either through inheritance or in exchange for loyalty, labor, or tribute. In this world there was no universal human entitlement to an irreducible minimum. The supreme ruler was either god or god's appointed representative, who claimed all property as eminent domain, along with life-or-death power over everyone. There were new corporate groups such as towns, cities, kingdoms, temple societies, courts, palaces, armies, farms, factories, and merchant associations that formed the basis of new imperia. These were exclusive groups in which only certain people could be members. They were usually highly ranked internally, and were often structured to funnel material benefits to a single controlling family. Furthermore, a single family could control multiple corporate imperia through overlapping directorships. There were pervasive distinctions between *nobles* or *citizens,* who had privileged access to government, military power, property, and economic opportunity, and who despised *commoners* or *noncitizens,* such as peasant farmers, servants, and laborers, who were excluded and disadvantaged in multiple ways. Slaves, who were total dependents, were often a separate, most excluded category. The rulers, their households, close kin, and supporters were privileged and powerful people, forming an aristocracy with special inherited rights. These institutionalized forms of human injustice were virtually universal in societies of the ancient imperial world.

The power differential between households in the imperial world has its most remarkable expression in the reality that not everyone could marry and raise a family, and that for the first time vast numbers of people were treated like domestic animals, fit only for labor or slaughter. Today, this would be seen as a clear violation of the Universal Declaration of Human Rights. Servitude, serfdom, and slavery were not characteristic of tribal societies, although they existed in certain cases, but they were endemic in the imperial and commercial worlds. In ancient China, Egypt, Greece, and the Islamic world rulers used eunuchs to guard their harems, effectively subordinating some men's reproductive potential in favor of others' in a fundamentally inhuman way. In many ancient civilizations large numbers of both men and women were separated into celibate communities. Most noncitizens were left with no meaningful material estate to pass on to their descendants, although their inferior and stigmatized social status was likely to be inherited.

The scale of direct violence perpetrated by ancient political rulers is difficult to comprehend, but it further demonstrates the fundamental inhumanity of the imperial world. Wars organized by rulers for purely political purposes and fought by large armies generated large numbers of casualties and great material waste and destruction, and were an intrinsic problem of civilizations. For example, Rummel (1997, 70) estimated that 34 million people were killed in civil wars in China between 221 B.C. and A.D. 1900, and another 30 million by Mongol armies. Violence was also a chronic problem in the tribal world, but in these smaller-scale societies the total casualties were much lower. In ancient civilized societies human beings were routinely sacrificed to accompany royals into the afterlife, or common people were simply killed in rituals that served to terrorize and intimidate. The Mesopotamian royal tombs of Ur in 2500 B.C. contained 74 human sacrifices along with the body of the royal personage. In 1500 B.C. Shang China more than 600 people were sacrificed in the foundation of a single building. When the Spanish arrived in 1519, the Aztecs were ritually slaughtering tens of thousands of people—some estimate as many as 250,000 annually. Rummel (1997, 70) conservatively puts the Aztec toll at 1 million. The commercial world did not reduce the slaughter. The Spanish killed millions in the Mesoamerican and Andean civilizations in a matter of decades. The European invasion of the tribal world may have killed tens of millions of tribals between 1780 and 1930. On a century by century basis, these figures are, of course, an order of magnitude below the more than 200 million soldiers and civilians sacrificed in wars, purges, and genocides in the twentieth century (Rummel 1997). Political violence directed by national leaders killed more people in that one century than twice the entire population of the tribal world at its peak.

The Commercial World and Capitalism

I have intentionally used the label "commercial world" rather than "capitalism" to denote a global-scale world dominated by commercial imperia whose leaders are dedicated to continuous expansion. As will be shown below, capitalism is a problematic label because it has such diverse meanings, not all of which get at the essence of commercialization as defined here. The point is that in the commercial world the leaders of commercial imperia operate on a greater scale, concentrate more social power, and have a greater impact on humanity than the leaders of political or religious imperia. In the contemporary world, commercial imperia influence virtually every aspect of everyone's daily life; they are omnipresent and virtually inescapable, but they were totally absent from the tribal world, and operated only in the margins of the imperial world.

The hallmark of the arrival of the commercial world was the identification of "the economy" as an object of scientific study by French physiocrat François Quesnay (1694–1774), with the publication of his *Tableau économique* (1758), coupled with the almost simultaneous revelation of the social benefits of the "invisible hand" of the "free market" by Scottish social philosopher Adam Smith (1723–90), as described in his *Wealth of Nations* (1776). These books were as important for defining the commercial world as were the works of Copernicus (1473–1543) and Galileo (1520–91) proving that the earth rotated around the sun, for advancing the world of science. Before the discovery of the economy, economic activities were so embedded within the practices of daily life or under so much political control as to be invisible. Previously, political rulers struggled over territories and peoples in order to accumulate wealth and power, but political power was central, and there was no detailed financial accounting. In the imperial world neither "the economy" as an independent entity nor economic growth could be the objective of policy.

This great transformation process that made commerce the centerpiece of cultural development will be examined in greater detail in Chapter 5, but at this point we need to characterize the commercial world more fully. Many historians have identified the transformation from imperial to commercial with the rise of capitalism, but capitalism means many different, often contradictory, things. Granted that commerce defined as trade is a human universal, many modern writers identify capitalism with *laissez-faire* economics, or free enterprise, free trade, and individualism, in contrast to state control or collectivism. This is an inadequate definition of the commercial world, because even with fully developed markets, political power is still needed to protect private property, enforce contracts, prevent catastrophic market collapses, undertake risky long-term investments, and supply services that have little commercial value. Only in the tribal world was trade truly "free" from state control because the state did not yet exist. Furthermore, individualism is not the center of capitalism, because commercial imperia invariably involve individuals operating not as individuals, but as members of multiple partnerships and corporations. Commercial imperia are power networks. Free market competition is also not the defining feature of capitalism, because the leaders of commercial imperia invariably seek to reduce competition, socialize risk, and concentrate profit through any politically supported institutional means, such as monopoly. Commercial imperia thrive in a world where the otherwise natural individual differences in energy, skill, and property can be overwhelmed by state-supported collective social power.

The commercial world has a different dynamic from the imperial world, because it creates opportunities for "commercial" expansion that are seemingly endless. This encourages perpetual growth in a way that was never possible in the imperial world, which was limited by the frailties of political power. Commercial imperia are personally directed social power networks based first of all on personal income, ownership of wealth and property, and control over people, resources, businesses, markets, and secondarily on political power. Wealth and property, however acquired, conferred political power in the imperial world, but in the commercial world wealth and property are forms of economic power based on commodity exchanges. As commodities in a market economy, wealth and property are commonly understood to be among the fundamentals of capitalism. In the commercial world income may be "earned" from professional salaries and wage labor, or it may be in the form of "unearned" rents, profits, interest, and royalties. Personal wealth may be measured as net worth (assets less liabilities), and includes tangible wealth such as real property, as well as intangibles such as money, stocks, bonds, patents, copyrights, trademarks, and business enterprises.

Wealth has been called *capital* at least since the thirteenth century, and as *human* capital, capital can include individual knowledge and skills. Capital can also mean *cultural* capital, or cultural hegemony in the form of ideological power, in reference to control over the information and ideas that direct human behavior. Even though the contrast between tangible and intangible property seems obvious, both are artificial legal concepts based on relationships between people, and they must be institutionally supported by formally organized markets and the coercive political power of law, police, and courts. Of course, control over other people's wealth and property gained by directors of commercial corporations, bankers, and financiers, or by individuals who form business partnerships or client networks, may be a far more important source of economic power than personal wealth and income by themselves.

Speaking of the *commercial* world calls attention to the commercialization process and its distinctive subprocesses, and emphasizes the unprecedented and overwhelming scale and scope of commercial influences. Commerce is an enormously efficient means of meeting human needs by promoting human creativity and stimulating production and distribution, but commerce can be easily subverted for imperial purposes. It is critical to distinguish commerce from *commercialization*, because it is possible to imagine a world in which commerce plays an important role, but does not overpower households, communities, or governments. The concept of commercialization, as used here, describes the condition that occurs when commerce becomes the dominant cultural process such that the success of commerce itself becomes more important than the well-being of people or governments. Commercialization in this respect is the cultural process of producing and maintaining business enterprises in order to concentrate social power. In this process elites construct imperia by coopting both the humanization and the politicization processes. The closely linked subprocesses of commodification and financialization are essential features of the commercialization process. Elites have expanded the scale and power of commercial imperia using the secondary subprocesses of capitalization, industrialization, externalization, corporatization, and supralocalization. All of these subprocesses will be discussed briefly here, but they are so important to understanding the contemporary world that they will be examined in operation, and in greater detail, in later chapters.

Commodification—turning things into marketable commodities—is the central feature of the commercial world. Extreme commodification would make every physical thing, conceptual object, and service a marketable commodity exchangeable for money. This can seriously undermine the humanization process, because when basic human survival items such as food, water, and shelter become commodities, they may not be equally available to everyone. Commodification can thus produce poverty conditions that lower life expectancies. For the commercial world to operate fully, all the factors of production including land, natural resources, labor, and money need to be exchangeable with each other through organized markets. In this system things have value as objects of exchange, not for their consumption value. Again, this is a matter of degree, because in the tribal world a few things did have exchange value, but never land, labor, or money. In the imperial world foodstuffs and luxury goods routinely entered the market, but there was little wage labor, and very few individuals could purchase land or legally borrow money at interest.

Commercialization creates unlimited opportunities for power seekers who want to build ever larger imperia, because the exchange transaction is what counts, and in a sense the physical commodity is irrelevant. Transactions are cultural conceptions involving social relations between people, and thus they have no natural limits. Financialization is the conceptual counterpart of commodification that makes perpetual growth seem possible. Infinite growth appears possible in an otherwise limited physical world because money is a symbolic cultural construction with no necessary material reality. Money was always a counting device, but when it was legally disconnected from gold or silver, it became simply a quantity recorded in a ledger. Ultimately, commercialization is about the accumulation of money, and this is accomplished by *arbitrage,* in which one buys low in one market and sells high in another. The remarkable disconnect of commerce from the real world is demonstrated by the fact that in the 1990s as much as 90 percent of the monetary value of commercial transactions involved financial intangibles such as stocks, bonds, and commodity futures. Many observers consider such transactions to be the essence of capitalism, but they have no necessary connection either with human needs or the physical world, and they thus can generate endless potential for imperial expansion. The big problem with such unlimited opportunity is that unless people set cultural limits to power, individuals will be naturally driven to build greater and greater imperia, and out-of-control imperia can be very destructive to the human values of freedom and democracy.

Early in the twentieth century, German sociologist Max Weber (1930) described capitalism as a state of mind—a *geist,* or "spirit," that made moneymaking the meaning of life. This leads to some less than obvious key points about the commercial world. For Weber, capitalism was unique because it made money making an end in itself. Money, not goods, mattered most. The crucial element of capitalism was the drive for perpetual acquisition *beyond all natural human need.* Like Karl Marx, who contrasted the *use value* of consumer objects with their *exchange value* as commodities, Weber contrasted the *economy of needs* in the precapitalist world with what he called the capitalist *economy of acquisition*. Commodity exchange is correctly identified as the means, and monetary acquisition the end, by Weber's "spirit of capitalism." The important point is that commodity exchange is also the means to the end of constructing commercial imperia. Recognizing this is a useful corrective to the misleading popular conception that commerce is driven by consumer demand. The question is, whose human needs does commerce serve most bountifully? The evidence will show that those who use commodities to build commercial imperia gain more social power and enjoy greater freedom and independence than the majority who merely consume commodities and remain dependents.

Weber stressed that the capitalist pursuit of money was carried out in a highly rational, calculating way. He thought that workers with a precapitalist mentality worked to satisfy their limited needs and would "irrationally" work less if their wages were increased. Of course, this was mainly a matter of whether or not workers perceived opportunities in available markets. However, Weber correctly noted that under a capitalist state of mind there would be no shut-off point to acquisition. One could argue that the unlimited acquisitiveness of capitalism was an irrational goal in a finite world, but rationality is not the issue; it is the means and ends that matter. Given the chance, people will amass as much social power as possible. We can safely assume that informed people will always act in a rational, economic way to meet their power goals, according to their perceived best interests and to the limits of their knowledge and ability. What Weber could not explain was why people adopted a capitalist state of mind in the first place. We will return to that question in Chapter 5 and later chapters.

Four interconnected subprocesses—capitalism, externalization, corporatization, and supralocalization—clearly demonstrate that concentration of social power may be one of the most important outcomes of industrialization and commercialization as they have developed. There is no reason why these particular subprocesses would be required in an alternative world in which industrialization and commere were geared to the production and maintenance of human beings. Capitalism in its most specific meaning refers to Adam Smith's original observations that industrial society was "naturally" divided into the "masters," who were landlords and manufacturers, and the "laborers," who did the productive work. This is the essence of serfdom. Karl Marx described this in class terms as a division between the bourgeoisie ("capitalist" owners of the "means of production") and the proletariat (workers). Capital, understood as productive goods, is a human universal, but *capitalism*, defined as only a few owning capital while the mass of society are workers, would appear to be an outcome of the operation of imperia, not an inevitable law of nature.

Externalization, corporatization, and supralocalization are functionally connected with capitalism. The externalization subprocess involves spreading the costs and human risks of commercial activities throughout society at large, while concentrating the benefits in the capitalists. Externalities are negative byproducts of commercial activities that are not charged as costs to the capitalists responsible. For example, based on careful calculations, economist Ralph Estes (1996) estimated that large corporations charged the American public at large $2.6 trillion in 1994 dollars (40 percent of GDP) for "externalities" such as workplace accidents and illnesses, dangerous products, pollution, crime, and monopoly price-fixing. It makes sense that these costs would be charged to society at large in a social system directed by capitalists, but accomplishing this requires considerable social power to produce the necessary legal and institutional support. Capitalists need to dominate the political process.

Corporatization refers to business enterprises organized as corporations, rather than as sole proprietorships or partnerships. This makes possible the creation of enormously powerful and infinitely expandable business imperia because corporations can be given the rights of individuals, yet they are legally immortal. Corporations are ideal capitalist business forms because a few "capitalists" with relatively large holdings can easily control and direct them as part of their imperia, even when millions of people own very tiny shares. Furthermore, corporations allow capitalists to limit their personal liability for financial loss or damages, making externalization even easier. Sole proprietors bear the full risks of their businesses, and of course their businesses die with their owners; thus they have only limited opportunity to accumulate power. Partnerships are equally short-lived. As corporations, businesses can easily become supralocal, that is, they can be detached from particular communities. Supralocalization is the pathway to global expansion. The case study on the United States in the following chapter will illustrate many of these key features of commercialization.

2

Imperia in Three Worlds

The following sections will present ethnographic case studies chosen to represent each of the three cultural worlds in greater detail, in order to examine comparatively the distribution of social power to individual households and the quality of life for people in each world. The tribal world is represented by the Ashaninka of the Peruvian Amazon, based on the author's fieldwork in the 1960s. The Chakri dynasty of the Thai kingdom (1782–1932), represents the imperial world, based on historical, archaeological, and anthropological descriptions of this politically organized agrarian civilization. The United States in 1998 represents a modern society in the commercial world. I use business records, census data, and analysis by the Federal Reserve to show important similarities and differences between the power distribution of American household imperia and Ashaninka and Thai imperia. These examples demonstrate that as the scale of society increases in successively more complex worlds, the largest imperia gain disproportionately greater power. Each case study is preceded by a general overview of relevant theoretical issues. The detailed role played by the directors of the largest imperia in constructing the imperial world, and transforming it into the commercial world, will the subject of later chapters.

Domestic Imperia in the Amazon Rain Forest: The Ashaninka

My understanding of Ashaninka imperia comes from the anthropological literature (Johnson 1975, 1983, 1985; Johnson and Behrens 1982), as well as from direct experience living with the Ashaninka during repeated research visits to the Peruvian Amazon over a period of many months from 1964 to 1969 (Bodley 1969, 1970, 1972a, 1972b, 1973, 1981, 1992, 1993), and with their neighbors the Shipibo in 1976–77. The Ashaninka illustrate the scale limits of political power in the tribal world and demonstrate the realities of tribal life as a basis for comparison with the imperial and commercial worlds.

In 1969, when my wife and I encountered a small group of light-hearted Ashaninka with red-painted faces, carrying bows and arrows and baskets filled with squirming honey ants that they had just collected for dinner, I knew they were self-reliant people whose daily lives were only minimally connected with the global market economy. We were in the Gran Pajonal, on the Amazon headwaters in Peru, fifty air miles from any roads or towns, and a long day's walk from the nearest landing strip. After a tense and ritually hostile greeting with Chonkiri, the group's arrogantly self-confident leader, we were allowed to visit their households and gardens and collect basic life history information. Although we could see that significant changes were occurring all around them, the daily life of this remote group was not substantially different from what the first Franciscan missionaries found when they entered Ashaninka territory in 1673, nearly three centuries earlier.

During our research with the Ashaninka, we talked to scores of people, systematically mapped communities, studied the language, collected genealogies and family histories, and measured economic productivity. We learned that although the influence of the global market was intruding everywhere in the form of missionaries, colonists, merchants, lumbermen, ranchers, oil prospectors, and leftist guerrillas, most Ashaninka were not abandoning their way of life to join the commercial culture. They fiercely defended their own cultural system because it worked well for them. The Ashaninka successfully drove out foreign invaders with an armed uprising in 1742 and repelled new invasions throughout the nineteenth and early twentieth centuries. Unfortunately, with the penetration of new roads, airplanes, and motorboats, after 1940, it became more difficult for the Ashaninka to hold at bay an ever increasing number of outsiders. By the 1960s only a few thousand Ashaninka were still remote enough to maintain full autonomy and self-sufficiency. However, outside of the colonized zone, every Ashaninka household still enjoyed easy access to the productive gardens, rivers, and forest resources needed to meet all their material needs for food, shelter, and clothing.

We were interested in this fiercely independent people because the global commercial economy had everywhere become so pervasive that it was almost impossible to study any community living successfully without money and capital-intensive technology. Most modern ethnographies, as valuable as they are, usually describe people who earn wages or sell products, pay taxes, attend school, and buy their food and clothing as commodities in markets. The Ashaninka gave us a rare view of a way of life where local people and individual households still controlled all the basic resources needed to meet their daily needs. We found other Ashaninka householders who, like those in Chonkiri's group, were skillfully supporting themselves in the rain forest with only the simplest of imports from the commercial world. These people not only had no cash incomes, they used no electricity, no telephones, no fossil fuels, no petrochemicals, no plastic, and their only running water came from a stream. Some had never seen a printed page. Chonkiri's group was tribal, but they were not living in the "Stone Age." They had previously bartered labor and local products in exchange for a few steel axes, machetes, metal cooking pots, and shotguns, but they maintained no direct or permanent contacts with the market economy. They were deliberately keeping the commercial world at a distance in order to maintain their freedom, while selecting from it what they found most useful.

The individual family household of husband, wife, and children, sometimes extended by additional wives and children, was the minimal independent social unit in Ashaninka society. For example, I counted twenty-two people, in seven households in Chonkiri's local extended family group, including men, women, and children. Named or localized lineages or clans did not exist. Each household owned its own house, kitchen, and garden, but no one "owned" the forest where everyone hunted and foraged. Married children or siblings lived in close proximity to one another and frequently drank manioc beer and feasted together and formed joint task groups and foraging expeditions.

Because of the requirements of shifting cultivation, hunting and foraging, and the dynamics of the domestic cycle, Ashaninka settlements were impermanent and changed composition frequently. More distant households might come together sporadically for parties or to form raiding or self-defense groups, but such groupings were even more unstable than local household groups. A prominent "big man" with an especially forceful personality, like Chonkiri, might form the nucleus of a dispersed local group, but this would be only a temporary and unnamed alignment and constituted a weakly extended imperium. At best an Ashaninka big man could seldom count on "commanding" more than the five to ten warriors from his own local group. Organizing a raiding party of twenty-five, to a maximum of perhaps 250, was a rare accomplishment.

An Ashaninka big man's imperium was maintained by a fragile balance of strength and generosity that came from developing a small retinue of supporters based on his personal charisma, family ties, and good fortune. This meant building a reputation for festive hospitality with kin and allies, and for besting and intimidating opponents in aggressive displays of strength, such as exchanging blows, dodging arrows, and engaging in shouting matches with trading partners. A big man had to persuade his married sons and son-in-laws to live nearby, and he had to maintain friendly relations with his brothers. Extra wives gave an aspiring big man the possibility of raising more sons and attracting extra son-in-laws as supporters. Extra wives could also brew more manioc beer, which was the basis of hospitality. An aggrandizing man might also claim supernatural powers, or lead raids to exact revenge and capture women and booty, but all of these displays were risky because people valued their autonomy and a bully might be shunned.

After 1900, when the rubber boom suddenly brought hundreds of outsiders into Ashaninka land and created a demand for labor, some Ashaninka big men gained reputations for special ferocity. They led small raiding parties to take captives from distant Ashaninka and from other tribes to barter with the rubber barons in exchange for rifles and other manufactures goods. As long as it was directed against outsiders, such raiding served a public purpose because it brought useful manufactured goods into Ashaninka hands. Successful raiders then distributed these goods to all households by means of kinship reciprocity and trading networks.

The absence of a cash income qualified these people as the "poorest of the poor," according to the World Bank experts who in the 1960s were beginning to funnel massive loans into Amazon development to promote highways, colonization, and agribusiness. Commercial development was supposed to enrich everyone's lives. Yet the Ashaninka were already living rich lives. Theirs was a luxury economy, even though they were officially poor. They hunted, fished, and gardened, built their own houses, wove their own clothing, and except for a few trade goods, made their own implements and weapons. There were no homeless and no one went hungry. Every adult was a member of a household, and households were self-sustaining. Chonkiri's group purposely lived in the remote headwaters because it was distant from the foreigners who traversed the main rivers; even though their refuge was fish and game deficient, they had plenty to eat. The bulk of their diet came from their gardens where they raised twenty major cultigens and dozens of varieties. The annual yield from manioc, their primary stable, was five times more than they could consume, and required remarkably little effort to produce. Their gardens were small, easily cleared temporary openings in the forest needing little cultivation and no additional inputs of commercial energy or materials. They allowed the forest to regrow in a successional process that maintained soil fertility while providing a long-term yield of diverse foods. This left the Ashaninka free to pursue an exciting and varied round of hunting, fishing, and foraging for edible insects, palm hearts, fruits, and nuts.

The Ashaninka way of life afforded maximum individual autonomy. People were in control of their own activities. There were no written laws, no police, no courts, and no taxes. Ashaninka men and women typically spent eight hours a day on such productive activities as subsistence, domestic manufacturing, food preparation, childcare, housekeeping, and hygiene. This satisfied all their physical needs, and left them with eight hours free a day to play, socialize, and rest, while still getting a full eight hours of sleep every night. They spent their leisure hours napping, drinking, partying, and telling stories. People traveled frequently on trading expeditions, to visit kin, and on extended treks to hunt, fish, and forage in more productive areas.

The Ashaninka represent a society characterized by anarchy (no government), autarky (self-feeding), and autonomy (self-law, independence). Anarchy means that each household performs all the functions of government including the use of violence, legislation, and justice, and of course has the right to appoint higher-level civil servants in the form of temporary war leaders and village heads for public purposes. This is maximum individual freedom and democracy, and government by and for the people. A tribal leader who abuses his authority can be instantly "recalled" when people chose to ignore him. In a sense, the Ashaninka have no economy because the household is the entire economy, combining all production and consumption functions in a single unit.

For millennia the Ashaninka were part of a much larger tribal society. Before Europeans entered Amazonia in 1541, most of that vast river system was an interconnected tribal world of perhaps a million people, adjoining the Inca Empire in the neighboring Andes, and bordering densely populated chiefdoms in the more productive lowland riverine zones. Amazonia is the world's largest river system, the largest tract of unbroken tropical rainforest, and probably the most biologically diverse terrestrial ecosystem. The archaeological record shows that tribal village people have lived in the Amazon by gardening, fishing, hunting, and foraging for at least the past 5,000 years. Cultural diversity matched the biological diversity. By 1500 there were five major language groups, at least 200 major languages, and more than a thousand self-designated "tribal" groups throughout Amazonia. Materials, people, and ideas moved throughout this vast region. Tribal identity was based on common language and culture, but a "tribe" was not a unified political unit, except for the chiefdoms, and tribal members only acted as a community temporarily and under extraordinary circumstances. There were tribal "big men" throughout, like the Ashaninka leaders, who were more successful warriors and more persuasive than others, but they could not speak for everyone nor compel anyone to do anything against their will. Each household could act alone. Social power was thus dispersed as widely as possible, as evidenced by the reality that every household possessed the same range of material resources.

The archaeological evidence shows that the Amazonian tribal way of life had endured for millennia. Amazonian villagers were in the business of meeting human needs over the long haul. They succeeded because kinship, household well-being, and decentralized decision making were their supreme cultural values, and because they had no cultural incentives for intensifying their productive activities or expanding population beyond the levels that their resources could easily support.

The sixteenth-century Spanish and Portuguese explorers were so impressed with the health and vigor and leisured contentment of Amazon Indians that they described them as noble savages living in a terrestrial paradise. Today's development workers, whether missionaries or economic planners, are promoting their own utopian visions of the world and they all see the Indians, and all self-sufficient tribal peoples, as poor, ignorant, and backward. Small-scale cultures like the Ashaninka mutually modify and evolve with local ecosystems, and they resist changes that would threaten household sustainability. The key factor is that Ashaninka households retain the power to protect their self-defined interests. This is "family values" supreme, but it does not produce "noble savages." The Ashaninka human nature is the same as ours. Without police and courts, the Ashaninka would sometimes kill each other for personal reasons in chronic feuds that were difficult to stop, and occasionally they would burn orphans to death as witches. The Ashaninka would convert patches of forest into permanent grassland, would over-hunt local areas, and sometimes would fell wild fruit trees for convenience. They died prematurely from diseases that commercial medicine could cure easily. Nevertheless, any culture that could reproduce itself and equitably sustain households for millennia without seriously degrading regional ecosystems must be considered a great human achievement.

Circles of Kings: Political Imperia in Southeast Asian Kingdoms

The ancient agrarian civilizations of Southeast Asia provide diverse examples of the organization and function of imperia in politically centralized, non-commercial "imperial" societies. These imperia were shaped by political power and operated in striking contrast to both the domestically organized imperia of the tribal world, as exemplified by the Ashaninka, and the commercially based imperia in the contemporary United States to be examined below. The Hindu and Buddhist kingdoms that maintained their political independence into the twentieth century in Southeast Asia were based on cultural foundations dating back more than 2,000 years. They offer excellent case studies because these literate civilizations left abundant historic records, and they have been well described by both native and foreign observers and scholars from diverse perspectives for centuries.

Culturally diverse Southeast Asia is home to the important Sino-Tibetan and Austronesian language families, and over the centuries the peoples of this region have drawn variously from Chinese, Hindu, Buddhist, and Islamic civilizations, as well as from Europeans. The descendants of these cultural groups today constitute well more than half of the world's people. Given this diversity, it is remarkable that a common social structure persisted throughout the region into modern times, consistently based on a pervasive system of social ranking, elite control of land and labor, and patron–client relationships closely resembling European feudalism. Throughout, as in medieval Europe, a small nobility used religiously legitimized political power and supernatural benefits, backed by harshly enforced legal codes, to control the land and dominate the majority of the population for its personal benefit. Between A.D. 500 and 1400 a succession of power-seeking rulers developed nearly a hundred urban political and ritual centers in mainland Southeast Asia alone, including some two dozen relatively large centers (Hagesteijn 1989). Most centers scattered through this vast 876,300 square-mile (2,270,207 square-kilometer) area were fortified settlements with a ruler, walls, and moats, complete with palaces, temples, and elite residences. Centers were strategically located near rivers and arable land, where they could best dominate intensive wet rice agricultural systems, dense labor forces, and trade routes, which were the ultimate sources of political power. Autocratic rulers, claiming divine authority, positioned themselves as politically superior "lords" over the surrounding populations and attempted with varying degrees of success to construct dynastic kingdoms and empires that asserted control over neighboring centers.

Scholars have variously described the ancient kingdoms of Southeast Asia as examples of an "Asiatic mode of production" (Karl Marx), "oriental despotism" and "hydraulic civilizations" (Wittfogel 1957), "theatre states" with "exemplary centers" (Geertz 1980), "contest states" (Adas 1981), "galactic polities" (Tambiah 1976, 1985), and "circles of kings" (Hagesteijn 1989). These interpretations range between two extremes. A crucial difference in perspective is whether researchers favor either a symbolic, idealist, or interpretive approach to understanding cultural development, or whether they favor a purely materialist, political-economy understanding of culture. Specialists emphasizing cultural meanings and symbolic views have sometimes described Southeast Asian political rulers as benevolent figureheads who were primarily concerned with building temples, hosting ritual spectacles, and protecting the populace, whereas critical theorists have sometimes depicted them as despotic tyrants who ruthlessly exploited the population. Both

Marx and Wittfogel emphasized the importance of technology and political economy in producing social inequality, but they minimized the role of ideology. They considered these civilizations to be despotic and exploitative. In contrast, anthropologist Clifford Geertz focused on ideology, symbolism, and ritual, to the virtual exclusion of the utilitarian objectives of individual actors and their material outcomes, and suggested that state ceremony was an end in itself intended to symbolically mirror a cosmic order. To the extent that he considered economic and political activity, Geertz located these at the village level, and he minimized the possibility that exploitation was a problem because presumably villagers equitably shared their poverty.

The imperia and scale theoretical perspective departs from previous approaches in that it recognizes the equal importance of ideology, technology, and political economy, but treats all of these as tools that individuals use to build their personal imperia, and as cultural variables that limit both the scale of society and the amount of social power that can be concentrated in the largest imperium. Cultural development is itself a tool, not the inevitable expression of "cultures" adapting. This instrumental view of cultural development seeks to identify the most influential individual decision makers, and to demonstrate how they construct and use culture for their own benefit, but does not demonize power seekers as evil exploiters even though the cultural and social systems they construct may often have serious negative human consequences. The elite have simply taken advantage of the opportunities available to them, just as would anyone else. In politically organized cultures members of a political elite gain the opportunity to design large imperia that allow them to personally: (1) enjoy extraordinary human advantages; (2) influence events in their favor; and (3) escape many of the negative consequences of historical events and processes. In A.D. 1600 there were some 15 million people in Southeast Asia (Reid 1992, 463). The top 5 percent of households used their relatively powerful imperia to live in comfort and security, but only the very top 0.25 percent super-elite commanded extremely large imperia that afforded them truly magnificent levels of power and great luxury. Perhaps 95 percent of the population were able to maintain themselves only marginally with imperia of the most limited sort. There was effectively no middle class.

Viewed as forms of political organization, or galactic polities, these Southeast Asian kingdoms contained ruling elites who used both symbolic, expressive cultural features and politically instrumental action in combination to concentrate and legitimize their power. The kingdoms were designed symbolically to be mandalas, representing a cosmic order of concentric rings centered on mythic Mount Meru as the divine center. The divine king, the royal palace, the capital city, and subordinate centers all physically replicate this pattern.

Michael Adis (1981) calls these societies "contest states" because they are characterized by relatively weak central governments and because the power of elites at all levels, from king to village head, was perpetually contested. Kingship itself was constantly challenged because there were always contenders in the royal lineage and because even nonroyal nobles could sometimes mobilize sufficient power to take advantage of any perceived weakness in the royal center. Political control over people was more critical than control over land, and the technical limits of communication, transport, and the military made it impossible for the king to exercise direct administrative control over outlying lords and territories. Kings were dependent on local lords, and the lords were dependent on local officials. Every official funded his own activities by extractions from below. Thus, protection and patron–client relationships were the order of the day. The dependent received protection rather than power. Protection for the peasantry meant a reduction of oppressive extractions of their time, labor, and production by the central government, but in exchange they were forced to accept similar extractions by their local elite protectors. Peasants could sometimes reduce their burdens by appealing for relief directly to higher-level lords and, when possible, by shifting to less demanding lords, joining temples or monasteries, fleeing into the forest, or becoming bandits or vagabonds. Paradoxically, they could also opt out of the forced labor situation by becoming debt-slaves—permanent dependents of a particular lord in exchange for subsistence. Flight was a difficult choice for peasants in areas with intensive wet rice agriculture where they had cross-generational investments of labor in irrigation systems, temples, and houses, or when people were tattooed and registered.

Life at the village level was strikingly different than in domestically organized tribal society because in these kingdoms power inequalities were pervasive and poorly mitigated. Everyone was individually centered on their patrons, and this weakened village-level social supports. In most cases, villages were dominated by the more powerful imperia constructed by large land-holding families that treated other families as dependents. Peasant mobilization for direct, militant protest movements was uncommon and difficult to organize because the vertical patron–client relationships that permeated the entire society left little room for horizontal connections between individuals at the same social level. Peasants were concerned with local, village-level affairs and the particular patrons they were aligned with. People at the lower levels of society did not think of themselves as members of an exploited social class. It appears that aggrieved peasants accepted the legitimacy of the fundamental order of their society, but resisted oppression from particular rulers. They allied themselves with local elites when conflicts arose between elites.

The Thai Kingdom, 1782–1932

The kingdom organized by the Chakri dynasty in Thailand will be presented as a specific case study to evaluate competing interpretations of the role of individuals, technology, ideology, and imperia in the development of cultural systems. These are not purely academic issues because theory, ethnography, and historical narratives do have power. Thai radical theorist Jit Poumisak was imprisoned for treason in 1958 for publishing *The Real Face of Thai Saktina Today*, a book arguing that the ancient Thai kingdom was an oppressive feudal monarchy. He wrote in Thai under a pseudonym. At that time any offense against the person or dignity of the Thai king was "high treason," comparable to the Latin *læsa majestas* in medieval England. Poumisak was imprisoned without trial from 1958 to 1965, and then was shot to death as an antigovernment rebel in 1966. Poumisak's book was banned in Thailand in 1958 and rebanned in 1977, but reappeared in 1979 and was translated into English in 1987. His work stands in conspicuous opposition to orthodox Thai scholars who objectify and glorify Thai culture. For example, Thai architectural historian Sumet Jumsai (1988, 71) denies the reality of Thai feudalism in *Naga*, his book on Thai cultural development, by declaring: "Thai feudal estates or *sakdina* were purely symbolic, being imaginary collections of title deeds conferred on princes and noblemen without any physical plots of land to hold on to." As will be shown below, *sakdina* was actually the basis of Thai imperia, and had enormous human significance. The following account will draw primarily on the descriptions and interpretations of British scholar H.G. Quaritch Wales (1934) and Thai researchers Akin Rabibhadana (1969) and Jit Poumisak (1987).

Among the largest historically documented Southeast Asian imperia were the personal households and extended power networks of the kings, princes, and nobles. For example, the king in nineteenth-century Thailand (Siam) resided in the Grand Palace within a hundred hectare (247 acres) walled royal compound with his personal household of thousands of dependents, royal pages, slaves, and personal retainers, as well as some members of his royal lineage. For example, King Mongkut, who reigned from 1851 to 1868, officially produced eighty-two children from thirty-five mothers, and there may have been as many as 9,000 women in his harem, including wives and concubines with their slaves and retainers (Landon 1944; Leonowens 1870, 1953). Mongkut was the fourth king of the Chakri dynasty that ruled Thailand as absolute monarchs from 1782 to 1932. He was also head of a royal lineage with a series of successively more distant, less noble sublineages headed by princes. The palace compound and associated temples were surrounded by a moated urban center enclosing an area of 8.75 square kilometers along the Chao Phraya River, with a resident population of some 50,000 people, and another 300,000 living in the immediate suburbs. The extended royal domain, which was controlled directly by the king, was centered on the lower reaches and delta of the Chao Phraya, and encompassed some 50,000 square kilometers (19,312 square miles). It may have contained a million people, given that this was the heart of the prime wet rice producing zone in the country.

The king governed through six top ministers who were responsible for the palace and the royal domain, and controlled the more distant centers. The kingdom contained some 116 urban centers outside of the capital. These centers were grouped in four ranks by size and importance, but none was larger than 10,000 people, and all but twenty-eight were smaller than 2,500 (Sternstein 1966). Most people lived in small villages and were controlled by an eight-level (counting king to subject) administrative bureaucracy that combined territorial features with a decimal hierarchy reaching to households at the village level in the greater kingdom of some 4 million people spread over 200,000 square miles. This political structure produced an enormous revenue for the king, in addition to the land and goods extracted by the nobles for their own support. King Mongkut's annual revenue of 30 million ticals in tribute, taxes, and fees was the monetary equivalent of three months annual corvée labor service by 1.6 million men at six ticals per man per month. This power made it possible for the king to live in absolute luxury, supporting extravagant court ceremonials while donating to the temples and maintaining a costly program of construction and canal development.

Using a Marxist framework, Poumisak treated land as the primary means of production in old Thai society. He described a two-class society in which the large landowners were the ruling exploiters and the ruled, landless, or smallholders were the exploited. The king was the largest landlord, holding the entire kingdom as his absolute domain and literally holding life-or-death power over his subjects. Poumisak equated the majority, who paid rent for the use of the land (*phrai*, or *lek*), with agricultural serfs in the historic European tradition of feudalism. This kind of historiography was considered treason in modern Thailand, but it was ethnographically accurate. Poumisak argued that human wealth, happiness, and merit corresponded to the level of land or labor that one controlled. The key concept in Thai society was *sakdina*, "power of fields," which was a land measure based on the *rai* (1 *sakdina* = 1 *rai* = 0.4 acres, the amount of land a water buffalo could plow per day). A commoner was not allowed use of more than 25 *sakdina*, and most received only 15. Slaves were allowed only 5, whereas officials were allowed from 50 to 100,000 *sakdina,* and the king's *sakdina* was infinite. *Sakdina* thus served as a literal measure of the power of every household and ruler in the kingdom, and Poumisak emphatically equated the Thai system of *sakdina* (as *saktina*) with the English term *feudalism*.

Poumisak emphasized that the land-controlling elite sought to "train" the commoners to emulate and accept as superior the elite way of life or "culture," as defined by elite speech, etiquette, music, and literature. This meant that in practice *sakdina* referred to more than economic power in the sense of control over land. It also referred to control over the people on the land, and control over the Thai way of life, or Thai culture. There were multiple social hierarchies in which people were distinguished by legal categories such as prince (*hao*), noble (*nai*), commoner (*phrai*); by rank or title; and by their *sakdina,* which were also sometimes appropriately called "dignity points." For officials these rankings correlated with the relative rankings of the domains that they administered, as well as with their general position within the bureaucracy. There were more than a thousand different *sakdina* ranks, but more than half were reserved for some 1,500 men in the nobility down to the level of 400 *sakdina*. Most of the others went to some 36,000 petty officials down to the level of 50 *sakdina*. This suggests that perhaps only 1,500 men headed super-elite and top elite imperia—fewer than 0.25 percent of all households. All nobles and petty officials combined probably constituted a total elite of no more than 5 percent of households (Soltow 1983).

The *sakdina* land allotments can be put in perspective by considering rice yields in relation to human needs. Annual food requirements for a household of five members were approximately 2,000 lbs. (909 kilos) of rice (Hanks 1972, 48). This included seed for replanting, but made no allowance for debts, taxes, or other expenses. The timing of labor inputs and the weather were crucial variables, however, and households needed a wide security margin to remain viable. Assuming wet rice agriculture and traditional methods of cultivation with adequate labor inputs, per *rai* yields might average 624 pounds and ranged from 264 to 1,600 pounds. This suggests that the fifteen *sakdina* allotted to ordinary commoners should have produced a generous surplus. However, several estimates suggest that as many as half the population were legally slaves (*that*) or indebted dependents in nineteenth-century Thailand. Most households were perpetually in danger of slipping into debt, because a very large "surplus" was in fact extracted by the elite.

Apologists for the monarchy like Sumet Jumsai sometimes maintain that the *sakdina* were not land distributions but were only rights to purchase land, intended to prevent land hoarding. Poumisak argues persuasively that the *sakdina* system was indeed an intentionally constructed land distribution designed by successful conquerors to reduce competition among rival princes, to provide gifts to maintain the loyalty of lower-level followers and retainers, and to extract tribute. Clearly the system accomplished these goals. As evidence that this was an ongoing process, Poumisak cites a decree issued by King Mongkut in 1861 allocating ten square miles of land (16,000 *sakdina*), tax-free, to several of his own sons, after it was opened for development by a royal canal construction project.

Little social mobility was possible. The land-holding nobility consisted of those with a *sakdina* rank of 400 or higher, and was effectively open only to descendants of nobles. A royal proclamation by King Chulalongkorn in 1880 increased and extended the *sakdina* allotments within the royal family. The highest offices in the royal service required formal training in the school for royal pages, and this was open only to sons of the highest officials. The royal princes often held high offices, but top administrators were selected from a limited pool of nobles on the basis of ability. Most analysts who describe the *sakdina* land distributions assign the value of twenty-five *sakdina* (10 acres) to the commoners, using this figure to estimate the number of subjects each ruler controlled and assuming that most people were relatively comfortable. However, Poumisak observes that twenty-five was the *maximum sakdina* for commoners, and was received only by commoners who served as petty foremen, or otherwise managed dependents such as refugees. Most people were entitled to only fifteen, and many were under various forms of demeaning servitude qualified for only five or ten.

It was the unequal distribution of land rights, and the arbitrary manner in which produce and labor could be legally extracted by the rulers, that made the system both "feudal" and oppressive. It was difficult for people to move to less demanding overlords, because they were marked on the wrist with a tattoo designating the name and domain of their lord. Administrators also kept detailed census rolls of all individuals. Rent, or taxes in kind (*suai*), varied from 16 to 80 percent of the rice crop, depending on whether one was legally a serf, a free renter, or a small independent landholder. Serfs were also obligated to work their landlords' fields for three to six months a year, and they were subject to forced corvée labor for the king. Slaves were incorporated into their masters' households but were exempt from rent and taxes. Their subsistence needs were provided for, but they worked at the whim of their masters.

The legitimizing ideology supporting the *sakdina* system was the belief that the ruling elite reciprocated the peasant's labor by maintaining the social order, guaranteeing natural fertility, and granting people use of the land. The distribution of households by level of imperia demonstrates that this was an extremely unequal exchange. At every level the dominant party received greater benefits, and was able to amass greater effective power, than the lower-level partner.

When Thai households are sorted by culturally defined categories of class, title, and rank, the major types of imperia sort themselves readily into four groups that cross-cut the other categories (Table 2.1). Thai imperia provide a measure of the material level of households that is more useful for cross-cultural comparison than either the Thai internal categories of class (nobles, commoners, slaves), or the complex ranking of titles in multiple hierarchies that were the cultural framework of daily social interaction. Thai imperia can be distinguished according to the amount of surplus production that each household commanded, based on *sakdina* rank and available dependent labor. The head of an average super-elite imperium commanded hundreds of dependents in the form of extra wives, concubines, full-time retainers, servants, slaves, and part-time corvée laborers. The ordinary elite, who commanded only tens of dependents, was an order of magnitude less powerful. This imperia classification highlights the reality that elite standing reached down into the upper range of the commoner class, and suggests that most commoners were closer to slaves than to the lowest elite. Both maintenance-level and poor imperia were distinguished by the absence of command over non-kin dependents. Maintenance-level households could meet their basic needs most of the time, but were always at risk of falling into debt and dependency because they were so close to the subsistence margin. Poor households had so little social power that they were almost entirely dependent on subsistence support provided by patrons.

Another important feature of elite imperia is that, even though an imperium was commanded by a single individual, because they were more powerful, elite imperia were frequently transmitted intact cross-generationally. Furthermore, elite imperia often cross-cut diverse power hierarchies in ways that would not have been visible in the formal structure of Thai society. Elite political imperia formed covert dynasties that were quite distinct from the formal royal dynasties that figure so prominently in historical narratives. For example, according to detailed genealogical research by David Wyatt (1968), in the Thai kingdom a single nonroyal family continuously maintained a powerful position within the key ministries in the royal palace from 1782 to 1886 by means of family heads carefully manipulating their wealth, kinship relationships, and marriage connections. A total of only four families formed a tight monopoly over the six most important ministries. Power, not wealth accumulation, was the objective of these power seekers, but wealth had to be conspicuously expended to demonstrate status and maintain the prestige of political office.

The coercive use of state power against the less powerful makes it clear for whose benefit the system was designed. Throughout Southeast Asia, legal codes were modeled after the Hindu Code of Manu, which explicitly favors the upper castes over the lower. For example, it was four times more

Table 2.1

Thai Households by Class, Rank, Title, and Imperia During the Chakri Dynasty, 1782–1932

Classes	Titles	Sakdina ranks	Households	Dependents	Imperia
Nobles (*nai*) 0.2%	Universal Monarch, Lord Buddha, Great Ruler, Lord of the Land, Lord of Life	Infinite	1	225,000	Super-Elite 0.2%
	Royal family and Top officials, Crown Prince, *upparat*, Prince *chao, chao phraya*	Average 5,000; Range 100,000–5,000	500	Average 500	
	Nobles (*khunnang*), Lesser royalty, *phraya, phra, luang, khun, mun, phan*	Average 500; Range 5,000–400	1,000	50	Elite 5%
Commoners (*phrai, lek*) 75%	Petty officials, *khunmun*	Average 65; Range 50–300	36,000	7	Maintenance 45%

	Category	%	Number	
	Labor supervisors, *phrai hua mgan, nay sip*	25	120,000	
	Freemen, *phrai som, phrai rap*	15	242,500	
	King's men, servants, *phrai luang*	10	200,000	0
	Poor, beggars, *yachok, waniphok*			Poor 50%
Slaves *(that)* 25%	Slaves *(that)*, bond slaves, criminals, captives	5	200,000	

Sources: Data from A. Rabibhadana 1969; Poumisak 1987; Wales 1934.
Note: Perhaps another 100,000 people were living as monks.

costly in monetary fines and physical punishment for a low-caste person to assault a high-caste person. A sudra (the lowest caste) might forfeit a limb for striking a brahmin. In nineteenth-century Bali, fines for offenses against the social order were also inversely proportional to rank, declining step-wise through the hierarchy from commoner to royal priest for the same offense, as follows: 10,000, 8,000, 4,000, 2,000, 250 kèpèng (Schulte-Nordholt 1996, 154). The poor were generally allowed to substitute body parts for fines they were unable to pay, or they could allow themselves to be sold into slavery. The laws of King Mang Ray, who presumably founded the city of Chieng May in upper Thailand in 1296, unflinchingly demanded death for such felonies as damaging an image of Buddha, trespass, robbery, killing a lord, and adultery (Griswold and Nagara 1977).

Modern Thai and Balinese Imperia

Researchers have described contemporary Southeast Asian societies in ways that closely match the concept of imperia. For example, Lucien Hanks (1975) describes modern Thai society as based on superior-inferior, patron-client (čhao–lūk) relationships with the "entourage" (bōriwān) and the "circle" (čhak) as the basic building blocks. In contemporary Thailand the word *chao* means both prince and patron, and thus perpetuates the *nai–phrai* (noble–commoner) dependency relationship from ancient Thai society. Hanks points out that modern Thai clients can freely switch between patrons, unlike most European serfs who were rigidly bound to their lords. A large "entourage" is clearly an elite imperium. It is a multifunctional, temporary collection of clients or followers (bōriwān) centered on an individual patron. An entourage is different from a social class, because an *entourage* is composed of otherwise unconnected, but dependent, individuals, each maintaining a patron–client connection with the patron. If they were powerful enough, the members of the entourage in turn maintained patron–client ties with their own dependents. Collectively, all of these individuals were effectively part of the ruler's imperium or circle of power (čhak). It then becomes a large imperium, "the group of people who respond to a command" (1975, 203), and is symbolically equated variously with the circle of power (*cakra*) held by the Hindu god Visnu, the mandala, and the Hindu-Buddhist *cakravartin*, world ruler, which is the title adopted by the Chakri dynasty. The circles of power become progressively smaller, and the imperia weaker, as one descends the social hierarchy.

A smaller version of the elite and super-elite Thai imperia are found on the island of Bali in Indonesia, at the furthest extension of the Hindu-Buddhist circle of kings cultural model. The Balinese *dadia* described by Clifford and

Hildred Geertz (1975) closely resemble Thai imperia, even though the Geertzes downplay the economic significance of power inequalities in Balinese society and claim that the small regional Balinese polities are not "miniature *imperia.*" According to their finely detailed ethnography, *dadia* were the most important competitive social units on Bali. They were endogamous, patrilocal, corporate, patrilineal descent groups. The most powerful were ranked royal and noble houses directed by their firstborn male heads. Noble *dadia* were called *batur.* They were regionally dispersed, genealogically deep descent groups, whereas commoner *dadia* were much smaller, shallow, localized groups operating at the village level. *Dadia* heads competed in a "struggle for position" for control over *people* rather than territory. They attempted to dominate the entire society, judging by the Geertzes' comment that "the dadia is set within, and in a sense in opposition to, what one can only call the general community, against which it is constantly seeking to assert itself and by which it is constantly being restrained, even undermined" (1975, 5–6).

The head of the main family of the main sub-*dadia* of the hamlet's main *dadia* was usually the most prominent man in a hamlet. Lower-ranked village officials were also most likely to be *dadia* members, and constituted what the Geertzes refer to as a "ruling elite." Whereas in theory, hamlet-level decisions were made by consensus, in practice everyone followed the lead of the most prominent *dadia* heads, who can reasonably be called local elites. Only a few people headed elite *dadia,* and many commoners did not even head sub-*dadia.* The well-documented differences in Balinese household compounds suggest that Balinese imperia can be sorted into the same categories of super-elite, elite, maintenance, and poor that characterized ancient Thai society.

Commercial Imperia: The United States, 1998

The United States is an extreme example of a successful commercial culture and a perfect place to examine commercial imperia in action. The United States is the epitome of capitalism and growth on virtually every measure, whether in population, total economic output, per capita output, investment, or capital accumulation. Not only did the United States grow from a pioneer population of 3.9 million in 1790 to 270 million by 1998, but total national income expanded from billions to trillions in comparable dollars, even as per capita income increased perhaps twentyfold. By 1998, the U.S. gross national product (GNP) of nearly $8 trillion was $3 trillion ahead of Japan's, its closest competitor, and exceeded the combined GNPs of all 5 billion people living in all of the world's low- and middle-income nations. Only Japan,

Norway, Singapore, and Switzerland exceeded the United States' per capita GNP of $29,340. What is remarkable about America's economic achievement is how few Americans were in a position to actually direct these changes as the primary capitalist investors, managers, and financiers, and what a disproportionate share of the rewards these few received, even though the risks and the labor were widely shared.

A visitor from Ashaninka land—where everyone lives in family households, all adults are married, and parents take care of their children—would find daily life in America to be very odd, quite apart from its obvious material plenty and conspicuous social inequality. American society in 1998 was composed of many small households, incomplete families, disconnected individuals, millions of institutionalized people; many children were being raised by incomplete families. According to census figures, more than 10 percent of Americans over the age of fifteen (26 million people) lived alone in isolated, single-person households, and nearly one-third of all households were not composed of kin. Twenty-seven percent of men over eighteen, and 20 percent of women had never married, and 18 percent of family households were headed by women with no husband present. Nearly one-third of American children under age eighteen (23 million) were living with only one parent, and nearly 3 million children were not living with any parent at all. These statistics would seem shocking and inhumane to the Ashaninka, but are functionally related to gross disproportions in the distribution of social power and the unrestrained formation and operation of commercial imperia.

Americans are either producer-consumers or capitalists according to the ranked economic imperia they command and the level of economic independence they consequently enjoy (Table 2.2). Economic or financial independence is a critical variable. This was recognized long ago by Adam Smith when he observed that manufacturers and landlords had a natural advantage over workers because they could survive longer on their stock of food and capital than their workers who were living from one payday to the next. In a fully commercial society such as the United States, people may have the legal freedom to find employment, but most are not free to be unemployed and still live comfortably. The only fully financially independent households are those that can survive indefinitely without an earned income. Households that control only producer-consumer level imperia are economically dependent and in that respect resemble the serfs of medieval England, because their freedom of action is limited by low earned incomes, low net worth, and very small, or nonexistent, investment portfolios. The great division is between those who command only their wages and those who command their own businesses and properties, and perhaps other people's money, businesses, and properties as well. This difference is reflected in the portfolio, which is the total of investable, income-generating assets, excluding the value of homes and cars that contribute only to net worth. Households commanding capitalist imperia can be economically self-sufficient because they have high earned and unearned income, high net worth, and large portfolios.

Producer-consumer imperia can be further subdivided by their level of commodity consumption as determined by income rank. The very low incomes of under $10,000 earned by unskilled workers support "poor" households that may have difficulty meeting basic needs for food, shelter, clothing, education, and healthcare. Skilled employment may produce successful consumers who live comfortably, but they can accumulate very little net worth beyond the value of homes, cars, and small retirement funds, and they cannot exercise strategic control over the direction of their culture. Self-employed owner-operators of small sole proprietorship businesses generating less than a million dollars in revenues may have some potential of becoming capitalist entrepreneurs if they can strictly limit consumption and invest in growth. Most Americans have difficulty saving because capitalist imperia devote vast marketing resources to promote elevated levels of commodity consumption by low- and medium-income households.

Large capitalist imperia can be readily constructed by those reaching incomes of over $100,000, but there are important differences in scale and organization among these very powerful imperia. Entrepreneurial imperia in which a single individual owns and directs a rental property empire, or a local or regional business empire generating over $1 million in revenues, can command steadily expanding multi-million-dollar portfolios, especially when these elites reinvest their profits rather than expending them on high-status consumption commodities. These elites include the 3.5 million successful American entrepreneurs with portfolios of 1 to 10 million dollars described by Stanley and Danko's (1996) *The Millionaire Next Door.* An example of an entrepreneurial imperia that I identified in my research in Washington State in 1997 was the $90.7 million in assessed urban property value spread over two counties that was held by one man. This was more property than held by all 10,200 people living in twenty small towns in the region. Other individuals owned empires of metropolitan commercial property, chains of post office buildings, chains of fast food restaurants, or parking lots. Such imperia have an enormous impact on local communities, but they are virtually invisible to casual observers.

The much larger imperia commanded by great corporate directors and financiers who control other people's capital assets are equally invisible even though they are of national scope and are orders of magnitude greater than small entrepreneurial imperia. At this higher level, incomes may routinely exceed $1 million, net worth may be in the billions, and decision-making control

Table 2.2

American Imperia, 1998

Classes	Economic type	Income range	Net worth	Households	Portfolio	Imperia
Capitalist (8%)	Directors	$1 million+	$ millions–billions	0.4 million	$ million $ trillions	Super-Elite (0.5%)
	Owners	$100,000–999,999	$100,000–millions	5.6 million	$ millions	Elite (8%)
Producer-consumer (92%)	High consumers, skilled wage and salary, small entrepreneurs	$10,000–99,999	median $60,000	55.8 million	None	Maintenance (79%)
	Low consumers, unskilled wage-earners	<$10,000	median $3,600	8.9 million		Poor (13%)

may be exercised over billions or even trillions of dollars in capital assets. A few super-elites have constructed truly extensive imperia, just as in feudal England, where there were several thousand manor lords but only a handful of great barons. For example, in 1997, out of some 4 million American corporations there were 12,953 publicly traded companies with assets of $5 million or more. These elite companies were directed by some 114,000 directors, but only 350 directed five or more corporate boards. One man was a member of twenty boards. Looking just at Fortune 500 corporations as examples of the very largest companies, and sorting carefully, I found that ten corporate directors served on the boards of thirty-seven companies with combined assets of $2 trillion in 1994. One man directed five companies with combined assets of $549 billion, but in 1998 the chief executives of the three largest Wall Street investment firms controlled assets of $1 trillion each (Califano 1998). Remarkably, almost none of these very powerful men, and the occasional woman, is a widely known public figure, but their influence on American culture is profound.

In spite of America's great economic success, in 1998 more than 35 million Americans (13 percent of the population) were living below the most conservative official poverty level, and by other official measures more than 56 million (21 percent) were poor. The disadvantaged economic status of the bottom 15 percent of American families—those with incomes of less than $10,000—is dramatically profiled by data contained in the 1998 survey of consumer finances conducted by the Federal Reserve (Kennickell 2000). These data show that the median annual income of these 10 million families was only $6,200 dollars. Half earned less than this amount, half more. Not surprisingly, the median *net worth* of these poor families was only $3,600— barely enough to pay for a very simple funeral, and not enough to qualify one as an American capitalist, especially given the form of their economic assets. Fewer than two-thirds of these families even had checking accounts, only half owned cars, and only one-third owned their residences, whose median value was only $38,900. None owned any other real estate that might generate rents. Fewer than 8 percent held stocks in any form, and the median value of these few holdings was only $4,000, no greater than the median value of their vehicles. Fewer than 4 percent had equity ownership in a business of any form. The limited opportunities for economic advancement by these families, and the prospects for their children, were hardly an improvement over the outlook of the landless serfs in medieval England, although their material conditions were greatly improved.

At the other extreme of American society, the top 6 million families, which comprise less than 9 percent of all families—those with incomes of $100,000 or more—received 39 percent of total personal income and held 52 percent of all family-held net worth. In addition to their high incomes and capital gains, they also held 56 percent of all family-held *unrealized* capital gains, calculated as the appreciated value of their unsold assets, such as stocks or real estate. These elite were the leaders behind America's economic growth. The few in this top American group were also the prime beneficiaries of the rapid economic growth of the late 1980s and 1990s. These high-income families were members of the small segment of people who were the real American capitalists, and their position in society bore a striking structural resemblance to the super-elite in the Thai kingdom, or the Norman aristocrats who ruled medieval England, America's ancestral culture. It is almost as if nothing had changed in the fundamental arrangement of society after more than 900 years of cultural development, except that the American capitalist elite were commercial elites rather than just landlords. Furthermore, they were often also political elites and exercised disproportionate control over government. They owed their predominant position to their ability to create and manipulate highly profitable commercial imperia in a way that placed their households on a steep upward material growth trajectory, whereas most households were either maintaining themselves at a relatively constant, but comfortable, material level, or were declining in economic power under the burden of accumulating debt.

The bottom 91 percent of the American population, like the lower 95 percent with maintenance- and poor-level imperia in the Thai kingdom, or the lower 98 percent who were commoners in Norman England—who will be examined in Chapter 4—had such small incomes and held so little in economic assets that their prospects for ever joining the top strata were statistically exceedingly small. Of course, the majority of Americans were living at a material level that was vastly more comfortable than that of commoners in medieval Europe, or ancient Thailand. Average life expectancy was much greater, food more varied, abundant, and nutritious. Virtually all Americans lived in residences with indoor plumbing, hot water on tap, automated central heating, refrigerators, electric power, televisions, and telephones. Most Americans owned motor vehicles and enjoyed the luxury of consuming enormous amounts of energy. These comforts and luxuries would astound a Norman time-traveler from 1089 England. However, these obvious material advantages should not obscure the crucial underlying parallels between medieval English serfs and nobles, and American producer-consumers and capitalists. The cultural role of people who are primarily producer-consumers resembles serfdom, if serfdom is strictly defined as economic dependency. Structurally, most American households depend on wage and salary incomes, and neither own nor control the businesses or resources that are the sources of their employment. This is the same kind of economic powerlessness experienced by English serfs who were not landowners, or commoners who did not own enough land to increase their wealth.

Employment is a critical resource in America, because the cultural ideal in America is that people are expected to "earn" a living, just as medieval peasants earned their living from the land. However, for most, just having a job is not a sure path to the upper economic ranks of American society. According to the census (U.S. Bureau of the Census 2000, 403–446), in 1998 the official labor force consisted of those civilians ages sixteen and over who were either employed or actively seeking employment. This group represented about two-thirds of the potential civilian labor force and half of the total resident population. Well-paid, full-time jobs were not abundant. One-third of the labor force was either unemployed, underemployed and working part-time, or holding multiple jobs. The top 15 percent of full-time jobs were executive and professional positions held mostly by men earning a median weekly salary of at least $895. Of these top positions, 15 percent were held by women earning only $626. Even in the highest-paid occupational category, a household in which both husband and wife earned the 1997 median professional income of $50,402 and $35,417, respectively, the combined income of $85,819 would still fall far short of the capitalist growth threshold. In 1998 a family income of at least $100,000 was a virtual prerequisite for active participation in America's capitalist economy. Upward mobility was possible for those few who managed to save and invest 15 percent or more of their income in the face of pervasive advertising pressures to engage in status-seeking competitive conspicuous consumption.

The existence of commercial imperia makes sense of this inequitable distribution of social power. In America, personal economic imperia are constructed from family income, assets, and net worth, but these were very unevenly distributed. Most American families did not have enough economic power to be capitalists in any meaningful sense and were unable to pass on a significant estate to their children. Less than two-thirds of the middle-income families in the $25,000 to $49,999 range, (roughly the middle third of the population, bracketing the median income of $33,400) were able to save anything, and their savings were very small judging by their limited assets. This explains why the median net worth of middle-income families in 1998 was only $60,300, primarily equity in home and car, why only two-thirds of these families even owned a residence, and why the median value of that property was only $85,000, why that net value was reduced by a median mortgage debt of $45,700. The $152,500 median sales price of a new single-family residence was a difficult financial barrier for these families.

The limiting factor that prevented most American families from becoming capitalists with income-generating assets was that they derived their incomes from wages and salaries that were too low to allow them to save and invest. The link between low income and inability to save is an example of Engel's law, named after the nineteenth-century statistician Ernst Engel, who observed that lower-income people must spend a higher proportion of their income on basic consumption, leaving little for the luxury of investment. Families that cannot save and invest are perpetually locked into wage and salary incomes, which may only meet their immediate consumption needs, whereas those with high enough incomes to allow them to invest can gain "unearned" dividends, rents, and profits. In this regard it is significant that tax return data for 1996 show that more than 90 percent of individual tax returns—those returns reporting earnings of less than $100,000—derive more than 80 percent of their income from wages and salaries, versus only 56 percent for those earning $100,000 or more. These figures show that the top 6 million individual filers—a mere 7 percent of total filers—report receiving more than 50 percent of all unearned income. There are also important differences in the source of "unearned" incomes for the groups on either side of the $100,000 line. Those earning less than $100,000 derived one-third of their "unearned" income from retirement pensions and annuities, whereas those with incomes over $100,000 derived one-third of their income from capital gains from the sale of assets. "Low-income" filers did not have enough capital assets to provide a significant source of unearned income.

Stock ownership, the prime symbol of American capitalism, was remarkably underrepresented in the middle range of American families in 1998. Only about half of these families held stocks in any form—directly, as mutual funds, in retirements funds or other managed accounts—and their median value was only $11,500, barely more than the $10,200 median value of their cars. Stock ownership declined rapidly in lower-income brackets. In contrast, among the 6 million families at the top, with incomes of $100,000 or more, more than 90 percent owned stocks, and their median value was $150,000.

Financial assets of different types are distributed among families according to income level such that for 90 percent of all families in 1998 the only financial asset was a checking account with a median value of $2,300. The next most common financial asset was a retirement account with a median value of $18,100, but fewer than half of all families even had a retirement account. Other financial assets in descending order were even less common: term life insurance (30 percent), savings bonds (19 percent), stocks (19 percent), mutual funds (17 percent), certificate of deposits (15 percent). When families are sorted by income level a remarkable degree of economic inequality emerges. The median value of financial assets held by families with incomes of $100,000 or more was $218,500, whereas families with incomes of $25,000 to $49,000 had financial assets with a median value of only $13,300. The increasing overall importance of financial assets is reflected in the fact that by 1998 financial assets made up 40 percent of all family assets, whereas in 1983 they constituted only 25 percent.

The American example raises troubling questions about the impact on humans of commercial culture, and begs a comparison with America's parent country, medieval England, organized as an imperial culture. Can the new commercial culture really be considered a progressive change in absolute human terms when the number of Americans in prison probably exceeds the number who were serfs and slaves in Norman England, and when the 35 million Americans who were officially living in poverty in 1998 represents more than the total population of the British Isles in 1875? It is sobering to realize that in America, just as in medieval England, the majority still have little control over the conditions of their daily life and are not in a position either to meaningfully invest and thereby influence cultural development, or to make more direct decisions concerning their country's great wealth. In both cultural systems the top 2 percent of the population constituted an effective aristocracy and a ruling elite of a few hundred people held enormous power. It is fair to ask in what sense the great transformation to commercial culture can be considered human progress.

3

Why Scale Matters

Human societies and cultures are significantly influenced by scale. The fundamental principle is that a larger society is not the same thing as a small society grown larger. Bigger societies are different from smaller societies, but scale differences are intrinsically almost incomprehensible because they exceed ordinary experience and perception. Growth necessarily produces scale increase, and growth will change internal relationships. In this respect, scale follows natural laws. Individual organisms naturally grow, but growth eventually stops when genetically defined points are reached and maintenance functions must take over. Likewise, human societies grow until they meet thresholds. Societies do not naturally grow forever, and perpetual growth in a finite physical world is impossible. These are truisms, but in the commercial world perpetual growth is curiously assumed to be both a natural and an ideal condition. Growth is culturally identified with "progress," but the negative human consequences of the scale change that growth produces are culturally either disregarded or viewed as natural and inevitable. This chapter critically examines the concepts of progress, growth, and scale, demonstrating that scale does matter because throughout human history it has affected the quality of human life. This discussion of scale theory is a necessary prelude to later chapters that ask the why and how questions about growth and scale change.

The crucial insight of scale theory is that growth changes the quality of human relationships between households and individuals, as was shown in Chapter 2's comparison between life in Ashaninka society and in the Thai kingdom. The size of human societies and cultures matters because larger societies will naturally have more concentrated social power. Larger societies will be less democratic than smaller societies, and they will have an unequal distribution of risks and rewards. Aggrandizing individuals will have the possibility of constructing larger, more powerful imperia in larger societies. These changes in power will be a natural function of size, but democratic countermeasures can prevent scale increases from occurring and may be able to moderate their negative consequences. It is a cultural illusion to imagine that growth will necessarily improve the quality of human life for everyone.

Power Laws, Energy, and the Disproportions of Scale

Scale theory uses simple mathematical power laws and log graphs to demonstrate that societal growth disproportionately concentrates social power as scale increases. Scale refers to the size or dimensions of an object. Scale can be measured by magnitude in powers, or multiples of ten. Scale differences are best displayed on a log graph where the value of each major grid line increases by one power of ten. Whenever scale differences span several powers of ten, they can*not* be effectively displayed as conventional numbers on a standard linear graph. For example, the population size of typical tribal societies, chiefdoms, kingdoms, agrarian empires, colonial empires, and the global society can be ranked respectively by order of magnitude in the sequence 500, 50,000, 5,000,000, 50,000,000, 500,000,000, and 5,000,000,000 (Figure 3.1). The global society is larger than a tribal society by seven orders of magnitude, or powers of ten, which is expressed by the addition of seven zeros. These scale differences are so vast that they cannot be comprehended or visualized within our ordinary perception. However, using a log scale, where each grid line is a multiple of ten, we can visualize societies at all six scale ranks on the same graph.

These scale differences are crucial because we can assume that the largest society at each of these size ranks is approaching a scale threshold beyond which further organizational changes would be required. These societies cover the entire span of human cultural development and call attention to the fact that the shift from ancient agrarian empires to the largest colonial empires (British empire, 500 million people by 1930) was an order-of-magnitude change that required extensive exploitation of a new energy source such as fossil fuels. The shift to the commercially organized contemporary global society (5 billion people) required electric power, air travel, computerized information systems, and giant transnational commercial corporations. These six cultural-scale transformations also depended on drastic organizational changes that shifted the locus of social power sequentially upward

Figure 3.1 **Social System Scale Thresholds**

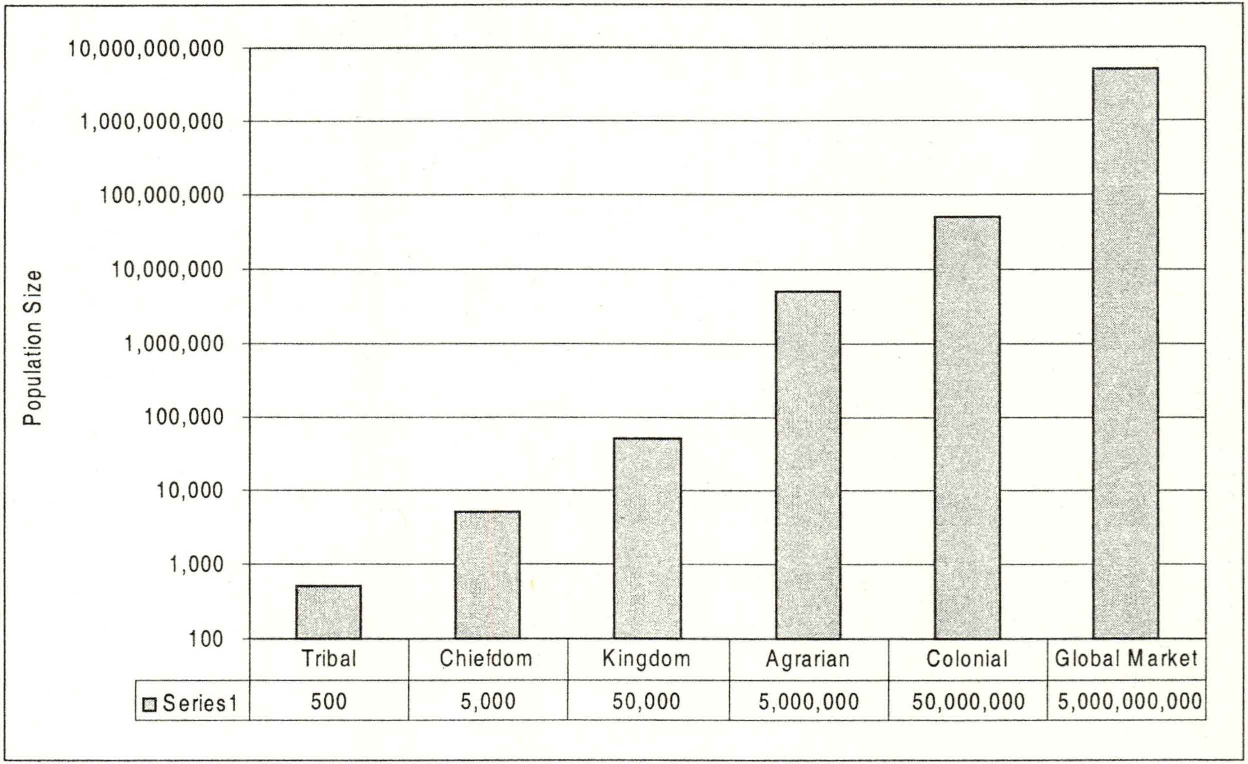
Population Size
10,000,000,000
1,000,000,000
100,000,000
10,000,000
1,000,000
100,000
10,000
1,000
100
Tribal
Chiefdom
Kingdom
Agrarian
Colonial
Global Market
Series1
500
5,000
50,000
5,000,000
50,000,000
5,000,000,000

from households, to political rulers, to commercial elites. In thinking about such scale differences, it is important to remember that the same principles also apply to scale differences in individual income, wealth, or the assets and revenues of the commercial businesses that dominate the contemporary world.

The distribution of many forms of individual human variability, such as size, weight, and test scores, can often be described by the familiar bell-shaped curve, in which the average value is the most frequent value and there are relatively few individuals with very large or very small values. In sharp contrast to this "normal" distribution, the frequency of many things in nature is characterized by a lognormal distribution in which small values are most frequent and higher values are increasingly infrequent. This means that the mathematical average is not a useful measure of distribution. A lognormal distribution is skewed far to the right by a small number of cases with very high values. This is where the power elite are located. Any lognormal distribution produces a straight sloped line when plotted on a log log graph. This trend line is the signature of a lognormal distribution and it expresses a power law. The lognormal distribution is a law of nature with important human implications. It will turn up again and again in the following chapters.

This skewed lognormal distribution is crucial for understanding the social theory of scale and power because it applies to cities by size, countries by GDP, numbers of persons in occupations, ranked positions in a hierarchy, income, wealth, and other measures of human achievement (Zipf 1949). This was first discovered in the 1890s by Italian economist and sociologist Vilfredo Pareto (1848–1923), who found a "natural" skewing in the distribution of income where there were a small number of very high incomes and progressively more numerous smaller incomes. Pareto developed an equation that described the long right tail of the income curve, showing that it produced the signature straight sloping line on a log log graph. Pareto (1896–97) found that the upper end of income distributions was relatively constant in nations as varied as France, England, Belgium, Germany, Switzerland, Austria, Peru, and the United States covering a time span from 1471 to 1894. This distribution proved to be so constant that economists have called it Pareto's law. For example, above the median the distribution of American incomes as reported to the Internal Revenue Service in 1995 clearly shows a Pareto distribution (Figure 3.2). This means that the top few, in this case the 400 richest Americans, receive average incomes that are four powers of ten greater than the average maintenance-level taxpayer. The average revenues of the 500 largest American business corporations show the same relationship to small businesses (Figure 3.3). Pareto's law may be "natural," but these distributions are not inevitable, because government policies such as steeply progressive income taxes, or other forms of social redistribution, can intervene to alter the pattern.

These comparisons reveal that the differences between the average wealth or income of the top 400 individuals in the United States and the average for the bottom half of society, between the revenue of giant corporations and small businesses, between the population of villages and megalopolises, and between small tribes and giant commercial nations is as great in cosmic terms as the difference in the thousand light-years between earth and the Orion nebula, and the 150 million light years across a supercluster, the largest identifiable form in the universe. It is no exaggeration to say that these social scale differentials have reached cosmic proportions. The differences between rich and poor households, large and small societies, and small and giant businesses have literally become astronomical.

Social power is distributed in hierarchical societies according to mathematical power laws resembling the distribution of solar energy through the food chain in a natural ecosystem. Following the laws of thermodynamics, as solar energy moves through an ecosystem from the sun, to the earth's surface, through green plants and herbivores to the top consumer there is a power of ten decline in the quantity of available energy, and a power of ten increase in energy concentration (Odum 1997, 89). Following the "energy equivalence rule," the few individuals of a large species collectively use as much energy as all the more numerous members of a small species in the same environment, but larger species use much more per capita (Marquet 2000). Therefore, like the richest nations or households, the few top consumer species individually consume a far more concentrated diet of solar energy than species lower on the food chain.

Per capita energy consumption increases by powers of ten in step with increases in social organizational scale and complexity from 8,500 kilocalories in the tribal world, through 26,000 kilocalories in the imperial, to 230,000 kilocalories in the commercial world (Cook 1971). This trend parallels scale increases in global population, but of course elite consumption levels are orders of magnitude higher than average. For example, in the year 2000 the household of a billionaire in Washington State used 604,960 kilowatt-hours of electricity, which was fifty times the average household usage in the state (*News Tribune* 2001). In general, within the commercial world individuals in the largest-scale societies with the largest economies use more energy per capita than individuals in smaller-scale societies, with energy use increasing by powers of ten. This means that the largest commercial cultures are functionally equivalent to top carnivores, making them very costly members of global society.

Pareto's discoveries were brought together under even broader mathematical principles that have infelicitously been labeled "chaos theory" (Gleick 1987). For example, Benoit B. Mandelbrot (1977) used the phrase "fractal

Figure 3.2 **American Taxpayers by Size of Income, 1995**

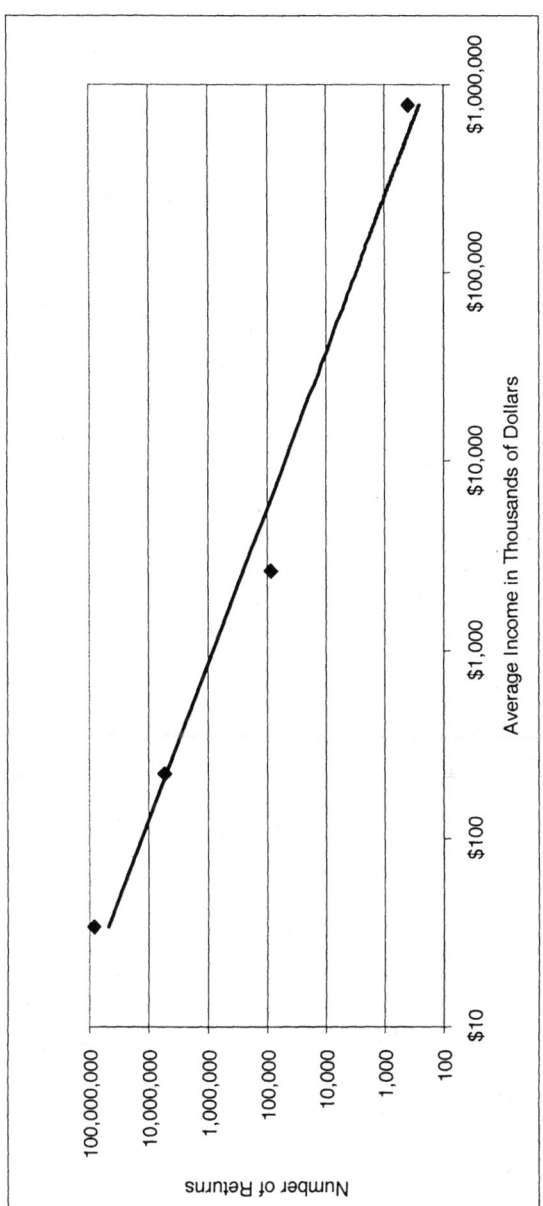

Figure 3.3 American Business Corporations by Size of Revenue, 1994

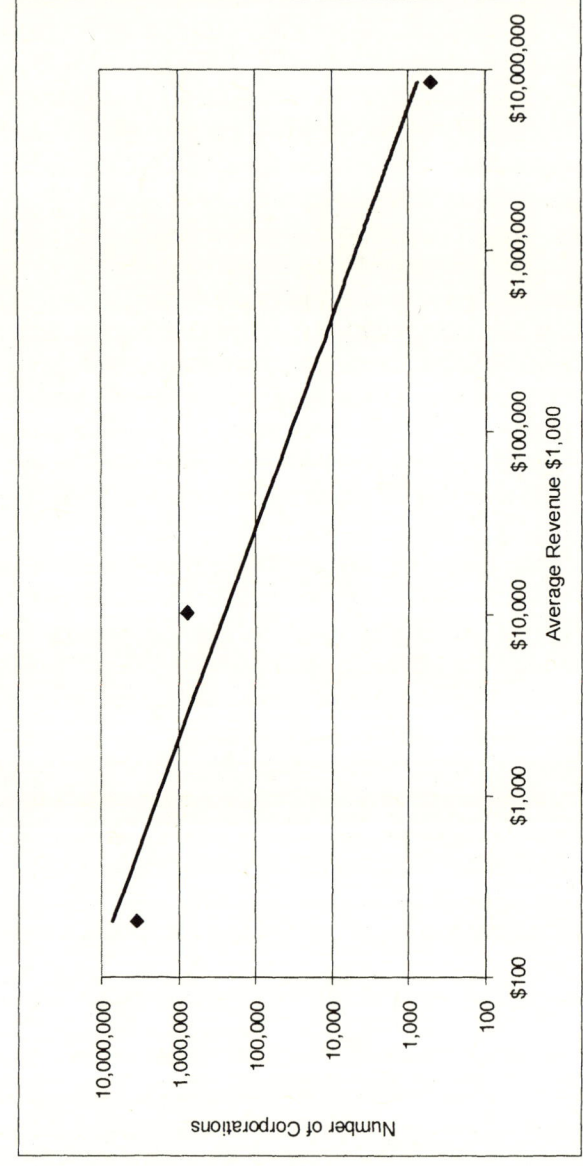

geometry" to describe the amazing regularities in natural patterns that describe everything from snowflakes, coastlines, the shape of clouds, constellations, and income distributions. Mandelbrot observed that fractal patterns are "scale free," in the sense that they maintain their shape regardless of the size or scale of the object. This suggests that social power is also "scale free" and the shape of its distribution does not "naturally" change as societies grow larger, and this causes growth to concentrate social power.

The actual mechanisms producing power distributions in human societies have been widely debated, but it is clear that scale itself is a crucial variable. Many social theoreticians, including Pareto, have assumed that extremely unequal income distributions can be attributed to natural variations in ability among individuals. However, other theorists have argued that random chance in combination with growth in scale is all that is required to produce skewed distributions of wealth and power. Bruce H. Mayhew and Paul T. Schollaert (Mayhew 1973; Mayhew and Schollaert 1980a, 1980b) developed mathematical models showing that purely on the basis of random chance and probability theory, political and economic power becomes more concentrated as societies grow larger, or as total wealth increases. Expressed more simply in reference to political elites, Mayhew (1973, 468) declared, "The relative size of a ruling elite is a decreasing function of the size of the system it governs." This means that fewer and fewer gain more and more power, purely as a function of scale. Mayhew and Schollaert (1980a, 8) conclude: "by chance alone, an increase in population size creates an increasing concentration of wealth, ultimately pressing the system toward maximum possible inequality. . . ." This of course assumes that there are no cultural interventions to redistribute power.

Whether skewed social power distributions are ultimately explained as the outcome of mathematical laws or of natural variation in human ability, there is a consensus among theorists that increasing concentration of power is a predictable outcome of growth. This is the power of scale. Sociologists have been aware of these principles for some time, but their human implications are not widely appreciated by policymakers or the public in general. These insights on scale and power are profoundly significant for any understanding of world history and will be explored in more detail below and in the following chapters.

The Illusion of Evolutionary Progress

Growth in social and cultural systems leads to increased scale and complexity, and invites deceptively easy comparisons with the evolution of life and the appealing illusion of progress. People commonly assume that the cultural developments unfolding all around us are natural, inevitable, progressive, and good for humanity. By extension, it is often thought that specific recent developments such as globalization and the introduction of new technology that sustains globalization likewise simply happen as the natural outcome of an inevitable drive toward complexity and material progress. Such beliefs can lead to ominous conclusions. Bill Gates, a prominent exponent of this progressivist viewpoint, declared in *The Road Ahead* that we have no choice—technology-based "productive change," or progress, "will come no matter what; we need to make the best of it—not try to forestall it" (Gates 1996, 11).

This self-serving interpretation of human history echoes an earlier generation of social philosophers led by Herbert Spencer, who misapplied Darwin's theories of biological evolution and natural selection to human societies. At the end of the nineteenth century Spencer was convinced that the British Empire had achieved global supremacy through a natural process of "survival of the fittest." Spencer mistook the imperial policies of a small ruling elite for the natural order. In the case of England's colonial expansion, as will be explored in some detail in Chapter 5, English *culture,* designed and directed by a few key individuals centered in London, not *nature,* produced the British Empire. There were many other more just, and more democratic alternative cultural designs for Britain and the world, as will be shown in Chapter 7, and individual intention ultimately brought the empire down. A belief in the inevitability of progress may be some comfort for the vast majority who play no direct role in the high-level decision making that actually causes cultural development, but it would be unfortunate if the belief in natural progress silenced people who envisioned a more humane and sustainable world.

Anthropologists were widely influenced by the evolutionary beliefs that directed colonialism. For example, in 1877 American anthropologist Lewis Henry Morgan constructed a sequence of developmental stages to describe the history of human progress from savagery, through barbarism, to civilization. He confidently placed European civilization at the top of the hierarchy. Morgan argued that these stages combined moral and technological improvement and represented a natural unfolding of God's plan for humanity. Morgan's work was largely ignored in the United States until 1949, when Leslie A. White revived the concept of cultural progress. At that moment America's global military supremacy had just been demonstrated, and it was widely believed that a nuclear age of peace and prosperity had dawned. In his influential writing, White used improvements in technological efficiency, increased per capita energy consumption, and increased scale of society as measures of progress.

White's "neo-evolutionary" students devised a new sequence of band, tribe, chiefdom, state to replace Morgan's stages of general cultural evolutionary progress. Progress came to mean scale increase, and it was defined as greater physical and biological complexity, "higher" forms of integration, specialization, more energy use, reproductive success, and greater adaptability. However, complexity may reduce adaptability, too much reproductive success can lead to extinction, and greater energy use may prove suicidal. Overspecialization may make it impossible for a culture or species to respond to a sudden environmental change. These measures of evolutionary progress may not be adaptive for either people or animals.

Cultural imperialism is not a law of nature, although those who espouse it may inappropriately borrow from the biological concept of *competitive exclusion,* according to which similar species are unlikely to occupy the same place. The imperial culture might also be said to resemble an ecological dominant, the most numerous species in a community. However, in nature successful ecological dominants outnumber, but they do not eliminate, the many nondominant species. Biologists who argue that larger-scale organisms are more progressive have sometimes explained this in terms that resemble explanations for the existence of large predatory corporations in the commercial world. For example, Brown and Maurer (1986) speculated that the ability to "monopolize" and "dominate" resource use will be a selective advantage for larger organisms. However, even neo-evolutionary cultural anthropologists acknowledged that smaller and "weaker" cultural systems were sometimes adaptively superior:

> Nor are those cultures that we might consider higher in general evolutionary standing necessarily more perfectly adapted to their environments than lower. Many great civilizations have fallen in the last 2,000 years, even in the midst of material plenty, while the Eskimos tenaciously maintained themselves in an incomparably more difficult habitat. The race is not to the swift, nor the battle to the strong. (Sahlins and Service 1960, 26–27)

Successful cultural adaptation displays the branching pattern of development characteristic of biological evolution. This is represented in the rich cultural variation that has characterized domestic-scale cultures for millennia. Branching and cultural diversity provide a means of sustaining people in diverse environments. This process of segmentation, diversification, and adaptation is the opposite of both "progressive" centralization and increase in scale and complexity, which is more likely to be maladaptive over the long run.

Evolutionary psychologist Robert Wright (2000) repeats the progressivist argument in even more exuberant terms. According to Wright, life is a non-zero sum, win-win game. Like Morgan, he argues that the history of all life and culture can be understood as an irresistible progression toward greater complexity, cooperation, and increasingly beneficial outcomes for humanity. Scale increase is good. Over the long run people have in sum been getting richer, and more moral, as the scale of culture has increased. For Wright, economic globalization represents more progress and was "in the cards" from the moment life appeared. In contrast, the present book argues that all of these assumptions about progress are probably illusions, perhaps dangerous illusions. Even the very notion of progress is an illusory cultural construct. Furthermore, there is abundant evidence that scale increase in human affairs is a problematic process, because it is directed by individual human beings with human weaknesses.

Looking at biological evolution, paleontologist Stephen Jay Gould (1996) argued that biological progress is a human illusion based on a pervasive progressivist bias. He does not deny that through time more complex organisms evolved from simpler, single-celled organisms, but he stresses that small-scale organisms have remained the dominant, and most successful, life forms. Complex organisms, such as humans, represent extreme forms and are not a progressive *trend*. Biologist Sean B. Carroll (2001) pointed out that 3 billion years of biological evolution were required before macroscopic, motile organisms based on modular designs appeared on earth, apparently quite by chance. Humans are very late arrivals in 3.5 billion years of life history, were probably also produced by chance, and may ultimately not prove successful. The chance appearance of more complex organisms does not mean that life as a whole has progressed simply because the great mass of simpler organisms remain "behind." This entire analysis can be seen as a metaphor for the extreme material success of the core capitalist members of the contemporary commercial world in comparison with the great mass of the world's peoples who exist at much lower levels of material consumption. Average consumption has increased, but humanity as a whole has not moved up the ladder of consumption because the curve is skewed far to the right. There is also steadily increasing evidence that high consumption is unsustainable.

Culture, Biology, and the Problem of Size

Evolution, whether cultural or biological, means change through time, but implies no inevitable drive toward complexity, or toward larger-scale organisms or societies. In nature, small, simple organisms are often better able to survive adverse changes in the environment, such as droughts, because their higher reproductive rates allow them to rebound more quickly, and they require fewer resources than larger animals. The smallest organisms, such as viruses and bacteria, are objectively the most successful life forms in the universe in terms of total individuals, species diversity, biomass, and overall adaptability. Objectively, we live in the "Age of Bacteria," as Gould (1996) is fond of pointing out. For the same reasons, it is likely that small-scale cultures and societies are more adaptive than larger ones. It was not an accident that domestic-scale cultures existed in great diversity and occupied most of the world until a mere 200 years ago. Growth in the scale of cultural systems may be maladaptive for humans overall because growth concentrates power, reduces cultural diversity, and makes it possible for larger, less sustainable cultures to unnaturally overpower smaller, otherwise longer-lived cultures. Growth also increases the number of people who live in absolute and relative material deprivation. These matters will be explored more fully in later chapters.

It is misleading and inappropriate to impute personality to societies or civilizations, and to treat them as adaptive units operated on by "natural" selection. Individual humans and cultural ideas are the primary units of cultural selection and evolution. Unlike genes, culture consists of purposefully created, socially transmitted symbols, information, and norms that shape what individuals do and regulate society so that people can successfully maintain themselves and reproduce. People change culture by deliberate invention and imitation. This is humanly intentional cultural selection, not natural selection. Natural selection operates on individuals as biological organisms. Cultural selection means that individual humans select and reproduce cultural ideas. Nations, or civilizations, may be imagined to be entities in competition with each other, but their individual human leaders are the decision-making competitors. Civilizations are artificial cultural constructions, not biological organisms, and they would be poor biological performers if we insisted on considering them as organisms. Domestically organized tribal societies segment when they grow too large, but politically centralized societies do not generally split and reproduce themselves. They grow larger in territory and population until they disintegrate or are absorbed by other civilizations. This is why the total number of polities has declined over time. There may have been as many as 150,000 autonomous polities in the world 10,000 years ago, but by the year 2000 there were only 188 member nations in the United Nations. This reduction in number and diversity was a humanly directed cultural process, not a natural evolution. Imperial civilizations are not better adapted than tribes, because empires are more costly to maintain, they break down more easily, destroy their natural resources, and have shorter life-spans. Political empires are grossly oversized, extremely vulnerable dinosaurs that cannot stand major environmental perturbations.

Under the influence of commercially organized cultures humans have recently begun taking far more of the earth's energy and resources than any other species, in a way that appears objectively maladaptive. In addition to the very recent human use of fossil fuels, it was estimated in the mid-1980s that humans overall were already appropriating nearly 40 percent of the net primary biological production of global terrestrial ecosystems, either directly as food crops and domestic animals in highly simplified, immature ecosystems, or indirectly through nonconsumption uses and habitat destruction (Vitousek et al. 1986). A mature, highly evolved ecosystem should shift energy resources from growth (reproduction) functions to maintenance functions (basic metabolism), leaving less for human consumers. This is precisely the kind of stable ecosystem that domestic-scale cultures depended on. All of this suggests that cultural "progress" is unnatural. Our cultural metabolic rate is too high, our reproductive rate is too high, we take up far too much of global biomass, and we have reduced global cultural and biological diversity in ways that threaten the well-being of all life forms. These are unnatural and maladaptive trends, but they do promote greater scale and greater concentration of social power. This raises the question of who would promote such growth.

Human Community, Society, and Scale

When the scale of human societies increases, at least five things are likely to happen: (1) per capita economic productivity and consumption increases, but the product becomes more inequitably distributed; (2) democracy declines, because decision making becomes more cumbersome and more concentrated; (3) institutions and technologies become more specialized, more complex, more costly, and more vulnerable; (4) the pace of change and instability increases; and (5) all types of social power become more concentrated. The evidence presented in this and the following chapters suggests that these scale effects are due to the nature of scale itself as well as the nature of human beings. Growth is a disruptive and expensive process. Many scale effects are negative for human society as a whole because they mean that more people will be disempowered and impoverished by growth, and society and culture will become less resilient and less sustainable. Culture plays a crucial role in mitigating these detrimental effects of scale by preventing growth beyond optimum levels, and by redistributing power.

There is a general consensus in the social science literature on the significance of size for human societies, and that two scalar types can be distinguished: large and small (Berreman 1978a, 1978b). This scale distinction readily identifies the line between the tribal world and the imperial world. The differences between large and small societies were brilliantly captured in the 1880s by German sociologist Ferdinand Tönnies's (1957) concepts of *Gemeinschaft* (community) and *Gesellschaft* (society). This is the same distinction that I draw between domestic-scale and political-scale culture, and that anthropologist Robert

Redfield (1947) made between folk and urban societies. For Tönnies, *Gemeinschaft* was a "real," organic, face-to-face community integrated by shared sentiments of personal familiarity and kinship. It was an intimate, private, and exclusive society focused on the domestic life and local place. Redfield emphasized that folk societies tended to be culturally homogenous, relatively stable, self-sufficient, and egalitarian. Only a few hundred people could live comfortably in such a society. A *Gesellschaft* was an artificial, imaginary, impersonal, public society because it was too large to sustain the interpersonal human qualities that were possible in a *Gemeinschaft*. Urban life, with its cultural diversity, personal anonymity, impermanence, and inequality captures the essence of *Gesellschaft*. If societies grow larger they will eventually cross the scale threshold between *Gemeinschaft* and *Gesellschaft*.

All the things that matter for people, including connubia (mating networks), subsistence security, kinship reciprocity, settlements, production systems, communication, and social solidarity, have scale limits, with size optimums, minimums, and maximums. For example, scale influences the relationship between leaders and followers, as well as among followers and leaders. As productive systems become larger, diversification and divisions of labor will be required, and scale efficiencies may be obtained until diminishing returns set in. Population growth changes the face-to-face domestic community into an impersonal society, because people cannot effectively remember and relate personally to more than 500 individuals (Kosse 1990).

Organizational theorists have classified social organizations as small, medium, large, and giant, according to the possible forms of leadership (Caplow 1964, 25–28). A small organization of up to thirty members could function without any formally delegated authority because everyone would know everyone else. In a medium-sized organization of up to a thousand people a leader could interact with everyone, although he could not recognize or know everyone well. A small "inner circle" of leaders who know each other and the primary leader well would be likely to emerge. A large organization of 1,000 to 50,000 members would be too large for any one person to know all the other members, but one leader could still be recognized by everyone. Most people would know the leader, but the leader would not know them. In giant organizations of more than 50,000 members, mass communication would be required for the leader to even be recognized by most members, and an inner circle of subordinate rulers would be essential. The implications of many of these scale relationships will be explored in this and later chapters.

Scale Limits in the Tribal World: Australian Bands

The size and shape of human residential groups reflect the organization and distribution of social power in a society and are very conspicuous scale phenomena. The size of the minimum residential group in forager societies throughout the tribal world has been found to be a remarkably constant figure of only 25 to 50 people (Steward 1936). This is the optimum size for the domestic group that camps together and daily forages and shares food, given the cultural objective of satisfying basic human needs with maximum human freedom and personal autonomy, and assuming solar-based foraging technology. This number provides the optimum number of people to be supported by the natural food supply in the tribal territory, and allows them to coordinate their activities with informal leadership. Band mobility is a big social advantage for tribal societies, because frequent movement means that people will accumulate little movable property, and portable wealth will be an unlikely source of rivalrous display and competitive emulation. Furthermore, mobility allows people to solve interpersonal conflicts and incompatibilities by separating and joining other bands. The tribe is an interacting network with an average of 500 people in ten or more bands held together by kinship, marriage, reciprocity, and common language and culture. The average of 500 people is the minimum needed to maintain connubia, as well as a common language and culture.

The lower limit of band size was set by the minimum number of households needed to make sure that the group was large enough to carry out reciprocal exchanges of mates with the members of other bands, reproduce the culture, and obtain emergency assistance from the outside to assure biological viability. Individual psychological needs for daily sociability help set the band's lower limits, as well as the need to use reciprocity as social insurance to smooth out random variations in the economic fortunes of individual households. This kind of risk reduction is in everyone's interest.

The social and cultural limits to band size are constants, and they define a constant optimum population size, but the size of band territories varies widely in response to the natural environmental productivity of local ecosystems. Very rich natural environments make possible small, high-density territories and reduce band mobility, because no one wants to walk further than necessary for food. The advantage of a forager production system is that nature does the work of reproducing and maintaining the food supply. Solar energy purifies and recycles the water supply. The trade-off for nature's services is that under extreme desert or arctic conditions band territories must become very large, and bands become highly mobile. In desert environments, where water determines biological productivity, the relationship between rainfall and band density is so predicable that it can be described mathematically.

The Australian aborigines provide an excellent example of scale principles in operation among foraging peoples. Aborigines filled the Australian continent up to an optimum population of perhaps 300,000 people living in some 600 tribes and 6,000 bands. Tribal members spoke a common language and intermarried most often among themselves, while maintaining strategic connections with their neighbors (Birdsell 1957, 1971, 1973, 1979). Generally tribal territories were occupied at no greater than 60 percent of their average carrying capacity, in order to maintain a margin of safety during poor years. The scale of bands and tribes remained constant, although territories became huge and densities low in the driest desert regions, but tribal estates became very small in food rich, high rainfall zones. The spiritual ties between peoples, and between peoples and the land, were so important that bands could abandon drought-stricken areas for long periods and move in with better-off neighbors. Everyone understood that tribal homelands would be reoccupied when conditions improved. Any change in the scale of social units or total population would have totally transformed the scale relationships in this system. The archaeological record shows that the aboriginal system operated in basically the same form for 100,000 years, and for perhaps much longer.

It was possible for aborigines to maintain their small-scale social system over millennia because everyone was a decision maker and, most importantly, women were empowered to make family planning decisions. At the same time, the mobile culture provided natural incentives for a woman to limit family size, and made the task less difficult. Constant mobility in the absence of backpacks or baby strollers meant that a woman could not carry, or care for, more than one dependent infant at a time. Furthermore, there were no infant formulas or easily prepared baby food. Mothers nursed their infants for up to four years or more, providing virtually their sole source of nourishment. This prolonged lactation had the additional physiological benefit of inhibiting ovulation in the nursing mother by keeping her body fat levels low, and thus provided a natural contraceptive. In the event of an untimely birth that would threaten the well-being of an older child, the mother could resort to infanticide. Equally important, aboriginal culture provided men with no incentive to increase the size of the band, or the tribe, in order to gain power. Social power was derived primarily from the spiritual knowledge that an individual could accumulate, as well as their kinship and marriage connections. Polygynous households gave old men the opportunity to multiply their social ties, but this benefited everyone except the young men who had to delay their own marriages. Women provided the bulk of calories, and co-wives foraging together made the food supply more secure and the task more pleasant. Beyond the optimum, larger band size benefited no one, and more importantly band size could not be increased without intensifying technology, or installing political rulers, but aborigines apparently rejected such changes. Presumably they did not want to increase their workloads, and did not want to surrender personal autonomy.

Scale Limits to Power in the Tribal World: The Ashaninka

Settlement in relatively permanent villages can change the scale of society and create a radically different way of life in comparison with mobile bands. Dispute settlement, access to resources, and use of time all change. Permanent settlements also facilitate trade between groups, as well as the accumulation and storage of food and goods. Food storage gave individual households a greater interest in maintaining control over resources, and in some marginal or very unpredictable areas may have somewhat relaxed concerns about subsistence risk. These changes may have weakened some of the anticompetition, antigrowth elements of forager societies. The important question is, who would benefit from such changes? Why would foragers want to make such changes? The effects of scale changes on the distribution of power seem to be the key.

The Ashaninka example demonstrates the limits that scale imposes on power seekers. The independent Ashaninka resembled foragers, even though they lived in relatively permanent houses. With very small, widely dispersed settlements there was no basis for Ashaninka big men to accumulate more than a minimum level of social power, and consequently their imperia remained very small. Households averaged only five persons, and this was perhaps high for tribal societies. The largest polygynous households had four to six wives with at most eight to twelve unmarried children at a given time. A local household group based on such an extended polygynous family might be an aggregate of up to forty people, which was about the same size as an aboriginal band.

Raiding for revenge and booty was apparently much more common in Amazonia than in Australia. Over 100,000 years of living in the same territory, aborigines had perfected a cultural system that apparently minimized conflict and maximized leisure and social stability. Amazonians have probably occupied the rain forest as villagers for a mere 5,000 years, and when Europeans arrived, tribal conditions remained unstable and intergroup hostilities were common. Under these conditions a man's social power could be enhanced if he could command a group of warriors, or call on them as allies. The small size of Ashaninka settlements and the low overall densities meant that a big man might mobilize five to ten warriors from his own local group, but calling on more from neighboring local groups would be an uncertain proposition.

I estimated that in the 1960s there were approximately 21,000 Ashaninka scattered over 20,000 square miles (52,000 square kilometers) of forested hills, although there may have been more people in 1500 before Europeans arrived. This was an area nearly half the size of England, but with a density of just over one person per square mile. This low density meant that an Ashaninka big man would have found very few potential warrior allies within an easily accessible distance of his home. If he traveled only by foot and were able to command the support of all men living within a 6.2 mile radius (10 kilometers)—the maximum foraging distance that people can typically range on foot from their camps and return in a day—there would be a maximum of only twenty-five men available. Even if an extremely ambitious leader managed to command every man within the twenty-mile radius that he could conveniently reach on foot in a single day, there would be no more than 263 men. This would be an extremely small imperium, and it would be very difficult to hold together. Another crucial limit on the concentration of social power for the Ashaninka was that there was no way for even a big man of great renown to pass his success on to a son so that power could accumulate across generations. Every aspiring big man had to start from scratch.

Population density could have been increased in Ashaninka land if people had opted to domesticate peccaries, agoutis, ducks, or guans by feeding them surplus manioc and kitchen scraps, or if they had farmed fish. We can only assume that this did not happen because people preferred the freedom and excitement of hunting, fishing, and foraging to the dull routines of sedentary farm labor and village life. Furthermore, people wanted leaders to be public servants who served the community at their will. As long as people had only limited fixed capital investments in a particular place, and natural resources were abundant and freely available, they could easily withdraw their support from an oppressive leader by simply moving away. This explains why a tribal big man had to be persuasive, and generous, as well as successful in dealings with outsiders. Such qualities were uncommon, difficult to maintain, and almost impossible to reproduce.

The Power of Scale in the Urbanization Process

When aspiring rulers succeed in creating larger urban places above the level of undifferentiated tribal villages, they can concentrate vast amounts of political and economic power. Geographer Walter Christaller (1933) discovered that urban places in southern Germany were lognormally distributed by increasing scale and he attributed this to the random outcome of optimization behavior in which farmers exchanged rural products for urban commodities (King 1984). Christaller

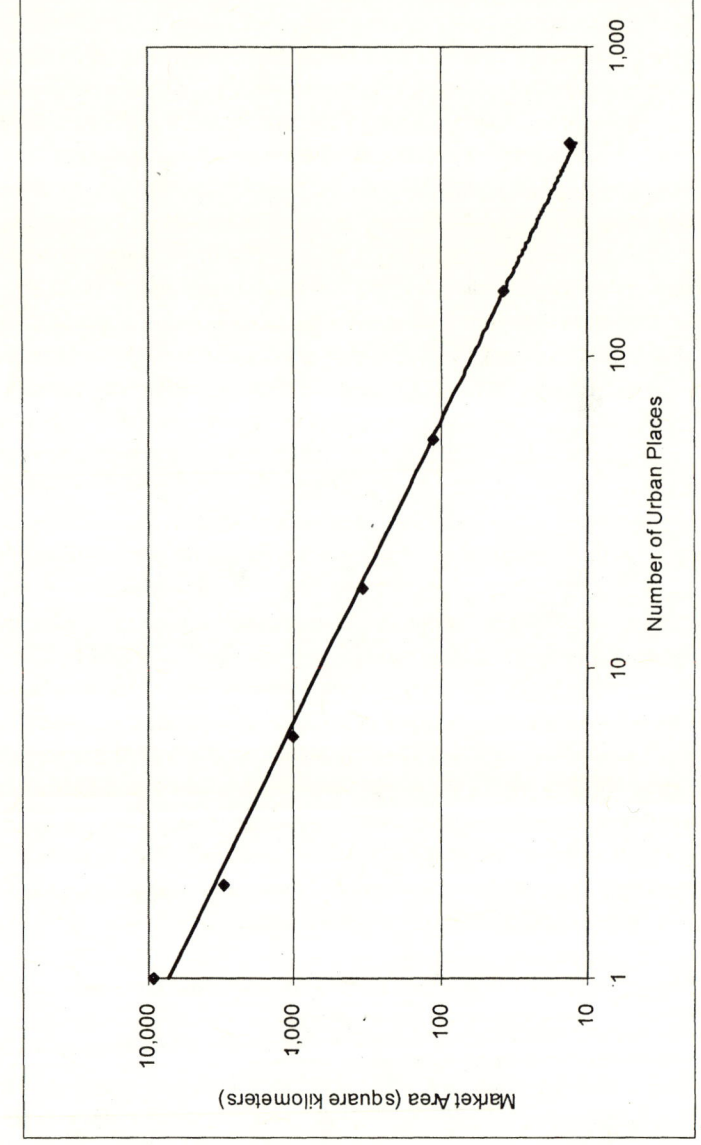

Figure 3.4 The Distribution of Urban Places by Size of Market Area, Germany, 1930

described urban growth as a centralizing process rather than simple segmentation and reduplication of tribal villages, and thought that urban market networks were self-organized systems. Christaller's central place theory assumed that multiple human decisions determined where urban places of different size could best be located, and collectively created market areas based on transport costs, price, and consumer demand. The invisible hand of the market would thus produce the optimum urban landscape. However, central place theory pretended that all individual decision makers had the same power to influence the outcome, and could not explain why urban scale changed in the first place.

Christaller was able to show empirically that the 729 urban places in his German study area were lognormally ranked into seven size classes, with their larger members spaced at ever greater distances, and with their respective market areas ranging in size by orders of magnitude from 12 to 9,161 square kilometers (Figure 3.4). Although these urban rankings resemble the rank order distributions found in nature, and have functional significance, they are created by central decision makers. Ever larger urban centers have important consequences for the concentration of social power because they create positions for high-level managers and strategic planners who can profit enormously from large-scale exchanges or from the politically enforced extraction of "surplus" production. Not all producers and consumers have the same economic or political power, and not all commodities are consumed by everyone. How such urban systems develop, and why they should not be considered the natural result of self-organization, are important issues to be explored more fully in later chapters.

Other examples of ranked urban systems in very different cultures help illuminate the scale and power issues involved with urban growth. Historian G. William Skinner (1964, 1977) described central places in Imperial China in the 1890s, showing how Chinese cities combined both political administrative and economic market functions. With a much larger population (215 million people) and a larger area than southern Germany, Imperial China had 316,785 urban places grouped into ten size ranks with populations ranging from villages or "central market towns" of under 500 people to the imperial capital of perhaps a million people. Chinese urban places were also lognormally distributed. Market areas ranged in size from 2,860 square kilometers in central market towns to 589,482 square kilometers in central metropolises. At this time China was still a solar-powered ancient agrarian system, although commercial exchanges were certainly important. Administrators and merchants who commanded larger market areas would have clearly enjoyed social power that was orders of magnitude greater than those in smaller centers. An urban hierarchy of this scale is created by imperial rulers; it is not produced by the decision making of peasant farmers. Such urban systems also require vast bureaucracies.

Bureaucracy and Domination

The power-concentrating effects of growth in scale are most fully realized through the creation of hierarchy and bureaucracy. Bureaucracy is an institutionalized form of domination. Max Weber defined domination as a special form of power, as "imposing one's own will on the behavior of other persons" (1968, 942). In this respect, domination can be viewed as the operation of an imperium. Weber identified domination as "authoritarian power of command" in which there is a ruler and a ruled who must obey. He notes, however, that formal administrative domination could potentially remain so narrow in scope that the official would be a servant rather than a master if he were appointed by direct democracy. This is only possible in a small-scale society. A tribal village headman is such a "servant official" in that he has limited power and may be readily replaced. His position is so precarious that most anthropologists would not call a village headman an official at all.

In some societies officials may be selected at random or serve in rotation for short terms. Direct democracy of this sort assumes a small-scale society. Weber argued that mass societies were likely to be ruled by a small minority, according to the "law of the small number." This was because a few people, perhaps under a single head, could quickly organize rational action against opposition and could readily keep their intentions secret. Weber felt that dominant rulers needed a small circle of obedient subordinates set apart from the ruled masses. The members of the ruling circle were conditioned to following the orders of a master and had a personal interest in maintaining the apparatus of domination that they constituted because they benefited from it. According to Weber, every privileged dominating group must justify its position to those in less privileged groups either by appealing to rational rules or to norms that everyone accepts as legitimate, or by appealing to personal authority based either on sacred tradition or personal charisma.

For Weber, a bureaucracy is based on a formally defined hierarchy of salaried professional offices under a single top ruler, with official jurisdictions, official duties, carefully delimited authority, strict qualifications, record keeping and formal rules, and regular supervision, all supported by subofficials and specialized staff persons. Modern bureaucracy replaced systems based on notables who served as part-time officials as an avocation and an honorific duty, and who dispensed personalized judgments based on personal loyalties. In modern bureaucracy, the public sphere of the bureaucrat is distinct from the bureaucrat's private household. In principle, at least, this kind of rationalized structure is distinguishable from the highly personal, informal structures of domination often maintained in the ancient imperial world, which were based on patronage, nepotism, and favoritism. Bureaucracies succeeded and expanded because they were technically superior to less rationalized forms of domination, although modernization did not eliminate abuses of power. A bureaucracy is a machine. Bureaucrats strive to operate objectively, "without regard for persons," and to the extent that they succeed, bureaucracy becomes a "dehumanized" system eminently suited to the demands of domination in a large-scale system. In Weber's words:

> Bureaucracy develops the more perfectly, the more it is "dehumanized," the more completely it succeeds in eliminating from official business love, hatred, and all purely personal, irrational, and emotional elements which escape calculation. This is appraised as its special virtue by capitalism. (Weber 1968, 975)

More recently, organizational specialist Ralph P. Hummel (1987) also stressed that a bureaucrat was a technician, devoid of individual will and human emotion. Hummel calls bureaucracy "the bomb that threatens humanity" (1987, 2), arguing that bureaucracy alters the human psyche by replacing one's autonomous will with the identity of the organization. The rational, scientific, and legal human technician replaces the emotional, feeling, human person. Bureaucracy also replaces an individual's conscience, his or her internal sense of right and wrong, and the sense of mastery over daily tasks, with decisions made by remote superiors. The bureaucratic experience makes the individual dependent on the bureaucracy for his/her identity and survival, thereby creating a powerful existential anxiety that keeps the bureaucrat subservient.

Growth placed ordinary people in the unhappy situation of choosing between having social functions such as justice "administered" on the basis of favoritism by traditional, self-interested aristocrats, as hereditary elites, or by professional bureaucrats serving as unfeeling technicians. Bureaucracy reduced certain traditional social differences, for example by applying the concept that everyone was equal before the law, but it made other abuses possible by facilitating ever greater concentrations of power in fewer hands.

Power laws are clearly visible in the construction of bureaucratic social structures and provide useful insights on the natural limits to their size and shape. The number of ranks or levels of organization and the span of bureaucratic control, or the number of immediate subordinates each official directs, consistently fall within narrow ranges. The number of officials at each power rank, measured by the aggregate number of bottom rank people they ultimately command, are lognormally distributed. This provides a precise measure of the power of bureaucratic imperia. Empirically, the maximum number of ranks even in the largest bureaucracy, is unlikely to exceed eleven, and the span of control exercised over subordinates by any official ranges from two to twenty individuals, but typically does not exceed five. The natural mathematical limits to bureaucracy can be readily demonstrated. For example, a system of ten ranks with each official having ten subordinates would produce a pyramid with 1 billion workers at the base, one emperor at the top, and 10 percent of the total population as the bureaucrats. If each official had 500 subordinates—the maximum number of people that anyone could know personally—a mere five ranks could control a pyramidal society of 62.5 billion people.

A few empirical examples drawn from different social power domains shows how closely the real world follows these theoretical natural limits. The Inca emperor controlled an empire of some 16 million people with a bureaucracy of eleven ranks from top to bottom, and with only one rank of officials having as many as twenty subordinates and most having only two to five. Likewise, the 675,000 men in Napoleon's Grand Army were organized in a bureaucracy with ten ranks. Most Napoleonic officers dealt with only two to six subordinates, and never more than twenty. This command structure became the basis for modern political and corporate business bureaucracies in the nineteenth century. A modern corporate business enterprise with 390,625 bottom-level employees could be organized in nine ranks, with five subordinates for each.

Napoleonic armies represented the summit of early modern bureaucratic military organization and became the model for all modern armies. Napoleon's total imperial forces amounted to some 880,000 men (Chandler 1966, 333), only slightly more than the maximum 650,000-man military strength of the Romans under the Emperor Diocletian in A.D. 300 (A.H.M. Jones 1974, 129). During World War II, 6 million, 12 million, and more than 20 million troops were mobilized respectively by the French, Germans, and Soviets. Such vast numbers were made possible by the use of fossil fuel-based transport systems and electronic communication, but remarkably, the human command structure remained basically the same as in the Napoleonic era. The reality of bureaucracy is that a branching network of power can readily bring millions and even billions of people under a single centralized command.

Scale, Imperia, and Growth Trajectories

Scale theory and power laws matter because they help explain why growth occurs in human societies. The power-concentrating effects of growth provide positive feedback to those in control, allowing some individuals and their households to become much more powerful than others. This is a reflection of the natural law of allometric growth, in which different parts of a complex system grow at different rates, as in the example of length, surface, and volume in a cube. As the side of a cube increases linearly ($x + 1$), surface increases as the square of the length (x^2) and volume as the cube of length (x^3). The social power of elite households expands on a steeply upward growth trajectory, whereas other households maintain a constant level or fall behind. Scale theory also calls attention to multiple overlapping power networks rather than single power hierarchies, and forces us to recognize that a few individual decision makers at the apexes of the largest power networks are those who primarily determine the direction taken by entire cultures and societies. As individuals, these elites command networks that may cross-cut social classes, ranks, statuses, and multiple institutions and power hierarchies, drawing together numerous people operating within different power domains under a single human director.

Scale theory allows ever larger imperia to be viewed as the mathematically predictable outcomes of growth in the scale of human social groups, production, markets, and capital in the absence of democratic counterforces to compel the redistribution of social power. Because of natural biological factors, the vagaries of fortune, and historical or situational advantage, at any particular time some individuals and households might be expected to acquire extraordinary social power in the form of income and wealth, measured in kilocalories, kilowatts, or money, whereas others fall short. The "natural" skewing of power distributions displayed by lognormal distributions occurs partly because there is no *natural* upper limit to social power, but there is a lower limit, a left-wall on the power axis, beyond which no one can survive. In domestic-scale tribal societies the effects of these inequalities are leveled out by the household and by kin-based redistribution practices, but larger-scale societies can exist whenever the majority allows elites to create expanding imperia by retaining and amplifying these otherwise natural inequalities. Even if the percentage distribution of power remains the same, the top-ranked individual will receive an increasingly disproportionate share as growth in the total society occurs.

Scale ultimately determines how big imperia can become, or how much absolute power is available to the top ranks. Scale gives elites a powerful incentive for growth, but other scale-related effects are also important. Further power amplification is produced for the elite by culturally constructed class differences, institutionalized inequalities, or the adoption of intensive new technologies. For example, in politically organized societies, rulers further amplify their power by using the institutions of government to extract taxes or tribute from citizens. In commercial societies economic elites can amplify their income by means of "unearned" income in the form of rents, interest, and dividends. Even very small percentage returns can produce great capital accumulations when the scale of taxed populations, markets, or investments can be increased by powers of ten. A crucial feature of imperia is the ability of their heads to gain even further scale effects by creating dynasties that transmit and accumulate power transgenerationally. All of these effects make the power of scale one of the most important driving forces behind cultural development.

4

The Political Elite Take Power

The contemporary world system did not emerge naturally, and it was not the inevitable result of technical innovations. It was an intentionally designed framework of social institutions and cultural symbols and beliefs constructed by particular individuals to maximize their social power in all its forms: ideological, economic, military, and political. Throughout world history, opportunistic individuals have successfully designed and used cultural meanings, social institutions, governments, and business organizations for their own purposes. Elites took political power, but people also gave them power. Understanding how this came about, who the designers were, and what their objectives were is crucial if we, as citizens, are to regain control and assume an active role in creating better, more humane societies and a better world.

In this and the following chapters it will be shown that individual elites and elite families were often interconnected to form powerful imperia. This is not conspiracy theory. Elites have taken a dominant cultural role in human affairs, but their intent may not be evil, their actions are often open and public, and they often compete against each other. In this analysis elites are treated as competitive individualists and natural opportunists, not as evil people and not as conspirators. Groups of people may have mutual interests, and they may sometimes act in common, but conspiracy is a legal concept describing a group acting together with illegal or malevolent intent. Elites who design and enforce social systems are not normally acting illegally, although they may. Scale and power theory does not assume that the system itself is illegitimate. This does not ignore the reality that illegitimate, even criminal, regimes have sometimes perpetuated enormous evil, as in the infamous examples of Nazi Germany, the Soviet Union under Stalin, and Maoist China, but these extreme cases demonstrate the urgency of our task.

Scale and power theory is also not a Marxist, class-struggle theory of world history because it treats *individuals* as the agents of historical change, not social *classes*. Social classes emerge in the following chapters as formal analytical units and cultural constructions, not as agents in themselves. This approach is also not orthodox materialism, although political economy, material resources, and wealth will be featured prominently as these affect the well-being of individuals and their households and are important sources of social power. The symbolic cultural constructions that motivate people will necessarily be prominent variables.

This chapter examines the role played by individual elites in directing the world's major cultural developments from the rise of trans-egalitarian (beyond egalitarian) societies in the late Neolithic world 10,000 years ago to the first politically organized chiefdoms, beginning 7,000 years ago, to the ancient agrarian empires such as the Romans, and the aftermath of their collapse. The objective is to use archaeological, ethnographic, and historical case studies to demonstrate that individual power seeking is the principle driving force behind the great transformations in world history.

Scale theory assumes that everyone is biologically driven to promote their own and their children's life chances for survival and reproduction. People may also have an innate drive to dominate and exploit others in order to minimize their own energy expenditure. Culture is a social enterprise that rewards cooperation, but competitive individuals can manipulate cultural beliefs, technologies, and institutions to gain a disproportionate share of the benefits of growth and shift the costs to society at large. Growth in the scale and complexity of societies and cultures is primarily the result of this competitive struggle between individuals because it is the most efficient way for elites to win power, but there is nothing inevitable about the triumph of elites.

Scale theory argues that power elites have been the primary intentional designers and directors of the great transformations that have shaped cultural development since the Neolithic, but even as a group, elites have not acted alone, and they have not always been in control of events. The nonelite majority has always influenced and empowered the elites who direct. It is the nonelite majority, as well as other elites, that the elites seek to command. Historically, pressures from commoners have repeatedly forced elites to diffuse their social power, and this diffusion has repeatedly counteracted the otherwise natural tendency for growth in scale to concentrate power. It must also be acknowledged that culture itself can in many respects be considered a self-organized system. This was recognized by pioneer anthropologists

Alfred Kroeber (1917) and Leslie A. White (1949), who treated culture as a "superorganic" entity in its own right. Culture, whether conceived of as pure information existing in collective human minds, or as a transcendent system, is in some respects effectively beyond the control of any single individual or any small group of individuals. When culture is conceived of as the events of history, it is also not fully under human control. The crucial questions are: To what extent does change in scale unfold as a self-directed process creating and maintaining a natural system, controlled in effect by natural laws? To what extent is development a cultural process directed by individual human decision makers and constrained by cultural laws? This book takes the position that both processes are at work, but power-seeking elite individuals are decisively important human agents and thus deserve to be singled out for special scrutiny.

Social scientists have defined elites in many ways. As a minimum, they must number fewer than half of the reference social group, and they must have high status, wealth, or power (Burke 1994). These three indicators of eliteness are in theory independent, but they are often combined. Just as a very wealthy person might simply hoard and never convert wealth into status or power, a high-status person might have little wealth or power. Individuals with the largest imperia will likely combine high status and wealth to produce their extraordinary power. Mills (1956) and Domhoff (1983) have appropriately identified "ruling elites" or "power elites" as those who gain disproportionate social benefits, occupy controlling social positions, and prevail in disputes. Throughout this book the term "elite" is used repeatedly as a convenient shorthand for *individuals* with similar social power characteristics but who are not necessarily members of a social class. The focus is on elites as influential individuals who use their imperia in ways that, intentionally or not, may transform whole societies and cultures. This is an important distinction because it means that elites can "rule" in the absence of overt social conflict, and they need not self-consciously coordinate their activities with other elites. This avoids the debate over whether or not a ruling *class* always exists or whether a particular society is oligarchic or "pluralistic" (Dahl 1958, 1961). These issues will be examined in greater detail in later chapters.

Crossing the Great Divide from Tribal to Imperial Worlds

Historians commonly speak in exuberant but passive terms of civilizations arising, growing, and collapsing, or they describe kingdoms and empires competing, trading, and growing rich and powerful, as if these cultural constructions were themselves agents and everyone was a player. This deceptively simple picture implies an inevitability and naturalness to the whole process of cultural growth and development, and shifts attention away from the actual human decision makers. In reality, the great transformations of cultural evolution are not driven by natural selection, by random chances of cultural diffusion, or by some inevitable drive to complexity. Human decision makers produce, reproduce, and transform culture, and individual humans are primarily responsible for the particular path that cultural development follows.

Humans have always responded creatively to dynamic social and natural conditions, but for most of human history all households participated in development decision making, and therefore the risks and rewards were broadly shared. In this respect, social equality was the norm for most of the human past. Many historians mistakenly assume that cultural development lagged behind until a creative genius produced a brilliant invention. However, anthropologists have long recognized what Levi-Strauss (1966) called the "Neolithic paradox": that many of humanity's most fundamental technologies including fire, ceramics, weaving, farming, and herding, and basic institutions such as marriage, kinship, villages, clans, and lineages, were anciently produced by tribal people. Paradoxically, these creative people intentionally stopped short of inventing the foundations of civilization such as kingship, writing, monumental architecture, social class, capital-intensive production techniques, and cities. Neolithic technology was at the threshold of civilization, but Neolithic societies were not politically centralized. Neolithic people had to deliberately and continuously refuse to provide power seekers with the tools for creating and maintaining centralized, coercive cultural institutions.

The reason that such obviously capable people did not immediately go on to invent civilization is that civilization did not obviously serve a broad human need, and it directly threatened the personal independence, moral self-direction, and egalitarian social support systems that people enjoyed in small-scale tribal societies. The great Neolithic inventions were broadly shared domestic inventions, designed to sustain human life generally by supporting local communities of up to 2,500 people. As we have seen, this scale limit represents the upper threshold for consensus decision making within a small society, or direct participatory democracy at the local level. Growth beyond that social scale threshold meant crossing what Ferdinand Tönnies called the great divide between *Gemeinschaft* and *Gesellschaft,* between small, domestic, rural communities, and large, public, urban societies as discussed in Chapter 3. Societies larger than 2,500 people were unlikely to benefit everyone because they required formal political elites, a political economy, and ritual specialists, all supported by taxes, tribute, and military power drawn from the nonelite majority. Large-scale societies required physical coercion, ideological domination, and a corresponding suspension of individual moral direction and personal autonomy. The majority had to be compelled to accept economic inequality and dependency. Thus, civilization was commissioned by elites to serve their exclusive interests in growing larger power bases. Proof of this contention can be seen in the extent to which the number of the poor and dependent multiplied as the scale of culture increased.

The real mystery is how elites were able to take control of cultural evolution, overcome village and personal autonomy, and produce the imperial world in the face of perpetual resistance. The best explanation for the successful assertion of elite control seems to be Carneiro's (1970, 1988) concept of "circumscription," which suggests that people accept domination when they feel that they have no reasonable alternative, or it may be that the personal costs of surrender seem lower than the cost of resistance. For example, a family might be reluctant to abandon a permanent house and irrigated farm and flee to the desert in order to escape oppression. People have fewer options to resist when they are surrounded by hostile environments or neighbors. Circumscription may mean that accepting an overlord's authority becomes the lesser of evils, particularly in a crisis situation. The presence of hostile neighbors and a perpetual threat of war would make a leader's promises of "security" seem more appealing. Mann (1986) refers to this process as "social caging," emphasizing that reluctant individuals can become locked into oppressive social systems. People may even be persuaded to accept tyranny as legitimate. People can also be persuaded to believe that they will personally benefit from accepting elite authority. There will always be examples of individuals who have benefited dramatically from alliances with tyrants. The loss of human freedom was probably a gradual process. Tribal societies thrived as long as villagers were able to limit the power of their leaders and depose them, or withdraw their support by walking away from tyrants.

The roots of the great transformation from tribal to imperial societies can be traced back to more than 10,000 years ago when interhousehold competition for status and prestige gradually became more frequent and open. The archaeological evidence for this interpretation has been reviewed by Peter Bogucki (1999). At the end of the Ice Age people adapted to new environmental conditions by settling in villages and relying on risky, but sometimes very productive, gardening, farming, and herding technologies. This created new opportunities for especially competitive, aggrandizing individuals to organize factions, accumulate property and privilege, and attempt to transmit them to the next generation. Prehistoric hordes of wealth objects in burials, and the construction of great megalithic tombs and burial mounds, suggests that successful power-seeking individuals were becoming prominent by the late Neolithic, but the scale of their imperia remained small. However, as soon as invidious rank distinctions were socially tolerated, it was then but a short step from these unstable transegalitarian societies to the creation of chiefdoms with inherited offices, elaborate ranked statuses, and the beginnings of social classes. Aspiring Polynesian chiefs convinced their fellow islanders that they were descendants of the gods and thus the rightful owners of the land. They offered ritual protection in exchange for tribute payments. Some societies became divided into a small nobility and more numerous commoners. Successful power seekers could then grow larger chiefdoms and turn them into small kingdoms, and so on.

The big question is whether the imperial world was created by uniquely inventive people in response to popular demand and general human need, or as primarily an instrument of domination. There is a dynamic to the development of civilizations, and there is a set of functionally interconnected institutions and processes that make it happen, but it seems clear that it is not driven by popular demand toward the goal of general human benefit. If civilization arose spontaneously to meet human needs, it is odd that it took 6,000 years before the material level of the majority was substantially improved in any region of the world.

Village Headman to Divine King in Southeast Asia

British social anthropologist Edmund Leach (1964) observed firsthand how aspiring elites constructed imperial power out of the everyday culture of the tribal world. Leach discovered that the development of politically organized chiefdoms and kingdoms out of tribes in Southeast Asia was an elite-directed process, not the result of a "natural" unidirectional evolutionary process. Using historical data and drawing on his field experience with the Tibeto-Burman speaking Kachin peoples in highland Burma during World War II, Leach found that individuals and whole communities periodically shifted back and forth across the great divide between tribal and imperial worlds. Depending on circumstances, people moved between three different types of societies constituted respectively as: (1) small-scale egalitarian tribal villages known as *gumlao*; (2) moderate-sized chiefdoms known as *gumsa*; and (3) large-scale, hierarchical, Shan Buddhist kingdoms.

For aspiring Kachin leaders, these different social forms were steps to more powerful personal imperia. Leach views *gumlao, gumsa,* and Shan not as an evolutionary progression, but as alternative phases, or positions within a dynamic regional social system along a continuum of increasing social scale and power. At the lower extreme, *gumlao* Kachin lived in low-density societies, in autonomous villages based on shifting cultivation in the hills. At the upper extreme, Shan Buddhist kingdoms were high-density societies based on wet rice cultivation in the valleys. *Gumsa* chiefdoms were intermediate between these two extremes and were formed by opportunists when and where geography and historical circumstances made it possible for them to take advantage of variable agricultural potential, trade routes, or other special opportunities for concentrating people and social power. The *gumlao/gumsa* distinction was the difference between a domestic scale society where the village headman was a relatively powerless coordinator, and a society with multiple villages under a hereditary chief who asserted ownership rights over land, collected tribute, and claimed religious privileges based on a special connection to the supernatural. From the perspective of ordinary villagers this was the difference between tribal independence and subordination and domination. The process of social transformation from one type of society to the other was reversible, and it was possible for states to devolve into chiefdoms, and chiefdoms into tribes, and so on.

It is remarkable that *gumlao* and *gumsa* Kachin shared the same basic culture, for the human differences between the two social systems were profound. The potential for rank and inequality always exists in tribal society, but it can be resisted as long as there is a consensus against it. For example, when two groups exchanged wives directly, as was the case in the tribal world where marriage was often based on symmetrical cross-cousin marriage, the members of each group remain equals. This is true for the Ashaninka and most Australian aborigines. However, the Kachin practiced asymmetrical, or matrilateral, cross-cousin marriage. This meant that each group received wives from one group, and married their own daughters into a different group. This could lead to inequality because the Kachin considered wife receivers (*dama*) to be inferior dependents of their wife-giving (*mayu*) partners. In *gumsa* society the *mayu–dama* relationship provided an easy transition to tribute payments and ritual inferiority. However, because receiving a gift put one in debt to the giver, a chief who was by definition the top gift receiver was expected to be extra generous or he would lose status. This was a potential check on chiefly power.

A. Thomas Kirsch (1973) argued that Kachin social transformations were not just about politics. Shifting from one social form to the other depended on the ability of the aspiring *gumsa* chief to successfully mobilize a repertoire of economic, social, and ideological cultural elements in order to concentrate social power. This involved changes in political economy and ideology. Kirch argued that the "power" that the hill tribesmen competed for was a religious value, which he characterized as "potency" or "fertility." This was conceptualized as grace, merit, spiritual virtue, or ritual efficacy, all of which resembled the Polynesian concept of *mana*. This kind of power could be attributed variously to households, lineages, and clans, but it ultimately resided in individuals. One's spiritual power was assumed to be an innate quality—that is, people were born spiritually unequal, yet inherent power had to be demonstrated and perhaps enhanced at the same time by success in feasting, hunting, head-hunting, sexual prowess, and the number of dependents one could accumulate. Potency or merit could also be lost suddenly, as shown by extreme misfortune. This kind of power was potentially unlimited, and only measurable relative to the amount others held. Competitive feasts of merit were performed by individual households. They involved animal sacrifice and were held in a graded series of increasing size. Those who performed bigger feasts demonstrated their enhanced prestige by wearing special adornments, house ornaments, rights to better land, rights to larger shares of feasts, and more prominence in village affairs.

The Kachin vividly demonstrate the microcosm of daily human activities that enterprising individuals could manipulate in an effort to enlarge their imperia by creating rank distinctions and social class out of an otherwise egalitarian tribal society. Rivalrous potlatches on the Pacific Northwest coast and pig feasting in New Guinea are similar cultural patterns. Given the right conditions, such competitive displays must have been repeated many times throughout the tribal world over many thousands of years, and in a few cases they made it possible for individuals to construct relatively long-lived, politically organized imperial societies. Leach believed that individual striving for social power was the driving force behind social change of this type. In Burma, the move from *gumlao* to *gumsa* occurred because it produced a striking enlargement of a village headman's imperia, turning him into a chief. Under the right conditions a *gumsa* chief could successfully become a self-styled Shan prince.

Kachin *gumlao* villages contained only 50 to 100 persons, and village headmen resembled Ashaninka big men in their limited powers. However, *gumsa* chiefs could amass substantial, highly visible power, perhaps commanding tribute from thousands of people in multiple village clusters. The Kachins distinguished between the large houses of chiefs and those of ordinary people. An especially successful chief with pretensions of being a Shan prince might build stone walls around his house to mimic the royal palace of a divine king after the Hindu–Buddhist model. Chiefs' households were larger because chiefs could have more wives, dependent households, and guests, and because they included extra space for special shrines. The Kachin chief had followers who paid taxes for use of rice paddy, on the assumption that the taxes would be returned in feasts sponsored by the chief. The Kachin chiefs thought of themselves, and were treated, as small-scale Shan princes, and were actually called "prince" or "father of the domain."

The *gumsa* Kachin recognized four social classes: chiefs, aristocrats, commoners, and slaves. Leach argued that Kachin social classes were not directly correlated with material level or standard of living because wealth in exchange objects did not automatically mean that one could enjoy greater luxury, or be an aristocrat. In such small-scale chiefdoms aristocrats, commoners, and slaves all enjoyed basically the same material level. However, a rich chief was also a powerful chief, and under the right conditions a very powerful chief would form a kingdom.

The archeological record suggests that orthodox evolutionary interpretations of cultural development based on particular technologies do not explain the appearance of the chiefdoms and kingdoms in Southeast Asia. Highly productive wet rice agriculture and metallurgy, usually taken as preconditions for centralized political organization, were present in this area by 2000 B.C., but kingdoms did not appear until A.D. 500. Furthermore, long-distance trade and specialized craft production developed as decentralized activities, apparently conducted at the village level by independent specialists, perhaps as individual household production units. It appears that domestic consumer goods such as metal objects, textiles, and ceramics may have been distributed by means of decentralized exchange networks that were not controlled by elites. After ruling elites established kingdoms and created a "demand" for elite consumer goods, this new demand could have been met by specialist village-level producers as well as by slaves or dependent producers attached to the royal palaces or noble houses, or by merchant traders operating in long-distance trade.

Beyond 500: Scalar Stress and Urban Growth

Given the choice, it is not obvious why people would want to live in settled groups larger than 500 people, even though it might seem that larger-scale societies would provide increased prosperity and security, and would make certain cultural goals more readily attainable. However, a larger number cannot be sustained without more intensive communication and transportation technology, and without formal leadership. More intensive technology itself requires more work, more energy and materials; while it may provide material returns of questionable utility, it raises the political question of how to allocate social costs and benefits. As a result, interest groups and factionalism are likely to arise where they never existed. This is in response to the problem of who benefits from growth and who pays the costs. Formal leadership itself is a costly, energy-intensive enterprise, and leaders are potentially dangerous and difficult to control. The primary defining feature of forager bands in the tribal world was that they were mutually constructed in a common process in which everyone did what best met their personal needs—somewhat like an ideal free market in which everyone is both a buyer and a seller. In the case of foragers there was no conflict between self-interest and the interests of society because social costs and benefits were shared equally among all households.

When settlements grew beyond 500 and crossed the line between *Gemeinschaft* and *Gesellschaft,* people had to deal with the scale problems of power inequities and the increased possibility of catastrophic social collapse. In an important study of settlements, archaeologist Roland Fletcher (1995) demonstrated that the size and density of all human settlements, whether bands, villages, or cities, directly reflects scale principles and growth thresholds. In addition to the factors discussed above for foragers, the upper limits of settlement size and density are determined by disproportionate increases in the stress of interpersonal communication and interaction as population grows. Just as the volume of a cube grows exponentially while length grows linearly (Chapter 3), according to "network law" an increase in settlement population to the second power of ten (10^2) is accompanied mathematically by a third power of ten (10^3) increase in potential human interaction: hence, there are 5 billion possible interactions in a city of 100,000 people. When the interaction between people as members of subgroups or alliances is added to one-to-one relationships, the interaction possibilities and the potential for discord and social disintegration become astronomical.

This is the same physical relationship that exists between an individual body's ability to resist strain and maintain its integrity, and the greater strain of increasing weight as it grows larger. Likewise, a larger settlement or society is mathematically more difficult, per capita, to hold together. This means that as settlements grow larger social transaction costs increase disproportionately. This aspect of growth is so striking, and so obviously related to size, that it has been called "scalar stress" (G. Johnson 1982). A small group of twenty-five to fifty people can camp comfortably together in mobile forager bands at densities of more than 1,000 people per hectare, but sedentary communities of more than 500 require much lower densities, and may average only 100 people per hectare. Daily life in a village of 5,000 people is potentially a hundred times more difficult and costly than life in a village of 500 people because there are that many more possible pathways and connections between people. Following these scale principles, we can infer that the human costs of overcoming communication and interaction stresses help explain why many people decided to keep their settlements as very small, domestically organized villages.

Anthropologist Robert Carneiro (1967) discovered that the cost of growth in tribal societies, measured as increasing social complexity, was so regular and predictable that it could also be expressed mathematically. He examined an assortment of 100 tribal societies, including a few small chiefdoms. He compared the size of the largest integrated community in each society with the number of organizational traits starting with the nuclear family and including such variables as special religious practitioners, trade between communities, social segments above the family, and the presence of formal political leaders. Carneiro found that the number of organizational traits (N) in a given community could be expressed as the square root of its population (P), as in the equation $\left(N = \sqrt{P}\right)$. As settlement size increased from bands of twenty-five people, and to villages from 500 up to 2,000 people, organizational traits increased from five, to twenty-two, to fifty. The equation predicts that a small city-state of 50,000 people would need 224 organizational traits, indicating a power of ten increase in organizational complexity over the tribal level.

Turning villages into cities was an expensive scale transformation that was necessarily part of the change from the tribal world to the imperial world. Cities required new technology, new social structures, and further economic growth to overcome the cultural as well as physical limitations to settlement growth. Unless the costs and benefits of this kind of culture change were equitably distributed, it is unlikely that people would have unanimously chosen to create cities. Even full equity would not make large cities attractive, because the equitably shared costs would probably outweigh the shared benefits. It is more likely that cities could have only been created by the decisions of power-seeking elites who deliberately set out to overcome the limits to urban growth in the process of creating and expanding the political imperia that they controlled. They first accomplished this difficult task some 6,000 years ago on the lower Nile and in Mesopotamia with the successful development of the earliest large bureaucratic political economies, using monumental architecture and writing systems to allow people in large, dense urban settlements to communicate effectively and interact with minimum interpersonal stress.

Fletcher (1995) showed that the total area of urban places and their rate of growth are limited by communication technology, with development occurring as expensive order-of-magnitude transformations across growth thresholds. He distinguished three historic phases of urban growth, each with its respective upper size limit set by technology and form of organization. The upper population threshold for each urban growth era (first cities, then agrarian cities, then industrial cities) is separated by two powers of ten—10^2, 10^4, 10^6—in a logarithmic scale progression (see Table 4.1). Given an average urban density of 100 persons per hectare, this suggests upper city population limits of 10,000, 1 million, and 100 million people respectively for each phase. Fletcher's calculations suggest that historically, the growth rate of cities by area in hectares per century increased by large orders of magnitude of 5×10^{-1}, 5×10^2, and 5×10^5 respectively. The populations of most "large" cities remained well below the maximum for their size ranges, probably averaging 1,000, 10,000, and 100,000. As cities became larger, commercial exchanges had to be elaborated and formalized because production by politically directed command can be extremely expensive. Only a very few cities actually ever reached the maximum size limits for a given era, and then they were likely to collapse quickly because the life expectancy of cities appears to decline as they become larger. Moving beyond the size limits set by a particular organizational level is a rare event because it is so costly.

In the long run of world history, the evidence is overwhelming that urbanization was an elite-directed process and that the benefits went primarily to the elites. Evidence that the first cities were created as administrative centers is found in the Mesopotamian archaeological record, which contains a size hierarchy of settlements by 3500 B.C. (G. Johnson 1973). Susa, a single urban center of some 2,400 people, stood as a central place with three smaller outlying centers and forty-five small tributary villages distributed in a way that facilitated communication with the primary center. This suggests that an administrative hierarchy of three levels was already in operation, coordinating the activities of a regional population of perhaps 25,000 people. This conclusion is supported by the presence of clay seals with identifying marks, and counting devices, as well as mass-produced ceramic bowls of a design used for the distribution of grain rations to laborers. Ceramics were also being mass produced in the center for distribution to the smaller centers and villages. The center of Uruk also in Mesopotamia may have grown to 40,000 people by 2500 B.C., and would have required an extensive exchange network to meet all of its material needs (H. Wright 1969). Significantly, Uruk is considered to be an "Early Dynastic" center, indicating that urban civilization had finally arrived in the form of monumental architecture, writing, and well-organized dynastic rule with palaces and temples.

Cities with populations of 100,000 or more, which were in existence in Southwest Asia by 500 B.C., could only be supported by a material exchange network and transport infrastructure extensive enough to be called a "world system." Such large urban centers also imply the existence of monetary systems and commercial markets for foodstuffs. Steady growth in the world system over the last 4,000 years is reflected in the increase in the number of cities of 25,000 or more from 2000 B.C. to A.D. 1500, when more than 7 million people were living in some seventy-five large cities averaging 100,000 people, with the largest containing 500,000 (Chandler 1987; Wilkinson 1992, 1993). Imperial Rome at its peak may have briefly contained a million people, but that number was not regularly sustained anywhere until the appearance of industrial cities by the 1850s, and the effective development of fossil fuels

Table 4.1

Major Settlement Size Increases (hectares)

Urban growth stage	Area limit (maximum population)	Secular growth (hectares per century)	Examples
First cities (10,000–3000 B.C.)	100 hectares (10,000 people)	0.5	SW Asia
Agrarian cities (3000 B.C.–1600 A.D.)	10,000 hectares (1 million people)	500	China, Peru, Mesoamerica, Ancient Rome
Industrial cities (1840–2000 A.D.)	1,000,000 hectares (100 million people)	500,000	Europe, North America

Source: Data from Fletcher 1995.

and electricity for the mechanization of transportation and communications, with railroads, electronics, printing, and large-scale business corporations. The scale of urban places is perhaps one of the most important variables determining the quality of human life, and the urbanization process deserves a very close look to identify both the driving forces behind urban growth and the human consequences of change in urban scale.

Elite Payoff: Mates, Servants, and Palaces

There is a well established tradition in the social sciences of attributing the rise of civilization to the benefits that it presumably provides the majority, such as secure food, shelter, protection from enemies, improved living standards, and the enjoyment of "high culture" in the form of great monuments and the arts (Service 1975). However, the real question can be expressed in the legal phrase "*cui bono?*" ("for whose benefit?" Nolan and Connolly 1979, 340). Both the human value and the necessity of many of the presumed benefits produced by the imperial world can be questioned given the inequity that accompanies the benefits. Historically, the payoff to the elite in social power, as compared with the cost to the majority, was so disproportionate as to call into question the likelihood that the majority would have freely embraced civilization if given the choice.

The improved life chances enjoyed by elites in the imperial world are reflected directly in estimates of life expectancy. Roman tombstone inscriptions and written records suggests that elites may have lived an average of about thirty years, whereas the average for the "servile" masses may have been only twenty years (Duncan-Jones 1990, 102–104; Hopkins 1966). Elite life spans were probably little different from those experienced by tribals, as noted in Chapter 1, suggesting that the physical superiority of elite lifestyles was only relative to the absolute deprivation and material impoverishment endured by the lower classes, where many were pushed below the tribal level. Citing the Roman case, some authorities argue that the imperial world brought tangible improvements to the living conditions of the majority. The great abundance of metal and ceramic consumer goods in Roman archaeological sites and the obvious upswing in long-distance trade—together with population increase, greater density, more urbanization, and widespread literacy—suggest that overall improvements in living standards may have been widely shared. However, the luxuries were concentrated at the very top, and it would be difficult to argue that the Roman consumer goods received by slaves, serfs, and the disenfranchised non-noble citizenry were superior in quantity or quality to those goods that still independent peoples living in small-scale societies beyond the Roman frontier were able to produce directly or obtain by trade. Furthermore, Rome itself was a remarkably unhealthy city because of poverty, disease, pollution, and poor sanitation (Duncan-Jones 1980) and an especially unsavory environment for the poor. Population growth and urbanization in and of themselves were hardly human benefits because they meant that more people experienced less freedom. Human impoverishment and dependence were outcomes of political decisions made by a tiny Roman elite that transformed independent farmers into full-time soldiers, rural serfs, and urban poor, and gave them no voice in policy making.

In his comprehensive review of the origin of despotic civilizations, Karl Wittfogel (1957) observed that rulers do some things that may benefit the majority when it is in the ruler's own perceived self-interest. Wittfogel, who was inspired to study despotism and political power after he was imprisoned by the Nazis, noted that even the most oppressive rulers sometimes find it useful to dole out benefits. The Romans themselves gave us the word "dole" for the "free" grain that they distributed to the poor citizenry of Rome. Likewise, the Nazis found it cost-effective and nonthreatening to allow concentration camp inmates to form their own internal organizations. For Wittfogel, such politically irrelevant freedoms merely created a "beggars' democracy" that served its captors. Likewise, pirates who keep their ship afloat are not being benevolent toward their captives. Given the choice, a despotic ruler "will further his own interests, and not the interests of others" (Wittfogel 1957, 126).

It is easy to imagine three objectives for running an empire: (1) to maximize benefits to the populace at large; (2) to maximize benefits to the rulers;

and (3) to balance benefits between rulers and populace. Always critical of despots, Wittfogel concluded that rulers are most likely to "consider the needs of their subjects in the light of their own needs and advantages" (Wittfogel 1957, 126–127). He concluded that despotic rulers will invariably choose the second option. The question for rulers then becomes, what is the maximum that they can safely extract from the peasantry? It is in ruler self-interest to: (1) keep the productive economy functioning; (2) keep taxes below the point that would discourage production; and (3) maintain external peace and internal order.

That rulers generally chose their personal interests above those of the commoners is well illustrated by contrasting the conspicuous consumption and splendor of royal courts with the poverty of the peasantry, combined with arbitrary confiscation of peasant wealth and the prohibitions on competitive emulation by the lower classes. Differential consumption in the ancient imperial world was legally sustained by sumptuary regulations that specified fixed forms of dress, housing, furnishings, food, and transport for each social category.

Awesome prestige and public responsibility are often regarded as the just reward for imperial leadership and sufficient explanation for why people seek power, but the private rewards may be the most important underlying personal motivations for empire building. Expanding personal imperia follow a natural sequence: first, the ruler enlarges his household by the addition of extra wives and concubines; then he adds domestic servants; and finally he turns the house into a walled palace, and his personal lifestyle becomes one of extraordinary luxury and conspicuous consumption. Throughout the imperial world it is remarkable how so few enjoyed so much privilege.

From the perspective of scale theory it is significant that even as rulers expanded their imperia, the absolute number in the top leadership remained relatively constant. There was always only one emperor at the very top who also headed a personal dynasty, and there were seldom more than 500 noblemen, each heading their own noble lineages. For example, the 50 million people in the Roman Empire were governed by the emperor and a few hundred senators and top bureaucrats. Well-off Roman citizens in the upper strata represented no more than 2 percent of the total population (Table 4.2). In fourth-century A.D. Rome, a city of a million people, only a tiny elite of fewer than 2,000 were prosperous enough to live in mansions (Stambaugh 1988, 90). Likewise, there were only 700 people in the Ch'ing clan at the top of Manchu China in A.D. 1900, and another 40,000 top bureaucrats in an empire of 400 million.

The physical rewards and enhanced "life chances" for imperial leaders are striking in a purely biological sense. The size of the personal households

Table 4.2

Roman Imperia by Wealth, Income, and Social Class, A.D. 100

Class	Rank	Households	Population	Wealth (sesterces)	Income	Imperia (% population)
Upper strata Ruling elite Nobles	Emperor Consuls Senators	1 160 440	5 800 2,200	1 billion 250 million 10 million	500 million 15 million 600,000	Super-Elite (0.00%)
	Equestrians Decurions	20,000 150,000	100,000 750,000	500,000 100,000	100,000 50,000	Elite (1.76%)
Lower strata	Wealthy entrepreneurs	5,800	29,000	100,000	30,000	
Ingenui liberti servi	Poor entrepreneurs	52,200	261,000	50,000	15,000	Maintenance (0.5%)
	Urban poor Legionares Rural poor Rural slaves	855,399 300,000 6,988,800 2,912,000	4,276,995 900,000 34,944,000 8,736,000	750 500 250 50	1,200 900 500 375	Poor (97.7%)
Totals		11,284,800	50,000,000			

Sources: Data from Alföldy 1985; Carcopino 1940; Hopkins 1978a, 1978b.

of rulers, including wives, concubines, servants, slaves, and potential offspring, increased by powers of ten in direct proportion to the scale of empire (Betzig 1986, 1992, 1993, 53). In tribal societies leading men would be unlikely to have more than three wives, but in chiefdoms, the chief's wives might be numbered in the tens. Within a given imperial society, low-level elites might have tens of women in their households, nobles hundreds, kings thousands, and the great emperors up to ten thousand (Betzig 1997b, 400). This means that imperial elites were able to command the human and material resources to sustain such hypertrophied domestic establishments. The Aztec emperor at the time of the Spanish conquest reportedly had 4,000 women in his personal retinue (Betzig 1997a, 7), and Chinese emperors had access to more than 10,000 women. From a biological evolutionary perspective Betzig (1986, 1992, 1993, 1997a, 1997b) argues that the whole point of a man accumulating greater social power is to allow him to produce more offspring, and more successful offspring. There are surely other psychological motives behind the drive for power, but there is abundant indirect evidence for the reproductive success of those with the largest personal imperia. Betzig (1997b, 399) summarizes the evidence for the Romans as follows: "rich Romans were promiscuous; they had sexual access to tens, or hundreds, or thousands of slave women; and by those women they begat tens, or hundreds, or thousands of slave children."

The apparent domestic prosperity that is suggested by such extravagant biological success can be readily inferred from the expanded domestic space of elite households. Universally in the tribal world people required domestic floor spaces of approximately 50 square meters for an average household of five persons (Naroll 1962). The ruling family of the Andean city-state of Chan Chan in A.D. 1000 occupied a walled residential compound of 140,000 square meters—sufficient space for a royal household of 14,000 people (Day 1982). One of the Emperor Hadrian's (A.D. 76–138) private residences was a 60–hectare (150-acre) country villa pleasure palace, the equivalent of a small city of luxury apartments, pools, baths, temples, courtyards, statuary, and libraries centered in 18 square kilometers (7 square miles) of landscaped gardens, parks, and waterworks outside of Rome (MacDonald and Pinto 1995). Hadrian's extravagance was later equaled by French monarch Louis XIV's (1638–1715) Versailles, which occupied 15.5 square kilometers (6 square miles) and contained monumental buildings with perhaps 93,000 square meters (a million square feet) of living space. The French king was personally attended by 500 servants, a court of 1,000 nobles, and 10,000 groundskeepers, all sustained by taxes extracted from a nation of 18 million people.

The correspondence between scale of political domain and spatial scale of the domestic household can be demonstrated using historical data from

Asia. The walled domestic compound of a Balinese commoner household in nineteenth-century Bali covered approximately 375 square meters. A Balinese noble household compound of 1,815 square meters and a royal household palace compound of 22,400 square meters were each a power of ten greater than the preceding household (Figure 4.1). Given that a nineteenth-century Balinese king typically commanded fewer than 100,000 people, it is not surprising that his palace was overshadowed by the 210,000 square-meter Thai royal palace, which was a power of ten greater, reflecting an empire of some 5 million people. The Chinese Empire, with a population of 300 million, supported an imperial palace of a million square meters, a power of ten greater than the Thai palace. A palace of this magnitude probably approached the practical upper limit for a single domestic compound. The Chinese emperor maintained additional palaces and rotated between them seasonally, following an elite residential pattern shared by the Roman aristocracy and many elites in the contemporary commercial world.

The relative proportion of elites and super-elites to maintenance-level and poor household imperia in Norman England in A.D. 1086 was virtually identical with their proportion in the Roman Empire (compare Tables 4.2 and 4.3). Most people were poor in Norman England, but there may have been a higher proportion of maintenance-level urban households in the cities and towns than in Rome. Per capita economic production was apparently about half the Roman level, and the level of commercialization was much lower. Nevertheless, the Norman aristocracy lived very well. The lavish incomes of the Norman aristocrats supported bloated households and touched off a building spree in which the elites constructed multiple fortresses for their personal protection. By 1154 here were 49 royal castles and 225 baronial castles, almost entirely constructed within less than a century (Gies 1994, 141). In addition to the exchequer and the army, the king had expanded the royal household into multiple departments including the chancery, steward, pantry, larder and kitchen, buttery, chamber, constabulary, and the hunting staff. There were 98 named offices, from the cupbearers to the dispensers of bread, laundresses, feeder of hounds, and leash holders, and perhaps 250 people or more working as personal retainers (C. Johnson 1950, 129–135). While this was an impressive display, it was a only a shadow of the personal splendor surrounding the Roman emperors.

Strategies of Domination in the Ancient Imperial World

The expansions of imperia are almost universally resisted by the majority who do not directly benefit from them. Grossly inequitable social systems are difficult and costly to develop and maintain, and this is particularly true

Figure 4.1 **The Scale of Residential Space in the Imperial World**

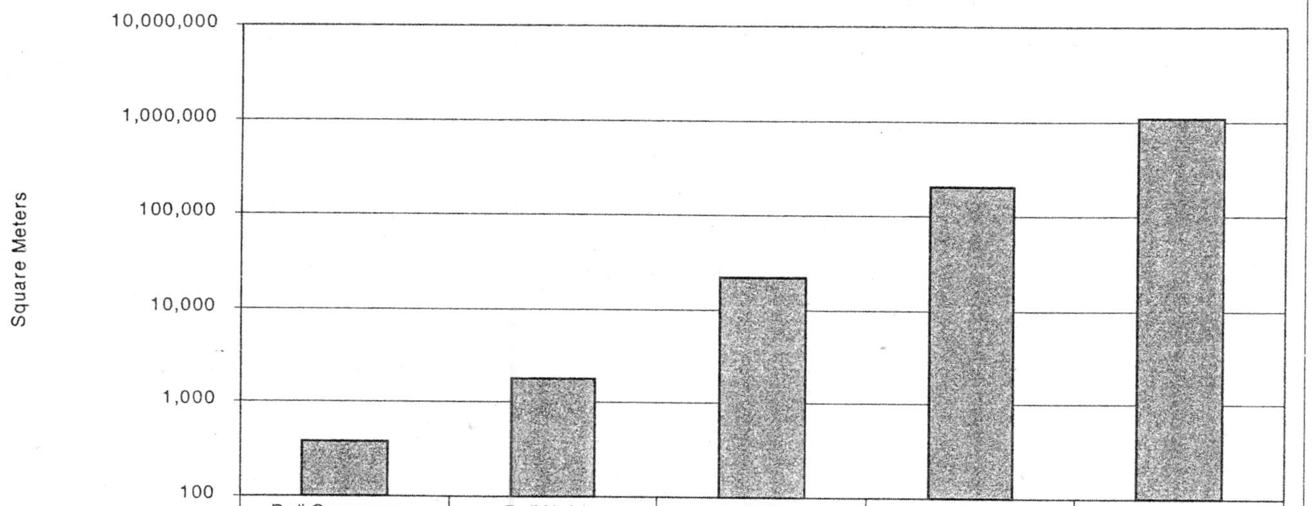

	Bali Commoner	Bali Noble	Bali King	Thai Palace	Chinese Palace
Area Sq. Meters	375	1,815	22,400	210,000	1,092,000

Table 4.3

Norman England Imperia by Wealth, Income, and Social Class, A.D. 1086

Class	Rank	Households	Population	Wealth	Income	Imperia (% population)
Aristocracy	King	1	5	£17,650	£20,000	Super-Elite (0.06%)
	Barons	10	50	£1,500	£1,500	
	Magnates	171	855	£115	£130	
	Lords	900	4,500	£20	£8	Elite (2%)
	Subtenants	6,000	30,000	£2	£2	
Commoners	Burghers	24,000	120,000	£1	£0.3	Maintenance (8%)
	Free peasants	38,511	192,555	£0.25	£0.22	Poor (90%)
	Unfree peasants	236,568	1,182,840	£0.05	£0.2	
Totals		306,161	1,530,805			100%

Sources: Data from Snooks 1993; Roberts and Roberts 1980.

when tyrannical dictators monopolize power. Mann (1986, 143) notes that rulers have historically used at least four ways to expand and maintain their power: (1) Indirect rule by developing patron–client relations with subordinate local elites; (2) use of direct military power in strategic strongholds; (3) forced economic cooperation; and (4) development of a widespread ruling-class culture.

The first two methods were widely applied, producing what have been called "hegemonic empires" or "empires of domination," but over the long run they proved to be relatively ineffective because resistance and rebellion remained difficult to prevent. The third method, forced economic cooperation, involves the creation of "territorial empires" with a political economy in which the ruler uses the institutions of government, such as the law and organized violence, to enforce peace, build communication routes, and promote and regulate production and trade in support of the ruler's personal structures of power. It seems unlikely that exchange would have developed beyond the simple reciprocity of the tribal world in the absence of government intervention to establish coinage, standardize weights and measures, enforce contracts, defend property rights, and set the rates of exchange. The royal household, retainers, political agents, as well as the military and religious imperia that the ruler or his kin and allies also controlled, were collectively the most important consumers of labor, staple production, and luxury goods beyond the subsistence needs of the peasant population. Modern economists call the outcome of this centrally directed, coercive form of economic growth the "multiplier effect."

The decisive requirement for empire building was for aspiring leaders to gain monopolies over the sources of social power, be they kin, land, labor, water, tools, agricultural production, exchange, armaments, political institutions, or the institutions, symbols, and physical media that persuade people to believe that the elite view of the world is natural, inevitable, and irresistible. Civilization is about control over people and maintaining systems of inequality. For emperors to succeed, the commoners must accept their inferior status and be willing to work for the benefit of those at the top. Leaders in the ancient world relied initially on two broad imperial strategies that were variants of hegemonic empires. Divine kings in China and the Andes resided in a central royal city and extracted taxes from a widely dispersed but self-sufficient village-based peasantry. These far-flung hegemonic empires have also been called "village-states" (Maisels 1990) and were held together from the center by a powerful ideology backed up by military force. The Mesopotamian and Greek alternative was to maintain economic and political dominance over dependent households and slaves within a localized city-state that under the right conditions could be expanded into vast territorial empires. Roman and Hindu rulers used variants of both strategies. Andean rulers such as heads of the Inca dynasty dominated by constructing an ideological system in which the populace acknowledged the Inca to be divine emperors.

In constructing politically centralized systems of domination, imperial elites designed a political economy consisting of two parts: a staple economy and a wealth economy (D'Altroy and Earle 1985; Earle 1987). The staple economy allowed rulers to gain direct control over the production and distribution of the most important staple foods and to extract "surplus" foodstuffs from the primary producers. For example, controlling the food supply allowed the Inca rulers to accumulate the strategic reserves that they used to support full-time specialist slaves, servants, soldiers, priests, and artisans. The artisans were used to produce wealth objects such as expensive jewelry and fine textiles, which were given out to buy the loyalty of imperial bureaucrats and provide them with distinctive marks of high status. The commoners who built and maintained the Inca roads and filled the storehouses were rewarded with beer and work clothes.

The growth of elite imperia in the ancient imperial world was paralleled by the growth of military technology, because a ruler's ability to command labor and extract food and material from other people ultimately depended on violence and the threat of violence. As historian William H. McNeill (1982) observed, imperial rulers were human "macroparasites" who preyed on other humans, often by means of "organized robbery" and pillage. The development sequence of military technology in ancient Eurasia from 3500 to 500 B.C. was from simple bronze armaments to chariots based on horses, spoke wheels and axles, and the compound bow, through light and heavy cavalry, and the use of iron armaments. These technological developments required long-distance trade and full-time specialists but were relatively inexpensive for elites to implement, and they diffused quickly because they conferred specific tactical advantages. However, the lethality and overall battlefield effectiveness of individual military weapons did not change dramatically until approximately A.D. 1600, when Europeans began to make effective use of gunpowder, mobile artillery, and iron cannonballs (Dupuy 1979, 7).

By 1500 B.C. the most powerful Eurasian elites were those who directed forces of charioteers and commanded the supporting specialists who could supply the necessary material. McNeill suggests that the widespread shift to iron armaments by 1200 B.C., briefly produced a "democratization of war" because iron was more readily available than bronze. The Iron Age created new opportunities for aspiring military elites and made it easier for people to become warriors, but it did not make everyone equal. By 700 B.C. heavily armed Greek hoplite infantry units organized into phalanxes set the standard for land warfare in the Mediterranean region. Iron plows also permitted farmers to expand into otherwise marginal soils and increased densities and overall population, making possible larger-scale societies with more warriors. Rulers such as Genghis Kahn, who could obtain iron armaments while still remaining mobile, and who commanded hoards of light cavalrymen raised on the Eurasian steppes, were able to raid and pillage settled farming districts for centuries. The continuing success of imperia based on pure pillage certainly retarded the development of commercially based imperia. Likewise, with military support many urban-centered empires that relied on taxation, bureaucracy, legal, and religious authority could also suppress the emergence of powerful commercially based imperia.

The Romans: Conquerors and Slaves in a Legionary Economy

The Roman Empire, which expanded and contracted over some six centuries from approximately 200 B.C. to A.D. 400, exemplifies an elite-directed territorial empire that was based almost entirely on military power and perpetual conquest. At its height in about A.D. 100, the empire brought some 50 million people and 2 million square miles (5 million square kilometers) of territory in 43 provinces under a single political administration and a single deified emperor. At that time perhaps one-third of the world's people were under Roman rule. An empire of this scale was unequaled in the world until the Sung Dynasty in China by A.D. 1000. By comparison, the United States did not exceed 1.7 million square miles (4.4 million square kilometers) until 1850, and 50 million people until 1880. It is fair to ask how this vast empire was designed and directed, and to what ends.

Rome started out as a relatively democratic city-state with egalitarian tribal roots and a volunteer citizen army. Rome's early leaders selected an expansionist policy of military conquest that yielded a wealth of land, slaves, subjects, and booty, which flowed disproportionately to the elite. Early Rome was an empire of domination with client states and local rulers, not unlike the Southeast Asian kingdoms examined above and in Chapter 2. The important Roman innovation was turning newly conquered client states into provinces, thereby creating a territorial empire administered directly by governors and bureaucrats. This made it possible for Roman administrators to enrich themselves with impunity by extortion, violence, excessive taxation, direct plunder of conquered lands, and oppression of their fellow citizens. The wealthy were able to purchase offices and tax-farming positions, or they obtained them through bribery and favoritism from patrons. Authorities at all levels were expected to profit from their offices, positions, and wealth.

Continuous wars of aggressive conquest initiated by the emperors promoted urban growth, poverty, and wealth concentration through a complex feedback process, the intricacies of which were probably not understood by those commanding specific military campaigns. The key to Roman military success was superior organization and logistics rather than technology. As described by historian Keith Hopkins (1978a, 1978b), the booty generated by perpetual conquest was grossly inequitably distributed and became the means by which elite individuals operating as private citizens were able to buy Italian land, displacing smallholders and creating large estates and luxury country villas. The new landowners turned war captives into domestic slaves and laborers on their new estates. Slaves proved to be economically more productive than either free peasants or wage workers because slaves had no families and could be compelled to work harder and at less than the maintenance cost of a household. Slave owners did not need to pay the cost of reproducing the labor supply because war produced a constant supply of new captives. Meanwhile, the dispossessed smallholders who were forced off their land had to either join the legions, move into towns and cities to become poorly paid wage workers, or remain on the land as poorly paid serfs. They were also encouraged to colonize the newly conquered provincial lands whose former residents had been enslaved and removed. Thus, slavery was functionally related to the artificially produced scarcity of free peasants and wage workers in the countryside. Citing Beloch (1886), Hopkins (1978b, 101) estimates that there were some 2 million slaves in Roman Italy in 31 B.C., an astounding 35 percent of the total population of 5.5 million people at that time.

Mann (1986, 250–300) extols the Roman "achievement" and argues that the masses measurably benefited from empire, pointing to improved agricultural productivity, population growth, and the apparent greater availability of consumer goods. Roman engineering and slave labor did improve agricultural output, as shown by yield ratios of seed to harvest that were higher than in medieval times, but this merely brought higher rents to landlords and slave owners, and directly benefited neither the serfs nor the slaves. There was increased flow of coins, coin hoarding, and an upswing in trade and shipwrecks, but much of this activity reflected taxes, military expenditures, and luxury goods consumed by the elite. In Mann's terms, the Roman system is best described as a "legionary economy" where the emperor as supreme commander is the driving force and he and his agents the prime beneficiaries. The empire was a slave society and a command economy. Ultimately, grain, produced on confiscated land by slave labor, was the source of energy and social power. Land ownership was the foundation of elite status and social power because the population of Imperial Rome was

90 percent rural and agricultural production was the principal economic activity. The emperors distrusted merchants and managed the economy to ensure the steady flow of taxes, tribute, and slaves. In order to prevent profiteering, Diocletian (emperor A.D. 284–305) issued a detailed list of maximum prices covering everything from sow's udders to the daily wages of camel drivers. Infractions were punishable by death. Even though there were coins, markets, and long-distance trade, the Roman Empire was not a capitalist commercial political economy, and the benefits to the masses were few and indirect.

The imperia of the ancient world were sustained by the political and economic power of the state and state-connected religious institutions, but these political systems were limited by scale thresholds and often proved short-lived. Most empires lasted no more than 130 years, and very few endured more than 300 years. Perhaps more importantly, political empires left little room at the top for new power seekers, and the very existence of conspicuously wealthy elites created a powerful emulation effect that inspired innumerable others to construct their own imperia. Those who had accumulated private wealth, especially large landowners and merchants, were eager to expand their economic power, and these were the few who eventually succeeded in transforming the ancient imperial world into the modern commercial world. In Europe even after the Roman Empire collapsed, strategic resources such as land continued to be narrowly controlled by the church and the landed aristocracy. This meant that only a few could hope to become commercial elites.

5

The Rise of European Commercial Elites

By A.D. 400, when the Roman Empire was collapsing, it was clear that the political world produced great opportunities for only a limited number of power seekers. Furthermore, politically based imperia obviously became increasingly more expensive and potentially less sustainable as they grew larger. Eventually those power seekers who succeeded in developing commercial imperia gained scale advantages and greater opportunities for themselves, and in the process unintentionally constructed an entirely new, much larger-scale and more dangerous world order. Medieval and early modern commercial elites did not set out to construct a global capitalist system. They simply sought personal power. There was no grand vision. No one could have foreseen the ultimate consequences of commercial expansion. Individual actors simply took advantage of opportunities as they appeared, but only a few had such opportunities, and fewer still could intentionally create new opportunities for themselves. Individuals developed great commercial imperia because it became possible to do so and because those who may have been negatively impacted by such developments did not have the power to resist.

There was no sharp dividing line between the imperial and commercial worlds. Rather, there was a gradual transformation from one to the other after A.D. 1000 as the leaders of urban-based European commercial imperia began to gain strength and were able to coopt and dominate the leaders of more exclusively political imperia. The perpetual violent competition between Western European political elites seeking military domination facilitated this transformation during the 600 years from A.D. 1000 to 1600. Their increasingly violent power struggles generated increasing opportunities for a few commercial elites to construct their own ever more powerful commercially based imperia. Eventually the capitalist heads of the largest commercial imperia began to command members of the old landed political aristocracy and the religious establishment until their personal commercial interests came to dominate political decision making throughout Europe.

Urban Growth and the Origins of Capitalism, 1100–1600

The medieval European towns that aspiring commercial elites designed after the Roman collapse allowed elites to create the peculiar power structures that made commerce dominant. Burghers were in effect seizing power when they created medieval towns. Urban powers included market monopolies as well as the right to regulate trades and artisan guilds, collect urban rents, hold courts, collect and spend taxes, confer citizenship, and form and direct military forces. In early medieval Europe these rights legitimately belonged to royal monarchs, who might grant them exclusively to their feudal lords or to burghers in formal written charters, or franchises. Some kings consistently refused to issue city charters, but it was the relative weakness of kings and clerics that gave the burghers an opportunity to build power. Frequently, burghers were able to first independently turn towns into their own "legal" corporations and then later seek royal approval. Either way, by creating municipal corporations, burghers secured crucial political and economic powers that made them effectively independent from feudal monarchs and lords, and allowed them to command the labor of now dependent artisans and peasants. A crucial step toward commercial domination was taken by a tiny handful of self-interested people who shifted many of the social costs of economic growth to the weaker and more numerous. The freedom of action gained by the burgher elite created oppression and dependence for the majority while at best allocating them minuscule benefits.

The growth of cities was a crucial aspect of the commercialization process because as urban populations became larger, their inhabitants necessarily became more and more dependent on markets and commodities. Elite decision making created the conditions that both promoted urban growth and made growth possible. Villages became towns when particular elites made them their headquarters. The presence of the wealthy set off a multiplier effect because the elite demand for luxury goods and services created opportunities for many small suppliers who moved to towns with their families. When the great English landowners decided that it was more profitable for them to convert their vast holdings to large-scale wool production and collect cash rents rather than labor dues for use of their lands, masses of the rural poor were uprooted and forced to seek a better life in the cities. At the same time, elites, including many of the same great landholders who were enclosing their fields to raise wool-producing sheep, were also constructing great houses in the cities, thereby creating new subsistence possibilities for the urban lower classes. Elites, in their self-interested pursuit of power, set in motion processes that resulted in urban growth and ultimately transformed European society and culture.

Only a handful could play the growth game. Eighteenth-century French physiocrat (nature rule) theorist Richard Cantillon (1755, 1959) argued that it was "natural" that an elite few would own private property and dispose of the "surplus" product as they saw fit. The presence of large landowners, nobles, and secular and clerical officials would "naturally" generate a larger city. Following Cantillon's lead, historian Josiah Russell (1972, 34–36) identified a hierarchy of ranked social positions whose presence determined the size of urban places by the combined size of their retinues, assigning a multiplier for the local residents required to provision each. This represented the power of the personal imperium of each individual occupying each rank in a particular place. For example, they ranked by scale: king, 3,500; merchant/magnate, 350; small merchant/official, 35; farmer, 3.5. By 1300, after a few centuries of elite-directed urban growth, nearly 40 million people lived in western and central Europe, which was divided into twenty large market regions, each focused on an urban center and a simple rank hierarchy of smaller cities, market towns, and villages (Russell 1972). Most people supplied the bulk of their needs locally. Long-distance trade moved between the largest centers, was still poorly developed, and large merchants focused largely on providing luxury goods and financial services for the landowning elite and clergy. There were only three urban centers with 80,000 people or more, and another sixteen with 40,000 or more. There were probably only a few hundred large merchants whose trading activities reached beyond their local regions, and only a handful who could have accumulated significant social power.

The interests of urban-based merchants in extracting profits by expanding trade and promoting the independent use of money might seem to have conflicted with the interests of feudal landlords, monarchs, and clerical authorities, who were all dependent on labor, rents, and tithes extracted from the peasantry. However, as events unfolded, it became possible for a few powerful individuals to construct personal imperia that brought these diverse interests within their own family-centered networks of power. These power networks came to be driven predominately by monetary considerations. This power shift required an increasingly urbanized cultural world with an expandable demand for commercial products and services. Merchants needed enough political autonomy to support commercial institutions, to protect luxury consumers, and to maintain access to markets and resources. They could not dispense with government because commerce and wealth accumulation required law and order. As urban scale increased, commercial rather than political or ideological elites gradually became the principal growth-directing agents. Investment decisions made by the largest commercial elites assumed a disproportionately important role in larger places. The crucial condition was that a few large merchants were highly successful at accumulating commercial power, and there were few cultural limits on either their numbers or their total power. In effect, the newly emerging commercial elites had identified a growth opportunity and were taking advantage of it. In contrast, there were severe cultural limits on the number and power of political rulers and clerical elites, and ultimately they became financially dependent on, and even joined with, the great merchant-financiers. This unbalanced growth process, favoring commercial elites, ultimately produced the global capitalist system and continues to shape the future.

Many small market towns grew organically from villages, but in England the king still had to approve town charters, and this meant that a developer needed political influence. This public-private partnership of government and commercial elites became the prototype for virtually all commercially motivated expansion. For example, from approximately 1066 to 1370 some 380 new towns were deliberately "planted" in England, Wales, and Gascony (France) by English kings, clerics, and private entrepreneurs who enjoyed royal favor (Beresford 1967). Financial gain was the objective of this unfolding urban revolution, which was directed by some of the earliest capitalist real estate developers in European history. Increased profits for merchants also meant more rents for urban landlords and more royal revenues. All successful towns produced revenue for the king from taxes, tolls, and fines. The new towns also became an abundant source of rents for the great landowners. Rents and revenues accruing to the king, who at this time was still the largest urban landlord, were a significant source of royal income. In 1334 the king received as much in taxes from new towns as he did from London. Revenue farmers also profited from the urban growth bonanza.

The case of Sir Henry le Waleys (died 1301) illustrates the emerging power of commercial imperia and the cross-cutting of political and commercial interests in medieval Europe, showing its international character. Sir Henry made his fortune as wine merchant to the English Royal Household from 1252 to 1272. He was also a diplomat, royal advisor, alderman, and periodic lord mayor of London (1273–99), and he became mayor of Bordeaux, France (1275) (Beresford 1967; Williams 1963). In 1284 Sir Henry also became an important revenue farmer for six new towns in the Bordeaux wine-growing district. This meant that he had the right to collect revenues for the king and enrich himself at the same time. It is not surprising that King Edward I summoned him in 1297, along with some twenty-five other prominent citizens, to an urban planning conference focused on how best "to devise, order and array a new town to the greatest profit to Ourselves and merchants" (Beresford 1967, 3–13).

Medieval City-States and the Medici Imperium

The commercialization process was greatly accelerated by the unique circumstances of medieval Italy. In the chaotic aftermath of the Roman collapse, from A.D. 875 to 1100, the titled nobility in Tuscany were able to position themselves as rulers over relatively autonomous city-states and went on to create a great commercial dynasty based on the wool trade, banking, and the production of luxury commodities and various consumer goods (Lachman 2000; Lansing 1991). In 1296 the largest merchants in Florence created a chamber of commerce as a court to regulate, promote, and defend their commercial interests, and they sought to control the municipal government. They also organized themselves into commercial companies and guilds to combine political and economic power and promote the professions and the production and marketing of everything from armor and crossbows to bridles and bits (Staley 1967). The guilds were hierarchically arranged, with political and commercial leadership coming from the powerful master merchants, bankers, textile manufacturers, judges, and notaries. The leaders of the textile guilds imported raw wool and yarn from London and turned it into finished cloth for export back to London. The Florentine elite also constructed a network of family offices with some 300 agents scattered throughout Europe, and they became the bankers and financiers to the popes and kings who directed the Crusades and the dynastic Hundred Years War. This continental network of commercial power was the prototype for the global network that the great London commercial dynasties constructed 500 years later. The commercial boom and obvious prosperity created by these organizational changes caused the city of Florence to swell to a peak of some 100,000 persons before the Black Death of 1347.

By 1434 the political and commercial institutions of the city-state of Florence, as well as greater Tuscany, was dominated by a single dynastic family, the Medici, whose members remained in almost uninterrupted control for three centuries (1434 to 1737). The family's great wealth and personal artistic tastes made them the center of the Italian Renaissance. Their commercially dominated imperium became a vast network of political, commercial, and ideological power that reached throughout Europe far beyond Italy and helped create the infrastructure of the capitalist world system.

Cosimo d'Medici (1389–1464) represents the Medici imperium at its height. Cosimo commanded a cluster of some ten clans and sixty families connected by ties that cross-cut family, class, neighborhood, and wealth. It was a complex of interests that included political partisans, business partnerships, bank employment, mercantile exchanges, and real estate deals (Padgett and Ansell 1993). Standard categories such as feudalism, nobility, and social class do not adequately explain the structure of the Medici elite. They were opportunists building their own personal imperia. Religious ideology and prevailing cultural customs were no barrier to Medici expansionism. They bypassed the Church's opposition to usury and the charging of interest on loans by making no entry in their account books for "interest." Rather, they referred to "profit and loss on exchange" (Roover 1963, 12). The widespread concept of "just price" and regulations against price-fixing and monopoly were overcome by their political power, because no one could seriously challenge them.

There were fourteen family members in Cosimo's immediate extended household, and he supported an additional thirty-five domestic servants and retainers, including four slaves. He owned two palaces in Florence, three country villas, and residences in Pisa and Milan. This was a vast circle of power, with Cosimo at the hub and many disparate individuals and organizations occupying the spokes, not unlike the Hindu-Buddhist *cakra,* but in the Medici case it was commercial, not political power, that was primary. Eventually the Medici imperium reached far beyond Italy. In addition to economic wealth, the greater Medici extended family included dukes and grand-dukes scattered across Europe, as well as cardinals and popes, and a queen of France.

In some respects the key institutional structure of the Medici imperium was the Medici Bank, which was a money-generating complex of business partnerships at the heart of the greater imperium (Figures 5.1 and 5.2). This was in many respects a modern, multidivision, multinational business organization. In 1451 the Bank was headquartered in Florence and directed by Cosimo and his general manager partner. It consisted of three branch partnerships focused respectively on silk, wool, and banking. The windfall profits that banking produced were entirely contingent on the historical circumstances and the decisions of a handful of political and religious rulers and other wealthy elites. Foreshadowing an ominous process that would later become very significant in England, a growing portion of Cosimo's financial assets were in his marketable shares in the Florentine city-state's public debt, much of which went for military expenditures. Public debt was a safe investment for the Medici, because they also controlled the government that issued and secured the debt. Medici headquarters and agents spanned eight of the twenty market regions of medieval Europe, putting the business in contact with a total urban population of nearly half a million people. This was far more extensive power than exercised by any other contemporary political ruler and clearly demonstrated the great potential of commercially organized imperia.

The general upturn in European commercial activity increased total wealth, and it became highly concentrated. Florentine income tax records for 1457 reveal an astounding shift of wealth into the Medici imperium and into elite hands in general (Roover 1963, 27–31). At the top of the social hierarchy, the super-elite composed of Cosimo and the top ten wealthiest households held 11 percent of assessed wealth, although they constituted a mere 0.1 percent of households (Table 5.1). The elite and super-elite represented only 5 percent of households, but they controlled 63 percent of wealth, whereas the bottom 82 percent had only 11 percent. The maintenance-level "middle class" was very small (13 percent). Nearly one-third of the population were considered paupers, too poor to pay any taxes. By 1691 the largest Florentine fortunes exceeded a million florins. The 5 percent income from a fortune of that magnitude would have supported more than 16,000 poor people. These fortunes spurred a spree in luxury spending on art, architecture, and elite conspicuous consumption that historians call the Renaissance, and indeed it was a return to the splendor of Rome, albeit on a smaller scale (Goldthwaite 1980, 1993). The accompanying official corruption, poverty, and social injustice certainly contributed to the Protestant Reformation.

Crisis as Opportunity: England, 1500–1688

The scale increases related to the commercialization process in England were conditioned by the extreme social inequality that was still in place centuries after the Norman Conquest. Only a very few were able to direct the great social transformations that lead England into the modern age of commercial capitalism, and these few benefited enormously while relatively powerless millions paid disproportionate costs and struggled to receive the smallest benefits. Commercial elites owe much of their success to their opportunistic response to crises of various sorts during this period. Everyone suffered in these crises, but the least powerful suffered the most, and had the least ability to direct corrective action.

Wallerstein (1976) sees a long economic crisis extending from 1300 to 1450, caused in part by elite overconsumption and overexploitation of the peasantry. Under normal conditions, after the elite extracted their feudal rents, tithes, labor dues, and revenues, the peasants were left with a very small subsistence margin that was easily threatened by any perturbations in the system. During the fourteenth century all of Europe was engulfed in peasant rebellions, plagues, bad weather, famine, monetary instability, and seemingly endless wars between rulers (Tuchman 1978). Fischer (1996) shows that rents and prices steadily rose throughout Europe from 1475 to 1660 even as wages fell, causing enormous social distress. The end of Fisher's sixteenth-century "price revolution" corresponds with what Lawrence Stone (1965) has called the "crisis of feudalism," and highlights the almost continuous social turmoil that created growth opportunities for economic elites throughout this period.

These multiple crises were not primarily a Malthusian problem of population pressure. They were largely problems of social and cultural organization that could have been solved by a devolution of political and economic power. The situation was obviously exacerbated by elite decision making, but crisis also presented prudent landed elites with new incentives to turn to political and economic expansion to safeguard their threatened income. At the same time, the responses of rural elites created new opportunities for urban-based merchants. It was in the interests of the landed nobility and the merchants to find a larger, more manageable labor force and draw in more remote resources. In effect, urban and rural elites worked together as they attempted to stabilize and enlarge their imperia. The crucial choice that elites made was to expand the scale and scope of their personal commercial activities. They sought new places to invest their money, new and larger markets, and more effective government support for their commercial interests. The elite devised new government and commercial institutions to support larger urban places and larger markets. These new institutions became more bureaucratic, more powerful, and more intrusive in everyone's lives. Ultimately the scale of both government and commerce increased. Power became more concentrated, and the elite formed new interest groups to protect their gains.

Shortly after the rise of the Italian city-states and the Renaissance, the city of London became the center of the great cultural transformations that created the modern commercial world. The London elite created a unique culture and provided a place where a new commercial elite could develop—an elite not totally dependent on landholdings. By 1600 London had grown to 200,000 people. In 1650 there were only eight European cities with populations of 100,000 or more (London, Paris, Amsterdam, Naples, Palermo, Venice, Rome, and Lisbon). By 1700, with its population reaching 575,000, London surpassed Paris as the largest European city. The rapid growth of London, and its disproportionate size, promoted commercial development throughout the country (Wrigley 1967). It also shifted power away from the rural sector. London had always been the central urban place in England, but before 1500 there were some 800 market towns in the country and fifteen

Figure 5.1 **The Medici Imperia: Locations of Offices of the Medici Bank, 1451**

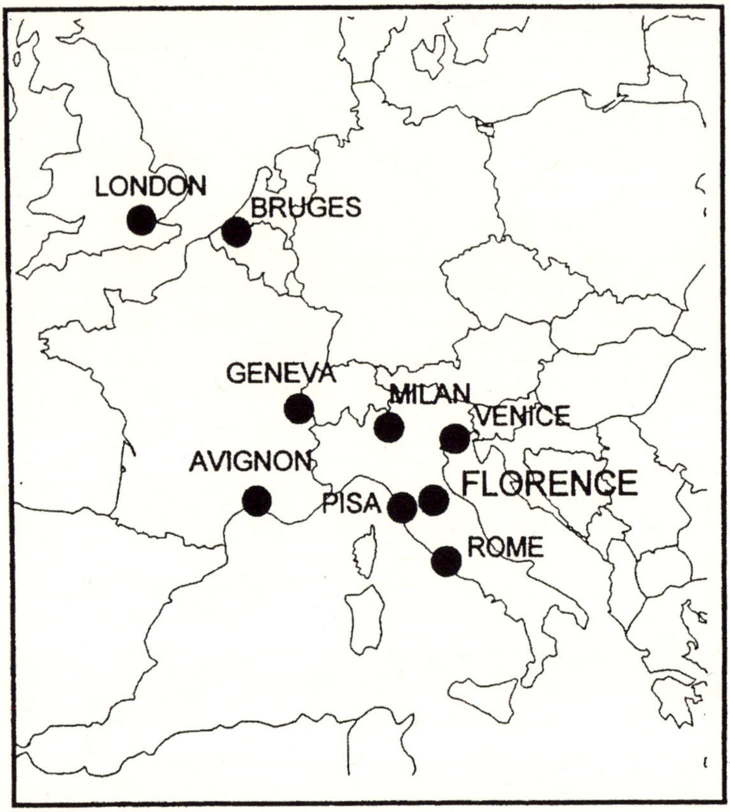

Source: Roover 1963.

separate grain markets, each operating under their own price structures (Gras 1915). In 1250 Londoners drew their grain from producers within a twenty-five-mile radius of the city, but by 1500 grain had to be shipped to London from all over England. Soon there was only one national grain market, and London was the center of an international grain import/export market spread over Europe, North America, and the Caribbean. By 1680 four great merchants handled half of the total volume of London's international grain trade (Gras 1915, 197).

Tudor England (1485–1603) spanned the most crucial foundation phases in the creation of the modern world system. Tudor England's 4 million people were controlled by a mere 120 great landholding nobles and a few hundred lesser elites under an absolute monarch. The world was changed by the

Figure 5.2 The Medici Imperia: Organizational Structure of the Medici Bank, 1451

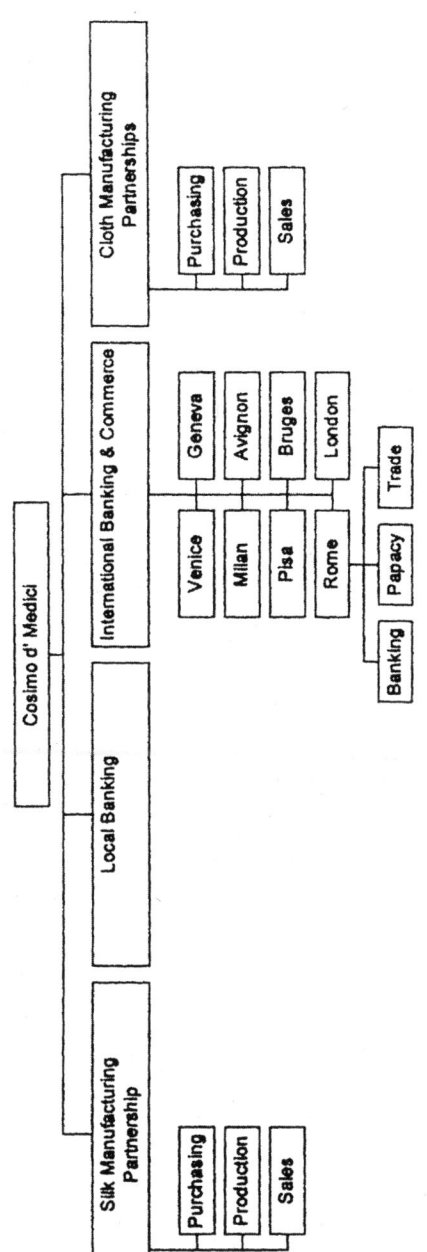

Source: Roover 1963.

Table 5.1

Florentine Imperia by Tax Rate, Wealth, and Income, A.D. 1457

Rank	Households	Average tax (fl)	Average wealth (fl)	Average income (fl)	Imperia
Cosimo	1	576	115,200	8,064	Super-Elite
Top 10	10	80	16,040	1,123	0.1% of Households
					11% of Wealth
Wealthy	216	20	3,944	276	Elite
Upper middle	317	8	1,500	105	5% of Households
					52% of Wealth
Middle	711	3	660	46	Maintenance
Lower Middle	661	1.5	300	21	13% of Households
					26% of Wealth
Poor	5,720	0.25	50	3	Poor
Paupers	3,000	0	0	0	82% of Households
					11% of Wealth
Total households	10,635	Total wealth	2,555,210		100%

Source: Data from Roover 1963, 27–31.
Note: Clergy excluded; fl = gold florins.

cumulative effects of decisions made by these few top elites in response to historical contingency. For example, the crisis of the Protestant Reformation gave Henry VIII the opportunity to seize the Church's monastic properties in 1539. The monasteries held about one-third of all manor lands in England and perhaps 16 percent of all the wealth in the country (Lachmann 2000, 99–100; Roberts and Roberts 1980, 252). The largest portions of this great bonanza, reminiscent of the division of the spoils in 1066, went to a relative handful of already powerful individuals. Between 1558 and 1641, Henry and Elizabeth I gave an average of £30,000 (in 1603–28 values) to 117 individuals (Stone 1965, 776). They each received sufficient capital to build a great country house, but the top nine recipients averaged £177,000. This great windfall was instrumental in persuading the great English landlords to give up their fortress castles, private armies, and county-level focus in favor of ostentatious country estates and participation in the splendors of the royal court. This transformation helped make Britain a modern nation-state and encouraged further growth in London while at the same time giving a strategic few the means to invest in commercial expansion.

In Wallerstein's view, the elite-constructed world system that eventually emerged had several important features: (1) it was larger in scale than any previous world system; (2) it sorted people in different parts of the world into unequal social and economic roles; (3) it was expanded and sustained by strong nation-state power; and (4) it was based on monetary exchanges. In Wallerstein's terms it was a "capitalist world system." In this new world order the elite partnership between political and economic power was critical. Lachmann (2000) persuasively argues that the English elite succeeded because they directed political power in support of economic growth. English rulers promoted commercial interests when they ordered military invasions of Wales, Ireland, and Scotland to create the United Kingdom. This was the growth logic that led eventually to the British Empire.

Landed and Monied Interests in the London Financial Revolution, 1600–1900

More costly wars and the discovery of the "New World" were the two most important historical contingencies that created growth opportunities for London's economic elites. By 1600 it became obvious to potential investors that overseas ventures would yield great financial rewards. There were also perhaps 15,000 elite household heads with enough disposable wealth that they could imagine deriving a profit from new institutional structures designed to pool, coordinate, and protect their investments. Within a remarkably short time, a handful of the largest of these investors and their supporters organized a financial revolution, forging the financial tools of corporate capitalism. They created and directed the key financial institutions of the country, making it possible for people to readily buy and sell securities, including stocks, mortgages, and government bonds. It was these institutional tools of capitalism that made the world system function. As the center of long-term capital, state finance, and overseas commercial finance, London quickly became a "city of capital," as Carruthers (1996) aptly described it. London was also the center of government and the primary port. The London-centered financial revolution gained momentum after the "Glorious Revolution" of 1688 removed King James II, who undermined investor confidence because he was Catholic and pro-French. The financial revolution also depended on limiting the financial power of the king and vesting it primarily in Parliament in order to develop a system of state finance based on improved taxation measures, long-term government borrowing, and the effective administration of a greatly expanded public debt.

The financial revolution was carried out by the elite few who designed and assembled in London all the essential institutions of capitalism, in sequence: the joint stock companies such as the British East India Company (1600) and the Hudson's Bay Company (1670), the Bank of England (1694), the Royal Exchange (1695), Lloyd's of London (1769), and the Stock Exchange (1772). This crucial series of organizational transformations was the infrastructure that made global-scale commercialization possible. The financial revolution made all monetary exchanges easier and promoted the use of credit, allowing the government to a create massive public debt. These new institutional structures were supported by the creation of a distinct service sector in the economy with a public administrative bureaucracy, mercantile bureaucracies, and many new categories of professionals. With these corporate institutions in place, a wealthy few were in position to develop and profit from the newly discovered opportunities presented by the land, resources, and peoples of the New World, Africa, and Asia.

How few were involved in these momentous decisions can be illustrated by the example of the Bank of England, which was designed by two men—London merchant Michael Godfrey, the bank's first governor, and future bank director William Paterson. Their associate Charles Montagu, then Treasury Commissioner, and future Chancellor of the Exchequer, used his personal influence to gain parliamentary approval for the bank, thus securing its corporate charter (Dickson 1967, 54–55). Their immediate purpose was to provide a corporate structure to coordinate government borrowing from wealthy citizens to meet the rapidly escalating costs of European wars. Many people criticized their decisions at the time and objected to the ominous link between investors, rulers, and war. However, the monied interests had the political power to silence their critics. Parliament shared power with the monarch, but the political system was only a limited democracy. Parliamentary decisions were made by 186 hereditary aristocrats, or Peers, in the House of Lords, and by the 513 men holding elective seats in the House of Commons. Lords and Commoners were virtually all great landowning elites and super-elites drawn from the top 0.5 percent of the population. Because of property ownership requirements, only about 278,000 men were even eligible to vote in parliamentary elections, and thus represented the wealthiest top 5 percent of the population. Candidates for election to the House of Commons were selected not by the electorate, but by the most powerful local elites, who effectively commanded electoral empires where votes were routinely purchased.

In 1697, three years after the Bank of England was founded, only about 5,000 individuals bought government bonds through the bank, or even owned bank stock, and ownership remained very concentrated. Ninety percent of the original subscribers to bank stocks lived in or near London. The forty-four largest owners controlled 27 percent of the stock (Dickson 1967, 254–255). By 1752 the total number of public creditors had grown to about 60,000 owners, however, the top 2 to 3 percent of owners with individual holdings of £10,000 or more consistently held 25 to 30 percent of total value (Dickson 1967, 284–285). Colquhoun (1815, 80–81) shows that by 1812 some 75 percent of the £33 million in capital held by all 732 banks in England was in the Bank of England. This gave tremendous power over other people's money to the directors of a single great bank.

British Colonialism: Merchant Capitalists Transform the World

Over the four centuries from 1500 to 1900 the capitalist world system assumed its essentially modern form propelled by colonialism and economic growth funded by a frenzy of investment by a wealthy few economic elites. In the process some 50 million tribal peoples died (Bodley 1999a, 43), along with millions in the ancient empires of the Aztecs, Maya, and Inca. Fifteen million Africans were enslaved and transported to the Western Hemisphere (*Encyclopaedia Britannica* 1975, 862). This was surely the most rapid and profound cultural transformation humanity has ever experienced.

In A.D. 1500 most of the world's 500 million people were still evenly divided between various domestically ordered tribal worlds and politically controlled ancient imperial worlds. European commercial elites had significant political influence in only a few areas of Europe. Four centuries later the autonomous tribal world had been virtually destroyed and, except for

China and Japan, most of the ancient imperial world was politically and/or commercially dominated by Europeans. Most of the world's 1.4 billion people were under the formal political control of fifty-two independent states and political empires, but the global system was designed for commercial profit. Seventy-five percent of humanity—more than a billion people—were controlled by the Chinese, British, Russian, American, French, and German empires. All of these nations were drawn into a network of commercial exchange that was directed by a very small number of very influential economic elites, operating from the great urban centers in Europe and the United States. Some sixteen interconnected dynastic noble families still held formal political control over most of Europe, but more than 200 million people were already living under formal democracies, or republics, primarily in North and South America, and were now governed by presidents rather than kings (*World Almanac* 1900, 369). The emergence of formal democracies after the American and French revolutions was a clear measure of the collapse of the ancient, politically based imperial world in favor of a commercially ordered world order directed by private economic elites.

During Elizabeth I's reign (1558–1603), with royal beneficence still flowing freely, a handful of wealthy English merchants and landed aristocrats pooled their wealth to finance the early stages of English overseas colonial mercantile expansion. This was a crucial moment in world history. Flynn and Giráldez (1995) note that 1571 was the year that Spanish merchants founded the port city of Manila in the Philippines, completing a secure maritime link between Mexico and Asia. For the first time, Africa, Asia, Europe, and the Americas were part of a single global trade network. This was also the moment when Mu Tsung, the emperor of Ming China (1368–1644) decided to convert his tax and tribute system to silver coin and began to import silver on a vast scale. This decision was a great stimulus to all forms of global trade. Flynn and Giráldez (1995) point out that China was a vast market, with one-fourth of the world's people; the Spanish merchants were the main suppliers; and gold was much cheaper (in silver) in China than in Europe. This caused great quantities of gold to flow into Europe via Manila and Mexico as silver flowed from Mexico to China. A few European middlemen were the immediate beneficiaries of these first steps toward economic globalization. Mexico City, which had grown to some 75,000 people by 1630, was the New World hub of the silver trade, but on the average only forty-four large Mexican investors handled more than 60 percent of all trans-Atlantic cargo passing through the city (Hoberman 1991).

Theodore Rabb (1967) developed an exhaustive list of 6,336 individual investors who ventured some £8 million in the thirty-three joint stock companies operating overseas out of London from 1575 to 1630. These companies funded the first English colonies in North America and sponsored ventures in Africa, Bermuda, East India, Guiana, Ireland, the Levant, Massachusetts Bay, Russia, the Baltic, Virginia, and elsewhere. Rabb found that in any given year there were no more than 2,500 investors, a mere 0.25 percent of the 5 million inhabitants of England. At the same time perhaps no more than a hundred men actually managed the companies. Eleven men directed four or more companies, suggesting the early presence of interlocking directories. There was obviously a minute number of very active, very influential investors behind England's great colonial adventure. Whereas the average individual investor ventured only £820, and one could buy in for as little as £15, a tiny number of big investors ventured £15–£20,000 each, and the queen personally invested £40,000. Most investors were wealthy merchants who contributed about 80 percent of the total capital, but they were joined by some 625 landed aristocrats. In 1604, when early investor enthusiasm for overseas ventures was at its height, nearly 40 percent of the Members of Parliament also bought stocks. At first, the most promising investments were in piracy, stealing the gold and silver that the Spanish had looted from the Inca and Aztec empires. Between 1500 and 1600 New World bullion "imported" into Europe increased the existing stock more than tenfold.

During the fifty years between 1735 and 1784 the interlocking imperia of just four individual London merchants—Augustus Boyd, Richard Oswald, John Sargent II, and Sir Alexander Grant—encompassed virtually all of the commercial activities represented by the early British Empire (Hancock 1995). These four men and their nineteen associates were among the primary creators and beneficiaries of the incipient global-scale commercial economy. They were, of course, not the only men actively shaping and directing the global market, but the total could not have been large. Pioneer statistician Patrick Colquhoun (1815) estimated that there were only 3,500 "eminent" merchants and bankers in all of Great Britain in 1812.

Hancock called the four London merchants that he studied "citizens of the world" because they directed such a far flung global trade network. For example, Oswald was in personal communication with forty to fifty "contacts" who acted as his correspondents, agents, and clients in England, Scotland, five North American colonies, three eastern Caribbean islands, eleven European cities in Germany, the Netherlands, France, Germany, and Italy, as well as in India and Africa (Figure 5.3). The geographic scale of this personal imperium was vastly greater than that of the Medici, and Oswald's wealth and power was at a comparable magnitude. At his death in 1784 Oswald left an estate valued at £500,000, which was sufficient to hire more than 10,000 workers at an annual wage of £46. The four London merchants were opportunists who made themselves fabulously wealthy by global real estate speculation, land development, plantation agriculture, slave trading, shipping, providing legal and financial services, and military contracting. The same men owned the ships, the land, the buildings and equipment, the commodities, the slaves, and the financial capital to make the global market operate. Among them, they owned 284,390 acres (444 square miles) of land in London, their country estates, and overseas plantations. They shipped guns, iron shackles, and provisions from England to their fortified slaving station in Sierra Leone, slaves to their plantations in the Caribbean, and agricultural products such as sugar and rum back to London. The occupied all points in the famous trade triangle.

Oswald and his associates also carried cloth from Calcutta and wine from Madeira. Between 1748 and 1784 they "exported" at least 12,929 slaves from Sierra Leone for a total profit of £30,841, averaging £857 per year. One associate averaged £3,450 per year from his slave-operated Jamaican sugar plantations alone. The role of the slave trade in promoting industrialization, capital accumulation, and overall economic growth in England has been widely debated (Williams 1944; Solow and Engerman 1987; Cateau and Carrington 2000), but it is obvious that it made some Englishmen very wealthy. Oswald also profited from war. He contracted with the British government to provision the troops in Europe during the Seven Years War. Employing some 300 bakers, he supplied nearly twenty bread depots and cleared £112,000. Many of the opportunities that the associates enjoyed depended on their extensive networks of personal contacts. For example, Oswald landed the lucrative army contract because his partner Grant had a friend who was a friend of the Earl of Bute, who was a friend of the Prince of Wales, who became King George III. It was also helpful that some of the associates served as corporate directors of the British East India Company and the Bank of England.

Throughout the colonial era the institutions of business and government worked in a close partnership and were cross-cut by personal connections. For example, the British East India Company operated as a commercial monopoly and a quasi-government under royal charter. The Company produced enormous financial returns to a relative handful of shareholders and officials from its commercial operations and the revenues extracted from the native populations of Bengal, Madras, and Bombay. By 1750 some 2,100 East India shareholders were receiving an average return on their investments of £1,160 annually. The forty-nine largest shareholders averaged £12,660, and received nearly one-fourth of the company's total annual dividends and interest payments (Dickson 1967, 287). Top owners participated in shareholder meetings to keep the rate of dividends up and to lobby for good positions with the company for family and friends. Bowen (1989)

Figure 5.3 **Agents in Richard Oswald's Personal Imperia, 1735–1785**

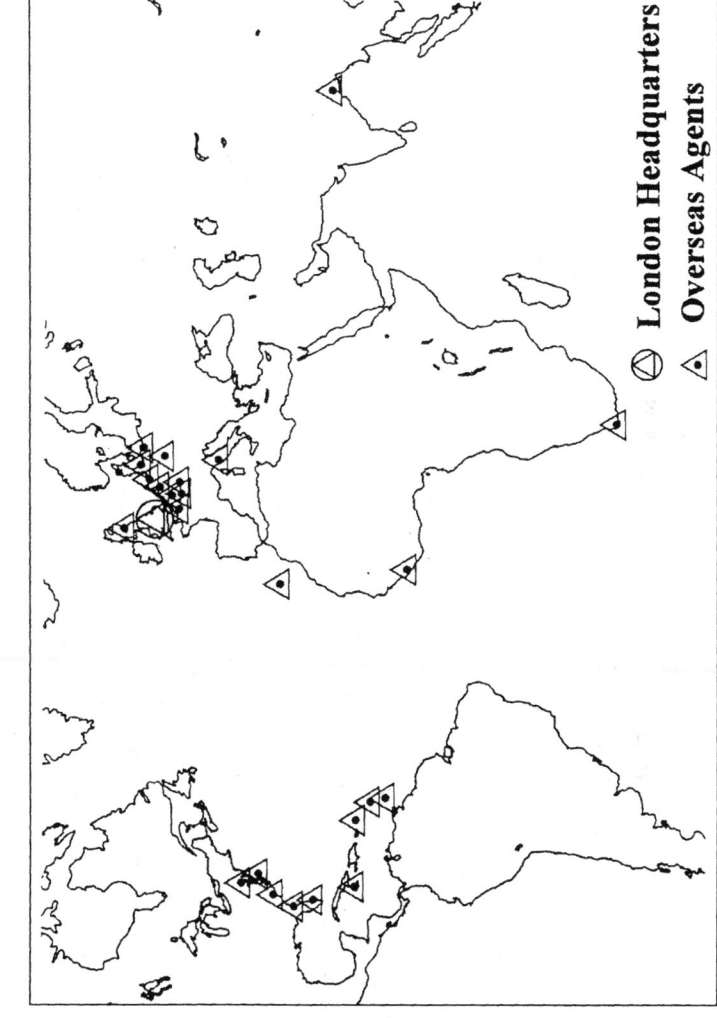

Source: Hancock 1995.

found that during the last half of the eighteenth century most stockholders in the East India Company were from the London area, and most were merchants and professionals.

There was one chief official of the East India Company, fourteen corporate directors, and 1,730 clerks at the London headquarters. In India another 3,000 company agents directed 12,362 native employees. Pay scales for company clerks ranged from £66 to £540, putting most at a maintenance level. A further 25,000 Europeans and natives found marginal employment in company shipping. In India, company operations were supported by a military force of 140,000 natives, 20,000 "King's Troops," and 913 marines. Revenues extracted from the native East Indian population of 40 million people largely supported the company's operating costs. Aside from the "employment opportunities" created by the company, records show that the top 162 shareholders were in effect commanding 45 percent of the financial gain extracted by the company from the labor of 40 million (Colquhoun 1815).

Government administration of the British Empire remained remarkably small. In 1825 the entire Colonial Office, except for India, contained just thirty-one people. In 1892 there were only 2,400 Colonial Office personnel in the entire empire, including appointed indigenous officials (Davis and Huttenback 1986, 12–13). The India Office contained another 3,000 people in 1896, including many Indians. There were at most 120,000 soldiers, including the 75,000 in India. India had been administered by the East India Company up to 1858, and then directly by the India Office. The government of British India was virtually self-sufficient, but most other colonies were subsidized by the central government in London.

During the nineteenth and early twentieth centuries the financial reach of London-based commercial imperia penetrated far beyond the formal British Empire into the newly independent countries of South America and the only partially commercialized empires of the Ottomans, Persia, and China. The London merchants, financiers, and private investors who directed the massive concentration of finance capital flowing overseas gained enormous benefits from the power of scale. For example, Argentina's rulers borrowed heavily through British bankers to fund a genocidal military campaign against the Tehuelche Indians in the 1870s. Annihilating the Indians improved Argentina's credit rating and virtually doubled the amount of land available for commercial agriculture. By 1900 one London financier, banker, and warehouseman, Charles Morrison, controlled some 10 percent of what had become very substantial British investments in Argentina (Cain and Hopkins 1993, 290). By 1913, some £23 million in British manufactured goods and £480 million in British investment funds moved to Argentina, and £43 million in wheat and beef flowed back. Even a modest return in commissions, interest, and dividends on sums of this magnitude proved richly rewarding. Morrison was already a rich landholder in the 1870s, owning more than 118 square miles of land in Great Britain (Bateman 1883, 321), but when he died in 1909 his personal estate was valued at £10.9 million. He was one of some thirty multi-millionaires in Britain in 1895–1914 (Rubinstein 1981, 41–44). In Argentina, a country of some 5 million people, the benefits of this development bonanza went primarily to 400 great land barons and a few bankers and merchants.

The British colonies were not profitable for the government, British taxpayers, or the natives, but a few individuals benefited substantially. This was possible because the costs of police, military, and legal services to protect private property and enforce contracts and public infrastructures that supported commerce in the colonies were paid by society at large, either in the form of taxes levied on the native population or subsidies from Britain. The latter costs were borne by British taxpayers. Numerous other public expenditures on education, public health, and social welfare were required to make labor more productive. Government also provided direct subsidies, loan guarantees, discounted rates, and various tax advantages to businesses, support for science and technology, and special marketing and information services. Some of these public expenditures were reflected in the extraordinary £1.4 per capita annual tax burden carried by British taxpayers for "national defense" in comparison with £0.42 in other developed countries and £0.02 in the colonies between 1860 and 1912 (Davis and Huttenback 1986).

Those who profited most during the height of colonialism during this period were some 200,000 top shareholders composed of bankers, military officers, government officials, Members of Parliament, peers, and large property owners. In 1867 these super-elite households represented perhaps no more than 0.6 percent of the total population (Baxter 1868), yet they held more than half of the shares in imperial enterprises. Working-class people held less than 1 percent of the shares, the middle class about one-third, and foreigners held the balance (Davis and Huttenback 1986, 251–252). Comparing the taxes that different British social groups contributed to the empire with their return on colonial investments, the 29 million workers and middle-class people were in effect redistributing their taxes to the elites because elite investors received a £7 million bonus from their colonial investments above their tax contribution.

The Business of Government in the Fiscal-Military State

The British imperial system was a totally unique cultural construction in the history of the world because it was a commercial empire serving a tiny commercial elite, but it was sustained by political power and a publicly financed military force. The ties between military power, government, financial institutions, and wealthy individuals were so closely interconnected through overlapping personal imperia that it is appropriate to describe the British Empire as a "fiscal-military state." After 1688, a landed and financial elite was firmly in control of the British state. By the eighteenth century the government and the military, and the financial sector that sustained them, were tightly interdependent, forming a sector of the economy that was more important than either agriculture or manufacturing. Historians have called this connection between the military, the rulers, and the finance capitalists, the "fiscal-military state" (Cain and Hopkins 1993; Brewer 1989). This network of financial interests existed in a delicate balance. It was based on private wealth and public taxation, but too much taxation was likely to create social turmoil that would undermine the state's ability to protect private wealth and would shake investor confidence. At the same time, investors engaged in destabilizing financial speculation that sometimes produced "bubbles" that burst, as in the infamous case of the South Sea Company. The economic elite and political rulers were often the same people, but their social roles were also mutually interdependent, linked by common interests that transcended the claims of the mass of working people.

It is apparent that the fiscal-military state was designed by and primarily benefited two interest groups: the landed elite who enjoyed a major tax break, and the financial elite who received interest on the national debt and profits from overseas trade. Large landed interests supported the fiscal-military state because the government kept land taxes low, and because other taxes were generally regressive. Politicians also offered the aristocrats the benefits of patronage in the form of positions in government service. Government appointments and sinecures helped keep landed estates intact because they provided "places" for noninheriting second sons. Manufacturers supported politicians who protected their interests by selectively imposing protective tariffs on imports. Arms manufacturers benefited directly from military contracts. Tariffs also generated revenues that were redistributed to the financial elite in the form of interest payments on the national debt, which they in turn had capitalized. Rulers who borrowed for military purposes also benefited because borrowing created a constituency of creditors who had a financial interest in keeping a ruler in power (Carruthers 1996). The mass of the population bore the burden of taxation (Mathias and O'Brien 1976; O'Brien 1988), and the entire system was heavily subsidized by the cheap labor and resources gained overseas. The operation of this vast social power redistribution system was, of course, ultimately sustained by military power. The obvious injustices generated by the fiscal-military state prompted widespread social unrest, radical criticism, and calls for reform, and were partly responsible for the American Revolution.

The large-scale demand for armaments and the great cost of raising and supporting armies and navies had social and economic repercussions throughout the commercially organized world. War is implicated as one of the causes of price revolutions and of the cycles of economic expansion and contraction, capital investment and depreciation, prosperity and decline known as Kondratieff waves—also called K-waves or long waves. In the 1920s Russian economist Nikolai Kondratieff described such phenomena as fifty-four–year cycles and identified three long waves between 1790 and 1925 that peaked respectively in 1814, 1864, and 1920 (Kondratieff 1984; Mager 1987; Goldstein 1988). Whereas war was a long-term benefit for the great financiers and generated boom and bust cycles for the armaments manufacturers and military contractors, it caused extended hardship, unemployment, and poverty for ordinary people because of higher taxes, breakdown of trade networks, and material shortages.

Capitalist Manufacturers: Canals, Pots, Guns, and Lobbies

A few key individuals directed the new developments that collectively produced the Industrial Revolution in England. The nationwide "fuel crisis" produced by the continued rapid growth of London after 1750 opened profitable opportunities for great landlords who were already in possession of rich coal deposits. For example, Francis Egerton, third Duke of Bridgewater (1736–1803), built a commercial empire that rivaled any in the country during the early phases of the Industrial Revolution (Hadfield 1969; Mather 1970). The duke's rise to power came from his successful coordination of the construction of a complex series of canals, complete with locks, aqueducts, and tunnels, to connect his Lancaster coal fields with Manchester and the wharfs of Liverpool. The canals revolutionized transport, driving down costs more than 80 percent. Soon Bridgewater was the largest barge owner in this now strategic industry, and he controlled much of the barge traffic in fuels, produce, and manufactured goods that sustained London. In 1837 the Bridgewater Trust was still one of the largest commercial establishments in England, and the Bridgewater canals carried about one-fourth of all the raw cotton consumed by all the textile factories of Great Britain (Mather 1970).

Josiah Wedgwood (1730–95) is a prominent example of an English entrepreneur who created a global market for ceramics (McKendrick 1959). He started with a small partnership producing for a regional market in 1754, and within forty years his ceramics were in use throughout the world. His personal fortune of £500,000 placed him at the very pinnacle of social power.

Josiah's family was part of a long tradition of small-scale pottery manufacture in Staffordshire. However, before 1750 some sixty potteries were selling less than £10,000 in annual production in a market of only 340,000 people. In 1765 Wedgwood began selling very expensive, limited-edition dinnerware sets to the nobility, and then used emulation effects to market cheaper sets to the lower ranks. He used newspaper advertisements, special catalogues and samples, money-back guarantees, traveling salesmen, and free delivery until he controlled a truly national market of more than 6 million potential consumers. He then teamed up with 240 private investors to finance construction of the 93-mile, £296,000 Trent and Mersey Canal to connect London with the Duke of Bridgewater's system. Wedgwood could then ship his wares cheaply to London and import tons of clay from as far away as the Carolinas, Australia, and China. Wedgwood extended his marketing strategy overseas using political influence with the British government to gain favorable trade policies. By 1795 Wedgwood pots were sold throughout Europe, Russia, America, the Caribbean, China, and India.

British naval expenditures were dominant influences on the early industrial English economy. In 1765 a single large gunship cost as much as £63,000 to build, when iron works and textile mills averaged only £10,000 to £12,000 (Brewer 1989, 34). The number and tonnage of warships increased tenfold, from 42 ships and 22,411 tons in 1641 to 411 ships and 402,555 tons in 1793. During the Napoleonic Wars the naval fleet nearly doubled to 776 ships and 724,810 tons (Hannay 1926, 303–305). The military demand for cannon and military hardware was an incentive for iron producers to boost the scale of their operations, but only a few were the prime beneficiaries. For example, three Walker brothers and a partner formed a small foundry in 1746 capitalized at £600 and producing 64 tons of cast iron, by 1766 they were able to increase production to 622 tons and their capital to £31,000 (Ashton 1968, 47–48). The wars with America and the French were good for the Walkers. By 1781 they were producing over 1,000 tons of steel, with 60 percent for cannons. After the war their business was worth £213,393. The Carron Company, another early English armaments partnership, saw its capital soar from £12,000 to £150,000 between 1760 and 1773, even before the American Revolution. The armaments industry was already an international business, with British cannon being shipped to Russia and Spain. However, workers received few of the benefits. In the 1830s they worked 80 hour weeks for £30 a year.

The early military-industrial complex had a synergistic effect. The development of the cannon-boring lathe by John Wilkinson in 1774 provided the boring technology needed to produce reliable cylinders for the first commercial production of the steam engine designed by James Watt. Watt's engines would soon be used to operate blast furnaces and milling machines in the iron industry and provide locomotion for the first railroads. The switch from charcoal to coal for smelting made even larger-scale production of iron and steel possible, and made it attractive for big operators to integrate their operations vertically by taking possession of coal mines and ore fields. An Ironmasters Association was operating by 1777, and manufacturers created a Birmingham Commercial Committee in 1783 and a General Chamber of the Manufacturers of Great Britain by 1785. Manufacturers designed such groups to lobby Parliament for the approval of their favorite canal projects, for favorable tariffs, tax breaks, controls on international labor migration, and whatever policies suited their immediate self-interest.

These organizations covered all the major industries and were scattered throughout the country. They were created as corporate bodies with formal constitutions, officers, membership fees, and regular meetings. They were successful tools that individual capitalists used to secure their interests. James Watt and Josiah Wedgwood were prominent among these early political pressure groups. Their efforts were often very successful in molding policy and thereby creating the conditions that would promote the growth of their particular industries and increase their personal wealth and power.

The Power of Scale in Britain, A.D. 1066–2000

A clear measure of the power of scale in Britain can be seen in the relationship between the size and composition of households of different rank and the distribution of wealth and income over the millennium between 1066 and 2000. The scale of English society increased by an order of magnitude from 1.5 million in 1066 to nearly 60 million people by the year 2000, and the economy grew by six orders of magnitude from a gross domestic product (GDP) of £2.3 million to more than £2 trillion (Snooks 1993). However, the majority of Britains did not enjoy a meaningful share of the benefits until after 1950 because growth concentrated power for those who directed the process. For example, Gregory King (1696, 1936) estimated that in Stuart England in 1688, 160 super-elite households averaged forty persons, counting family members, retainers, and servants, and were supported by incomes of £2,590, whereas the 430,000 households of poor cottagers, paupers, and vagrants at the bottom of society averaged only three persons supported by incomes of £6 (Table 5.2). Poor households outnumbered all 306,161 households in Norman England (Table 4.3). Colquhoun's (1815) estimates show that after 125 years of growth, by 1812 there were some 5,000 super-elites, but 2.4 million poor households, 841,000 homeless people, and 1.2 million menial servants. Super-elite households swelled to fifty persons each, and

Table 5.2

Stuart England Imperia by Income and Social Class, A.D. 1688

Class	Rank	Households	Income	Imperia (% population)
Upper nobility	Monarch Peers, Lords	1 186	£1,000,000 £2590	Super-Elite 0.01%
Upper gentry	Baronets, Knights, Esquires	4,400	£555	Elite 2%
Lower gentry	Gentlemen Officials, Professionals	12,000 5,000	£280 £240	
Transitional	Capitalist merchants	2,000	£400	
Degree up	Merchant traders	8,000	£200	
	Professionals Farmers Shopkeepers Artisans	50,000 330,000 40,000 60,000	£82 £51 £45 £40	Maintenance 35%
Lowest class	Laborers, Soldiers, Servants Paupers, Vagrants	449,000 430,000	£15 £6	Poor 63%
Total		1,390,587		100%

Sources: Data from G. King 1696, 1936; Stone 1965.

the incomes of Peers averaged £10,000. There were more servants than all the "unfree" peasants and slaves in Norman England, and more vagrants than all the free peasants and townspeople in 1086 combined. This would seem to be a dubious form of progress, even without considering the human costs on the imperial frontier.

The scale changes in British society during the nineteenth century were also profound, and were made possible by the great commercially directed transformations in the organization, finance, technology, and energy base of production and distribution. Growth was reflected in the more than tenfold order-of-magnitude increase in the gross stock of fixed capital in buildings, machinery, and equipment from £493 million in 1760 in Great Britain (England, Wales, and Scotland) to nearly £7 billion by 1910 in the United Kingdom (England, Wales, Scotland, and Ireland) in constant 1910 values (Feinstein and Pollard 1988: appendix). Population increased sixfold from 7 million in 1760 to 44 million by 1910. By 1930, twenty years later, the British Empire peaked at some 500 million people, roughly one-fourth of the world's population and land area (Clark 1936). This was a tenfold scale increase over the benchmark for politically organized empires set by the

Table 5.3

Georgian Great Britain and Ireland, Imperia by Income and Social Class, 1812

Class	Rank	Households	Income	Imperia (%)
First class, highest orders	Royalty Peers, lords	12 564	£41,750 £9,575	Super-Elite: 0.1% of households, 5% of income
Second class, large incomes	Baronets	861	£3,510	
	Eminent merchants, bankers	3,500	£2,600	
	Knights, esquires Higher civil officials Lesser merchant traders	11,000 3,500 22,800	£2,000 £980 £805	Elite: 4% of households, 29% of income
Third class	Manufacturers, wholesalers Gentlemen and ladies Clergymen, ship owners	45,400 35,000 10,250	£804 £800 £618	
Fourth class, moderate incomes	Eminent educators Better farmers Professionals, artisans Shopkeepers and tradesmen	874 70,000 130,145 140,000	£600 £275 £269 £200	Maintenance: 29% of households, 40% of income
Fifth class	Lesser freeholders, farmers, manufacturers, shopkeepers	681,250	£111	
Sixth class, lowest	Laborers	2,006,525	£46	Poor: 68% of households, 26% of income
	Paupers, pensioners	407,100	£26	
Total households		3,568,781	£110	
Total nonhousehold individuals		841,227	£36	
Total menial servants		1,279,923		

Source: Data from Colquhoun 1815.

Romans, and required commercial organization backed by political and military coercion, as well as the use of fossil fuels.

Even as the British population and economy grew over the centuries, land ownership continued to be extremely concentrated, such that in 1790 perhaps 5,000 large owners held three-quarters of all agricultural lands. This resembled the situation in 1086 when the royal household held 27 percent and the top 181 barons held 47 percent. The great landowners dominated Parliament, the legal system, and state finance at least until the mid-nineteenth century. The "New Domesday" survey of land ownership conducted for 1873 showed that the top 400 individual owners in England and Wales held an average of more than 14,000 acres each and collectively controlled more than 18 percent of total acreage in the country, outside of London (Bateman 1883). The top 4,000 owners held more than half of the land area of Britain. Given that there were fewer than a million owners (958,552) out of some 4.3 million households outside of London, it seems likely that only 22 percent of households owned any property. This figure is virtually identical to the 20 percent ownership rate that Soltow (1981) calculated for England and Wales, including London, based on the 1798 land tax. Apparently the basic power structure remained unaltered by the early Industrial Revolution and by centuries of economic progress and empire building.

Growth was also reflected in the increase in the number of British leaving estates of £100,000 or more, from fifty in 1858 to 540 in 1935 (Rubinstein 1981). There were eight millionaires in 1809 and one hundred in 1900. The old landed aristocracy dominated the millionaire ranks until the second half of the nineteenth century, when they were overtaken by millionaire merchants, bankers, shipowners, stockbrokers, and insurance agents. The new capitalist millionaires were primarily in commerce and finance, not manufacturing. Furthermore, the accelerated pace of economic growth in Britain and the world since 1800 produced a striking concentration of social power in London. The "naturally" unequal effects of scale appear in the disproportionate elevation in English property values as urban places grew larger. Growth in per acre and per capita real estate values increased rapidly in larger-scale urban places, creating an opportunity for elites to further increase their power. In 1900 the assessed value of British county lands and villages, which were primarily rural, averaged about £3 per acre, whereas towns averaged £10, cities £110, and London £491 per acre (Whitaker 1900, 746–762). Even before the age of skyscrapers, urban land values soared to staggering heights in the square mile (671 acres) of "The City" of London, where the *average* value per acre was £7,240, and individual building lots sold for as much as £3 million an acre at £70 per square foot! This created a fabulous windfall for London's largest landholders.

Not surprisingly, by 1900 there had been remarkably little improvement in the highly inequitable distribution of land in Britain since 1086. Offner (1981) estimated that the largest property owners, a mere 0.86 percent of all owners, still held about 30 percent of all land value nationally, much of this in great family estates. Landed property represented 40 percent of national wealth in 1885, and 88 percent of agricultural land was still cultivated by tenants in 1908. The heritage of William's conquest had enduring for nearly a thousand years, and this left most of the population at a distinct disadvantage. London also remained the property wealth center, with more than 20 percent of all privately held property value in the country well into the twentieth century. The degree of land concentration in London in 1910 was astounding. In a city of 4.5 million people there were only 38,200 property owners. This forced 90 percent of the population to pay rent for their residences and businesses (Offner 1981, 272–274).

A Tale of Three Families: Grosvenors, Rothschilds, and Bonapartes

Two European families, the Grosvenors and the Rothschilds, show commercial imperia-building processes and their human consequences at work across the centuries and generations. The Grosvenor family claims descent from a nephew of William the Conqueror, and like the famous Norman Duke, they created an enormously successful imperium based on real estate. Their lands were held intact thanks to the judicious use of land trusts and leases and the pattern of eldest sons perpetually inheriting their fathers' estates by means of periodically renewed "entails," or legal settlements that effectively prevented fragmentation. The 480-acre London estate of ancient manors on what was then the outskirts of London, which the Grosvenors acquired by marriage in 1676, proved to be a tremendous real estate bonanza for the family. Much of this land still belongs to the Grosvenor family and is now located just half a mile west of the world-famous landmarks of Parliament, Westminster Abbey, and Buckingham Palace, bordering Hyde Park and the Thames. The second Earl Grosvenor began to develop these properties in 1826, turning them into some of the most exclusive residential properties in London. The Grosvenors and ten other great landlords there owned 8 percent of the total land area of London and a mere 700 owned another third (Offner 1981, 272–274). By the end of the nineteenth century the Grosvenor family had accumulated some 20,000 acres of largely rural land in England and Wales, and a 100,000-acre estate in northwest Scotland (Sutherland 1968, 96). Their London property had soared in value to some £14 million.

Hugh Lupus Grosvenor, then the Grosvenor family head, was made the first Duke of Westminster in 1874 and was considered to be the wealthiest private person in the country, perhaps in the world (Rubinstein 1981, 44). In 1990, Gerald Grosvenor, the sixth Duke of Westminster, was worth £3.7 billion and was still the wealthiest private person in the United Kingdom (Beresford 1990, 19–21). At that time the Grosvenor landed estate had expanded to 150,000 acres (234 square miles) in Britain and included 12,000 acres in Canada, with prime properties in Hawaii, Florida, and Spain, and a 10,000-acre sheep ranch in Australia.

In the year 2000, Gerald Grosvenor was the forty-fifth richest person in the world, with a net worth of £10.5 billion ($6.5 billion). This was a gain of £6.8 billion since 1990. To handle his sprawling real estate empire, in 2001 Gerald created and directed Grosvenor Group Holdings, an international real estate investment, property management, and fund and asset management company, with five operating companies headquartered in London, Vancouver, B.C., Paris, Sydney, and Hong Kong. The company implemented worldwide the Grosvenor "vision" of shopping centers, commercial skyscrapers, high rises, and industrial parks in such diverse places as London, Edinburgh, Dublin, Lisbon, Madrid, Brussels, Brisbane, Singapore, Los Angeles, Pasadena, Washington, D.C., Tampa, Florida, and Eugene, Oregon. Few families have had such a global impact.

In contrast to the Grosvenors, the Rothschild family built their powerful imperium from scratch, from large-scale high finance and speculative investments in a fully commercialized world. Like the Medici, they provided financial services to aristocrats and rulers, but in a much larger world, and their activities promoted further growth in the global economy in ways that allowed them to capture staggering windfall profits. They rose to power very quickly from obscure beginnings in the Frankfurt Jewish ghetto after 1795 and placed themselves in a position to finance many of the most important, and profitable, events of the nineteenth century and beyond. Two hundred and fifty years and some eighteen generations later, members of the family were still among the world's wealthiest and most influential. The Jewish religion and a high proportion of cousin marriages helped integrate the family into a single, transgenerational personal imperium, perpetuating high income, great wealth, and property in a continuous estate.

Mayer Amschel Rothschild (1744–1812), who became the patriarch and founder of the Rothschild clan, had the great good fortune of becoming factor to the wealthy court of Duke William of Hanau. Well-connected Duke William was the son of Landgrave Frederick of Hesse-Cassel and was a grandson of England's George II and a cousin of George III. William and his father controlled Hesse-Cassel's principal exportable product—highly trained professional soldiers whom they rented to needy rulers at very profitable rates, even claiming special indemnities in the event of their death or injury (Morton 1961). George III hired some of these "Hessians" for use against the rebellious Americans. Duke William replaced his father as Landgrave in 1785, and his rent-a-soldier business proved so successful that he soon became one of the wealthiest noblemen in Europe. William proceeded to loan money to kings and nobles throughout Europe, using the services of Mayer Rothschild as his financial intermediary.

Mayer had five sons and placed them strategically in the major commercial centers of Europe. After Napoleon conquered Europe, Duke William went into hiding and asked Nathan Rothschild in London to manage his fortune. Nathan profited handsomely by investing the Duke's funds in British treasury bonds. He also profited from arbitrage on currency, gold, and commercial bills of exchange, buying low in one market and selling high in another, and speculating and manipulating the stock and bond market. The scale of these transactions produced tremendous profits. During the Napoleonic Wars the Rothschilds became paymasters to the British allied forces on the continent and again gained fabulous profits from the vast scale of the sums handled. From 1818 to 1844 the five Rothschild banking houses in Frankfurt, Paris, London, Vienna, and Naples together averaged profits of £204,000 a year. Working together, they were the largest banking house in the world, and their combined capital grew rapidly from under 10,000 in 1797 to £7.7 million in 1844. Between 1818 and 1846 they loaned £130 million to governments and £25 million to private investors (Ferguson 1998, 269–273). After Waterloo, Mayer's son James provided financial services to a succession of French political rulers from his banking office in Paris. James's personal wealth was estimated at over 600 million French francs, which was nearly three times Napoleon's final estate (Morton 1961, 68). Son Salomon served the Austrian Chancellor. The family was unfazed by, and even benefited from, the wars, revolutions, and financial crises of the time.

The Rothschilds helped construct an efficient international credit system and floated the loans that financed many of the major developments projects of the nineteenth century both in Europe and worldwide, including railroads, steamship lines, hospitals and municipal water systems, mercury mines, copper mines, and diamond mines in southern Africa. They propped up the credit ratings of various national treasuries and initiated Jewish immigration to Palestine. The family helped reimburse slave owners after Britain banned slavery throughout the empire in 1833. They helped the government raise money to assist the Irish during the potato famine of 1845–46. They helped Britain finance the Crimean War in 1854 and organized the French reparations after the Franco-Prussian War. In 1875 the N.M. Rothschild and Sons London bank made an emergency £4 million loan to the British government to purchase a commanding share in the strategic Suez Canal. In 1886 the Paris Rothschilds formed a petroleum company to produce and export Russian kerosene, shipping it by rail and tanker ships from the Baku oil fields on the Russian Caspian Sea to Europe via the Suez Canal. At that time the primary use for kerosene was for lamp oil. This new commercial venture made Rothschilds major players in the pre-automobile shift to oil as the world's most important fossil fuel, and put them in direct competition with John D. Rockefeller's Standard Oil for the suddenly expanding world oil market.

In 1911 the Rothschilds became the largest shareholders in Royal Dutch/ Shell Oil, controlling much of the vast oil resources in Romania, Russia, and East Asia, as well as the tanker transport business (Yergin 1991, 133). The family owned the largest coal and steel works in central Europe, an important vineyard in Bordeaux, and mansions and palaces all over Europe. They gained titles of nobility, a position in the House of Lords, and residences in London's exclusive Grosvenor Place.

Nathan's estate was estimated by contemporaries to have been about £5 million at his death in 1836 (Rubinstein 1981, 44), but the total family fortune in the nineteenth century has been estimated at as much as £400 million (Morton 1961, 56). Even if this were divided among the five brothers, the resultant £80 million each would be more than four times the wealth of the richest Roman citizen in labor value equivalents. In 2001 Benjamin de Rothschild was among the world's 500 billionaires (Dolan and Kroll 2001). The N.M. Rothschild bank still exists as an international merchant banking group controlled by a holding company, Rothschilds Continuation Holdings, with subsidiaries and affiliates operating in more than thirty countries and five Rothschilds on the board. The group provides banking, treasury, investment banking, fund management, private banking, and trust management services to governments, corporations, and very wealthy individuals worldwide.

In contrast to the commercially successful Grosvenors and Rothschilds, Napoleon Bonaparte used military power to subjugate and loot the peoples of the European continent and create his vast personal imperium. Napoleon's personal empire lasted barely fifteen years, from 1800 to 1815, but with a subcontinent of some 175 million people within his grasp, he was able to amass enormous power, however briefly. During the Napoleonic Wars some 10 million men were mobilized throughout Europe, and there were some 2 million battle casualties (Sorokin 1962, 306–331). This was a very high human cost to catapult a single man and his family and close associates to super-elite status. Napoleon declared himself emperor and turned his four brothers, three sisters, and their spouses into kings, princes, dukes, and grand duchesses (Seward 1986). In addition to some fifteen members of his immediate family who instantly became imperial nobility, Napoleon surrounded himself with an expanded personal retinue of some 4,000 people, including household staff and servants. He confiscated properties in the conquered territories at will, adding them to his personal domain, maintaining forty-four royal palaces throughout Europe for his own use and giving another forty-one to his extended family (Mansel 1987, 27, 61, 64, 131). Napoleonic conquests produced what was "probably the greatest single accumulation of property in European history" (Mansel 1987, 27). With his personal income of 36 million francs (£1.4 million), drawn from the state payroll as well as his private property, Napoleon had no difficulty supporting this enormous personal establishment. He bestowed wealth, power, and titles on his favorites, creating seven Princes of the Empire, and twenty-eight Dukes and Marshalls in addition to his ennobled family (Chandler 1966, 1122–1125). Some of his closest non-kin collaborators were also richly rewarded. For example, Archchancellor Jean-Jacques Cambacérès saw his assets soar from 50,000 francs (£2,000) in 1792 to 5.3 million (£20,000) by 1813 (Woloch 2001, 142–145).

Napoleon was a dictator who transformed French society and culture, the French legal and administrative system, and the economy, but in the process Europe was plundered by what would today be considered a criminal regime for the primary benefit of a single family. In his last will before his death on St. Helen's in 1821, Napoleon disposed of what remained of his estate, which he estimated at 206 million francs (£8 million), by giving it to his family, former associates, and veterans, war orphans and widows (Jonge 1977). This last noble gesture was appropriate given that there were more than 40,000 French casualties at Waterloo in the final defense of his empire. Although Napoleon's nephew Louis-Napoleon briefly reclaimed the imperial title from 1860 to 1871, the Napoleonic dynasty demonstrated the great cost and vulnerability of politically based personal imperia in an industrialized commercial world.

Commercial Elites in Control: Summary and Assessment

The transformation of the politically organized imperial world into the commercial world marks a clear shift from a world in which the elite demonstrated their power by the number of men and women they controlled and the children they produced to a world in which pure economic power measured by command over accumulated wealth became the primary measure of personal power. It took some 500 years after the Norman conquest before the balance between political and commercial began to move in favor of commercial imperia. The most powerful individuals in the commercial world took controlling positions in important political, commercial, and ideological imperia at the same time. It may be helpful to think of elites shuffling diverse power assets in their "investment portfolios." The mix of assets in a given personal imperium might include any and all the elements of social power, be they political, economic, or ideological, but the best mix shifted unpredictably according to the changing historical context of events and opportunities that defined the greater world in which powerful individuals operated.

In its totality, the social world that emerged under commercialization was never completely under the control of any unified social class, particular group of elites, or any single powerful individual. Most significantly, since 1500 commercial imperia began to operate on a global scale. By 1900 those who headed great commercial imperia had clearly become more influential over the course of cultural development than those commanding political imperia, purely political interests, or established religious imperia. We are describing a modern world in which commercial imperia are dominant. This organization of social power creates a highly dynamic, highly unequal, and dangerously volatile world that is unique in human history and prehistory. Commerce and economic elites define the modern world, and economic growth, not territorial conquest, has become the essence of modern political policy. Business enterprises, instead of nations, have become the tools of personal competition. It is this change in power structures and culturally defined priorities—not the mere presence of markets, money, or commerce—that matters. What counts most is the kind of imperia that control culture, and thereby control the future of humanity.

6

The Power Elite in Action: America's Commercial Revolution, 1787–1945

The American ideal is that the United States is a democracy in which the voting majority rules, determining the quality of public life in its states, cities, and local communities, and shaping the direction of the national government. The United States is also believed to be a free and open land of prosperity and equal economic opportunity based on free market capitalism and public education. According to this cultural ideal, consumers determine what gets produced and distributed by their free choices in the marketplace. Furthermore, it is assumed that anyone can be rich given the proper determination and hard work. If people are poor, it is because they have not taken responsibility for their lives and have not taken advantage of freely available opportunities. The power of scale made it possible for economic elites to control and direct America's growth in ways that gave them exclusive advantages that often contradicted American ideals. This chapter focuses on the scale effects of major, elite-directed transformations and the role of specific individuals. We will consider what changed, who most benefited, and what alternatives were bypassed. Scale theory is concerned with personal imperia and individual human agents, and does not treat social classes as decision-making agents. The "power structure" of powerful institutions will be treated as a tool that individuals used to gain their personal objectives.

The elite transformed America more rapidly and more profoundly than the earlier commercial transformation of feudal England, which unfolded over 800 years after 1066. American elites came to power in a world that was already almost fully commercialized; they were immediately drawing their power from commercial transactions. Mercantile ventures, finance, rents, land development, and land speculation were already the primary sources of elite fortunes in colonial America, rather than the agricultural production that predominated in England.

Founding Fathers and the Constitution

The few men who directed the famous events that gained America's political independence from Great Britain, and who then combined the separate states under a strong central government, were predominately economic elites. The fifty-six members of the second Continental Congress who in 1776 signed the Declaration of Independence in Philadelphia were all men "of substance and affairs" (Beard and Beard 1934, vol. 1, 233). They were primarily wealthy urban professionals and commercial men and included only nine farmers. Two-thirds were judges, lawyers, and other professionals. Another 20 percent were merchants and manufacturers. Taxation and trade restrictions legislated by Parliament were the inflammatory issues that pushed these men to declare their political independence, but the "abuses" and "tyrannies" that they perceived were part of a system of long standing, and the tax burden in the colonies was far lighter than in England. It appears that the scale effects of growth in England and colonial America may have produced unintended consequences that made war difficult to avert.

Before the war, American merchants protected their interests by relying on political lobbying on their behalf by mercantile groups in London and by maintaining pressure on local governors. This arrangement worked fairly well as long as there were relatively few American merchants and the total volume of trade remained small (Olson 1992). However, after about 1750 the scale effects of growth in both the economy and population on both sides of the Atlantic began to generate friction. By then the American population had surpassed a million people, and by 1752 total American exports exceeded 1 million pounds sterling, nearly a fourfold increase from 1697 (United States, Bureau of the Census 1960). It appears that increasing growth and complexity on both sides of the Atlantic as well as the effects of the expanding fiscal-military state eventually upset the balance of British and American elite interests. As decision making in London became more centered in Parliament, it became more difficult for American elites to influence events in their favor. Many specific new measures imposed on the Americans by Parliament—such as the prohibition on American paper money, Crown control over territories taken from the French in 1763, Crown patents required for fur traders, as well as many efforts to spread the tax burden—all tended to favor the interests of English elites over the Americans.

Events leading to the American Revolution unfolded in a remarkably interconnected manner that was related to scale processes in a thoroughly modern way. For example, Parliament's bail-out of the East India Company inadvertently led to the Tea Act of 1773 and the famous Boston Tea Party, which helped inflame American public passions for revolt. The "Too Big to Fail" principle was already at work in this dynamic process. The East India Company, the largest commercial corporation in the world at that time, was on the verge of bankruptcy because of famine in India and overgenerous stockholder dividends. In order to bail out this giant company and prevent a financial disaster, Parliament took over the administration of the Indian government, gave the company a refund on import duties on its huge surplus of tea, and allowed it to sell directly to America, thereby undercutting local merchants in London and America (Beard and Beard 1934, vol. 1, 223–224).

Very few people participated in the decision making that created the American nation, because power was already highly concentrated in colonial America. The distribution of colonial estates by size on the eve of the Revolution suggests that income distributions in 1775 broadly approximated the typical lognormal pattern existing in 1994 (A.H. Jones 1977, 1980). This meant that a super-elite of a mere 2,500 people were the primary decision makers, and they were supported by a total elite of perhaps 25,000. Just as the fiscal-military complex in England was designed and directed by a few individuals who disproportionately benefited, the course of the American Revolution and the new government that followed was heavily influenced by individual merchant financiers like Robert Morris (1734–1806), who also garnered huge, albeit temporary, personal rewards from the war. Morris was a Philadelphia merchant who signed the Declaration of Independence, served as Treasurer of the Continental Congress, helped to finance the Revolution and to draft the Constitution, proposed the nomination of George Washington for president, designed America's monetary system based on the dollar, and served in the Pennsylvania legislature and the U.S. Senate. Morris was Washington's first choice for Secretary of the Treasury but declined, perhaps because critics had unfairly accused him of taking personal advantage of his financial role in the Continental Congress. The problem was that he was personally wealthier than the government and had difficulty keeping his private affairs separate.

Morris is not a widely known Founding Father, but he played a crucial role in creating the United States and at the time was called a "Prince of Merchants," patriot financier, and a great man. His career approximates the careers of such London contemporaries as Richard Oswald and Nathan Rothschild, described in Chapter 5. Morris's personal imperium was based on his diverse commercial interests in England, France, and the West Indies, banking and finance, and speculation in currency, government securities, real estate, and the commodity markets. He brokered the government's provisioning of the French forces that fought with the Americans. He was wealthy enough to personally finance Washington's strategic troop movements to the Battle of Yorktown, ending the Revolution, and was an organizer and principal shareholder in the original Bank of North America, which was the first national bank in the country. He was a member of five major business partnerships, as well as many small partnerships, and maintained business connections with at least five delegates to the 1787 Constitutional Convention. After the war he financed the first American trade expedition to China in 1782, attempted to gain a monopoly over the tobacco trade with Europe, bought stocks in a London bank, and was heavily involved in real estate speculation. At one time he owned some 24,000 square miles of undeveloped land in five states and brokered land purchases for European investors. As soon as the site for the national capital was selected, Morris invested in property in the future Washington, DC (Beard 1913; McDonald 1958; Ver Steeg 1954).

Not surprisingly, Morris was aligned with Alexander Hamilton and other prominent Federalists, who wanted a strong federal government. His pro–economic growth stance and advocacy of free trade and global commerce was thoroughly modern. In spite of his personal attempts to gain monopoly power, he argued that commerce should be "free as air to place it in the most advantageous state to mankind," and was a firm believer in Adam Smith's concept of the invisible hand. He could not imagine any conflict between his private and public roles. Referring to American businessmen he declared, "Their own interest and the publick [sic] good goes hand in hand and they need no other prompter or tutor" (Ver Steeg 1954, 38). In his view, businessmen themselves were the best arbiters of public good and only they could understood the proper balance between public and private interests.

The Constitution, the legal framework of the United States as a federation of states, was drafted in Philadelphia in 1787 in a Constitutional Convention. At that time it was an open question whether the new nation would be a loose confederation of independent states or whether there should be a strong central government to promote the interests of private entrepreneurs and financiers. Some prominent anti-Federalist Founding Fathers, including Thomas Jefferson, author of the Declaration of Independence and third U.S. president, and James Madison, "father of the Constitution" and fourth U.S. president, recognized that the Constitution was a compromise, and although they approved of it they were fearful that unregulated commercial growth sought by Federalist merchants, financiers, and manufacturers would produce great wealth inequality that could undermine democracy.

The Federalists, led by Alexander Hamilton, who became first treasury secretary, wanted a national banking and tariff system to defend business interests and promote industrial development and a strong national army and navy to protect private property and American shipping. This was a radical departure from the existing political system. The Declaration of Independence called the former colonies "free and independent states" and this was affirmed by the 1783 peace treaty with Great Britain. Under the Articles of Confederation, which were still in effect, political powers operated primarily at state and local levels. The Continental Congress had no president, no power to tax, and no control over commerce, banks, or currency. Former Crown functions such as tax collecting, protection of property rights, and enforcement of debt payments were virtually suspended at the federal level. Farmers held their lands as a "natural" right of occupancy, protected by local authority under common law. This situation was fine for small landholders, small merchants, and artisans, but it presented only limited opportunity for investors seeking great wealth.

Federalists wanted America to become a wealthy nation and a great world power, and they correctly believed that rapid economic growth, supported by government power, was the fastest way to achieve their goal. However, the majority of Americans did not appear interested in supporting a great American empire. The anti-Federalists feared that a powerful central government would become as tyrannical and militaristic as the British monarchy, and would prove too expensive and difficult to control because a large government would not be democratic. They wanted the United States to remain a nation of small independent farmers. During the six years between the last battle of the Revolution and the drafting of the new constitution in 1787, the states remained politically independent and many small farmers and merchants were apparently prospering, even in the absence of a strong federal government. If, at this crucial juncture, the United States had rejected the proposed constitution and remained with the Articles of Confederation, the separate states might have become small, prosperous democracies like Switzerland.

The U.S. Constitution was drafted by just fifty-five men at the Constitutional Convention held in Philadelphia in 1787 (Collier and Collier 1986) in a process that was democratic only in a formal sense. A mere thirty-nine men actually signed their approval. Convention delegates were selected by only 160,000 electors because only free adult males could vote and many states had minimum property ownership requirements. Just as with the signers of the Declaration of Independence, urban interests and large wealth holders were clearly overrepresented among the delegates. There were sixteen large planters, but only two small farmers. The delegates were predominately large property owners, merchants, and professionals. Thirty of these wealthy men held government securities, 10 held bank stocks, 26 held investment real estate properties, and 19 were slaveholders. Scale laws applied even among this select group. A total value of $364,705 in financial assets was lognormally distributed among the 34 delegates who held significant financial assets. Robert Morris was the wealthiest, with $63,000 in financial assets, holding 17 percent of the total value; the top 5 men held 57 percent of the total (Beard 1913).

The Federalists had an advantage in the fight for ratification because they had many common goals, knew one another, and did business with one another. Anti-Federalists were more numerous, but were inherently scattered and unorganized. Nevertheless, it was a close struggle (McDonald 1979). The Constitutional Convention did not reach a unanimous consensus, and ratification proved difficult. Nine states had to ratify before the Constitution could go into affect, and it took nine months before New Hampshire, the ninth state, ratified on a margin of eleven votes. The State of Vermont did not ratify the Constitution until 1791.

Under the new constitution the weak Continental Congress was replaced by a strong federal government with the power to tax, borrow, regulate foreign and interstate commerce, issue money, run a national postal system, promote progress by issuing patents, declare war, and raise a national military. This was virtually everything the Federalists needed to create the institutional infrastructure that would promote their particular vision of national prosperity. A strong central government placed the country on the path of economic growth as the way to "secure the Blessings of Liberty to ourselves and our Posterity" (Preamble, Constitution of the United States). A particular set of Founding Fathers chose growth and the concentration of financial capital as the means to reach these laudable ends. This was surely not the only choice possible, but not everyone had a choice.

The 1790 U.S. population of 4 million doubled within twenty-five years. This dramatic growth was produced by massive immigration of impoverished peoples and forced transportation of slaves, as well as by rapid expansion into native American territory, which the European invaders treated as an open frontier. In the process more than 6 million native Americans probably died, and a continental-scale tribal world was ultimately destroyed (Thornton 1987). Massive and sustained intercontinental and transcontinental immigration of this speed and scale depended on the elite-directed exercise of commercial and political power in combination with the compulsion of mass poverty that forced people to choose emigration. Because the growing American population remained under a single federal system, the political structure changed from the direct democracy that was possible in the earliest New England colonies, none of which exceeded 400,000 people in 1790, to representative democracy. In 1790 one elected federal representative could speak for about 30,000 people, but in 1998 each represented 500,000.

As the nation expanded, the legal disposition of government land was a critical area for the exercise of elite direction. From the very beginning of European settlement, land was always held by the Crown or other government authority, or by commercial corporations operating under royal charter. Land was legally accessible to individuals only by special grant, rent, or purchase. Other lands belonged to the Indians. While colonial America was under British law, and up until 1871 when the U.S. Congress changed the rules, the Indians were treated as independent sovereign nations, owning their lands under customary communal title. The invaders could gain possession of Indian lands only by government-authorized purchase directly from the Indians, or from the government after formal treaties were signed, or after legal military conquest extinguished native sovereignty. The federal government used force to remove Indians and bring their lands under government control, and federal troops fought a long series of Indian Wars and military campaigns until the last Indian groups ended armed resistance in 1886. After further reductions the federally controlled Indian reservations represented only 2 percent of the original Indian territory by the 1960s.

By 1990 only about one-third of federal land remained under federal ownership; much of the remainder had been transferred over the years to private control under various land acts, either as outright grants or at give-away prices. In practice, land speculators were able to gain control over vast tracts of land through legal loopholes, political favoritism, bribery, and fraud. Two large federal programs—the various railroad land grants beginning in 1850 and the Homestead Act of 1862—gave away over 20 percent of the land area of the forty-eight continental states. The growth-promoting and wealth-concentrating effects of this legislated liquidation of public lands resembled the Stuart kings' give-away of monastic lands in sixteenth-century England.

The Rise of Big Business

By the beginning of the twentieth century a series of elite-directed cultural, legal, and institutional changes had transformed the United States from a collection of rural agrarian states into a national-scale urban commercial society dominated by a few giant commercial corporations. In 1790, 95 percent of the population was living in places with fewer than 2,500 people. There were only five cities with more than 10,000 people, and none larger than 50,000. Between 1781 and 1800 only thirteen commercial corporations were chartered for manufacturing, mining, agriculture, land development, and mercantile activities (Davis 1917, Table 2, 26). In 1813 the largest American industrial corporation was the Boston Manufacturing Company with an authorized capital of $400,000. This was a power of ten larger than other manufacturing firms of that era, but was overshadowed by John Jacob Astor's American Fur Company in New York, which incorporated in 1808 with an authorized capital of an astounding $2 million. In 1901 the U.S. Steel Corporation became the first industrial corporation to amass capital assets of more than a billion dollars. The transformation was virtually complete by 1920 when more than half of the population lived in urban places of 2,500 or larger.

The first step in what became a rapidly unfolding growth process was the elite creation of a national society with a cultural ideology and an institutional framework that legitimized elite-directed economic growth and the existence of giant corporations as a morally proper social imperative. This allowed a few to define the public interest for the many. The result was that the great majority of citizens confronted state-supported, corporately organized commercial power as separate, relatively weak individuals. The initial agents of this social revolution were an influential few New England merchants, investors, and intellectuals who from about 1810 to 1850 designed and directed numerous private institutions including universities, charities, banks, insurance companies, and factories (Hall 1982). These new institutions took on an aura of invincibility and inevitability, and thereby supplied a powerful legitimacy to what was actually a narrowly defined development program that precluded other options even as it generated profound human consequences.

The rise of American big business began in 1819 with crucial legal decisions by the John Marshall U.S. Supreme Court granting private rights to business corporations allowing them to make contracts, to own property, to extend their charters indefinitely, and to bring suit in federal court. Justice Marshall and U.S. Supreme Court Justice Joseph Story and his associates at Harvard Law School from 1829 to 1845 used their interpretations of the Constitution as instruments of social policy to promote big business (Newmyer 1987, 818). Harvard was a business-friendly institution given that 95 percent of the $142,000 raised by Harvard's fund drives from 1805 to 1846 came from just twenty-nine wealthy individual donors, many of whom were closely related (Hall 1982, 110). The creation of a big business–friendly national-scale economy required a series of federal court decisions that made it difficult for states to impose their own regulations on corporate businesses operating in interstate commerce. Early in the nineteenth century the first American business corporations were chartered by state governments as quasi-public, state-protected organizations for socially useful purposes. However, the state legislators who approved corporate charters were among the wealthiest citizens and benefited from big business. With favorable court decisions, business leaders were able to transform business corporations into a new form of private property designed to accumulate private wealth, in effect socializing capital to create the giant business corporation. After 1868 instrumentalist judges applied the "due process" and "equal protection" clauses of the Fourteenth Amendment to corporations, granting them the rights of individuals, especially the right to own other corporations. This made giant trusts and holding companies possible, even though the Fourteenth Amendment was originally intended to protect the citizenship rights of former slaves. More recently, political contributions by corporations have been defended as the human right of "free speech" under the First Amendment. These interpretations gave large business corporations legal immortality and omnipotence, making them superhuman. Corporations were legal fictions, created and protected by the state, ideally for the benefit of society at large, but in practice, they used the power of scale to disproportionately benefit the largest shareholders and managers.

Corporations became dominant in the United States after the Civil War, but not because larger businesses were more efficient or because new technology naturally gave them the upper hand. The Constitution prohibited the individual states from imposing tariffs on interstate commerce, but states could use taxes and licensing restrictions to protect local markets from cheaper out-of-state products thereby making large-scale production and marketing a less attractive growth option for investors. However, by the 1870s big businesses began to force their way into local markets in spite of local restrictions and used their financial power to lobby for legal protections in federal courts (McCurdy 1978).

The Singer sewing machine company and giant meat packers illustrate the early power of large corporations. By 1879 Singer had established a nationwide chain of 530 retail outlets. However, their door-to-door salesmen were blocked by state and county restrictions designed by local communities. By the 1880s Singer began to win its challenges of these restrictive state laws in federal courts. At the same time, the nation's four giant meat packers gained federal court approval to operate a national-scale meat market, overturning the ability of states to require state inspections that might exclude animals slaughtered out-of-state. Although previously the federal Supreme Court had ignored locally imposed commercial restrictions, now it began to assume that the Constitution intended to promote a national "free market" and favor large, national-scale business in competition with small-scale, local businesses. It was the federal courts, not Congress, that made the crucial decisions that favored very large-scale, vertically integrated corporate businesses over small local businesses. This was an unequal struggle because only very large businesses had the financial resources to sustain scores of court challenges over several years.

The legal victories of large corporate businesses changed the nature of property relationships in the United States. Corporate businesses became "socialized property" in the sense that a few very large owners control the company, dominate the board of directors, hire and fire managers, set broad corporate policy, and receive a disproportionate share of corporate profits, while many small owners and society share the risks (Zeitland 1989; Roy 1997). Individuals owning as little as 5 percent of the shares of a large corporation are conventionally considered to be "beneficial owners." They benefit, but avoid risk. If a 5 percent share of a corporation seems like a small amount, it is important to consider the significance of scale effects. For example, if a corporation with a billion dollars in capital assets produces a modest 5 percent return in profits annually that is distributed as shareholder dividends, a 5 percent owner would receive a hefty $2.5 million dividend. If the 5 percent owner is also a chief executive officer, he might receive even more in salary and bonuses. Because of their controlling positions, beneficial "owners" are insulated from adverse business outcomes that might be catastrophic for, lower-level managers, small shareholders, and employees.

Business historian Alfred Chandler (1977) attributed the rise of American big business to a natural, evolutionary response to the appearance of new technologies that speeded the rate and volume of commercial transactions. Large bureaucracies can be very efficient, but they are not the only way to organize an economy, and new technology and improved management are not the best explanations for the sudden domination of the American economy and society by corporate elites. However, emphasizing evolutionary forces makes it easy to overlook the role of human agents as well as the social consequences of their decisions. David Noble (1977) shows that technological change was called into being, directed, and "designed" by corporate business leaders. Giant corporations were also not the only way to organize new technological forms of production, distribution, and communication. They could have remained under the control of municipal corporations, state corporations, or other forms of public control. Industrial corporations could have been created as public utilities, with capital raised through taxes and bonds. Historically many state governments invested in railroads and canals in order to promote economic growth. However, corporations took the form they did because the largest private investors wanted private control, limited liability, and government subsidies, and they did not want to be accountable to the public.

How few individuals were involved in the early corporately organized businesses that initiated the first stages of the Industrial Revolution in the United States can be illustrated by the twelve people who in 1813 subscribed one hundred shares at $1,000 each in the newly incorporated Boston Manufacturing Company. The directors used their $100,000 in capital at Waltham, Massachusetts, where they built and operated the first American textile mill to integrate mechanized spinning and weaving operations. As the business grew, the directors ordered more mills constructed at Lowell, Massachusetts, and by 1820 they raised their total capital to $600,000 and increased the number of shareholders to twenty-four. Dividends averaged 19.25 percent, or $192.50 a share, and in 1822 rose to 27.5 percent. The manager and largest shareholder was making $27,000 a year in salary and dividends and lived in a company house rent free. His income was approximately 150 times that of the average factory worker. In 1836 women workers averaged $0.60 per day. At six days a week, fifty weeks a year, they could earn $180, less their room and board.

By the 1840s Waltham-Lowell textiles were being marketed globally to Latin America, Africa, India, China, and Russia. There were some nine textile companies in the Waltham-Lowell complex, and the total capital investment had expanded to $12 million. There were some 8,775 employees, primarily young women, who lived in company dormitories. Although these companies had different names, and separate corporate charters, they were linked by a small network of a mere seventy-seven interconnected shareholders, directors, and officers. Collectively, this group of wealthy capitalists was called the "Boston Associates." Between 1813 and 1865 they effectively initiated the Industrial Revolution in the United States, and expanded their investments to include railroads and banks throughout New England. They coordinated their interests by means of interlocking corporate directories and through cross-cutting family connections. For example, one man, Nathan Appleton, had interests in twelve textile companies and two banks. Nathan's cousin William also had interests in twelve textile companies, a railroad, two banks, and a Boston insurance company (Dalzell 1987, 233–234). As new mills were built, the investors simultaneously built dormitories for workers, set up real estate investments, and developed associated towns and waterworks. The town of Lowell grew from 200 in 1820 to 18,000 in 1836 (Dublin 1979, 21).

After their institutional framework, the transportation network, and industrial technology were in place, large corporations very quickly became the dominant form of business in America. Roy (1997) emphasizes the explosive speed at which large corporations were created, showing that this was not a gradual, inevitable evolutionary process. Roy pinpoints the greatest transformation as the seven years from 1898 to 1905. Over the decade between 1890 and 1900 the volume of the stock market changed from tens of millions of dollars in 1890 to hundreds of millions in the mid-1890s, to billions after 1900.

In the twentieth century, advertising specialists projected images of America's giant corporations that made them appear as all powerful, yet beneficent, public institutions, designed to serve the people (Marchand 1998). This image was of course quite the opposite of the ideology of free market capitalism in which corporations compete with each other to return higher dividends to their shareholders and capture larger market share. People needed to be persuaded of the social and moral legitimacy of giant corporations at a time when they were obviously disempowering and devouring small businesses, family farms, and small communities throughout the country. In 1886, in the *Santa Clara County vs. Southern Pacific Railroad* decision the U.S. Supreme Court had declared business corporations to be legal individual persons, with rights under the Fourteenth Amendment. To legitimize their existence they needed to be given corporate souls, and in the 1920s Bruce Barton developed an advertising campaign for General Motors that portrayed the company as one big family and the entire country as a neighborhood. Most other large corporations also quickly created wholesome family images for themselves.

Urban Elites and American Inequality: Boston, New York, and Philadelphia

The growth of American cities was an important indicator of the scale changes and the organizational transformation that was taking place throughout the nineteenth century. By 1890 there were twenty-three cities of more than 100,000 people, including three megalopolises, New York, Chicago, and Philadelphia, with more than a million people. These large cities, and especially the megalopolises, were the financial and commercial centers of the country, and the elites who made these cities their headquarters were those who directed America's urban-commercial transformation and in the process intensified preexisting social inequalities.

There was a widespread belief among contemporary observers—belief shared by many later historians—that before the Civil War the United States was a highly egalitarian, democratic society, full of opportunity and prosperity, where few were very rich or very poor. This belief was popularized by the works of the French political scientist Alexis de Tocqueville (1835–40), who toured the United States in 1831–32. In reality, social power was much more highly concentrated in the United States than the cultural ideal would suggest, but a smaller proportion were poor, and more were at maintenance

Table 6.1

U.S. Property Wealth Distribution by Households, 1850

Property wealth	Income range	Number of households	Households (%)	Property (%)
$100,000+	$5,000+	1,582	Super-Elite (0.03)	6
$10,000+	$500	77,506	Elite (1.6)	32
$100+	$250	1,814,358	Maintenance (39)	62
<$100	$50	2,758,755	Poor(59)	0

Source: Data from Soltow 1975, 178, 186.

level, than in Europe. For example, the 1850 census revealed that nearly 60 percent of free adult males owned virtually no real estate at all, whereas the top 2 percent of households owned approximately 40 percent (Table 6.1). Nevertheless, in comparison with Great Britain in 1812 (Table 5.9), Americans in 1850 were marginally better off, and this helps explain the steady flow of European immigration.

There were only 714 super-elite individuals with at least $100,000 in assessed property value in the principal cities of Boston, Brooklyn, New York, and Philadelphia in 1845 (Pessen 1973). These wealthy few were the principal investors in America's factories, real estate development, land speculation, railroads, banks, insurance, and global trade. At that time $100,000 was a substantial fortune and would have produced an annual income of $5,000 invested at a modest 5 percent. An income of $3,000 was considered sufficient to provide "the good life" of luxury food, clothing, housing, and servants. However, in New York City in 1845 the top elite also owned 90 percent of all unassessed personal property and at least 50 percent of all the capital held in banks and insurance companies. This gave the top 4 percent 80 percent of total wealth. These figures show that wealth was much more unequally distributed in America's urban centers than in the country as a whole. As America's early cities grew larger and more prosperous, wealth and power shifted dramatically to the top ranks of society and the lower ranks became increasingly impoverished.

America's rapidly expanding national society and economy created numerous wealth-building opportunities that were effectively open only to the elite. The urban elite were able to draw their wealth from a much larger area than the city itself, and from multiple sources. Urban real estate values in fast-growing cities quickly rose beyond most people's reach, and at $100 to $1,000 a share, most corporate stocks were also inaccessible to all but the very rich. The wealthiest urban Americans in 1845 were primarily merchants, bankers, lawyers, physicians, and widows, but not often manufacturers, because the Industrial Revolution was only just beginning. However, more than occupation, the crucial wealth-concentrating processes were investments, inheritance, and fortunate marriages. Historian Edward Pessen (1973, 85, Table 5.1) found that 92 to 95 percent of the wealthiest individuals in antebellum New York, Brooklyn, Philadelphia, and Boston were already well connected with rich or eminent parents or families, and only 2 to 3 percent started from poor or humble origins. He concluded, "Vastly rich or fairly rich, celebrated or obscure, it mattered not: the upper 1 percent of wealthholders of the great cities—the rich of their time—almost universally were born to families of substance and standing" (Pessen 1973, 86). This of course is quite contrary to the widespread belief that the wealthy were self-made, and it reaffirms the importance of the personal imperium. In New York there was a striking number of wealthy families with genealogies going back 200 years in America, including multiple wealthy households in the 1828–45 period. Boston and Philadelphia show similar trends (Baltzell 1958; Jaher 1972, 1982). According to this analysis, the wealthy hung onto their wealth, often increased it, and passed it on to the next generation. They were seldom hurt, and were sometimes helped, by economic crises.

J.J. Astor, Real Estate, and the Fur Empire

German immigrant John Jacob Astor (1763–1848), the United States' first millionaire business tycoon, provides an example of one of New York City's super-elites during the first half of the nineteenth century. Astor directed the United States' growth by taking advantage of a series of opportunities presented by pro-growth politicians and historical circumstances. He constructed a vast personal imperium that drew together multiple power networks in trade, real estate development, government, and finance, allowing him to accumulate the greatest American fortune of the early nineteenth century while shifting enormous social costs onto millions of people.

Astor came to the United States in 1784 in search of investment opportunities. He had brothers in London and New York, both of whom had small businesses, and he had credit arrangements with London merchants and enough capital to start up his own international import-export business centered on furs and pianos. Operating as an American, Astor was able to profit from the historical circumstance of war between Britain and France that closed the continental European markets to British traders. By 1794 he was buying undeveloped lots in Manhattan and was engaged in large-scale real estate projects involving nearly sixty square miles in New York's Mohawk Valley. The value of his Manhattan properties soared when the population of New York nearly doubled from 33,000 in 1790 to over 60,000 in 1800 and reached

96,000 in 1811. Carefully building his personal imperium, Astor joined the right social clubs and became a close friend of New York State Senator De Witt Clinton, who later became a U.S. senator, governor of New York, and a major promoter of the Erie Canal.

Jay's Treaty in 1795, restoring commercial relations between the United States and Britain, brought more benefits to Astor. The treaty not only opened the Northwest country to well-positioned American fur traders, but it also allowed Astor to import Canadian furs and re-export them to lucrative markets in London, Leipzig, and China. Within four years he was shipping furs to China in exchange for tea, silk, and Chinaware, which he shipped back to New York and London. He brought cheap manufactured goods from London to trade to the Indians for furs. This trade proved so profitable that by 1804 he was buying his own ships and increasing the volume of his transactions. He also benefited enormously from the opportunity for neutral American trade opened by the Napoleonic Wars, and took advantage of the government's policy of imposing steep discriminatory tariffs against foreign shippers and low, deferred tariffs on Americans. By 1807 Astor was a millionaire (Haeger 1991, 65). The Louisiana Purchase of 1803 and the Lewis and Clark expedition of 1804–6 opened the interior of North America to Astor's fur trading agents, offering a virtually unlimited supply of furs. With Governor Clinton's support, Astor incorporated his American Fur Company in 1808, then gained President Jefferson's permission to operate west of the Mississippi, where the Indian trade had been a government monopoly. Astor attempted to gain full control over the fur trade across the continent to the Pacific by creating a subsidiary, Pacific Fur Company, to be based at the mouth of the Columbia River in a port town that he immodestly named "Astoria." Pacific Fur would ship directly to China. Another subsidiary, the Southwest Fur Company, bought out Canadian interests in the Great Lakes region. Astor also negotiated a cooperative agreement with the Russian government and the Russian American Company operating in Alaska. This put him in the middle of what became a diplomatic struggle between Russia, the United States, and the British over control of the Pacific Northwest. The Astoria venture eventually failed, but Astor recovered his great fortune.

Astor's success as a businessman was due in part to the sheer size of his capital, which gave him tremendous bargaining power. He was also able to gain favorable government policies by cultivating personal connections with key officials. He loaned money to James Monroe and Henry Clay and became Treasury Secretary Gallatin's personal financial manager. Furthermore, Astor, with two other great capitalists, personally provided nearly one-fourth of the $45 million that the federal government borrowed to finance the War of 1812 and helped arrange the remaining bonds (Haeger 1991, 138–141).

Astor engaged in an extensive lobbying campaign, including a personal appeal to President Monroe, to persuade Congress to abolish the system of government trading posts in Indian territory in 1821. Operating his American Fur Company in a fully modern way, he expanded by buying out competitors or by negotiated partnerships. He divided the fur country into territories assigned to five departments, pitting each department against the others and cutting employees and shifting resources for maximum efficiency. Each department head fielded separate trapping outfits and traders who dealt directly with the Indians. At its peak in about 1830, the American Fur Company had some 750 employees who brought in hundreds of thousands of furs.

Astor was often condemned for exploiting the Indians, and the overall effects of the fur trade, including direct violence, alcoholism, disease, guns, and disruption of subsistence routines and social patterns, were devastating. But Astor was of course only indirectly responsible for the behavior of individual trappers and fur traders. As long as no money was involved, it was common practice for traders to overcharge and undercredit, and the Indians often had little defense against sharp trading practices. The fur trade bonanza was a short-lived phenomenon. With no protective trapping regulations the game were quickly depleted; likewise the Indians could be exploited for only so long. Furthermore, the market depended heavily on luxury fashions and volatile military contracts and uniform styles. Astor sold his American Fur Company in 1834, before the supply and market demand collapsed.

It was not just the Indians who were negatively impacted by Astor's company and other American merchant capitalists; the negative consequences were felt worldwide. For example, Hawaii became an important mid-Pacific stopping place for Astor's ships, and his agents quickly discovered that Hawaiian sandalwood brought a high price in Canton. They traded cash, china, muskets, alcohol, and even ships to chiefs such as Kauikeaouli (King Kamehameha III) for the valuable wood (Porter 1931, vol. 2, 1195; Sahlins 1992). The Hawaiian chiefs used this sudden windfall of new wealth objects to boost their personal power and mobilized their subjects to extract ever more sandalwood. This continued until the local forests were devastated. The new diseases and disruptive changes introduced by the Yankee traders and sailors caused a dramatic plunge in the native population from nearly a million in 1798 to fewer than 250,000 in 1823 (Stannard 1989).

The Rail Empires, 1840–1870

Many people believed that railroads were the irresistible force that inevitably produced the United States' economic growth and giant business corporations. For much of the nineteenth century the railroads were the principal companies traded on the stock market, and owners and directors of railroads constituted the most powerful economic elite nationally (Roy 1997, 79). The great railroads were an order of magnitude more costly than the small roads, canals, and local rail lines that preceded them. They were also organizationally more complex than any previous forms of business. A single mile of railroad cost $30,000 to build—which was as much as a local canal, road, or steamboat—and a local rail line cost more than ten times as much as the largest textile mills. Between 1815 and 1860 only $188 million was invested in canals, but between 1830 and 1859 some $1.1 billion was invested in railroads (Chandler 1977, 90). The scale of these huge investments generated a few private fortunes. Furthermore, railroads became so large that they had a profound growth impact on the total American economy, just as did the earlier British fiscal-military state. Wherever railroads were constructed markets expanded, and small farmers, merchants, and manufacturers found themselves operating in a new, vastly larger, and more uncertain commercial world. However, the United States could have been developed without the railroads, and railroads could have been organized and financed on a smaller scale.

Historian Robert Fogel (1964) estimated that even without railroads, if Americans had continued to expand and improve canals and wagon roads, all but 4 percent of the agricultural land that was developed by 1890 would have been profitably accessible. Even though railroads required larger amounts of capital than other enterprises, there were several possible ways to organize and finance them. The large integrated northeastern lines were funded by large investors and foreigners through the organized capital markets in Philadelphia, Pittsburgh, New York, and London rather than by local people. This concentrated the benefits in a few remote hands. In contrast, state and municipal governments and local people funded roads and canals, and even financed small regional rail lines. The Virginia rail lines were funded by local investors, and consequently developed slowly and remained focused on local markets (Majewski 1996). Small-scale infrastructural improvements provided long-term and widespread benefits to local communities because they stimulated regional markets and raised property values, but they did not produce immediate profits to large remote investors.

The rapid scale changes in the railroads were driven by the speculative interests of financiers and rivalries between lines rather than by market demand. Within a mere forty years from 1840 to 1880, numerous lines expanded from small fifty-mile independent roads to larger systems with hundreds of miles of track by the 1850s, to giant, transcontinental systems with 10,000 miles of track by the 1880s. The rail empires replaced the "invisible hand" of the market with the visible hand of corporate managers by the 1870s as the large lines standardized their equipment by mutual agreements and coordinated their schedules, fares, and freight rates to prevent ruinous competition and improve efficiency. A "managerial revolution" was required for operating large-scale railroads (Chandler 1977). Previous business forms were small enough to utilize the simple management forms and accounting procedures that had worked for Florentine merchant capitalists in 1450. Even the Boston Manufacturing Company was no more complex than the Medici Bank. However, the great railroads were so large that their managers were forced to adopt military-style bureaucracies, formal organizational charts, codified reporting procedures, and personnel management policies to make them work. Business management suddenly became a profession in itself. By 1891, the Pennsylvania Railroad was probably the largest business in the world. It had 110,000 employees, which was more than all of the U.S. military forces or postal workers, and its revenues were 35 percent the size of the entire federal government's (Chandler 1977, 204–205).

The railroads might never have developed as they did under "free market" conditions because giant lines would have been too risky for investors (Roy 1997). As great financiers gained increasing power over political decision making they were able to mobilize public resources for the railroads. Government support for the railroads included purchase of corporate stock by state and municipal governments, state guarantees for corporate bonds, and even allowing railroad companies to borrow against the value of essentially worthless stock and to issue currency and operate as banks on what amounted to the hope that they would eventually prove to be extremely profitable. The federal government gave nearly 10 percent of the land area of the forty-eight states to the railroad companies (Mercer 1982). There was widespread public resentment of and resistance to this outpouring of public support for the railroads, especially since many rural farmers believed the railroads benefited urban merchants and investors at their expense. However, the railroads were able to out-bargain the cities and states to reduce and even eliminate their taxes and public accountability (Goodrich 1960). By 1865 the railroads were fully under private ownership and management, and quickly merged into giant interstate systems that became as powerful as the federal government. As early as 1871, fewer than 450 men directed the twenty-five largest railroads that controlled more than a billion dollars in railroad capital—some 44 percent of all railroad capital (Roy 1997, 105). This was at a time when the total gross national product was less than $7 billion. This was the beginning of corporate capitalism in the United States. The owners of railroad capital could make money whether or not the railroads themselves operated at a profit, or even actually existed.

American Financial Imperia

In order to sustain power-concentrating growth and scale increase in the American economy, financial elites gained federal approval for a series of legislative changes to stabilize and centralize the monetary system, increase the efficiency of financial transactions, expand the money supply, facilitate capital markets for money and financial securities, make credit more readily available, and increase the public debt. These changes included the Legal Tender Acts of 1862 and 1863, the National Bank Act of 1864, the Gold Standard Act of 1900, the Federal Reserve Act of 1913, and the creation of the Federal Deposit Insurance Corporation in 1933. These elite-directed changes amplified and concentrated financial power, and reduced the financial control functions of legislators and local bankers.

The financialization process was accelerated by wars and periodic financial crises in 1873, 1893, 1907, and 1929. The Civil War added $2.6 billion to the $75 million national debt, prompting the printing of $431 million in greenbacks. The United States' money supply expanded by five orders of magnitude from $28 million in 1800 to $6.4 trillion by 1999 due to the legal fiction of counting credits and loans as bank deposits. This amplification of the apparent money supply was accompanied by parallel increases in the federal debt from a mere $77 million in 1790 to $5.5 trillion in 1998. Personal debt increased from $36.3 billion ($356 per capita) in 1916 to $1.7 trillion ($6,550 per capita) in 1998 (U.S. Bureau of the Census 1960, 664, 711, 2001, 346, 516, 517). Private creditors and financiers collecting interest and commissions on the U.S. Treasury notes, bonds, mortgages, and consumer loans were the directors and prime beneficiaries of this growth process.

The link between scale and finance capital was that financial elites were able to pool "other people's money" into great masses of capital, which they could then direct into large-scale activities that generated great fortunes. Local financial elites designed the earliest state-chartered banks to accumulate capital for small extended kin networks, but these banks remained very small and local until after the Civil War. In 1860 the 505 New England banks averaged only $250,000 in capital, and throughout the country there were 1,562 small, state-chartered local banks, each issuing its own bank notes (Lamoreaux 1986). This great diversity of American bank notes made interstate commerce cumbersome, but local finance markets remained competitive and small towns thrived (Grant 1992).

Financialization unfolded together with national expansion, economic growth, and the creation of the great rail empires, giant industrial corporations, monopolies, trusts, holding companies, and banking dynasties. These giant accumulations of capital were directed by a tiny handful of people and were so massive, and were created so suddenly, that they overpowered the American political system, encouraged graft and corruption, and left millions of ordinary people feeling totally disempowered and alienated. By 1904 8,664 industrial, public utility, and railroad companies with a total of over $20 billion in capital were combined in 445 trusts that were directly and indirectly dominated by just two interconnected financiers, John D. Rockefeller (1839–1937) and J.P. Morgan (1837–1913), through memberships on corporate boards and ownership of securities (Moody 1904). The seven largest industrial trusts combining copper, steel, smelting, oil, sugar, tobacco, and shipping, as well as the railroad trust, together represented nearly 60 percent of all the capital in all 8,664 companies. A mere fourteen great financiers, representing just ten families, dominated the railroad trust.

In 1912–13, in spite of Teddy Roosevelt's antitrust campaign, Morgan's personal wealth was estimated at $77.6 million, but through his various business partnerships he commanded a complex web of personal relationships and interlocking corporate directorships that gave him effective control over corporate assets of $45 billion. He did not own all of these assets outright, but held enough strategically placed loans and friendships, and sufficient stock, to assert direct and indirect personal control over the corporate boards of 34 large banks and trust companies, 10 insurance companies, 32 transportation systems, 12 public utilities, and 135 other corporations. The assets of these 223 corporations represented 27 percent of the United States' total national wealth of $165 billion in 1912 (U.S. Bureau of the Census 1960, 151). At a 6 percent profit rate, which was the typical annual return on corporate assets in 1914–16, Morgan-controlled assets would have generated $2.7 billion in annual profits, dwarfing the federal government's revenues of $77.6 million and equaling nearly 7 percent of GNP. By 1935, direct and indirect influence of the "House of Morgan," now directed by J.P. Morgan Jr. (1867–1943) and his thirty-nine partners, extended to 444 companies with some $78 billion in assets (Rochester 1936, 317).

Morgan's financial empire was a global system centered on J.P. Morgan and Company, a commercial banking partnership located in New York City, with interlocked banking partnerships in London, Paris, and Philadelphia. At that time just six banking houses controlled the marketing of stocks and bonds for the nation's largest corporations as well as the government. Morgan's imperium, called "the House of Morgan," operated much like the Medici and Rothschild imperia. Morgan maintained personal financial relationships with the United States' wealthiest families, the directors of the largest corporations in the United States, American presidents, other key federal officials, and prominent international rulers (Chernow 1990). Morgan used his personal influence to assemble vast transfers of capital between giant corporations and extracted profitable commissions in the process (Carosso 1970, 1987). Under J.P. Morgan Jr. the House of Morgan helped the British and French finance World War I by coordinating a $500 million private loan. Morgan's decisions thus impacted the incomes and employment conditions for millions of people throughout the country.

Rockefeller Imperium and the Fossil Fuel Revolution

Several members of the Rockefeller family have been among the most prominent financial elites to direct large-scale, capital- and energy-intensive economic growth in the United States and the world throughout the twentieth century. Whether acting as private entrepreneurs and financiers, as philanthropists, on government commissions, or as public officials, they have been central players in some of the most important cultural changes that have shaped the contemporary commercial world. They frequently used their influence in ways that increased the scale and concentration of financial power at national and global levels, while promoting elite solutions to the human problems that growth in scale produced. The connection between power and scale and the Rockefellers was established by the founder of the dynasty, John D. Rockefeller Sr. (1839–1937), who had already amassed a great fortune from the oil industry by the 1890s. His descendants successfully transmitted and enlarged the family fortune and influence across four generations up to the present time.

John D. Rockefeller Sr. was perhaps the most important of the handful of people who created the giant oil companies and developed a global market for petroleum products, effectively bringing on the Age of Petroleum. John D. Sr. made his fortune by using the Standard Oil Company, which he formed in 1870, to gain monopoly control over the American petroleum industry. Even though a 1911 Supreme Court decision dissolved the original Standard Oil for violation of the Sherman Antitrust Act of 1890, the Rockefellers maintained holdings in the separate companies created by the breakup of the Standard Oil trust and continued to profit from the development of petroleum. Petroleum initially was marketed as kerosene, or lamp oil, and then, as Standard Oil and Royal Dutch/Shell began to distribute it worldwide, petroleum rapidly replaced coal as a fuel for ships, then fueled motor vehicles and aircraft, replaced coal in railroad locomotives, and became fuel for electric generators. Petroleum also became the basis of the petrochemical and plastic industries. All of these were capital-intensive, high-energy industries organized by large corporations and designed for mass production, mass distribution, and mass consumption for very large-scale markets.

Petroleum, coal, and later natural gas were the fossil fuels at the very heart of the global commercial culture as it developed during the twentieth century. Giant corporations and multimillionaires would probably have remained relatively rare if fossil fuels had never been developed in this particular, large-scale way. As noted in Chapter 3, fossil fuels permitted an order-of-magnitude increase in per capita energy consumption in the United States, pushing consumption far above the level of solar-powered agrarian civilizations in the ancient imperial world. This raised the standard of living for many. However, because the use of this new energy source was elite-directed, elites used prodigious quantities of energy to overcome growth and scale thresholds while leaving unresolved the social costs of environmental degradation, social inequality, and the eventual depletion of energy supplies. Elite dominance of the energy system required the ruthless application of economic and political power that had little to do with "natural" evolution, greater efficiency, or superior adaptive value.

The energy made available by the fossil fuel revolution ultimately made it possible for American financial elites to transform the United States and the world, setting in motion events that were impossible for any individual to control. The mass production and distribution of fossil fuels transformed the U.S. food production and distribution system and made it possible to mobilize the vast armies that fought World Wars I and II and supply them with devastating new weapons. Petroleum fueled the automobiles that transformed American settlement patterns, encouraging the development of sprawling suburbs where people were separated from participation in municipal government and urban amenities. None of these changes were inevitable, they were directed by economic and political elites who made specific choices for other people.

Factory Farms and the American Food System

Factory farm agribusinesses and giant food processing corporations, supermarkets, and fast food chains were part of the same elite decision-making process that created larger-scale markets and a larger total economy. These developments overpowered small-scale family farms and forced many small farmers and business people into dependency on wages and salaries provided by big business. The new food system proved to be more costly and less energy and resource efficient. Small farms were often more energy efficient, did a better job of creating direct income for the maximum number of people, and supported more prosperous local communities (Madden 1967; Goldschmidt 1978, xxx–xxxix).

The essence of factory farming was that fossil fuel and capital-intensive manufactured products replaced self-maintaining solar-powered biological processes (Odum 1971). This meant taking over natural functions on a larger scale than ever before, supplying soil nutrients, water, and pest control functions that nature would normally provide for free. Factory farms were more productive per acre of land and per unit of human labor than smaller-scale, more labor-intensive systems, but were entirely dependent on the availability of cheap fossil fuel energy. By 1970, when the full energy costs of the large-scale American food system were computed, including production, processing, and distribution, it was found that eight to twelve kilocalories were expended to put one kilocalorie of food on the table (Steinhart and Steinhart 1974). In comparison, tribal shifting cultivators in the Amazon were much more energy efficient, producing eighteen kilocalories of food for every kilocalorie expended.

Farm mechanization was well under way by the 1850s thanks to the mass production of McCormick harvester machines, but it was another century before fossil fuel–powered machinery and capital-intensive systems completely replaced horses and simple machines, which proved very efficient on small farms. Horses were maintained on locally produced grains and hay, making them an independent energy source. Moreover, where there were many small farms, farmers could easily share machinery with kin and neighbors (Olmstead and Rhode 1995). Beginning in 1903 cautious farmers had to be "educated" to industrialize their farms by county agricultural extension agents supported by the U.S. Department of Agriculture and the state land grant universities. The Rockefeller philanthropies also funded county agents through their General Education Board (Domhoff 1996, 51–100; McConnell 1953, 24–25). By 1918 there were 2,600 extension agents organizing local farm bureaus to promote the utopian vision of large-scale, high-yield production. The Rockefeller interest in capital-intensive agricultural development was more than philanthropic because John D. Sr.'s daughter had married into the McCormick family, makers of International Harvester farm machinery, and Rockefeller's Standard Oil controlled the fuel supply.

Large farmers and their business supporters were closely connected with the Department of Agriculture and the Extension Service, they could lobby effectively in Congress, and had direct access to the Roosevelt White House. The Agricultural Adjustment Act of 1933, which set up the first farm subsidy programs, was heavily influenced by commercial interests that favored large farms over small (Domhoff 1996, 51–100; McConnell 1953). The outcome of decades of political support and subsidies for the largest farms was apparent in the fact that by 1987 the hundred largest corporate farms produced more than 10 percent of all farm products (Krebs 1992, 28, appendix C). Concentration characterized the United States's entire food system. In 1989 three packing houses sold approximately 90 percent of the United States's wholesale beef. In 1992, the top fifty-nine food manufactures produced 75 percent of revenues, and five private grain merchants controlled the national and global grain trade (Morgan 1979; Sewell 1992). By 1997 there were only 1.9 million farms, far below the peak of 6.8 million in 1935, and the largest 70,000, the top 3.6 percent, produced nearly 60 percent of total agricultural sales. The smallest 963,000 farms (50 percent), produced only 1.5 percent of sales. Small farms had almost totally disappeared. Many small farmers gave up competing with large-scale producers for remote urban and global markets because of the large investments in equipment, fuel, and agricultural chemicals that were required.

Factory farming reduced the number of people who were supported directly from the land, increasing social inequality and lowering the quality of life for many rural poor. High-tech agriculture produced wonderful crop yields, but the social cost was high. For example, in the Palouse country of eastern Washington, with some of the world's most productive wheat lands, the switch to factory farming between 1910 and 1987 caused per acre wheat yields to triple, but in the process nearly two-thirds of the farms were eliminated, forcing some 14,000 people off the land and threatening the economic well-being of local towns and villages. The farms that remained averaged three times larger, and the 180 largest farms, the top 15 percent out of 1,204, held nearly half of the land. Virtually all of the crop was shipped overseas, rather than into local and regional markets, and 65 percent of production costs were now in fossil fuels and agricultural chemicals, none of which were required in 1910 when 38,000 locally fed horses and mules were in harness. The new agricultural system contaminated the local streams and wells with nitrogen runoff, and erosion off the steep hillsides meant that every ton of wheat cost thirteen tons of topsoil, washed into roadside ditches and silting up local reservoirs for other people's tax dollars to clean up.

The Triumph of Cars over Rails

The replacement of rail and other forms of urban and interurban transportation by cars, trucks, and buses transformed urban and rural environments in the United States, encouraging the decay of inner cities and the rise of suburban sprawl. Automobiles also contribute to air pollution and consume irreplaceable fossil fuels, and became dominant elements in the ideology of perpetual economic growth. The triumph of the automobile over rails was engineered by combined financial and political elites, much as the earlier triumph of the railroads over boats. Henry Ford used assembly line manufacturing techniques, easy financing, and a nationwide chain of dealerships to make cars available to the masses with prices as low as $360 in 1915. The automobile had tremendous popular appeal because it empowered people who felt victimized by the railroads. Private cars became an attractive symbol of personal freedom, but their widespread use required all-weather roads. This precondition was met because of the demand for reliable mail delivery. Federal approval of Rural Free Delivery of the mails to rural residents in 1893 made it possible for even very remote farmers to shop by mail order from the Sears and Roebuck catalogue (Goddard 1994, 48–50). This created a powerful stimulus for better rural roads to improve mail delivery. Before the end of the nineteenth century bicycles and small touring cars were already on the road, automotive enthusiasts formed clubs, and zealous promoters within the federal government began to expand the role of the government in building paved roads. The first federally constructed paved road was laid out as a demonstration project at the New Jersey Agricultural College in 1897. Initially, railroad executives supported a national campaign for paved roads, assuming that they would help move freight to railheads, but within thirty years truckers were hauling more freight than the rails.

The growth in scale of motor vehicle registrations in the United States was phenomenal. Census figures show that in 1900 there were fewer than 10,000. By 1906 there were over 100,000, by 1913 more than a million, 10 million by 1921, and 100 million by 1968. Consumption of fuel soared from 2 billion gallons in 1919 to 10 billion by 1926 and over 100 billion by 1972. Most people recognized the advantages of good roads, but unlike rails, they were too expensive for most local communities to finance, and private investors were not interested. The federal government took the lead in 1905 by creating an Office of Public Roads. Government officials argued that federal taxes spent on paved roads would increase prosperity by replacing nature's "mud tax" of seasonally impassable roads (Goddard 1994). There were disagreements over whether federal money should focus on local or long-distance roads, but the Federal Aid Road Act of 1916 began funneling $25 million a year to state highway departments for road construction on a cost-sharing basis with state governments. The federal government set the standards, but the states maintained local control.

Before the automobile gained complete dominance, light rail—electric trolley systems in many cases owned by city governments—became a highly popular means of urban and short-haul interurban transportation. The trolleys were less expensive to build and maintain, and could operate more frequently for short runs than the standard steam railroads. Henry Huntington, who inherited his uncle's Southern Pacific railroad empire in 1900, sold his railroad shares, bought up undeveloped land and existing urban electric trolley systems, and then rapidly expanded trolley lines throughout Los Angeles County. His trolley system opened his newly purchased tracts of raw land to suburban development, causing their value to soar and making Huntington fabulously wealthy within ten years. The electric trolleys made Los Angeles a sprawling "horizontal city," but Huntington himself made his fortune from real estate development, much like Astor in New York, and sold his trolley system to the Southern Pacific in 1910 to devote himself to his art collection, library, and gardens. The trolleys died out as motorized vehicles, operating on taxpayer-supported public highways, steadily replaced them.

The American highway system was a monumental construction of unprecedented magnitude. In 1910 there were only 210,000 miles of surfaced roads, compared with 351,000 miles of railroad mileage. By 1935 there were more than a million miles of surfaced roads, and by 1950 more than 3 million. Almost from the very beginning the highway system was promoted as a private-public partnership directed by one unelected public official, Thomas Harris MacDonald, head of the federal Bureau of Public Roads from 1918 to 1953. MacDonald was also president of the American Association of State Highway Officials (AASHO). He was hardly a public figure and was not a wealthy capitalist, but he was a zealot with a personal vision who used his political authority and public money to further the grandiose goals that he shared with powerful highway lobby organizations such as the AASHO, the American Automobile Association (AAA), the National Automobile Chamber of Commerce (NACC), and the American Road Makers (ARM). Behind these groups stood the representatives of the auto industry and the rubber, steel, and cement industries, who uniquely benefited from an outpouring of public funds for highway construction and who formed their own lobby group, the Highway Industries Association. MacDonald directed what may well have been "the greatest public work projects in world history . . . and the greatest political lobby in world history" (Goddard 1994, 101).

MacDonald set up a Highway Education Board (HEB) to funnel pro-highway "information" to Congress via AASHO, and a Highway Research Board in the National Academy of Sciences to help develop more durable highways. The HEB also accepted generous donations from highway-related industries to promote the benefits of highways to schoolchildren through booklets and scholarships. Lobbyists declared that the popular demand for cars and highways was an irrepressible "instinctive desire for individual transportation" (Goodard 1994, 113). However, these visionary lobbyists had no interest in alternative, less capital- and fossil fuel–intensive transportation. They ignored the hidden costs of highways such as the land taken off tax rolls, traffic courts, highway police, and traffic accidents, and minimized the possibility that the one-sided promotion of unregulated long-haul trucks might damage highways and undercut railroads.

The highway–motor vehicle coalition involved government planners like

MacDonald, congressmen, industry executives, and private investors in virtually interchangeable roles. Executives from Ford Motor Corporation became U.S. senators and even chaired the Interstate Commerce Committee; other auto executives sat in the White House cabinet. A single individual's personal network might include close associates in all of these roles, and the same individual might occupy each role, sometimes simultaneously. For example, one public official, urban planner Robert Moses, gained so much personal influence that he was able to impose his personal vision for New York's major highways, parkways, bridges, parks, urban renewal, and public housing from the 1930s to the sixties (Caro 1974; Moses 1970). His work became a model for car-friendly urban development nationwide. For many of these planners, their power did not depend on personal wealth. MacDonald exercised enormous power over the United States's future but did not benefit financially. He left a personal estate of a mere $25,000 (Goddard 1994, 118). Likewise, Moses was not wealthy. However, everyone in such power networks had an interest in promoting an endless expansion of more highways and cars. Nowhere in this interlocking interest group was there a mechanism for defining a shutoff point, or recognizing when an optimum growth threshold had been reached.

The transformation of urban and interurban mass transit systems from the popular electric trolleys that prevailed in the 1920s to diesel buses and private cars by the 1940s was successfully carried out by a handful of people who directly benefited from the change. This was a conspiracy in the legal sense of the word. The great automakers and their allies used their financial power to oust the electric streetcars because they viewed the cities as a vast untapped market for private cars (Goddard 1994, 120–137). The executives of General Motors and its Greyhound affiliate, with Standard Oil, Phillips Petroleum, Mack Truck, and Firestone Tire acting in concert, created and poured millions of dollars into several seemingly independent urban transportation companies such as United Cities Motor Transit, National City Lines, and Pacific City Lines. These companies, under GM's technical supervision, were designed to buy up and dismantle trolley systems in cities throughout the country and replace them with buses operated at cut-rate fares.

The trolleys were an easy target. Like the railroads—except in the few cases where they were municipally owned—the trolleys already operated at a disadvantage because they were taxed, but unlike the highways they received no public transportation subsidies. Ironically, the trolleys were weakened by antitrust rulings breaking up the electric utility trusts. At the same time, suburbanization, promoted by the proliferation of roads and cars, dispersed settlement enough to reduce the efficiency of trolleys. Before 1940 National City controlled 29 trolley lines in 27 cities (Goddard 1994, 133).

164 THE POWER ELITE IN ACTION

The biggest trolley-to-bus conversions were in New York and Los Angeles. When the conversions were complete, GM withdrew and many of the new bus lines were sold to municipal transit companies. The real objective was replacing all forms of mass transit, buses included, with less efficient, but much more profitable, private cars. In 1949 the companies and key individuals responsible were found guilty of criminal conspiracy to exclude competition "in restraint of trade." The corporations were fined $5,000 each and the individuals one dollar, even though their profits were in the millions.

The Millionaire Imperia: Super-Elite Lifestyles

The great industrial boom of railroad construction, petroleum development, steel mills, and the automotive industry generated tremendous wealth for a tiny number of Americans. Income tax data show that between 1892 and 1917 the number of American millionaires soared from 4,047 to 11,800 (Lundberg 1937). The number peaked at 38,889 in 1929 and then receded with the economic depression to about 12,000. The federal government's extraordinary public disclosure of the names, amounts paid in tax, and hometowns of individual income tax payers in 1924 and 1925 made it possible for Ferdinand Lundberg to compile a detailed financial picture of the wealthiest American families. He assumed that taxable income represented 5 percent of taxable wealth and estimated the total gross fortune of super-wealthy individuals at three times taxable wealth to allow for wealth hidden by tax deductions and tax-exempt income. For example, John D. Rockefeller Jr. paid $6,277,669 in taxes for 1924, which was the highest of any individual in the country. This put him in the 50 percent tax bracket, with income approaching $15 million. Twenty other members of the Rockefeller extended family brought the family's total tax to over $7 million on income of $18 million, suggesting a total family fortune of more than $1 billion ($18 million = [5 percent of $360 million] x 3 = $1 billion).

During the economic boom between 1914 and 1929 the wealthiest Americans took a larger proportion of total income and wealth, and most households remained both relatively and absolutely poor. In 1924 only 7 million taxpayers out of 27 million households reported taxable incomes of $2,000 or more, suggesting that 73 percent of households did not earn enough to pay any income tax. By 1929 the top 1 percent of taxpayers with incomes of more than $5,000 held 83 percent of financial wealth. This wealth distribution was remarkably similar to that of Florence, Italy, in 1457 (Table 5.1) and meant that the vast majority were barely above the subsistence level and could save less than 5 percent of their income.

The absolute power of the American economic super-elite at the very top of the social hierarchy from 1914 to 1939 was unprecedented in world history. Lundberg (1937, 3) concluded that the United States was "owned and dominated" by a "plutocratic circle" of 60 super-wealthy great families, supported by 90 lesser wealthy families, and another 350 families with incomes of $100,000 or more and wealth of at least $2 million. This super-elite of some 500 great families at the top of the American oligarchy represented approximately 2,500 individual households and perhaps 12,750 people. Some of Lundberg's 60 families were extended families or business partnerships that could individually include as many as 38 households. All together, this super-elite represented less than 0.01 percent of the 128 million people and 32 million households in the United States in 1936. Marriage and kinship connections linked the top sixty families within a complex network intersecting and overlapping the boards of the great corporations. Lundberg called these families "the living center of the modern industrial oligarchy which dominates the United States" (Lundberg 1937, 3). He attributed their power to their concentrated control over the largest businesses, their philanthropy, and their influence over government. He stressed that "corporations are merely the instruments or tools of control behind which the living masters hide in discreet anonymity" (Lundberg 1937, 8).

Sociologist Pitirim Sorokin (1925b) compiled life history data on 668 American male millionaires born between 1761 and 1880, more than half (380) of whom were still living in 1923. His findings give an interesting profile of the many of the wealthiest Americans during the first quarter of the twentieth century. The birthplace of 173 living native-born millionaires was strikingly nonrandom. Over half were born in New York, Massachusetts, and Pennsylvania, even though in 1920 these states accounted for only 23 percent of the American population. This demonstrates the continuing importance of New York City, Boston, and Philadelphia as centers of American wealth. Over half of the millionaires held college degrees. Not surprisingly, 75 percent of the fathers of living millionaires were merchants, manufacturers, bankers, financiers, and businessmen. Fewer than 20 percent of 386 living millionaires started life poor, and over half were born to wealthy families. Also not surprisingly, 80 percent of those born to wealthy families were millionaires by the age of 40, but only 25 percent of poor millionaires had "arrived" that quickly. Millionaires lived an average of 69 years, which was much better than the 1920 average American life expectancy at birth of 56 years, but this is not a statistically appropriate comparison because age correlates with wealth.

For comparison, Sorokin (1925a, 1926) also examined the life histories of some 400 monarchs and kings from ancient times into the twentieth century and found that those who did not die violently lived longer than their contemporaries in the general population. However, it was striking that nearly one-third of the monarchs died violently, suggesting that the pursuit of political power was a high-risk, high-reward activity. American millionaires remained largely outside of the public eye and enjoyed the benefits of power without the danger of assassination. This points to the advantage of commercially based power over purely political power. The availability of energy-intensive health care in the late twentieth century gives today's millionaires significantly greater life chances over their predecessors.

As might be expected, the U.S. financial super-elite were concentrated in New York. In the 1890s, after London, New York was the largest and wealthiest city in the world and was fast becoming the capital of the global commercial culture. New York was the central commercial place in the United States and its primary overseas port. It was the largest urban center, had the largest state population, was the center of the greatest ethnic and religious diversity, and the dominant cultural center. New York was also a political center with the largest block of presidential electoral votes. Perhaps most importantly, it had the greatest concentration of private wealth in the country. New York's growth between 1845 and 1890 increased the number of millionaires from 20 to 1,265, but the overall distribution of wealth did not change significantly. Growth simply moved a few members of the upper 0.5 percent into even higher wealth brackets (Hammack 1982, 46).

A close look at New York's 1890 elite shows the limitations of treating a social class as a single agent of change. Many of New York's millionaire merchants, bankers, and large property owners were personally interconnected, but they were also cross-cut by economic and philosophical differences and belonged to diverse business and professional organizations. Some worried that national-level economic development was drawing economic activity away from New York toward urban rivals such as Chicago. They envisioned a public-private partnership to develop the city that could be called "municipal socialism," in which tax dollars and private investment would improve the commercial prospects of the city by developing public transit systems, public education, public health and housing, better municipal government, and cultural institutions (Hammack 1982). However, many of the largest economic elites were reluctant to support these proposals because they were suspicious of government involvement in the "free market," did not want their taxes to increase, and had much broader economic interests than in New York City itself. Others blamed New York's problems on immorality, rising ethnic and religious diversity, and socialist, anarchist activists. These people thought government should intervene in social, cultural, and moral affairs as a Christian charity in a limited way to prevent class conflict, but did not want it to interfere with the economy. Thus the elites were divided on what policies the city should pursue, and at the same time the ethnically diverse lower-classes could have increasing significance as voters and often influenced events. As a result, New York's wealthy did not form a single social elite. The political differences among New York's elite in 1890 are mirrored in current national debates between liberals and conservatives.

The great wealth accumulated by the richest families toward the end of the nineteenth century apparently exceeded the bounds of what could be profitably invested in new wealth–generated projects. Much of the excess was poured into the private building projects and lifestyles that sociologist Thorstein Veblen (1994), writing in 1899, called "conspicuous consumption," and many others simply condemned as wastefully extravagant. For example, Count Boni de Castellane, who married Anna Gould, daughter of railroad tycoon Jay Gould, in 1892, reputedly squandered $12 million of his wife's fortune "on my general existence, my chateaux, my palaces, my *bibelots* [knick-knacks], my race horses, my yachts, my traveling expenses, my political career, my charities, my fetes, my wife's jewels and loans to my friends . . ." (Beebe 1966, viii).

The super-elite built oversized residences that were properly called mansions and palaces, and they maintained multiple seasonal residences at key resort areas. Many of the New York elite maintained luxurious urban apartments in Manhattan as well as mansions on the north shore of Long Island, clustered in an area known as the Gold Coast (Randall 1987). The same people built summer mansions in elite enclaves at Newport, Rhode Island, and Palm Beach, Florida. Henry M. Flagler, John D. Rockefeller Sr.'s main Standard Oil partner, turned Florida into a prime winter resort and booming real estate market by building the Florida East Coast Railroad and a series of resort hotels (Beebe 1966, 344–363). Both the Senior and Junior John D. owned residences in Manhattan, New Jersey, Maine, and Florida, and John D. Jr.'s son Nelson developed huge cattle ranches in Brazil and Venezuela. The principal Rockefeller residence was their 3,600-acre Pocantico estate, located twenty-five miles from Manhattan up the Hudson River. There were six family residences at Pocantico, a guest house, a "million dollar" playhouse, orangerie, carriage house, barns, greenhouses, and a village for the support staff. J.P. Morgan Jr. built his principal fifty-two-room Long Island mansion on a north shore island equipped with a dock long enough to accommodate his 343–foot yacht, the *Corsair*.

Another Long Island resident, F.W. Woolworth (1852–1919), founder of the famous international chain of five-and-ten-cent retail variety stores, exemplifies Veblen's concept of conspicuous consumption. First he built the tallest building in the world, the fifty-seven-floor, 792-foot Woolworth Building in Manhattan. Then he built Winfield, a $9 million, fifty-six room Italian Renaissance-style Long Island mansion. The marble staircase alone cost $2 million. The kitchen stove was twenty feet long, and appropriately, there was a ten-foot walk-in safe. His emulation of imperial nobility was explicit. Woolworth modeled his personal suite at Winfield after "the highest moment of Napoleon's pretensions"—his remodel of the Louis XV palace, Château Compiègne, north of Paris (Dunlop 1985, 249). A further ostentatious touch was Woolworth's claim that he slept in a bed that had belonged to Napoleon and that Mrs. Woolworth used one of Marie Antoinette's dressing tables (Randall 1987, 48). Other rooms emulated Louis XV, the Renaissance, French Gothic, English Gothic, Georgian, Edwardian, and Ming dynasty styles. Woolworth modeled his formal garden after the noble Villa Borghese in Rome.

There were nearly fifty similar great estates built on Long Island during the 1880–1929 Gilded Age by members of many of Lundberg's sixty families, including the Goulds, Guggenheims, Kahns, MacKays, Mellons, Morgans, Pratts, Vanderbilts, Whitneys, and Woolworths. This was enough people to maintain an intense social life, which included such aristocratic English games as fox hunts and polo matches, great balls, and giant lawn parties that were frequently attended by European nobility, such as the Prince of Wales. These mansions and their social life were the inspiration for F. Scott Fitzgerald's *Great Gatsby*. Significantly, when Robert Moses first planned his Northern State Parkway, it cut through many of these Long Island estates, including the Morgan, Whitney, Phipps, and Kahn properties, but he rerouted it after owners protested in 1929; elsewhere his highway projects uprooted 250,000 people (Caro 1974, 302–303).

The giant households that occupied these palatial residences in every way equaled the scale and organizational complexity of the households of the European monarchy and nobility, demonstrating the effectiveness of commercial power for building personal imperia. The formal organization of these households was detailed in Emily Post's (1927, 142–163) famous etiquette manual. Post explains that the appearance of a Great House depends on the housekeeper, who directs the housemaids and parlor maids. The gentleman of the house directs the butler, head chauffeur, and head gardener. The butler is responsible for the pantry and dining room, the silver and wines, and directs the footmen. The lady of the house directs her personal maid, the nurse, and the cook. Such ostentatious living might seem out of place in the America described by Alexis de Tocqueville, but is a predictable outcome of the power of scale.

The conspicuous consumption lifestyles of New York's super-elite needs to be seen in contrast with the lives of those who were called "the other half" (Riss 1904). In 1900 the New York State Tenement House Commission found that 2.3 million people, 70 percent of the population of metropolitan New York, were living in crowded, dark, unsanitary tenements, often with no running water (DeForest and Veiller 1903). They were crammed into apartments equaling conditions in the worst London slums of the same period. New York was still a free market paradise for slum landlords because there were no building codes and rent limits. It is not surprising that labor unrest and union activism were constant problems for the New York elite.

7

Counter-Imperia: Imagining Alternative Worlds

The strongest evidence that perpetual growth in scale is neither natural nor inevitable is the fact that throughout history the growth process and the direction it has taken have been both forcibly and passively resisted. Tribal peoples were the first to resist, but many ordinary people in the imperial and commercial worlds joined revolutionary social movements such as the Protestant Reformation, the English Civil War, the English "Glorious Revolution" of 1688, the American Revolution, the French Revolution, the Revolutions of 1848, the Paris Commune of 1871, and the various socialist revolutions of the twentieth century. Many of the most historically prominent revolutionary movements were coopted by power-seeking elites and channeled into more growth, producing even greater concentrations of power. Nevertheless they demonstrated that the majority could effectively challenge established authority and effect radical change. The peaceful populist movements, utopian communities, anarchist philosophers, and progressivist social reformers that responded to the negative human impacts of concentrated political and commercial power may ultimately prove more significant than violent revolutions. Nonviolent counter-hegemonic philosophies and social movements were sometimes based on an explicit critique of concentrated power and large-scale social organization. They stressed local communities and democratic decision making. Their goal was cultural transformation to disperse social power and distribute the benefits of increased production more broadly. Humanitarian social critics were often marginalized by historians who saw them as irrelevant to the mainline of history, but they deserve careful attention because they understood that big was not necessarily better, and they imagined more humane, smaller-scale societies as a realistic alternative to infinite growth.

Tribals Against the State

One of the great ironies of the commercial world where increased productivity and efficiency are such important ideals is that it is widely believed that human needs can never be satisfied and poverty can never be eliminated. Yet the numerous tribal societies that Europeans destroyed to produce economic growth did in fact satisfy human needs, and they minimized social inequality. Since aggrandizing elites first began to successfully fashion large-scale politically organized societies, tribal peoples have resisted growth, scale change, and the concentration of social power. The devastating human effects of genocide, ethnocide, and ecocide that accompanied the ultimate incorporation of virtually all politically independent, economically self-sufficient tribal peoples into the global-scale commercial world by the end of the twentieth century illuminates a scale change process that has negatively impacted local communities of all types. Genocide meant that entire tribal communities were destroyed; whole tribes, peoples, and languages simply disappeared, in many cases before their names even entered the historic record. The small-scale cultures and self-sufficient lifestyles of tribal peoples who survived the initial holocaust of commercial invasion were then forcibly transformed to fit the needs of commerce. Likewise, the natural environments within tribal territories were devastated by commercial overexploitation, making it difficult or impossible for surviving peoples to support themselves on lands that had sustained their ancestors for millennia.

In 1800, at the beginning of the Industrial Revolution, in spite of vast territorial claims by colonial powers, roughly half of the world's land area was still controlled by some 200 million politically independent and economically self-sufficient tribal peoples who at that time may have represented 20 percent of global population. Over the next 150 years, 50 million tribals died in a perpetual war against invaders from the commercial world who came as traders, settlers, miners, missionaries, soldiers, and peaceful government agents (Bodley 1999a, 2000, 394–425). Tribals were unwilling conscripts of civilization who had to be either forcefully incorporated into the expanding commercial world or killed. Tribals and tribal territories were targeted for invasion by peoples who needed new territories and new resources to sustain their own continuous growth. Furthermore, many of the invading settlers and traders were the landless poor and unemployed who were unable to find a satisfying life in their own homelands.

The destruction of tribal cultures involved several distinct processes, with many variations depending on the policies of particular governments at particular times. The most frequent initial process was the "uncontrolled frontier," in which officials stepped aside and allowed private citizens to seek their fortunes in tribal territories with no legal impediments. Tribal people were subjected to a totally unregulated "free market" where the most powerful could exploit tribal labor at will and conduct trade in the most profitable way in the absence of police, judges, or law. Tribal land and resources were considered unowned, empty wasteland, there for the taking. On the uncontrolled frontier tribal peoples were dispossessed, enslaved, tortured, and killed with impunity. They were ruthlessly cheated and exploited by traders and died from new diseases for which they had no defenses. Whenever possible people survived and kept their culture intact by fleeing into remote refuges where the could avoid any direct contact with the outsiders.

When tribals fought back with spears and arrows they were confronted by overwhelming military forces armed with modern weapons. Sometimes government officials responded with retaliatory punitive raids to punish and demoralize resistant tribals, or they used military conquest to defeat or totally destroy them. The American Indian Wars were mirrored by the Argentine and Chilean wars against the Araucanian and Tehuelche Indians between 1872 and 1885, and by many similar conflicts worldwide. British authorities used military force against tribal groups in their colonial territories in India and Africa. From 1893 to 1907 the German military in Southwest Africa used artillery, machine guns, and poison, killing some 100,000 individuals in an attempt to exterminate the Herero people. Between 1895 and 1909 the Japanese encircled 120,000 Formosan hill tribe aborigines with a military cordon using land mines, barbed wire, guardhouses, grenades, and field artillery in order to open their territory to colonization. The Germans, French, British, and Americans used naval gunfire at various times to subdue "rebellious" Pacific islanders.

At the beginning of the twentieth century forces from the commercial world were clearly gaining the upper hand over the tribal world. Tribal peoples were everywhere being exterminated. But at the time most anthropologists assumed that independent tribal peoples were doomed to extinction because their cultures were obsolete and inferior, or because they were physically incapable of survival. The cultural evolution theories that then prevailed explained this unfortunate outcome as the inevitable result of the natural adaptive process of survival of the fittest, it being assumed that the European commercial culture was obviously the most fit. Today such inhumanity would be condemned as ethnic cleansing and genocide, but in retrospect it is remarkable that it was so easily tolerated even by intellectuals despite its being comparable to the worst atrocities that criminal regimes inflicted on their own citizens throughout the twentieth century. The total human loss in the tribal world exceeds the 21 million civilians killed by the Nazis between 1933 and 1945. It is exceeded only by the 62 million killed in the Soviet Union between 1917 and 1987 (Rummel 1997, 4, 70).

By the 1920s, in the face of rising humanitarian criticism of their harsh military policies, many government officials adopted "peaceful pacification" policies toward still independent tribals. Specially trained teams distributed gifts and medical attention to hostile natives in Brazil and New Guinea to persuade them to move into government-controlled areas. Colonial governments also hired anthropologists to develop culturally sensitive methods of colonial administration that would allow development of tribal labor and natural resources to proceed without unduly disrupting village life. Keeping village life intact to reproduce the labor force proved more cost effective than the wasteful excesses of the uncontrolled frontier.

By mid-century anthropologists concluded that tribals were undergoing a benign "acculturation" process. Acculturation theory suggested that tribals were voluntarily choosing to abandon their inferior cultures in order to gain the benefits of civilization. Anthropologists were convinced that when otherwise self-sufficient tribals eagerly bartered for metal cooking pots, steel knives, and guns they were renouncing their independence, but new technologies simply reinforced their existing lifestyles and gave people more leisure. Tribals were not automatically interested in increasing their total production.

As soon as tribals were brought under government control they were subjected to a wide range of ethnocidal policies designed to eradicate any cultural traits deemed unsuitable for their successful adaptation to the commercial world. Government administrators, development specialists, teachers, and missionaries zealously brought pressure against any aspect of tribal culture, whether language, religious practices, marriage patterns, or economic patterns, that they believed to be immoral, subversive, or a hindrance to progress. For example, in the Peruvian Amazon missionaries offered healthcare and education to Ashaninka who would discard their language, clothing, face paint, hair styles, dancing, shamanism, polygyny, and consumption of manioc beer. Forced culture change and all other such ethnocidal practices were violations of basic human rights as defined by the 1948 United Nations Declaration of Human Rights. Furthermore, the International Covenant of Human Rights, adopted by the UN General Assembly in 1966, declared: "in those states in which ethnic, religious or linguistic minorities exist, persons belonging to such minorities shall not be denied the right, in community with the other members of their group, to enjoy their own culture, to profess and practice their own religion or to use their own language."

As long as tribals retained the means of subsistence they were reluctant wage workers. Officials had to impose taxes on natives payable only in cash in order to force tribals into the workforce. Those who could not pay were jailed, as were those who walked off the job. Equally effective were reductions in tribal territories, reservations on marginal lands, and incentives for tribals to sell their land. Government posts and missions also distributed consumer goods in order to stimulate new needs. Often economic development projects intensified pressures on local resources, causing deforestation, soil erosion, resource depletion and pollution, local extinctions of wildlife, and destruction of ecosystems. Such ecocide further undermined tribal subsistence, making tribals dependent on the global economy for their survival.

When it became obvious that even the best-intended development projects caused many unintended negative consequences when imposed on tribal peoples, the experts concluded that, regrettably, it was too late for tribals to go back to their autonomous small-scale cultures. However, there were many cases of tribal groups who reoccupied their homelands and even switched from herding or gardening to foraging when necessary to maintain their independence. For example, the Ashaninka were totally missionized by the Franciscans in 1742, but they rebelled and reasserted their independence, reinstituting all the cultural practices that the missionaries had forbidden but retaining the iron tools and some of the domestic animals introduced by the Franciscans. The Ashaninka enjoyed complete independence for another century, until outsiders invaded their homeland once again. They expelled missionaries again in 1914 and in the 1990s drove out the Shining Path guerrillas. The Ashaninka demonstrate that small-scale cultures can maintain themselves in a world otherwise dominated by commercial power. Perpetual growth in scale is not inevitable, and may not be irreversible when confronted by a persuasive cultural model for a more humane society.

Plato's Republic and Medieval Utopias

Many believe that there can never be a truly just and humane society. *Utopia*, as an ideal society, is understood to be unattainable. Yet again and again European philosophers and social critics have reinvented such ideal societies, even before the development of the commercial world, suggesting that there are fundamental problems with all large-scale societies. Plato's *Republic* is perhaps the earliest known written description of an ideal society. It was discussed briefly in Chapter 1 to highlight the distinctions between societies in the politically organized imperial world and the commercial world. Plato considered commerce, merchants, and money to be necessary evils in his ideal society, but he understood the dynamics that contributed to growth and he imagined a simpler society where growth would be controlled.

Plato (428/7–348/7 B.C.) related the size and organization of society directly to the standard of living. He started by imagining a minimum "state" requiring only five men to provide for the most basic physical needs of food, housing, and clothing. This minimum society approximated the size of the smallest twenty-five-person tribal band and was a realistic minimum, but Plato assumed occupational specialization and a division of labor to produce cultivated crops, houses, and textiles. Although he is describing a small city-state, not a tribal society, he nevertheless has an optimum size in mind. He does not specify its absolute size, declaring imprecisely "it will not be very large . . . but it will not be so very small either." Maximum size would be determined by the rulers based on the limits of social integration. The objective of Plato's city-state was harmony, happiness, and security, not social equality as such, because there were distinct class divisions. This ideal city-state required merchants, farmers, craftsmen, foreign trade, marketplaces, currency, shipowners, shopkeepers, and hired wage laborers. Plato was an intellectual elitist, and thought that wage laborers were a class hardly worth including in the commonwealth on intellectual grounds, but they were still needed and were not to be denied their share of human happiness. As Plato explained, "our aim in founding the commonwealth was not to make any one class specially happy, but to secure the greatest possible happiness for the community as a whole . . . not trying to secure the well-being of a select few (Cornford 1945, 110).

Plato assumed that as long as people limited the size of their society and limited their wants, they would be able to meet all their basic needs for bread, wine, and merry-making, and could still live together "pleasantly" avoiding both war and poverty. He argued that such a small-scale society was the ideal and the healthiest society, but he declared that if you want to see a sick society, "Then we must once more enlarge our community." He implied that growth was inevitable because some people are invariably attracted to luxury and will want furniture, delicacies, perfumes, courtesans, rich embroideries and paintings, gold, and ivory. As a result, professional dancers, actors, artisans, nurses, maids, cooks, and servants would be needed. The unhealthy luxury lifestyle would also create a need for more physicians. Plato warned ominously that a society devoted to securing "unlimited wealth" would soon need to enlarge its territory, and war with its neighbors would be "inevitable." An army of specialist warriors would be needed to defend the citizenry and their property.

Plato then discussed at length the unique qualities of courage and wisdom needed in the rulers or guardians of such an enlarged state. The rulers would need to be especially vigilant to prevent the evil extremes of both wealth and poverty. The wealthy would pursue luxury and idleness, and the poor would not be good workers and would misbehave. A plutocracy, or rule by the rich, was specifically to be avoided, because it would lead to class warfare. Plato also rejected democracy because it conflicted with his belief that people were naturally suited for particular occupational classes. However, tyranny or absolute rule was bad because "absolute power corrupts absolutely" and would lead to despotism. Given that wealth was bad, it is not surprising that the rulers of the ideal republic were to be philosopher kings who were not allowed to handle money or engage in commerce. They were also not allowed to have their own households or families, thus removing any incentive for them to form personal imperia. Leaders were born to their role by their inherited gifts, and even women with the right abilities could be leaders.

Plato certainly anticipated the social power problems of increasing luxury, wealth, poverty, plutocracy, and war that have been intensified by growth in the commercial world. His radical solution of creating a ruling class whose members would have no incentive for personal aggrandizement shows how vulnerable political power is to cooptation by commercial interests. The actual Greek city-state attempted to marginalize commercial elites but never succeeded in preventing the emergence of a wealthy elite. Ian Morris (1994) suggests that, just as Plato warned, the wealthy were needed to help finance ever larger military operations and the Greek world fell into a series of ruinous wars and military dictatorships.

Sir Thomas More's (1478–1535) *Utopia*, published in 1516, is, after Plato's *Republic*, perhaps the best known premodern utopian society and originated the term "utopia." More was Lord Chancellor of England for Henry VIII and was executed because as a Catholic, he refused to support the king's claim to supremacy over Rome. The utopian society that he imagined was a confederation of fifty-four city-states located on a 200-mile-wide island, which had existed for nearly two thousand years. There was a centrally located capital city where representatives from each city annually convened to discuss common interests. There was no private property. Residences were all similar three-storied buildings, each with an adjacent garden, and were randomly redistributed every ten years.

The political system was constructed to maximize public control over officials. There was a hierarchy of officers, but except for the prince, who may serve for life, every official was elected annually by secret ballot. Most significantly, the prince had only two top councilors, and in order to prevent conspiracies, they were rotated daily. Other than in full public assemblies, no private decision making affecting the entire city could occur, under penalty of death. In every city there were 200 elected magistrates, one for every thirty extended families, representing approximately a thousand people. There were twenty senators reporting to the prince, one for every ten magistrates. Thus, the entire political bureaucracy from household to prince involved only four levels (extended family head, magistrate, senator, prince). The total population of Utopia approached 10 million, but no town was allowed to exceed 6,000 extended families. These were patrilocally extended families, occupying great houses and composed of between five and eight related individual households, including unmarried children, married sons, and grandsons of the household head. At any given moment a significant portion of a city's population would be living in the countryside, working on the farms. If a city fell above or below the optimum size, households were redistributed or allowed to immigrate to the mainland.

There were public dining halls and communal kitchens associated with each magistrate, and public markets, which served as storehouses and distribution centers where everyone could simply take what they needed. Theft was not a problem because everyone had what they needed; locks were dispensed with. Furthermore, wealth did not provide social status and there was no incentive to accumulate. Surplus production was traded for iron, which was the only resource the Utopians lacked. Slaves were condemned criminals imported from the outside to perform tasks that were considered unwholesome, such as slaughtering animals. Slaves and criminals were forced to wear gold and silver ornaments as an identity badge, while only children played with diamonds, rubies, and pearls. This practice took Plato's prohibitions on rulers handling money, gold, and silver to an extreme to give wealth objects a totally negative value. Without private wealth and property, the Utopians had few laws and no lawyers.

Learning had a privileged place in More's Utopia, and the constitution was dedicated to making sure that everyone's basic needs were met in order to free people from manual labor so they could improve their minds. Learning made people happy. Anyone who showed special talent for intellectual pursuits was recognized as a scholar and exempted from regular work, but otherwise, everyone worked two-year rotations on rural farms and practiced an industrial trade in the city. This device blurred the rural-urban distinction that had become so prominent in England. This, and the absence of private property, eliminated the landed gentry. In striking contrast to Tudor England, clothing fashions did not change, and dress distinguished only gender and marital status. Each family made its own clothes. People were expected to work only six-hour days in two three-hour blocks and get eight hours of sleep, but this left ten hours a day for wholesome pursuits such as reading and attending public lectures according to individual inclination. More drew particular attention to the high amount of leisure that Utopia enjoyed, arguing, much like efficiency expert Frederick Taylor (1911), that when everyone was employed according to their abilities overall productivity would be greatly increased. He also argued, like Plato, that when needless luxuries were eliminated, much less production would be needed.

More's *Utopia* showed that it was possible to imagine a realistic society that challenged virtually all of the assumptions sustaining English society in the sixteenth century. Utopians renounced aggressive war, although they were not pacificists and remained prepared to defend themselves and to help threatened neighbors. Both men and women were trained for military service. Even more remarkably, they tolerated religious diversity. Ironically, More himself was unwilling to carry out the logic of his argument by challenging the religious authority of Rome, even though his pro-Catholic stand cost him his life in the face of Henry VIII's ambition.

The English Revolution: Regicides, Levelers, and Luddites

The Protestant Reformation, begun by Martin Luther in 1517, the year after More's *Utopia* was published, was a popular revolution against concentrated religious power. It was perhaps the first great religious decentralization and power redistribution movement in human history. It represented a return to the humanistic ideals of the early Christian Church by simply bypassing the elaborate Roman bureaucracy. When common people realized that they could challenge established religious authority and win, it was a short step to imagine that established political authority could also be challenged; people took that step in seventeenth-century England.

Before 1688, in accord with Great Chain of Being cosmology, the English king in his kingdom was believed to be equivalent to, and of course subordinate to, God in the universe, just as the sun ruled the heavens, the lion ruled the animals, the father ruled the household, and the head ruled the body. In theory, the king ruled by divine right and was answerable only to God. Following the Reformation, a fierce debate arose in England over the moral and legal basis of state authority. Divine Right of King Royalists rejected the heretical political theory that "All civil authority is derived originally from the people." This statement, which today would be considered the very foundation of democracy, was condemned by a convocation of the Oxford University faculty in 1683 as a pernicious, damnable doctrine "Destructive to the Sacred Persons of Princes, Their State and Government, and of All Humane Society." The Oxford faculty posted lists of the offensive books that contained such dangerous ideas and ordered them all publicly burned (Wootton 1986). They argued that the desire for "liberty" was the original sin of Adam and Eve and warned that it was now finding favor among Catholics (Jesuits), some Protestants (Calvinists), and many common people. In fact, even at that time the idea that the state ultimately derived its authority from the people was already widely accepted among intellectuals. They realized, in effect, that the state was a social construction. It was not "natural." However, the Oxford establishment knew that this fundamental tenet of democracy was a threat to public order because it suggested the frightening thought that *people,* rather than *ruler,* were sovereign. If this was believed, then people could reclaim their sovereign power from rulers who abused their authority.

Dethroning the divine king helped to create the modern state with democratic institutions that for the first time made the well-being of all citizens and the recognition of basic human rights matters of public policy. By the end of the century it was possible to argue politics without appeals to religious authority. Tyrants were answerable to the people. Prosperity rather than godliness had become the objective of political systems. People therefore had the right to use political power to secure their material well-being. This was a revolutionary idea and a revolutionary practice that soon led to the American Revolution and further radical political reform in England. The Divine Right of Kings ideology was replaced by the political ideal of democracy, even though the Divine King was once a "well adapted and successful" idea (Wootton 1986). Ironically, this great ideological transformation prepared the way for the commercialization process, which was coopted by a new elite who substituted an all-powerful corporation for the divine monarch.

The English Civil War and the Glorious Revolution of 1688 shifted power away from the monarch to Parliament, making it possible for the landed aristocracy and emerging financial-mercantile interests to use political power to promote economic growth. This did not immediately usher in full democracy or create the modern state in England. The socially radical "levellers" and "diggers" saw the initial attacks on the English divine monarch as an opportunity to diffuse social power by moving directly to full democracy, liberty, and property equality, but their radicalism was too extreme for the power elite who remained in control. Prominent conservative Edmund Burke (1729–97) conceded that originally "the people" had agreed to a constitution specifying their rights and the limits of state authority, but it was an irrevocable contract. He advocated popular patriotism, Christian morality, and deference to authority to sustain the existing society (Pocock 1980, 1982). John Locke (1632–1704), declared that the only purpose of government was the protection of property, and the people had no natural right to revolt. English democracy required a long political struggle and incremental reforms in response to direct population protest. Englishmen could not all vote until 1918, and English women not until 1928.

English "popular contention" changed from mutiny by impressed, or forcibly recruited, and abused sailors to mass mobilization by the citizenry between 1750 and 1840 (Tilly 1995). This was a change from isolated, almost random acts of resistance by aggrieved individuals or small groups, to common laborers organized in great numbers to protest publicly and petition the government for specific rights. Public protests were collective, temporary, radical actions directed at institutional change. It was probably more than coincidence that this change toward radical protest came from those with the least social power at precisely the moment when the financial revolution was gaining momentum, the fiscal-military state was taking shape, and great masses of capital were accumulating in a few hands. The existence of dense urban populations made political mobilization easier, but clearly the great mass of the English people did not like the direction in which their society was moving and felt that the personal costs they were being forced to pay outweighed any benefits received. People were unhappy enough to risk their lives and property in street protests in the face of organized police repression. Protest put reform on the agenda, but it was always the political elite who made the final decisions.

In the early stages of the Industrial Revolution in England and America it was still an open question who would control the new technology and to what ends it would be directed. The English textile workers who were the first victims of the early Industrial Revolution resorted to direct sabotage to stall the new factory system in order to gain control over the process of technological change. They even invented a mythical champion, Ned Ludd, as their figurehead, and set about destroying machines with sledgehammers (Noble 1993). Unlike twentieth-century workers who were successively confronted with scientific labor management, industrial automation, and computerization, the Luddites were not yet paralyzed into inaction by the ideology of technological progress (Berg 1980). They understood that factory owners were using machines in ways that made their work more oppressive and caused their wages to drop and their jobs to disappear at a time when government aid for unemployed workers was virtually nonexistent. Luddites did not believe that every form of technological change was inevitable and they knew that new technology was a social and political issue, not merely a technical engineering problem.

Authorities called out 12,000 troops in response to a peak of Luddite actions in the northern industrial districts in 1811 and 1812, and a series of new parliamentary measures were quickly passed against machine breaking (Tilly

1995, 136, 421). Factory breaking probably did slow the introduction of machinery and was no doubt responsible for various "progressive" attempts to soften the harshest aspects of the factory system, but the upsurge in civil disorder at the time was met by a counterwave of government oppression that included numerous restrictions on freedom of press, speech, and assembly and bans on labor unions as well as new legal devices to bring offenders to trial more quickly and punish them more harshly.

English popular protest culminated between 1837 and 1848 with the Chartist movement. This was a sharply focused national struggle to gain parliamentary approval for a series of demands called the "People's Charter." The Charter was designed to give all British men the right to vote and proposed specific reforms, such as the elimination of property ownership requirements, to make it possible for anyone to be elected to the House of Commons (D. Thompson 1984). It was an attempt by common people to counter the concentration of political and economic power that was dominating Britain, and it offered a political framework for a major redistribution of social power and a downscaling of British society. The Chartist movement attracted thousands of supporters to mass meetings and marches, carnivals, camp meetings, conventions, strikes, petition drives, manifestos, and other public demonstrations throughout Britain, and was supported by nearly twenty different organizations. While often described as a labor-class political movement, Chartism also drew support from small independent business people, professionals, and artisans, and appealed broadly to women. Chartism was a community-based movement that was strongest in small towns and villages. Class consciousness was implied in the common understanding among Chartists that Parliament was jointly controlled by the landed gentry and monied interests, as shown by the words of a popular rhyme, "Whigs and Tories are united, we see it very plain" (D. Thompson 1984, 22). Many people reasonably believed that gaining political power would also gain them greater power over the material conditions of their existence.

Chartists specifically opposed laissez-faire political policies that consistently favored employers over workers. Chartists believed that large-scale production promoted by financial and political power was causing overproduction and driving down wages. The Chartist movement arose as an immediate response to the 1834 amendment of the Poor Law, which reduced government support for the poor by favoring the deserving, "industrious" poor over the "idle" poor. Workers believed that the intent was to force women and children to work and thereby drive wages even lower, but even with an entire family of men, women, and children working, many families could not earn basic subsistence. When the People's Charter was rejected by Parliament, protestors moved dangerously close to armed national insurrection, but stopped short when thousands of marchers were fired on by apparently unprovoked troops, killing twenty-six Chartists in 1839. Three of the march leaders were then arrested, charged with treason, and condemned to death. Although their sentences were later commuted and they were pardoned in 1855, these events blunted the movement. As late as 1848 Chartists were able to obtain more than a million signatures on a petition, but Dorothy Thompson (1984, 316) concludes that they ultimately failed because the middle and upper classes would not support them. After 1839 Chartists turned increasingly to self-help community development programs including cooperatives. They also developed a Chartist Land Company designed to counter the monopoly effects of the large landholders, by making land available to thousands of small farmers, but their efforts again evoked parliamentary opposition.

Clearly every household had neither sufficient capital to buy the new labor-saving machinery nor the labor force to operate it, but many different ways of organizing industrial production and mass distribution remained possible. For example, government was already running large-scale capital enterprises, such as military installations, roads, schools, and the postal service. Furthermore, religious communities had demonstrated that capital-intensive enterprises could be cooperatively owned. It was not difficult to increase production with new technology. The real problem was how to equitably distribute the benefits of production and protect workers. Individual workers gradually came to view themselves as members of a group with a common interest in opposition to their employers and political rulers, and eventually they organized themselves into unions and political parties in order to gain shorter working hours and better wages as the fruits of increased production (E.P. Thompson 1963).

Thomas Paine and the Rights of Man

Perhaps the most eloquent and persuasive advocate of human rights and democracy at the dawn of the industrial age, and the fiercest critic of absolute monarchs and tyranny, was humanist writer and journalist Thomas Paine (1737–1809). Paine was born in England and immigrated to America in 1774. He knew Franklin, Jefferson, Washington, and Lafayette. His radical 1776 pamphlet *Common Sense* helped inspire the Declaration of Independence and the American Revolution. He witnessed both the American and French Revolutions, and was imprisoned in France during the terror. His *Rights of Man* (1791) was a strong anti–absolute monarch and pro–human rights statement. Paine believed that there could be many variations in the constitutional forms of governments, but the definitive measure of their effectiveness was how well they promoted the "*general* happiness." He argued that the system was wrong and reform was needed whenever government "operates to create and increase wretchedness in any parts of society" (Paine 1961, 446).

Paine distinguished between the relatively inexpensive *civil* governments concerned solely with domestic law and order, public education, and social welfare, and the despotism of *national* "court and cabinet" governments like England, that engaged in international intrigue and war. The difference was clearly a matter of scale and power. He condemned the leaders of national governments for fostering an international "state of nature" leading to continuous war, which he believed consumed one-fourth of England's national economic product and significantly amplified poverty. Referring to England, he observed that "something must be wrong in the system of government" when old people end up in the work-house, while poor youths are executed as criminals. He estimated that 20 percent of the British population was impoverished enough to require public assistance, and was convinced that "a great portion of mankind in what are called civilized countries, were living in a state of poverty and wretchedness, far below the condition of an Indian. I speak not of one country, but of all" (Paine 1961, 446).

The great social problem in England, according to Paine, was the "combination of common interest" among the Peers in the House of Lords, which overrode Whig versus Tory differences. The aristocracy defended their inherited status as great landlords by replacing property taxes with regressive taxes on common consumer goods. This hurt the poor, who paid a much higher proportion of their very low incomes on taxable subsistence. By maintaining their great country estates, the aristocracy largely avoided paying the poor tax, which was imposed on residential property and fell most heavily on those with small, modest properties and the poor and maintenance-level residents of towns and cities, where most of the poor lived. Paine had scathing criticism of the tax on beer, malt, and hops, because it exceeded the land tax, yet the aristocracy avoided it completely by brewing their own beer and ale on their great estates. He estimated that the English poor paid about one-fourth of their income in taxes, and such a disproportionate rate kept them impoverished. Paine identified the operation of personal imperia that made aristocratic power so effective by noting that the Lords controlled the Members of Parliament through their influence in the election process and because they were connected with them by kinship and patronage. He identified primogeniture as the legal device that kept landed estates intact and condemned the practice as an injustice for the nation as a whole. He also pointed to the sinecures that the aristocracy held and the public support that they secured for their various relatives, estimating that the total cost of the aristocracy to the nation as a whole probably equaled the cost of poor relief.

Paine redesigned England as a small-scale democracy to promote "the general happiness of mankind." He assumed that peace would make it possible to reduce government expenditures to pre-1688 levels, leaving a £6 million revenue surplus to promote public well-being. The top official would be paid £10,000, which was the *average* income in the House of Lords. There would be only 300 elected representatives, rather than the thousand or so members of the two houses of Parliament. Each representative would receive a maintenance-level salary of £250. There would be a mere 1,700 salaried officials, arranged in a simple eight-rank bureaucracy with pay scales ranging from £75 to £10,000. He proposed abolishing the poor tax and replacing it with a direct payment, or "remission of taxes," to the poor of £4 million, twice the amount they were receiving in public assistance. This would return £2 million to homeowners, and the poor would receive an additional £2 million.

Paine considered old-age benefits to be a humanitarian right, but noted that anyone who reached old age could legitimately be supported by the interest on the total amount they would have paid in taxes during their working lives. All children of the poor under fourteen years of age, as well as children of maintenance-level families, would receive support for education. Paine's belief was that a well-run government would allow no one to be uneducated. From the remaining surplus he would provide modest pay increases to veterans and other military personnel and assistance on request to mothers with new babies and newlyweds, as well as burial expenses for those dying away from home. He suggested special shelters to offer work and food to the casual poor of London, many of whom were new immigrants without family or friends. He argued that this would reduce much petty crime.

Paine's most radical proposal was the introduction of a progressive luxury tax on estates. He designed this specifically to reduce the great landed estates and the practice of inheritance by primogeniture. He constructed it to bear lightly on small and moderate-sized estates, but to make it unprofitable to pass on intact estates valued at more than £12,000. This would force aristocratic families to divide their estates equitably among their children, thus making it unnecessary for the government to support them with meaningless public offices and sinecures. He also proposed a progressive tax on the interest on the national debt, with the savings used to reduce various other taxes. Finally, he advocated a mutual reduction of naval forces by England, Holland, and France to one-tenth of their strength, with no new construction of warships. Perhaps the strongest evidence in favor of his plan was his calculation showing that English households paid taxes averaging more than ten times the amount paid by American households. This scale difference corresponds to the tax comparisons in Chapter 5 for the decades between

1860 and 1912, based on Davis and Huttenback (1986), and was also a tenfold increase over English taxes before 1688. Understandably, *The Rights of Man* was not well-received by the English aristocracy and caused Paine to be tried for treason and exiled. He died in poverty in the United States.

Anarchists, Owenites, and Fourierists

English social philosopher William Godwin (1756–1836) helped Paine find a publisher for *The Rights of Man* and, like Paine, was inspired to respond to Burke's defense of the English aristocracy. Godwin argued that people formed governments to reduce social violence and injustice and increase their security, but politically concentrated social power led to oppression, plunder, war, and the restriction of human freedom. This was counterproductive because human freedom was an essential condition for human happiness. Improvements in the human condition could best be obtained through improving human knowledge, understanding, and reason, but this depended on an equitable distribution of property to provide everyone with the leisure to pursue understanding. Justice was the best measure of social conduct. Godwin opposed government because it was based on coercion and because "The rich are in all such countries directly or indirectly the legislators of the state . . ." (Marshall 1986, 89). Godwin's scathing condemnation of monarchy and aristocracy matched Paine's, but focused on the loss of leisure and reason that the concentration of wealth and political injustice caused for the majority: "Can any system be more worthy of disapprobation than that which converts nineteen-twentieths of them into beasts of burden, annihilates so much thought, renders impossible so much virtue, and extirpates so much happiness?" (Marshall 1986, 110).

Godwin's solution was democracy, human freedom, and anarchy in the sense of "a well conceived form of society without government" (Marshall 1986, 160). His anarchy was not about disorder, and he certainly did not advocate political violence nor violence of any kind. He advocated political decentralization, arguing that social units the size of English parishes would be the most ideal small societies, implying independent communities of a few hundred people. As neighbors, people in such small societies would be able to work out their affairs without outside intervention and with a minimum of formal social structure, assuming the existence of a general equality of material conditions among them. Godwin believed that equality, freedom, democracy, and small-scale societies were functionally connected. Such independent communities might send representatives to a general assembly, and he imagined that such an assembly would turn previous great empires into a "confederacy of lesser republics" (Marshall 1986, 164). In effect,

Godwin's ideal of anarchy and confederation would recreate the advantages of domestic-scale tribal societies, presumably without the disadvantages.

Godwin's anarchist philosophy highlighted the human advantages of small-scale political systems but did not include a plan for implementing such ideal societies. Some of Godwin's ideas were taken up and applied by social reformers, including Pierre-Joseph Proudhon and especially Robert Owen. Owen (1771–1858) was one of the most energetic and best known nineteenth-century radical reformers. He admired and was personally acquainted with William Godwin. Owen was a social theorist who attempted to use industrial technology and education to end poverty. In 1800 Owen formed a business partnership and purchased textile factories employing 2,000 workers in New Lanark, near Glasgow. He saw his mills as a social experiment in which he attempted, with some success, to improve the lives and working conditions of laboring people through good organizational practices that included paternalistic kindness, discipline, judicious rewards for good performance, and provision of education and medical care. These were capitalist enterprises, and he promised investors a 5 percent return. At this stage in his career he believed that poor environment was the primary cause of poverty and misery. His work force included some 500 children, many as young as ten, whose characters and prospects he hoped to improve through schooling. Owen's factory experiments were widely acclaimed and directly inspired the Boston Associates who established the textile mill towns in Lowell, Massachusetts. This was the beginning of the progressivist view that economic growth, science, and new technology could benefit everyone.

Based on what he considered to be the success of his experiments in New Lanark, Owen published *A New View of Society* in 1813, in which he advocated a national system of nonreligious public education to solve the moral problems of the poor. He was convinced that if the poor could be educated and properly put to work with new industrial technology everyone would benefit. He spoke extravagantly of how poverty could be eliminated by the tenfold, and even hundred fold, increases in wealth that could be produced under his plan (Claeys 1991, 175). Owen implied that the immorality and sin that afflicted the poor were symptoms, but not the basic cause, of social problems. This brought opposition from religious authorities because it suggested that the poor were not personally responsible for their condition. Owen also met with opposition from Parliament when he proposed new legislation to improve working conditions in the factories. Laissez-faire factory owners were in principle opposed to any government regulations. They specifically opposed Owen's proposals for shorter working hours and limits on child labor, and they did not want to spend their profits on worker education and healthcare. In their view, any free time created by shorter working hours would make workers more immoral and improvident.

Against this opposition, Owen concluded that religious sects, social classes, political parties, and nationalities had socialized people into the errors, distortions, and prejudices that were responsible for poverty. In order to overcome these difficulties, he turned in 1817 toward what would later be called "socialism" and publicly campaigned for a much more elaborate proposal in support of a series of agricultural and manufacturing cooperative communities of 500 to 1,500 people. He showed how individuals from all the old sects, economic classes, and political parties could be gradually combined and assimilated into his new system. The villages were to be laid out in great squares with factories in the center and the sides lined with apartments, surrounded by walks and gardens. People would sign up for membership in a particular type of village association at a central registry office in London. Communal dining, education, and medical care would be provided, and marketing would be cooperative with surpluses shared for greater economic efficiency. No one would work more than eight hours daily, and children would be trained for both agricultural and manufacturing work. Members were assigned to particular age grades, each with distinct social functions, and they were to be governed by a general committee drawn from the oldest grades. There were to be subcommittees for health, instruction, agriculture, manufactures, merchandise, domestic economy, and external communication. In spite of the age differences and internal rankings based on investment, the villages were to be highly egalitarian.

Owen campaigned unsuccessfully for several years hoping to gain wider political support for his proposals, making personal presentations before parliamentary committees, and writing letters to world leaders, including Napoleon at Elba. He even met with the Russian czar in 1818, and made a presentation before the American president and the House of Representatives in 1825. He founded and invested heavily in the community of New Haven in Indiana, which failed in 1828. After constant rejections and failures he came to believe that organized religion, individual profit seeking, and private property were all obstacles to human well-being. By 1835 he turned to communitarian principles and founded the Rational Society, which became one of the most prominent protosocialist organizations in Britain. In 1839 the Rational Society distributed millions of pamphlets and organized lectures that attracted tens of thousands of people, including Friedrich Engels. Owen's intellectual influence extended to the Chartists and democratic socialists and labor union organizers who helped construct Europe's modern social democracies. Owen's village communities lived on in consumer and farmer cooperatives. There were many other religious and secular utopian social movements and communities in the nineteenth-century that sprang from similar roots, such as the Mormons, the Amish and Hutterites, and Charles Fourier's phalangist communities (Poster 1971). All shared a conviction that a better life could be found in small-scale self-sufficient communities.

Did Early Industrial Growth Benefit the English Poor?

Alternative visions of society attracted wide popular support because the growth process greatly increased human suffering, and because the improvements in the material standard of living that growth promised were not widely enough or quickly enough shared to prevent serious social imbalance. The dissatisfaction of the English working poor suggests that they did not feel they were receiving an equitable share of national economic growth. Between 1688 and 1756 England's national income flowed primarily to the rich and the still small middle class (Dickson 1967). Government policy did not promote any meaningful redistribution toward the great mass of the poor. In 1688 perhaps only 35 percent of English society constituted the "middle sort" or "middling orders" of householders at the maintenance level (Table 5.2). They were small farmers, small landholders, and self-employed entrepreneurs and artisans—people who earned enough to enjoy a more comfortable living standard than the poor (Langford 1989, 62–63). The line between the middle class and the poor was an income of about £40, which was the level at which householders were expected to pay "poor-rates"—the locally collected poor relief tax that Paine wanted to abolish. People earning less than £40 could apply for poor relief. By 1812 Colquhoun's data suggests that under the influence of industrialization the proportion of English society living at the maintenance level may have shrunk to less than 30 percent (Table 5.3).

When industrialization began there were severe barriers that made it difficult for people to escape poverty. The working poor would have found it almost impossible to become self-sufficient entrepreneurs and move up into the middling orders. Starting a business in London in 1750 required an average capital investment of about £100 for a modest business, and entry costs ranged up to £10,000 or much higher for more profitable businesses. Apprentices were also expected to pay premiums for their training ranging from £5 to £500. This meant that only people who were exceptionally fortunate, or were born into middle-class families and had ready access to credit, could ever realistically expect to start a business and have a chance to become economically independent. Estates records show that in London between 1665 and 1720, just as in the United States a century later, those who started rich were more likely to end up rich (P. Earle 1989). Successful businessmen could double their investments within a lifetime, but depending on the starting point this might leave only a very modest fortune for the next generation. Having a rich father, marrying a woman from a rich family, and living a long time constituted the most likely set of wealth-producing circumstances.

Throughout English society scale effects created opportunities that constantly favored the wealthiest. As Engel's law predicts, those with small-scale incomes spent a larger proportion on their household expenses and thus had less to save and invest. For example, Gregory King estimated in 1688 that a poor household spent 85 percent of its £21 income on food and clothing whereas an elite household spent only 54 percent of its £455. After housing costs this left the poor with nothing to invest. Comparisons between the diets of the working poor and middling families showed that even though the better off spent a smaller proportion of their income on food, they were able to eat more than twice as much meat, fish, butter, and beer per capita than the poor, and they enjoyed tea and sugar, which were completely out of reach for the poor. The subsistence disproportions gave the rich household a superior diet and ten times more (£30 versus £0.3) to spend on other expenses. Likewise, small business owners had 14 percent of their average gross assets of £620 in domestic property, whereas larger business owners had only 2 to 3 percent of their average gross assets of £17,667 in domestic property (Earle 1989, 121). This gave the wealthier a disproportionately larger amount for their businesses and investments. Among those who could save and become investors, there was a clear distinction between small investors with assets under £1,000 who invested almost exclusively in loans and leases yielding modest returns, and larger investors who could invest in government securities, and potentially more profitable corporate stocks and ships. The overview of the United States in the 1990s in Chapter 2 showed that poor and middle-class Americans were in a similar situation relative to investment potential, although they clearly enjoyed a higher material level than the early industrial English poor.

Some contemporary theoreticians accepted poverty as a natural, and even necessary, condition. Adam Smith (1994, original 1776) felt that the minimum wage should be set by the "invisible hand" of the labor market in a way that would hardly have lifted the poor out of poverty. Labor scarcity in the free market caused wages to increase, so workers could feed their children better and more would survive. This improved survival rate would then increase the labor supply, wages would drop, and fewer children would survive, causing wages to rise again. With such a wage system in operation, it is not surprising that contemporary commissions and reformers were almost unanimous in their conclusion that early "industrialization" hurt the poor. However, Smith thought that economic progress was essential to keeping the poor happy because they were miserable when growth stopped or turned down. Arguably, the lives of the poor were eventually improved not by growth, but by social and political reforms that reduced the adverse scale effects of economic growth. Smith's contemporary, economist and demographer Thomas Malthus (1798, 1895), considered poverty to be nature's way of responding to overpopulation. Ignoring the social and political dimensions of poverty, Malthus argued that society was engaged in a hopeless race between food production and population growth. Malthus's argument contributed to Charles Darwin's theory of biological evolution, in which the genetically unfit were eliminated by "natural selection," and to Herbert Spencer's (1866, 444) concept of "survival of the fittest." Extreme forms of "social Darwinism" implied that the poor should not be provided with welfare. Such an approach would be unthinkable in the tribal world.

In contrast to these apologists for poverty, Sir Edwin Chadwick (1842, 1965), secretary to the Poor Law Commissioners in Britain, published a massive report to Parliament in 1842 that documented the crowded, unsanitary conditions, high morbidity, and premature mortality suffered by the poor. Although 1.4 million qualified for official poor relief, Chadwick found that the health effects were much wider. Laborers in Liverpool were dying at an average age of fifteen, whereas upper-class people died at thirty-five. He argued that poverty was killing more people than war and was a great waste of resources, but considered it to be primarily a public health problem. He concluded that the government needed to take a stronger role in funding and organizing public health measures.

There was a long-term trend for English wages to increase as growth occurred (Lindert and Williamson 1982, 1983). However, the life expectancy, infant mortality rates, and overall health status of the nineteenth-century poor demonstrate that real living standards remained marginal, whether or not "real wages" increased. Furthermore, the wage benefits of economic growth were very unevenly distributed, such that the majority of working people realized very tiny income gains even though average wages increased. Many factors made conditions bleaker for working people, including the widespread adulteration of foodstuffs, the generally poor health conditions of urban life and factory work, and the reduction in public welfare payments (Feinstein 1998).

Increasing income inequality apparently contributed to a decline in average physical stature in many countries between 1760 and 1800, and again between 1830 and 1860. Children of the upper classes were immune to the shrinking effect, whereas both rural and urban poor were impacted. The poor were shrinking in stature in comparison with their parents due to poor nutrition, in part because the economy was growing disproportionately (Komlos 1998). An optimally fed population would experience little increase in average height in an expanding economy. Likewise, the children born to households enjoying rich diets at the top of the social scale would contribute statistically little increase in average height, whereas large numbers of those born into impoverished diets would show large growth declines. Rapid economic transformations left many people with no marketable skills or productive capital. The poor were especially vulnerable to the adverse effects of regular business cycles and the more dramatic financial panics. Adverse weather conditions during these periods only aggravated the economic problems. Even a short period of low income could cause permanent stunting of growth in children. Similar vulnerability to the health effects of low and uncertain income is reflected in low birth weights and stunting in the contemporary "developing" world.

London, which was the center of global development up to the end of the nineteenth century, showed some of the most extremes of poverty. The reality behind wage averages was that the number of the London poor soared in the nineteenth century. Under existing social conditions, adequate employment, income, food, and housing were not available to the bottom third of London's population of over 4 million by the 1890s. The detailed ethnographic research of Henry Mayhew (1861–62) and Charles Booth (1892–1903) brought the realities of London poverty vividly before the British public. Mayhew wanted the wealthy to understand the conditions of daily life endured by the working poor and spent years observing, interviewing, and collecting life histories before publishing his four-volume *London Labour and the London Poor*. He vividly described children reduced to collecting rags, bones, cigar butts, and even dog feces to earn sixpence a day to pay for a little sugar, coffee, a pound of bread, and wretched lodging. Street vendors earned three times more, but still not enough for a decent living, and not enough to buy their handcarts. Vendors were forced to borrow at outrageous interest rates to pay for their goods, and had to rent their handcarts from small-scale capitalists who had amassed empires of up to 150 handcarts. Successful London businessman Charles Booth (1892–1903) thought the social reformers had exaggerated the extent of London poverty and spent seventeen years of his own time and money meticulously mapping income levels, occupations, and housing conditions, door to door, street by street, in the northeast quarter of the city. He counted more than 1.2 million people as poor. They were living in dilapidated four-story buildings at 320,000 persons per square mile. Whole families were crowded into eight-by-eight foot vermin-infested rooms. Fifty people shared one outside toilet and a single water tap drawing from a cistern.

Against this background of human misery it may seem inappropriate to speak of "growth triumphant" (Easterlin 1996), but historians who take a very positive view of growth have characterized the early phases of the commercialization process in Europe as a "consumer revolution" (McKendrick 1982), or an "industrious revolution" (De Vries 1993). The commercial products that diffused most widely were basic domestic articles such as cooking implements and other household items that everyone in the tribal world had enjoyed since the Neolithic. These were household necessities that people were *recovering,* not new benefits. Maintenance-level households did become more comfortable after the Industrial Revolution, but even they remained vulnerable to economic crises. Upward mobility and higher standards of living were illusory for most people because only a very few actually achieved elite status relative to the far greater and increasing numbers who remained poor.

The rise of commercial elites and commercial consumption is paralleled by a decline in the productive capacity of households. As European households lost control over their direct subsistence resources, they were forced into the commercial economy along with newly conquered tribal peoples. For most people, satisfying basic needs involved difficult trade-offs between leisure and the marketing of household products or household labor to obtain money to buy commercial manufactured goods (De Vries 1993, 108). People were forced to intensify their labor in what economic historian Jan de Vries (1993) calls an "industrious revolution." De Vries notes that church and guild leaders facilitated this labor intensification process by reducing the number of feast days, thereby increasing the maximum annual work days from 250 days in the 1400s to 307 days by 1650. It was labor intensification that caused the workloads of European working people to exceed those of self-sufficient tribals, yet it was accompanied by a decline in social power.

Marxists and Totalitarianists

Friedrich Engels (1820–95) and Karl Marx (1818–83) rejected Owen's confidence in gradual and peaceful reform and moved to a more radical and violent political agenda as spelled out in the Communist Manifesto. The Manifesto, commissioned by the Communist League, which was then a secret international revolutionary society, appeared in 1848. It laid out a program to establish a utopian socialist state and provided the ideological framework for Marxist revolutionary movements worldwide, including most prominently the Russian Revolution of 1917. Marx and Engels conceptualized all of human history as a materialist struggle between social classes. They characterized the modern era as a struggle between the *bourgeoisie* capitalists, who owned the means of production, and the working class *proletarians*, who had only their labor to sell. The bourgeoisie developed from the burghers, who ruled the medieval towns as merchants and guildmasters.

According to Marxist theory, industrial technology and the emergence of the global market allowed the bourgeoisie to overthrow the feudal aristocracy and become oppressive exploiters of the proletarians. Marx was inspired by his training in Hegelian philosophy to see dialectical swings between extremes, leading to a new synthesis. Class struggle between the bourgeoisie and the proletariat was a dialectic that would eventually produce a socialist utopia. Marx and Engels assumed that growth in the form of perpetually expanding production and markets as well as crises of overproduction were essential features of bourgeois capitalism and would be its inevitable downfall because of the social turmoil that such growth produced. The Manifesto described this in dramatic terms as: "Constant revolutionizing of production, uninterrupted disturbance of all social conditions, everlasting uncertainty and agitation. . . ." (Marx and Engels 1967, 83). Violent revolution to overthrow the government was imperative because the bourgeoisie controlled the government. However, the proletarians were not self-conscious enough to create their own revolution. They needed communist elites, like Marx and Engels, who would be the intellectual leaders of the revolution of the proletarians.

The Manifesto correctly identified many of the human problems that commercial growth, colonialism, urbanization, wealth concentration, and changes in the scale of production and distribution were producing. Marxist theory in its original form took a rigid, deterministic view of history that left little room for independent human agency. Marxism as a revolutionary political ideology objectified social classes, making them appear as agents even as it demonized the bourgeoisie. The inflammatory rhetoric of the Manifesto made all members of the bourgeoisie appear to be evil exploiters, whereas working people were portrayed as being incapable of taking political action on their own behalf. Perhaps the most important shortcoming of the Communist Manifesto from a scale and power perspective is that it advocates centralized political and economic power in a communist state. The Marxists did not consider growth in scale or concentrated power as such to be problems, at least not in the short term. The proletariat would simply replace the bourgeoisie as a ruling elite until a utopian communist society could be created. Power would still be concentrated, and the scale of society would still be large. Presumably, economic growth and "progress" would continue in the ideal communist state.

The Manifesto advocated a sweeping social transformation that included the abolition of private land ownership, abolition of inheritance, introduction of a heavy progressive income tax, free public education, and state control of banks and credit, communication, transportation, and manufacturing industries. Everyone would work, but child labor in factories would be abolished and agricultural and manufacturing industries would be combined, gradually eliminating the distinction between urban and rural. The proletariat would cease to exist as a ruling class as soon as the ideal of a classless society was reached, and "In place of the old bourgeois society, with its classes and class antagonisms, we shall have an association, in which the free development of each is the condition for the free development of all" (Marx and Engels 1967, 105). The ideal communist society incorporated some of Owen's vision, but the Marxist totalitarian state was not a promising route to utopia.

The unwillingness or inability of nineteenth-century political elites to respond quickly and decisively to the inequality crisis produced by rapid scale increase provided fertile ground for violent, extremist solutions and helped totalitarian regimes gain power in Russia, Germany, Italy, Japan, and China, among others, in the twentieth century. Totalitarianism refers to political power in the hands of a single absolute dictator, in contrast to an authoritarian monarch, whose power is moderated by legislative or advisory bodies of various sorts. Totalitarianism was common in the ancient imperial world, but it became especially dangerous in the commercial world, because the existence of big business suddenly made the instruments of violence so much greater. Great business corporations such as Alfred Krupp provided the military hardware that allowed Hitler to expand his vision of an ideal society (Manchester 1964; Schweitzer 1964; Turner 1985). The giant German multinational chemical manufacturer IG Farben produced Zyklon B gas used in the Nazi gas chambers and manufactured synthetic rubber and gasoline for the war machine (Hayes 2001; Dubois 1952). In 1925 Farben was the fourth largest corporation in the world after General Motors, U.S. Steel, and Standard Oil of New Jersey. Farben was linked to Standard Oil by shared corporate directors (Sutton 1976). The violence perpetuated by totalitarian regimes with industrial technology is difficult to comprehend, but Rummel (1997, 15) estimates that these regimes worldwide murdered 138 million people and killed another 14 million in wars between 1900 and 1987. The human cost of democratic, authoritarian, and totalitarian regimes shows an order-of-magnitude progression from millions, tens of millions, to hundreds of millions in numbers killed. Concentrated power, whether political or commercial, is dangerous, but the danger is greatest when both forms of power are combined within a single personal imperium.

American Populists and Progressives Challenge Big Business

Prominent American reformer and muckracker Howard Demarest Lloyd (1847–1903) helped mobilize popular indignation against corporate power with his book *Wealth Against Commonwealth* (1894). He denounced the price-fixing abuses of monopoly power by the great corporations and commercial trusts at the end of the nineteenth century. He declared emphatically in a speech in 1894 that "a few have obtained unchecked power," adding that those holding such economic power were driven to extend their control over everything: "Congress, the judges, presidents and governors, newspapers, schools and colleges, social leadership" (Lloyd 1910, 204). Lloyd explained that by taking advantage of the global scale of the grain market through the Chicago Board of Trade, a few traders could generate private fortunes by gaining a market "corner." He directly connected price manipulations by such cartels with low prices received by farmers, high prices to consumers for flour and bread, and increases in crime and infant mortality.

In contrast to the reformers, investment analyst John Moody thought that the consolidation process was inevitable and irreversible. Speaking of railroads he declared, "[C]ertainly no intelligent man can be blind to the fact that general railway consolidation in the United States has now proceeded so far that we can never go back to the old discarded methods of the many small competing lines.... [N]o amount of blind public opposition or restrictive legislation can prevent this constant change from small scale to large scale methods" (Moody 1904, 449). Citing Rockefeller's Standard Oil lawyer as his authority, Moody defended monopoly power as the product of a "natural law" and an essential element of progress. Logically, he asserts that Mr. Morgan and Mr. Rockefeller, "or any other leader of men" are not responsible for the trust movement but rather that "it should be laid at the door of nature" because "The modern trust is the natural outcome or evolution of society conditions and ethical standards which are recognized and established among men to-day as being necessary elements in the development of civilization" (Moody 1904, 449).

Moody's views were not shared by millions of small farmers who were among those most obviously disempowered by the growth of big business in America. The railroads did initially create new opportunities for farmers in the newly opened American West, but wherever the railroads held monopolies they began to charge exorbitant rates that victimized the farmers who depended on them to move their produce to the markets. Many farmers were also distressed because they had difficulty paying their mortgages and were in debt for expensive farm machinery. Furthermore, many lost money because they were among the small holders that lost their investments when the great speculative rail financiers inflated, or "watered," the value of their stocks and many overextended lines failed or were consolidated into the trusts. Beginning in 1868, Oliver Kelley organized the National Grange as a farmer support organization and a populist political force to confront the growing power of the railroads and financiers. By 1875 there were 20,000 local Granges throughout the West and Midwest, with some 800,000 members agitating for reform.

It was obvious that the railroads had become absolutely vital features of American life, but when allowed to operate in the immediate interest of stock speculators, they had become so big and so important that they could do enormous damage to whole sections of society and regions of the country. By choosing rail line routes and setting rates and rebates, the rail managers could alter the structure of local and regional markets and effectively determine which towns and cities survived and flourished and which farmlands could be successfully developed. It was not clear how best to limit their power and direct it to maximize the social benefits that the railroads were chartered to provide. Popular unrest forced Congress to create the Interstate Commerce Commission in 1887 to regulate the railroads by setting "just and reasonable" rates and to approve the Sherman Anti-Trust Act in 1890, but enforcement was lax at first, and court challenges continually favored the railroads. Chaffing at regulations imposed by federal commissioners, rail magnate James Hill arrogantly defended railroad monopolies as simple "barnraisings" in which neighbors helped each other, but the scale and power of those directing the railroads made such a comparisons ludicrous (Goddard 1994, 37).

The lines of conflict were drawn sharply in 1902 when the Farmers' Union was founded with the specific policy goals of securing equity, discouraging abusive mortgages, and eliminating "gambling in farm products by Boards of Trade . . . and other speculators" (cited by McConnell 1953, 37). The Farmers' Union denied membership to bankers, merchants, lawyers, and anyone who speculated in agricultural commodities, whereas they maintained friendly relations with organized labor. Other populist-like organizations from 1915–1920 were the Non-Partisan League, and the American Society of Equity. There were many other scattered farm organizations, including the Gleaners, the National Dairy Union, the National Conference on Marketing and Farm Credits, the National Milk Producers' Federation, the Farmers' Equity Union, and so on, but no single, united, national-level organization.

When Americans began to challenge the dominant role of big business in American society at the end of the nineteenth century, many critics of the misuse of corporate power accepted giant corporations, if not trusts, as both natural and inevitable. People assumed that giant corporations were the only way to amass capital for useful social purposes, even though there were many alternative forms of business already in use. For example, law professor Adolf A. Berle Jr. and economist Gardiner C. Means (1933) in their definitive book *The Modern Corporation and Private Property* observed that the business corporation had become an institution that effectively collectivized private property and created "huge industrial oligarchies." They called this a "corporate revolution" and a "great change in the tide of social organization," but felt that this was a "logical and intelligent" trend, although dangerous and irreversible (Berle and Means 1933, v). In their view, two-thirds of

America's industrial wealth had been transferred from individual to corporate ownership. This had profound implications for individual property owners, workers, and consumers. Remarkably, Berle and Means questioned whether this new economic form would "dominate the state or be regulated by the state," or whether the two would coexist. Berle and Means placed the "corporate system" on the same level with the "feudal system" as a major social institution. It is astoundingly prescient that they suggested that eventually the corporate system "may even determine a large part of the behavior of most men living under it" (1933, 1).

Berle and Means were progressivists who looked for means of balancing the diverse interests produced by large-scale business. Many progressivists argued that the government needed to control the market. Widely known Harvard economist Joseph A. Schumpeter (1942) predicted that the economic success of capitalism would lead inevitably to some form of socialism. Corporate capitalism would exclude and disadvantage too many segments of society. Economic historian Karl Polanyi's (1944, 1957) writing of the same period argued forcefully that society could not be based solely on unrestrained market principles. He attributed the "social catastrophe" of the eighteenth century to the triumph of the market economy. He asserted that when a society is turned into a market society by the "crude fiction" of treating land, labor, and money as commodities, people suffer because a self-regulating market is a mindless machine, a technology unconcerned with human wellbeing. Polanyi was emphatic that "the economy" had to be regulated by society and not allowed to run freely. He declared: "To allow the market mechanism to be sole director of the fate of human beings and their natural environment, indeed, even of the amount and use of purchasing power, would result in the demolition of society" (Polanyi 1957, 73). He stressed that labor could not be treated entirely as a commodity because people's lives depended on their income. Without cultural institutions to protect them, people "would die as the victims of acute social dislocation through vice, perversion, crime, and starvation." Likewise, if land were totally commodified, neighborhoods, landscapes, and nature's ability to produce food and raw materials would be threatened. Polanyi's and Schumpter's skepticism was widely shared by economists and political leaders through the end of World War II.

English economist John Maynard Keynes (1936), in his influential book *The General Theory of Employment, Interest and Money,* disavowed then prevailing laissez-faire economic ideology that unemployment, low wages, and low prices would naturally lead to a recovery and prosperity would return without government interference, thanks to the miracle of free market economics. It is generally recognized that the application of Keynesian economic theory ended massive unemployment and brought the world out of the economic depression of the 1930s. In Keynes's view the unemployed were not personally to blame for their fate. He argued, much like Robert Owen and other nineteenth-century social reformers, that it was bad social policy that caused human distress. Keynes considered aggregate demand, in effect "consumer spending," as the force maintaining the economy. He advocated full employment as a matter of public policy, with government creating jobs through public work projects or increasing income with direct subsidies if necessary. This approach was disparaged forty years later as "demand side" economics by "supply side" neoliberal economic theorists who argued effectively for laissez-faire economic ideology, setting the stage for the rapid expansion to full economic globalization after 1980. However, the economic views of Polanyi, Keynes, and Schumpeter were accepted by enough prominent progressive economic elites and political leaders to result in many industries such as railroads and other public transport systems, electric power, and telecommunications being recognized as "natural monopolies" that were best either owned and operated by government or heavily regulated as public utilities. In these cases it was naturally most efficient for only a single utility system to operate in a particular place, and the lowest price to the public could be assured only by government intervention.

The crucial institutional changes that can be attributed to American progressivist planners before World War II include creation of specific organizations to mediate labor disputes, antitrust legislation, the Social Security system, and the Federal Reserve system. Some critics charge that these prewar measures only softened the social conflicts generated by the Robber Baron era of American capitalism in the late nineteenth century and prevented a radical socialist revolution. Others condemned these changes as a sinister move toward totalitarian socialism and perhaps even communism. The contrast between populist and progressivist approaches to growth are illuminating. The populists repeatedly championed small farmers and the rural life. They fought against the "monied interests" and concentrated economic power. For many populists, size was the issue. In contrast, progressivists did not object to size as such. They felt that with "scientific management" and appropriate government intervention giant industries such as the railroads could be made to operate efficiently and in the public interest. However, when the automobile age began, the populists lost the political struggle and the progressives never fully resolved the problem of how to balance the interests of such totally unequal players as giant, seemingly indispensable corporate businesses and small business people and farmers who were now dependent on the giants.

8

Utopian Capitalists: Constructing and Reconstructing the World Order, 1945–2000

At the beginning of the twenty-first century the commercial world was dominated by the military and political power commanded by the leaders of the U.S. government and by the economic and ideological power of the few private elites who commanded the largest multinational corporations and the most important public policy–formulating institutions. To a considerable degree, individual private elites were also able to command government. Most of this international system was designed and redesigned by a small number of elite policy planners during the second half of the twentieth century to promote their goals of economic growth, technological progress, and cultural development. These planners were able to implement two massive cultural reorganizations in rapid succession that produced a truly global commercial system within a few decades, according to two distinct utopian capitalist models of world order: progressivist and neoliberal. Both approaches were designed to maximize economic growth and can be called "utopian capitalism" because their extravagant claims of benefiting humanity have been imperfectly realized. It will be argued that the global-scale cultural system that global elites designed since 1945 fell far short of their utopian objectives, primarily because even the best-intended planners were unable to deal with the unintended consequences of the power of scale.

The important point is that the world system did not reach its present form as a result of natural, inevitable evolution, nor by popular demand, nor because this particular form was the best possible human adaptation. It did so because a few individual designers were successfully able to impose their will on billions of other people. The modern world system was created by a relative handful of individuals who succeeded in implementing their visions where previous utopian planners had failed, because utopian capitalists were able to command overwhelmingly persuasive personal imperia. The power of scale made this possible. As a consequence of their success, more growth occurred, scale increased further, and social power became even more concentrated, but this only amplified the human problems of scale and power.

The following sections will examine the role played by progressivist elites in the initial design of the crucial institutions that produced the first stage of economic globalization early in the second half of the twentieth century, such as the United Nations, the World Bank, and the IMF. It will then be shown that this progressive model of world order, which was designed to promote universal peace and prosperity, was redesigned and retransformed by other elites who followed neoliberal economic theories in the last quarter of the century. The neoliberal economic order and the unbridled financialization process produced even more rapid economic growth, creating more elite and super-elite personal imperia but leaving far more people relatively even further behind. Examples of these transformation processes and the scale effects of growth will be examined for the United States and for the world as a whole.

The objective is to show how social power was organized in twentieth-century America in a way that enabled individual elites to direct growth in scale to increase their personal power, regardless of the particular legitimizing ideologies that were followed. This is not to argue that there was ever a single unified ruling elite or a ruling class secretly directing American public policy, or a conspiratorial ruling elite operating at the global level. Rather, there were diverse elites who publically promoted growth at all levels in the global system in ways that also advanced their personal power goals. They created personal imperia based on interlocking alliances with others who also realized personal advantages from the power of scale. Individual power seekers often disagreed on policy details and followed different growth ideologies. There were frequent disagreements over the specific role of government and the amount of social power that nonelites should be permitted. Power elites often had conflicting economic interests, and the corporate institutions that they directed sometimes competed, but they shared the common goal of overall economic growth, increased production, larger markets, and reduced government regulation, along with easy access to government subsidies and power.

Like their predecessors, the individuals who directed growth throughout the twentieth century shared the self-serving belief that their understanding of events, problems, and solutions was far superior to anything ordinary people were capable of and therefore they had a natural right to lead. Like aristocratic leaders throughout history, they saw no conflict between their personal interests and the broader human interest. Even though these leaders may have been well intended, they were only human, and they could and did make mistakes. It is difficult for the rest of humanity to disregard the arrogance and even hubris of anyone assuming such a powerful and implicitly dangerous role in human affairs. The global-scale commercial world of the twenty-first century is a much more complex and dangerous place than ever as a result of elite decision making.

Constructing Progressivist Global Institutions: The UN, IMF, and World Bank

Progressivist and neoliberal ideological perspectives offered profoundly different approaches to the similar utopian end of economic growth. Advocates for each approach portrayed each as natural, inevitable, and morally superior, although the reality of elite direction demonstrated that neither approach was natural nor inevitable. Ascendancy by elite advocates of either approach required successful application of ideological, economic, political, and military power. Furthermore, both approaches were clearly self-serving in that they promoted growth in ways that facilitated greater concentrations of personal power. The progressivist approach will be examined first because progressivists and progressive ideology dominated American policymaking throughout the century until neoliberals began to displace them in the 1970s. Progressivist thinkers laid the framework for the global institutions that shaped the global commercial system.

The progressivist vision of American society and the world in the postwar period was brilliantly expounded in the popular books of John Kenneth Galbraith (1952, 1955, 1958, 1967). His thinking was shared by many others who, like Galbraith, played leading roles in shaping and managing the United States and the world system through World War II and beyond. Galbraith was a Harvard "demand-side" economist in the Keynesian tradition who believed that government should manage the economy to benefit the larger society. During the war he directed the federal price-control system. He helped rebuild the postwar economies of Germany and Japan, and served as an advisor to President Kennedy. He attributed the Great Depression of 1929 in part to extreme wealth inequality, advocated organized labor as a countervailing force to the power of giant corporations, and argued that public service was a more important objective of economic policy than simply increasing production. Galbraith advocated full employment and high wages so that workers could satisfy their basic needs, minimize debt, and enjoy the affluence that industrialization makes possible. More widely shared higher incomes would allow more people to maximize personal freedom, and find personal fulfillment in aesthetic, cultural, and intellectual pursuits rather than in unlimited consumption and wealth accumulation. He emphasized that the affluent society was a realistic possibility and thought that government, as a democratic institution, should take a managerial role in the economy. Galbraith's liberal political, progressive economic philosophy remained a dominant force in American public affairs into the 1970s, when neoliberal economic theorists began to gain political support.

The United Nations and its affiliated financial agencies the World Bank and the International Monetary Fund (IMF)—the primary new global institutions created at the end of World War II—were designed primarily by progressivist elites who worked both within government and for privately funded policy-formulating organizations. These new global institutions were intentionally designed to promote world peace and postwar reconstruction and to smooth out destabilizing fluctuations in international currency flows. They were an acknowledgment that, like a nation, a global-scale commercial world could not function safely as a totally free market. The latter two financial bodies were especially shaped by British "demand-side" economist John Maynard Keynes and "New Deal" economists in the Roosevelt administration. Historian William A. Williams (1961) called those who worked to establish these progressive international organizations "corporate elites" because the changes they promoted also helped to sustain giant corporations and they precluded more radical social change. American corporate elites wanted the United States, and U.S. corporations, to remain dominant forces in the world and they later helped organize the Cold War to prevent the expansion of totalitarian socialism, which could threaten American access to global markets and resources.

Officially, these new international organizations were designed to serve governments, not corporate business, and governments were the official planning agents, but nevertheless, private citizens played a leading role in creating them. Among the most influential designers of the postwar world were the private specialists and planning groups connected with the Council on Foreign Relations (CFR). The CFR, founded in 1921, has been called "the principle planning association for the U.S. foreign policy elite" (Williams and Horowitz 1975, 764). It was a private planning group, funded in part by the Rockefeller and Carnegie foundations, and initially followed a strongly progressivist ideology. Its select membership was limited to 650 business and professional people, former and future high government officials, and foreign policy experts drawn from elite universities (Domhoff 1990, 113–144). The primary role of the CFR, which still publishes the influential journal *Foreign Affairs,* was to define American "national interest" in international affairs.

Norman H. Davis, a millionaire businessman and CFR president from 1936 to 1944, illustrates the profound personal influence that private individuals can exercise over the highest levels of governmental decision making. Davis was closely associated with President Roosevelt and Secretary of State Hull, and was financial advisor to the treasury secretary during World War I and during the 1919 Paris Peace Conference. He also served as assistant secretary of the treasury and undersecretary of state before 1921, and was associated with J.P. Morgan and Company. At the outbreak of World War II, under Davis's direction, the CFR organized the Rockefeller-funded "War and Peace Studies Project" as a policy planning advisory service to the secretary of state. This self-selected advisory group involved perhaps a hundred people from 1940 to 1945. They concluded that the United States needed to fight World War II because the Western Hemisphere's resources could not sustain U.S. economic growth indefinitely. This private civilian advisory group had direct connections with the State and Commerce departments, and played a crucial role in planning America's strategy during the war and in postwar global reconstruction (Shoup and Minter 1980). The Atlantic Charter, signed by Churchill and Roosevelt, spelled out the objectives of the war in terms corresponding to CFR recommendations. The charter advocated political self-determination for conquered territories and called for equal access to trade and raw materials, economic progress, and improved living standards worldwide.

CFR planners advocated increased trade in the postwar world, supported by international economic organizations, and sketched out the broad outlines of the modern world system to include the World Bank and the IMF (Domhoff 1990, 126). These private elites were remarkably close to the action for a group of citizens with private financial interests at stake. The structures of the World Bank (International Bank for Reconstruction and Development) and the IMF were agreed upon at the forty-four–nation Bretton Woods Conference in New Hampshire in 1944. The World Bank was designed to make loans to governments to finance postwar development, whereas the IMF was designed to stabilize international currency exchanges. CFR planners brought in prominent Keynesian economists Jacob Viner and Alvin H. Hansen to began preliminary designs for the International Monetary Fund in 1941. The American business community and Congress generally favored the IMF and World Bank proposals, although some large New York bankers and a few "isolationists" in Congress were critical because they feared that these new institutions might undermine their own role as currency regulators and lead to inflation. A compromise that satisfied the bankers and the isolationists was implemented with the help of advisors in another policy planning group, the Committee for Economic Development (CED). The CED was a domestically focused private organization, that shared members with the CFR (Domhoff 1990). Its members were corporate business leaders with links to the Commerce Department. They were interested in promoting free trade, while avoiding future depressions and minimizing the government's role in the economy. As implemented, the new international banking system did reduce the role of the old private banking dynasties like the Rothschilds and Morgans, but opened new opportunities for many other financiers.

The new global institutions implied a move toward decolonization and a reduction in the British, French, and Dutch colonial empires, which would have limited American access to potentially lucrative markets and raw materials. Private elite policy planners were clearly concerned with sustaining economic growth and protecting corporate interests through a difficult military and political crisis. After the war, a report developed by another private policy group, the Twentieth Century Fund, with members also connected to the CFR, concluded that an "expanding American economy" could be supported for decades, given continued access to foreign resources (Dewhurst 1947, 1955).

The Rockefeller family was indirectly involved with designing the postwar international system through their foundation support for both the CFR and the CED. They were also more directly involved with the formation of the United Nations. President Roosevelt appointed Nelson Rockefeller Assistant Secretary of State for Latin American affairs late in 1944, and Rockefeller served long enough to play a leading role in the final voting to establish the United Nations at the founding conference in San Francisco in 1945. Rockefeller was then appointed to the committee responsible for finding a permanent home for the UN headquarters. He initially offered the Rockefeller Center Theater, then proposed the family estate at Pocantico, N.Y., before John D. Jr. purchased and then donated the existing site in Manhattan (Collier and Horowitz 1976, 237–243, 246–247).

Prospects for America: The Rockefeller Panel Reports

Perhaps one of the most telling examples of personal imperia and how they intermesh with all forms of social power at the highest level in the commercial world was the 1956–58 Special Studies Project organized and directed during the Eisenhower administration by the Rockefeller brothers, acting as private citizens. This project helped to design and legitimize the postwar development path that the United States followed and the country's dominant position in the world during the critical years of the Cold War from approximately 1960 to 1975. In this case, the four Rockefeller brothers, John D. III, Nelson, Laurance, and David—grandsons of John D. Sr.—played an influential role in shaping many of the major growth- and scale-related events in the second half of the twentieth century. This is not to suggest that there was anything conspiratorial, or even sinister, in the Rockefeller imperium. The point is that the global system did not just happen. It resulted from a humanly directed development process. As heirs to John D. Sr.'s Standard Oil fortune, the Rockefeller dynasty had extraordinary social power at their disposal, and they used it to shape the global system from a progressivist perspective.

The Rockefeller imperium was a personally directed power structure. This kind of power and human agency cannot be adequately understood by "pluralists," who argue that no single power "interest" shapes national or global events, nor by Marxists, who see social classes or institutions as actors and who assign priority to high-level analytical constructions such as economics or political economies. Some might imagine that formal social structures or institutions, rather than classes, determine human events, but fallible individual humans still make crucial decisions. Arguing over whether or not "the state" or corporations are autonomous entities, capable of making decisions on their own, is also misleading, because particular elites often have multiple directing memberships in different institutional structures and can thus work beyond particular structural limits. An individual person can act idiosyncratically, even irrationally or illegally, for inexplicable personal reasons.

In the Special Studies Project we see the policy-shaping activities of a few very influential private individuals who directed powerful corporate institutions and were personally connected with other powerful individuals. The project assembled representatives of all major sources of social power in the United States into a tiny policy-making group at a crucial moment in history. Their policy recommendations ultimately influenced the entire world. This four-year project resembled the War and Peace Studies Project described above and was funded at more than a million dollars by the Rockefeller Brothers Foundation, which was then headed by Laurance. Brothers Nelson and Laurance chaired the project. John D. III served on the Foreign Policy Overview panel, and David served on the Foreign Economic Policy panel. Together the brothers selected and directed ninety-four "concerned citizens" to diagnose American and global problems and to propose solutions. In effect, they were designing an ideal world according to their personal visions. The architects of this report were not ordinary citizens; they were political, commercial, military, and ideological elites. Significantly, they represented all the major sources of social power and at this particular moment were literally united within a single policy planning power network under the direction of one family's personal imperium.

There were six separate panels in the Special Studies Project commissioned to deal with foreign policy, military security, domestic economic policy, domestic social policy, education, and democracy. These were sweeping issues with immense significance for the future of both the United States and the world. Many panelists had formerly served, or would later serve, in the top ranks of the federal government as ambassadors, members of the State, Defense, Treasury, and Housing, Education, and Welfare departments, and secretaries of the Army and Air Force, as well as expert advisors in the White House. They included people directly connected with the ultimate in military power. Nuclear physicist Edward Teller helped develop the atomic bomb during the 1942–45 Manhattan Project, and had just developed the even more powerful hydrogen bomb in 1952. He served on the panel for International Security: the Military Aspects. Others included Henry Kissinger and Dean Rusk, who between them would later serve as secretary of state to Presidents Kennedy, Johnson, Nixon, and Ford. Kissinger (1957) had just published a book advocating limited nuclear war as a rational military policy. Many panelists were presidents or board members for the largest and most powerful U.S. corporations, including defense-related companies, communications, manufacturing, banks, the Federal Reserve, and the most widely distributed magazines and newspapers. There were presidents, deans, and top professors from major universities, as well as representatives of America's major foundations and scientific associations. They were clearly members of "the power elite" (Mills 1956).

The panelists' elitist perspective on political dissent was very obvious. They considered popular belief in democracy to be essential for the success of their development objectives, but thought that democracy would be effective only as long as citizens did not waste time and effort with "irresponsible or foolish views" (Rockefeller Panel 1961, 463). They warned that citizens would need to distinguish between "dissent and obstruction" and remain within the "bounds of reason and decency."

The panelist defined America's national interest in grandiose humanitarian terms as "the development of a world order in which all peoples can live in security and realize their fullest potentialities," or simply, "peace and freedom for all" (Rockefeller Panel 1961, 17, 21). In more arrogant language they declared: "the world order shall be of a kind in which the United States can be at home—spiritually, economically, and politically" (Rockefeller Panel 1961, 16). The new American imperium was to be an economic empire rather than a direct political empire, but global poverty and political oppression would need to be eliminated because "It is impossible to conceive enduring prosperity for America when large parts of the world struggle in want or oppression" (Rockefeller Panel 1961, 24). The ultimate objective was an ideal world, conceived of as a diverse community of cooperating nations supported by new institutions and regional associations, building on other, newly created structures such as the United Nations, the British Commonwealth, the North Atlantic Treaty Organization (NATO founded 1949), and the Organization of American States (OAS founded 1948).

The concepts of an Iron Curtain and Cold War loomed large in the foreign policy planning of the Rockefeller panel, which is understandable in that the Soviet Union demonstrated its possession of nuclear weapons in 1949. Panelists believed that China and the Soviet Union were waging a single, coordinated conflict pitting the "communist camp" against the "Free World." It was assumed that the communists were seeking world domination. The Soviets were seeking to outstrip the United States in per capita production and draw the "underdeveloped" world into their economic sphere, while at the same time gaining military superiority over the United States in strategic weapons. This justified rapid economic growth by the United States and the creation of an immense defense industry. The communist threat also made international development in the American interest:

> The long-range interest of the United States is in economic growth throughout the world. It wants the continuing prosperity of its allies in the advanced Western countries; more than that, it wants the other areas of the world to develop both agriculturally and industrially to their fullest potentiality. (Rockefeller Panel 1961, 75).

Panelists discovered another argument for even greater development efforts when they projected growth trends to 1976 and found that the economic gap between developed and less-developed nations would widen. They therefore advocated greater international efforts and more planning to produce even more rapid rates of growth in less-developed countries. Ominously, to close the gap they advocated "accelerated" growth to be "achieved" by shifting to exotic sources of capital and selectively favoring economic elite in the developing world over the majority who might accumulate capital more slowly with savings from income rather than from accumulated profits to capital. This was the policy actually followed. It further concentrated power in elite hands and excluded the poor, as will be shown below.

In the new global system, small producers and domestic consumers were far removed from the exchange loop, but clearly this was not the only kind of world that could have been imagined. Elite planners understood that the new world order they were creating would transform the previous system of international trade that focused on the exchange of raw materials for manufactured consumer goods to meet household needs, such as cotton and wheat for textiles and flour, into a system in which large-scale investors would profit from exchanging industrial raw materials and fossil fuels for heavy industrial machinery.

The panel charged with examining the military aspects of international security found further justifications for accelerating American economic growth. They argued that the United States was falling behind the Soviets militarily, and this view was reinforced by the Soviet launching of the first artificial satellite in 1957, shortly before publication of the panel's first reports. The planners' argument was clear: "We require a growing industrial, technological, and scientific base in order to achieve a state of continual readiness for the long haul. Without an adequate industrial plant, we will not be able to produce the ever-increasing variety of weapons required for our protection" (Rockefeller Panel 1961, 100). The arms race of course quickly led to the creation of a greatly enlarged "military industrial complex" that President Eisenhower warned about in his 1961 farewell address as follows:

> This conjunction of an immense military establishment and a large arms industry is new to the American experience. The total influence—economic, political, even spiritual—is felt in every city, every statehouse, every office of the federal government. We recognize the imperative need for this development. Yet we must not fail to comprehend its grave implications. (U.S. Federal Register Division 1961, 1035–40)

Ending Poverty Through Globalization

The Charter of the United Nations specifically makes the promotion of "social progress and better standards of living" and "economic and social advancement of all peoples" one of its primary aims. There is no doubt that the immediate postwar world was a human disaster, after the destruction of war and decades of one-sided colonial development. The UN's 1948 Universal Declaration of Human Rights boldly stated, "Everyone has the right to a standard of living adequate for the health and well-being of himself and of his family including food, clothing, housing and medical care." Under the UN Charter, the Economic and Social Council was expected to "help solve international problems in the economic, social, humanitarian and cultural fields." In 1949, when the Council surveyed social conditions throughout the world, they found that more than half of the world's people were living under "inadequate" conditions in "underdeveloped" countries (United Nations, Department of Social Affairs 1952). Infant mortality rates were outrageously high, life expectancy at birth was less than half the average in the developed world, and per capita annual incomes were an order of magnitude lower.

Initially, UN development experts attributed these social problems to a vicious cycle of disease, underproduction, and poverty, and they recommended education, improvements in public health, and new technology to increase production. Planners took this as a mandate for global economic growth and a new global economic system to be administered by the same UN agencies that diagnosed the problem. Human success was to be measured by growth in total economic output at national levels. All of this had to be financed by massive transfers of capital, hardware, and technical expertise from the richest countries in exchange for raw material exports. This self-serving diagnosis and solution was congruent with the guiding philosophy of the leaders of the largest American philanthropic foundations and their most influential planning groups, and it fit well with American national interests, which the same foundations and associations had helped define. However, a new world order designed to produce a larger global economy was not the only possible response to global poverty. If American objectives had not dominated, it would have been equally plausible to have advocated internal development at local and national levels, import substitution, and self-help programs that emphasized labor-intensive production for domestic use and local markets. This would have encouraged nationalist decolonization movements, but it would also have made the World Bank and international capital transfers as well as large-scale production for export less crucial.

Paralleling the UN's development work, President Truman's Point Four program initiated America's international development program in 1949 as part of its policy of "Soviet containment." In his inaugural address Truman declared: "We must embark on a bold new program for making the benefits of our scientific advance and industrial progress available for the improvement and growth of underdeveloped areas" (U.S. Federal Register Division 1949, 114). Supported by the recommendations of the Special Studies Project, in 1961 President Kennedy launched the Agency for International Development (AID), the Peace Corps, and the Alliance for Progress, and began shipping billions of dollars in surplus agricultural production to developing countries. At the same time the UN designated the 1960s as a Development Decade, and specified a 5 percent increase in national income as a growth goal for developing countries. America's "foreign aid" program was justified as enlightened self-interest. Aid helped American farmers, opened new markets for American industry, and helped keep underdeveloped countries out of the Soviet sphere of influence.

U.S. and UN development goals were mutually self-supporting. Both endorsed a technological and capital-intensive solution to improving human well-being, and both were directly linked to the establishment of a new international "free trade" economic system dominated by the countries with the largest economies. The new order unquestionably helped the dominant powers retain their position. For example, in 1998 there were 182 member nations in the International Monetary Fund, but G-7 nations (the United States, Germany, Japan, France, the United Kingdom, Italy, and Canada) held 45 percent of IMF voting shares. The United States was the largest voting member with 18 percent. This is the kind of "natural" power distribution that scale theory would predict. Furthermore, the president of the World Bank was permanently to be an American. It is not surprising that such a power imbalance was reflected in the design of the global system and in the emphasis on "free trade." In such a system economic exchanges would likely benefit the strongest partner.

The United States was an obvious model for the global economy because it was large enough to have developed an internal domestic trade between geographically diverse regions in the absence of trade barriers. Planners envisioned a global free trade system incorporating American-style regional international systems based on monetary institutions, free movement of capital and labor, and free trade. These regional systems would then trade with each other on a similar basis. The trade liberalization component of the world economy was initiated in 1948 when the General Agreement on Tariffs and Trade (GATT) went into affect with twenty-three member nations agreeing to jointly reduce tariffs. Regional economic associations began with the European Economic Community (EEC), or Common Market, formed in 1958, which became the European Community in 1967. The North American Free Trade Agreement (NAFTA), created in 1994, formed a similar trade association. By 1971 there were seventy-eight nations trading under the GATT. In 1995 the GATT was replaced by the World Trade Organization (WTO). The WTO's stated goal is "to improve the welfare of the peoples of the member countries." In 2001, like with the IMF, G-7 nations provided 53 percent of the WTO budget and the United States 16 percent. By 2002 there were 144 nations in the WTO. The WTO secretariat operated with a staff of 552 people, under a director-general. Each member nation was represented by an ambassador, or trade minister, and trade disputes were to be settled by a seven-person appellate body. In many respects the trade issues decided by the WTO were as critical for human well-being as any issues dealt with by the UN, but it is difficult to imagine how a mere 144 trade ministers, as political appointees, could adequately represent the often conflicting interests of six billion people. Government ministers were invariably elites and were likely to benefit personally from global economic growth. After the public protests at its

1999 ministerial meeting in Seattle, the WTO began to speak of "democratic legitimacy and accountability" and "external transparency and public outreach" and stressed that its negotiations were based on "consensus," but unlike the UN, the WTO did not allow participation by nongovernmental organizations (WTO 2001).

The ease with which elite planners could imagine that their version of free trade and economic growth would benefit all of humanity is astounding. It is even more remarkable that these utopian growth models were developed in the absence of democratic input of any sort and without substantial evidence that social benefits would in fact be widely distributed. The Rockefeller panelists arrogantly believed that economic globalization was inevitable. As they explained, "Regional [trade] arrangements are no longer a matter of choice. They are imposed by the requirements of technology, science, and economics" (Rockefeller Panel 1961, 191). This brings to mind Bill Gates's (1996, 11) statement that "No one gets to vote on whether technology is going to change our lives. No one can stop productive change in the long run. . . ."

The new development programs initially focused on easily treated public health problems, infrastructure, and the widespread mechanization of agriculture. Development in these areas produced dramatic improvements in gross measures of production and living standards. However, poverty did not disappear and the number of poor actually increased. Development experts then attributed the persistence of poverty to a population crisis caused by mortality rates dropping faster than fertility. This revived Malthusian arguments about overpopulation and made technological improvement seem even more imperative. Later, some security strategists attributed poverty to "environmentally induced economic decline" (Homer-Dixon 1991), and warned that discontented people might attempt to impose "distributive justice." However, as early as 1963 it was clear to a few UN experts that poverty was not simply a population problem. They noted ominously that "growth in income appears to have been shared disproportionately by the minority already well-to-do, while in richer countries certain disadvantaged minorities have continued to lag behind the majorities in growth of income" (United Nations, Department of Economic and Social Affairs 1963, 2).

In spite of these warning signs of increasing inequality, in 1967 futurists Herman Kahn and Anthony Wiener of the Hudson Institute published optimistic predictions for social conditions in a "surprise free" standard world by the year 2000 based on a continuation of technological progress and economic growth. Their growth simulations resembled Walt Rostow's (1960) progressive stages of economic development in which societies moved in sequence from a traditional stage, to maturity, to mass consumption. Kahn and Wiener suggested that continued growth would dramatically improve human well-being, and predicted that within thirty-three years, 20 percent of humanity would enjoy the luxury of "post-industrial, post–mass consumption society," somewhat like Galbraith's "affluent society." They expected another 20 percent of the world's people to be comfortably situated in mass-consumption and mature industrial societies, and 50 percent would be fairly well off in partially industrialized societies. In effect, everyone would be progressively moving up. Only 10 percent would still be in "misery" (Kahn and Wiener 1967, 59–60).

Their predictions that world population would double and the global economy would increase roughly fivefold by the year 2000 proved remarkably accurate, but Kahn and Wiener were wrong about how the benefits of growth would be distributed. In order to compare the historic outcome of growth with Kahn and Wiener's optimistic predictions, Figure 8.1 draws on UN and World Bank data to sort global households for 1965 and 1999 by poor, maintenance, elite, and super-elite imperia rankings, representing approximate household income ranges of <$12,500, $12,500–$62,499, $62,500–$249,999, and $250,000+, respectively, in constant 1995 dollars. These rankings assume households of five persons and were calculated based on percentage share of income received by each twentieth percentile of population in each country. This yields average household income rankings of approximately $6,800, $42,000, $170,000, and $375,000 in 1999 for poor, maintenance, elite, and super-elite households, respectively. These differences in scale approximate relative levels of social power, economic independence, and investment potential that household imperia at each rank experienced in the United States at the end of the twentieth century. The imperia concept sets a higher threshold for global poverty than World Bank development experts employ. For example, the World Bank's 1995 classification ranked entire countries by high, middle, and low income according to national per capita incomes that would produce equivalent household incomes of below $3,500 for "low-income" poor and $62,500 and above for "high income." Such rankings minimize the extent of poverty and obscure the concentration of social power at the highest ranks. In a global economy it seems more useful to apply a global measure of effective household social power, even if it makes it difficult to be optimistic about the outcome of economic growth. However, these figures do show that if the 1999 global income of $29.9 trillion were equitably distributed it would provide every household in the world with a maintenance-level income of $25,000.

This comparison of households by income distributions shows that the number of global poor increased from 2.8 billion in 1965 to more than 4 billion in 1999. Over a billion more people had become poor by 1999, in

Figure 8.1 **Distribution of Global Household Imperia Rankings, 1965 and 1999, in Constant 1995 Dollars**

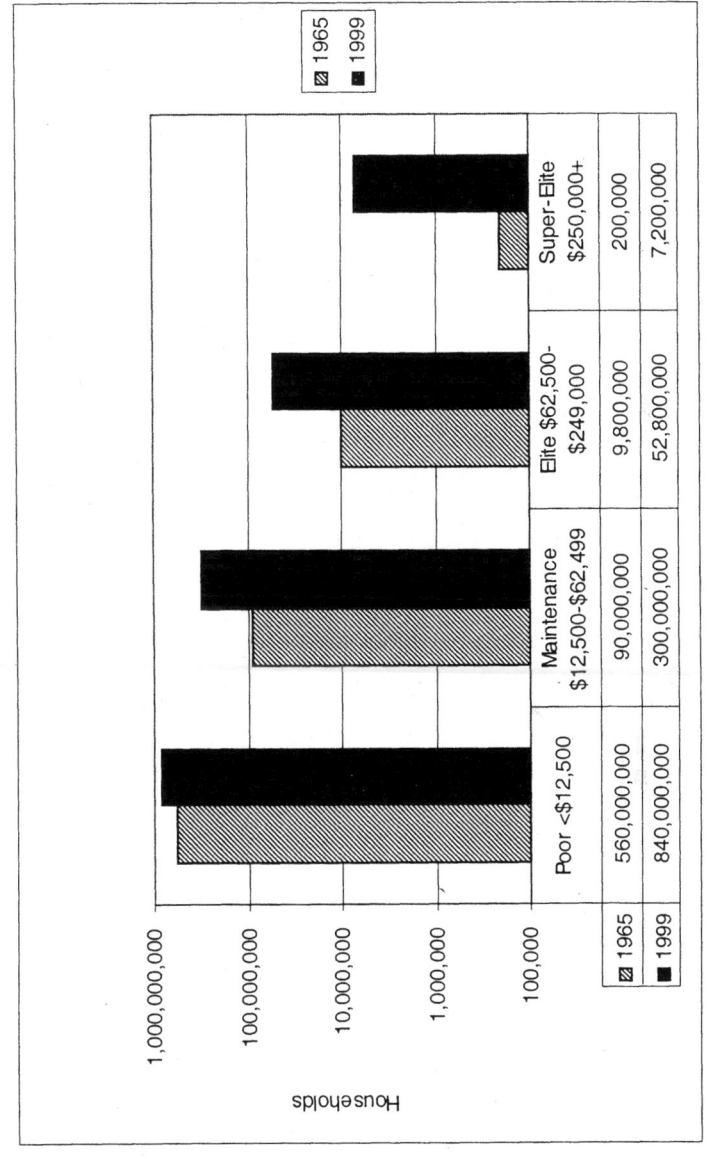

Sources: Bodley 2000; Gemini 2001; World Bank 2001.

spite of thirty-four years of economic growth. These new poor represented more than the entire population of the world in 1850. However, the poverty *rate* dropped from 85 percent to 70 percent. This could be seen as a 15 percent improvement, even though more people were poor. When growth optimists focus just on percentages, rather than taking into account scale effects on absolute social power, growth can appear deceptively beneficial to everyone. For example, World Bank researchers David Dollar and Aart Kraay (2000), carefully examined the effects of economic growth on the incomes of the bottom 20 percent of the population in eighty countries between 1960 and 2000. They found that "income of the poor rises one-for-one with overall growth," showing that the average income of the poorest 20 percent of global population increased at approximately the same rate as global per capita income over forty years of economic development. They concluded that growth-promoting neoliberal economic policy "increases the income of the poor to the same extent that it increases the income of the other households in society" (Dollar and Kraay 2000, 6). Even more emphatically, they declared, "growth generally does benefit the poor and . . . anyone who cares about the poor should favor the growth-enhancing policies of good rule of law, fiscal discipline, and openness to international trade" (Dollar and Kraay 2000, 6). Dollar and Kraay also conclude that democratic institutions and public expenditures on health and education produce no systematic effects on poor incomes.

This "one-for-one" outcome is what growth might naturally be expected to produce, and it naturally amplifies preexisting inequality. The optimistic view also masks an immensely disproportionate growth in top-rank incomes produced by the power of scale. Dollar and Kraay also observed that growth does not significantly alter the *distribution* of income. This could be bad news, because when the distribution is already grossly inequitable and everyone receives the same percentage raises, the absolute effects and power outcomes of such "equitable" growth are paradoxically even more inequitable. Figure 8.2 shows that the absolute income gain for elites and super-elites between 1965 and 1999 was a scale increase, boosting average elite and super-elite incomes from tens of thousands to hundreds of thousands of dollars. Poor incomes increased at a somewhat faster percentage *rate* than global per capita income, but in absolute amounts their average incomes increased only some $4,000 over the thirty-four years, whereas elites added more than $80,000 to their average incomes and super-elites gained $225,000. More significantly, the increase in poor income was temporary, because maintenance-level households in the global middle class increased at less than half the rate of global per capita income over the same period.

Between 1965 and 1999 the share of global income received by poor and

Figure 8.2 **Average Income of Global Households by Imperia Rankings**

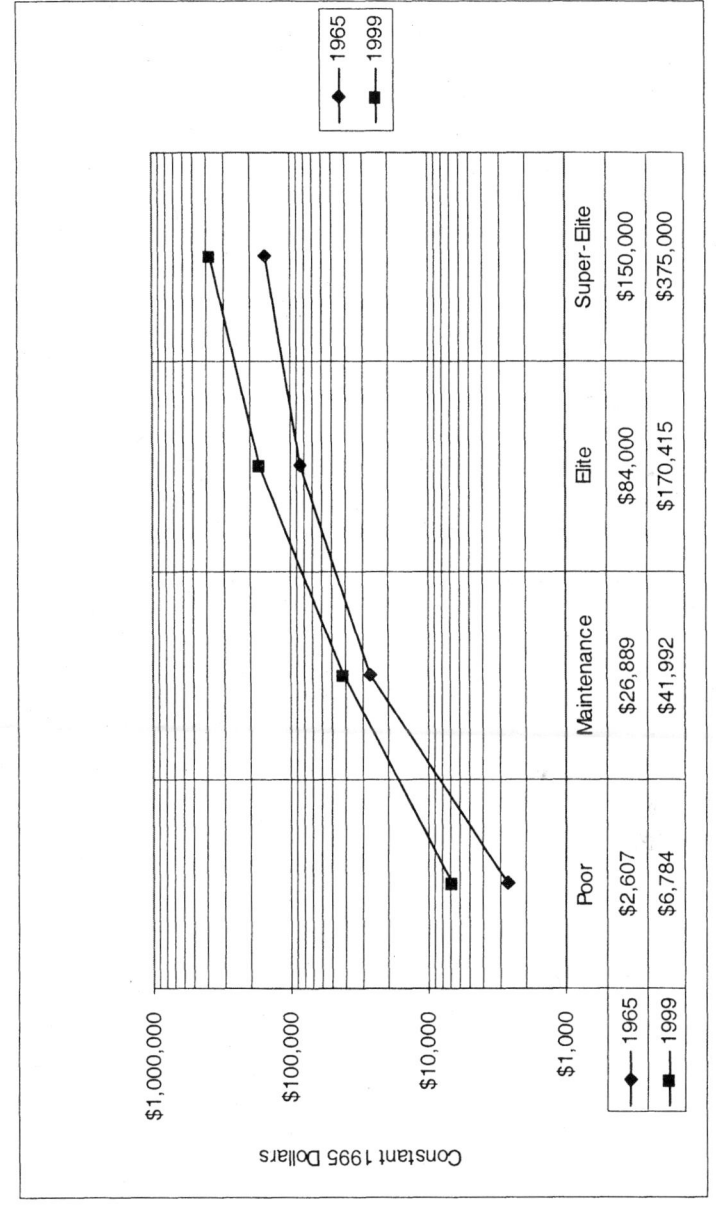

Sources: Bodley 2000; Gemini 2001; World Bank 2001.

maintenance level households declined dramatically, even as their average incomes increased slightly (Figure 8.3). Global economic development produced a massive redistribution that shifted some 43 percent of the new income upward to the elite and super-elites in the top 0.6 percent of global population. Such a growth outcome would not be surprising in an elite-directed development process, but it did little to benefit the global poor and middle class. These power-of-scale effects of growth show up most clearly at the highest levels of global wealth and income rankings. Between 1965 and 1997 the number of global elite and super-elite households increased from 10 million to 60 million, or from 1 to 5 percent of world population. Thus, although per capita income of the bottom 20 percent of global population may have increased at the same rate as per capita income overall between 1960 and 2000 as Dollar and Kraay suggest, nevertheless the top household imperia received a disproportionate share of global economic growth. The people who truly benefited from global growth and financialization processes were the super-elites at the very top of the economic hierarchy. Financial consultants estimated that in 1997 there were some 6 million high-net-worth individuals (HNWIs) holding $17.4 trillion dollars in wealth (Gemini 1998). By the year 2000 their number had increased to some 7 million worth $27 trillion (Gemini 2001). HNWIs held a million dollars or more in investable financial assets.

Power was even highly concentrated among the global super-elites and followed regular scale trends. In the year 2000 there were 538 global billionaires at the very top with an aggregate net worth of $1.7 trillion (Table 8.1). The average billionaire wealth of $3.2 billion would produce an unearned income of $321 million at a 10 percent return. The richest individual held $58.7 billion, and the top 10 percent held 40 percent of total billionaire wealth (Forbes 2001). One notch down were 56,462 ultra-high-net-worth multimillionaire individuals holding $6.5 trillion. The average multimillionaire wealth of $116 million would produce an unearned income of $11.6 million, at 10 percent (Gemini 2001). In 1998 experts expected HNWIs' wealth to increase annually at 10 percent, and the actual rate fluctuated between 6 and 18 percent. Calculating income as 10 percent of investable net worth produces an aggregate HNWI income of $2.7 trillion, which is an astounding 9 percent of the $29.9 trillion gross global income in 1999 (World Bank 2001). In contrast, HNWIs represented a mere 0.12 percent of global population. Viewing the world as a single society, this is very comparable to the proportion of super-elites in Rome in A.D. 100, England in 1086, 1688, and 1812, the United States in 1850, 1929, and 1997, and suggests that by itself growth does not improve the distribution of power, but does make it more concentrated.

Figure 8.3 **Percentage Distribution of Global Income by Imperia Rankings, 1965 and 1999**

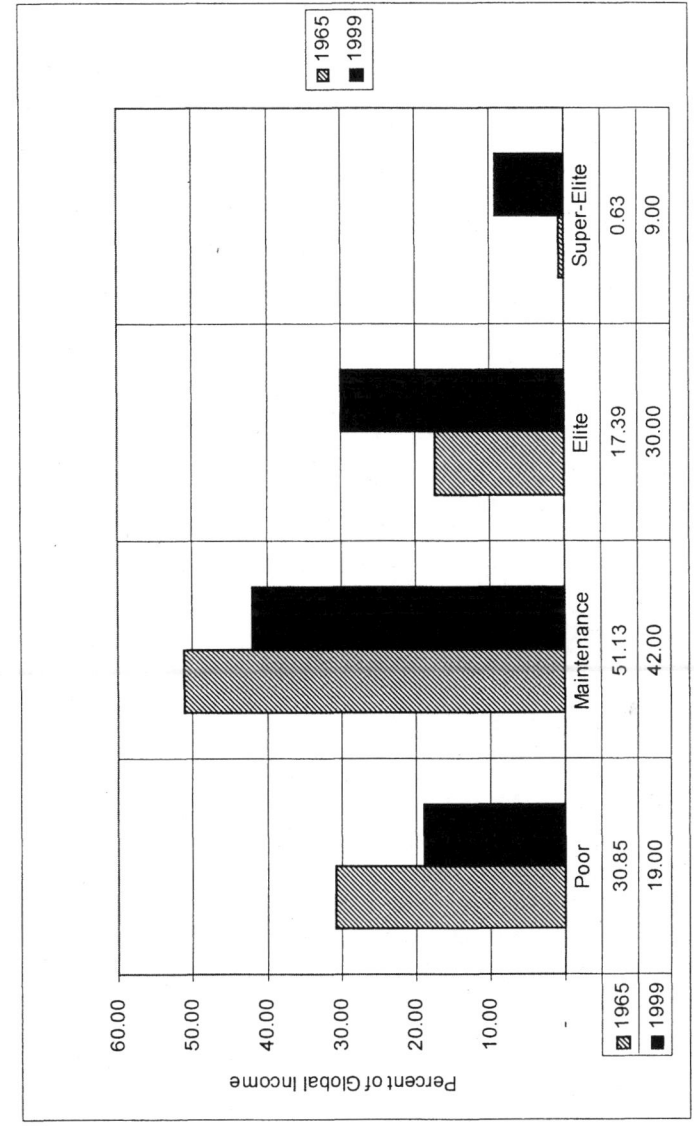

Sources: Bodley 2000; Gemini 2001; World Bank 2001.

Table 8.1

Distribution of Global Income and Wealth by Household Imperia, 1999

Rank	Households	Average wealth	Average income	Imperia
Billionaire	538	$3,213,011,152	$321,301,115	Super-Elite
Ultra HNWI	56,462	$116,386,242	$11,638,624	0.6 % of
HNWI	7,143,000	$2,617,948	$261,795	households, 9% of income
Elite	52,800,000	$100,000	$170,415	Elite 4.4% of households, 3 0% of income
Middle class	300,000,000	$50,000	$41,992	Maintenance 25% of households, 42% of income
Poor	840,000,000	$3,000	$6,784	Poor 70% of households, 19% of income

Totals: 6 billion people, 1.2 billion households, $29.9 trillion World Bank global income, 1999.

Sources: Super-Elite income (Gemini 2001); elite, maintenance, poor distributions (Bodley 2000, 378); global income (World Bank 2001).

Feeding the Commercial World

The dynamic growth processes that amplify poverty can also be demonstrated by examining the effects of economic growth on global food systems. Since Malthus first wrote about the potential for population growth to outrun food production, the need to feed the world has been used to justify the intensification of food production, the expansion of global markets, and economic growth generally. A tiny handful of people and a few large institutions have directed much of this global intensification of food production. However, a perpetual food crisis is not inevitable, and a fully globalized commercial food system may be a counterproductive solution. Feeding the tribal world was not a perpetual crisis because population planning and decisions to intensify production were made at the household level, and the long-run trend was toward balance with a relative absence of either malnutrition or famine. In contrast, in spite of all modern efforts at commercial development of food systems, hunger, like poverty, has increased. There are strong reasons for believing that the power of scale actually makes it more difficult to feed the world.

Global food surveys compiled by international agencies over the years since 1934 show persistent global malnutrition affecting millions, even though different measures of malnutrition and hunger have been used. As international development programs progressed, in addition to the Food and Agriculture Organization in Rome (1945), the UN set up three new bureaucracies to deal with the ever more obvious problem of malnutrition: the World Food Program (1961), the World Food Council (1974), and the International Fund for Agricultural Development (1977). However, malnutrition did not go away. By the year 2000 half the world's population—3 billion people—were officially considered to be malnourished, either from nutritional deficiencies or from overconsumption (Gardner and Halweil 2000). This figure equals the entire population of the world in 1960. Estimates of 790 million *under*nourished in 1997 exceeds the world population of 720 million in 1750. Making food a profit-making commodity in a global-scale "free" market created a human disaster. Protein and calorie deficiency is a predictable outcome when people do not have access to the direct means of food production such as arable land, labor, and tools, and when their incomes are too low to buy adequate food. Nobel Prize–winning economist Amartya Sen (1981) demonstrated that the people who starved to death in Bangladesh during the great famines of 1943 and 1974 died because they lacked land and money, not because of food shortages. When household income drops too low it may be impossible for people to purchase adequate food. Anthropologists have repeatedly shown that when subsistence farmers are forced onto marginal lands by large-scale commercial agricultural development, are forced to produce export crops, or must work for abysmally low wages, they often must replace more nutritious foods with cheap starch and children may be starved to keep parents at work (Gross and Underwood 1971; Scheper-Hughes 1992).

The Rockefeller Foundation initiated the search for more productive grain crops in 1943, believing initially that hunger was a food production problem. This research effort resulted in the development of new strains of high-yield wheat, corn, and rice crops that was implemented as the Green Revolution. This revolutionized agricultural production in much of the world, with very mixed human results. Taking a much broader and more direct commercial approach, the Rockefellers, led by Nelson Rockefeller, also formed the International Basic Economy Corporation (IBEC) in 1947 as a for-profit privately owned stock corporation "to promote the economic development of various parts of the world, to increase the production and availability of goods, things and services useful to the lives or livelihood of their peoples, and thus to better their standards of living" (Broehl 1968, 9). Here was a zeal reminiscent of Robert Owen's utopian experiments with textile factories, but with the capital to support it. IBEC was a pioneer project that set up mechanized farms, dairies, poultry producers, food processors, food wholesalers, and supermarkets with housing developments, industrial factories, and investment subsidiaries. By the 1960s IBEC had 119 subsidiaries operated in 33 countries. They had total assets of $219 million in 1966 and were producing 8 percent returns on stockholder equity of $42 million (Broehl 1968, 285). The Rockefeller family began to break up IBEC in 1973 but IBEC became a model for large-scale food production by global, multinational corporations. IBEC survived in 2001 as Arbor Acres Farms, a subsidiary of multinational poultry giant Aviagen, which called itself the largest broiler chicken breeding company in the world, controlling 44 percent of the global market in eighty-five countries. A food production system operating at this scale has little to offer the global poor and small farmers other than overpowering them with market competition, as shown by the negative impact of large-scale agribusiness on small farms in the United States (Chapter 6).

The Green Revolution and related economic development projects failed to solve the global problem of malnutrition and hunger because they made food a large-scale commercial enterprise far beyond the means of most of the world's poor. Commercial development did increase productivity, but at local levels it also increased risk, debt, landlessness, poverty, and malnutrition (Bodley 2000, 364–370). It was elites, not the poor, who had the advantage and profited most by the new global food chain, whether at the local, regional, national, or international levels. Ironically, in high-income countries such as the United States, fully commercialized food systems that are driven by profit-seeking investors, rather than nutritional needs, have contributed to a "nutrition transition." In this process diets based on complex carbohydrates, whole grains, and vegetables are transformed into more profitable high fat, simple carbohydrate, low nutrient diets (Drewnowski and Popkin 1997; Popkin 1998). Highly processed, advertised, and transported food products are very energy- and materials-expensive. Massive advertising campaigns to promote consumption of these foods, combined with higher incomes, urbanization, and the shift to dual-career households, have tended to remove even food preparation and consumption from the household, accelerating growth of the fast food industry (Schlosser 2001). It is not surprising that by 1999 1.2 billion people were considered malnourished from overconsumption (Gardiner and Halweil 2000), and that 55 percent of American adults and 20 percent of children were considered overweight.

An equally important problem of capital-intensive growth is that the scale of financial transfers required to support this kind of development also destabilized governments. Susan George (1992) estimated that between 1982 and 1990 high-income countries transferred $927 billion dollars in development assistance, loans, and private investment to developing countries for a payback of $1.3 trillion. Much of this development money enriched the multinational corporations that constructed large-scale infrastructure projects such as dams, highways, and power plants. However, by the 1980s many countries experienced difficulties with debt repayment. As a condition for loan refinancing, lenders such as the World Bank and the IMF imposed "structural adjustments" as "fiscal discipline" requiring governments to reduce social support programs and increase exports. These measures increased stresses on the poor.

The Triumph of Neoliberal Economic Theory: Wealth = Growth = Wealth

A number of national and global events beginning in the late 1960s that threatened elite security and economic interests contributed to the revival of laissez-faire public policy in the United States, which in turn helped push economic globalization to new levels, increasing the dominance of giant multinational corporations and shifting more global wealth and income to the top of the social hierarchy. Throughout the 1970s OPEC, the international oil cartel, steadily increased oil prices from three to forty dollars per barrel. Inflation soared, there were changes in the balance of international trade and more foreign competition in manufacturing, global economic growth slowed, stock prices stagnated, and corporate profits declined. All of these events constituted an economic crisis that some observers did not hesitate to call a crisis of capitalism (Castells 1998). The economic downturn of the 1970s was preceded and accompanied by a variety of other social upheavals that further alarmed economic elites, including increased public concerns over consumer safety and environmental protection, labor unrest, the civil rights movement, protests against the Vietnam War, urban riots, and the youth counterculture movement. Even the legitimacy of the presidency and the military was challenged by release of the Pentagon Papers in 1971, the Watergate affair in 1972–73 (Shapiro 1972), and the American withdrawal from Vietnam in 1973. Like the social disturbances during the early Industrial Revolution in England, elites saw all of these events as threats and challenges. Crisis gave political conservatives a renewed sense of mission and made neoliberal economic theory especially appealing as a global solution.

In response to the crisis, economic elites made immediate changes in corporate business strategies and began shifting manufacturing functions overseas where labor was cheaper and more docile. President Nixon precipitously abandoned the gold standard in 1971, even though it was established as a pillar of the global monetary system at the Bretton Woods Conference in 1945 (Judis 2000, 111). Economic elites also began reorganizing production and switched investments from manufacturing to computer-based information technology in order to support larger-scale enterprises in larger-scale markets; in addition, they demanded more concessions from government. These infrastructural changes were important, but what elites believed, and what they could persuade others to believe, ultimately made possible the triumph of the neoliberal globalization movement.

The shift to neoliberal economic policies was a remarkable ideological transformation that produced revolutionary outcomes. In 1945 most of the Western world was directed by policy makers who were inspired by the progressive synthesis of democratic socialism and Keynesian economic theory (George 1999). The prevailing belief of policy makers was that governments should intervene in the market economy to stabilize financial markets and, if necessary, with public work projects to keep people employed in order to maintain overall social well-being. Progressive political ideology still used economic growth as a measure of progress, but it was more likely to moderate the power-concentrating effects of growth than neoliberal "supply-side" or "new growth" economic thinking, which had become dominant by 1980. Neoliberal thought was a return to laissez-faire economic ideology from the eighteenth century. Economic elites now used it to legitimize massive tax reductions, reduced social benefits, and reduced government regulation of business. They argued that economic liberalism would increase production and stimulate growth, leading to increased employment and wealth. It did increase growth, but not everyone benefited.

The extreme form of neoliberalism, which in the United States became the political agenda of "right-wing conservatism," was considered a rather bizarre and very outmoded extremist idea in 1945 (George 1999). The intellectual roots of neoliberal economic thought were contained in two influential books—*The Road to Serfdom* by Austrian economic theorist Friedrich A. Hayek (1944) and Richard M. Weaver's (1948) *Ideas Have Consequences*—as well as a magazine, William F. Buckley's *National Review* (1957). Weaver argued that social democracy would weaken social hierarchy and inequality, and thereby undermine all motivation for human accomplishment. Writing during World War II, Hayek opposed virtually all forms of government-directed social planning, including those based on Keynesian economics, lumping them all with the totalitarianism of Soviet communism, German National Socialism (Nazism), and "socialism" in general. Hayek believed that free market competition would decentralize and diffuse economic power. However, he feared any form of concentrated power, whether in totalitarian governments or business monopolies. In the 1970s neoliberal economists selectively advanced Hayek's antiplanning doctrine to argue for market deregulation and smaller governments. Taking antisocialism to an extreme in defense of large business corporations, Hayek's student Milton Friedman (1970, 123), concluded that business corporations "cannot be said to have [social] responsibilities" at all because they are not persons. Friedman explained that the sole responsibility of corporate officers was "to make as much money as possible" in the interests of the owners of the company, albeit legally and ethically. This view contradicts other neoliberal legal arguments that corporations are persons with constitutionally protected human rights to free speech and to own other corporations. The ascendancy of neoliberal economic theory was signaled by the award of Nobel Prizes in economics to both Hayek in 1974 and Friedman in 1976.

The essential elements of New Growth economic theory included the following points: "Accumulate capital. . . . Keep government small. . . . Open the economy to foreign trade and investment. . . . Respect property rights and the rule of law. . . . Do not burden the productive sector with government regulations and controls" (Beach and Davis 1998, 4). Under such a regime, education was expected to increase worker productivity, not promote social justice. Competition was a central assumption of neoliberal economics, drawing on nineteenth-century social Darwinist survival-of-the-fittest evolutionary theory. The implication was that competition would eliminate inefficient firms, products, and presumably individuals, and would be the most efficient way to produce wealth and stimulate people to productive action. However, in practice the largest corporations proved themselves adept at using their great size and power to reduce competition. Under the influence of neoliberal policies many Progressive Era government regulations were dismantled, and many public utilities and healthcare institutions were "privatized," or turned into private for-profit companies. Privatization in Britain, implemented under Margaret Thatcher's government after 1979, was a massive shift of public assets into private hands, turning public revenues into private income on a scale reminiscent of Henry VIII's distribution of the monastic properties. Susan George (1999) called this the "surrender of the product of decades of work by thousands of people to a tiny minority of large investors."

Equally significant was the shift by financial elites away from long-term investments in the physical means of production to short-term speculative investments in financial securities as a means of turning a larger, more rapid profit. This new phase in the financialization process caused corporate executives to emphasize stock value over production, and helped initiate a series of widespread borrowing and mergers, or "leveraged buyouts," in the 1980s. In extreme forms of financialization, corporate securities and financial derivatives became products in themselves in what has been called a speculative "casino economy." The overriding objective of corporate decision makers was to assemble ever larger-scale corporations by mergers and buyouts, even though these new business structures did not increase efficiency of physical production.

Political analyst Kevin Phillips (1990) described the impact of the neoliberal approach implemented in America under the Reagan presidency. Phillips (1990, xvii) called the decade of the 1980s "the triumph of upper America," arguing that economic growth promoted by changes in public policy shifted wealth and income to the upper ranks of American society. Phillips stressed that those who controlled political power in Washington, D.C., would be in a position to design and implement public policies that would further concentrate their own social power. In this view the particular distribution of wealth and income in a democracy is a "political distribution" resulting from the relative political power balance between different segments of society. Phillips expected that public indignation would force a more equitable distribution, but this did not happen. The 1980s wealth surge actually continued longer than Phillips anticipated, and it produced an astounding concentration of wealth. *Forbes* magazine began publishing annual lists of the 400 wealthiest Americans in 1982, placing fourteen billionaires at the very top, with an aggregate net worth estimated at $15.4 billion and averages of $1.1 billion. By 2001 the number of billionaires had increased more than tenfold to 266 individuals worth a total of $842 billion. Their average net worth had almost tripled to $3.1 billion. The failure of a balancing swing in public policy in favor of the middle ranks and the poor reflects the dramatic increase in absolute power in elite hands, and their much more effective hegemonic control.

The politically liberal public policies of the federal government from 1932 to 1968, especially progressive income taxes and public assistance programs, had effectively redistributed wealth from the top downward to the middle and lower ranks of society, shifting money to consumers and thereby promoting the "demand" side of the economy (Phillips 1990). The political implementation of neoliberal ideology reversed these policies with a revolutionary and extremely rapid redistribution of social power back to the top, paralleling the global income redistribution process described above for the same time period, except that a progressivist policy was never fully implemented at the global level. The effects of the neoliberal transformation were immediately apparent in the growth trajectories of American personal imperia.

New technology was selected, promoted, and applied by elites to achieve their particular goals. Among the crucial technological changes were the use of "scientific" personnel management (Taylor 1911), followed by the application of automation to machine tool production in the postwar period (Noble

1984), followed by the widespread adoption of computers in all areas of business. Scientific management, as espoused by Taylor, was brutally elitist. Taylor advocated grading workers according to how well they performed in light of standards set by time and motion efficiency studies for each subtask in a production process. The assumption of this approach was that management must force workers to adopt the most efficient production methods, and workers would be rewarded by incremental differences in pay. Workers would still be dehumanized cogs in the industrial machine, but they would be graded cogs, each producing at its maximum efficiency and each receiving a "scientifically" established pay for his or her grade. It was assumed that instruction and incentive had to be imposed by management because an ordinary worker is "merely a man more or less of the type of the ox, heavy both mentally and physically" (Taylor 1911, 137).

Changes in the tax code achieved by lobbyists working for neoliberal organizations and corporations were central elements in the effort to redistribute income to the upper ranks of American society. The neoliberal argument was that the wealthy should keep more of their money as a reward for their entrepreneurial skills and because they would invest and produce more wealth, more growth, and more jobs. The income tax did not become a permanent feature of American society until 1913. During the Progressive years, income taxes became highly "progressive." Just as Thomas Paine had recommended, the wealthier paid a progressively higher proportion in taxes. This imposed some limits on total accumulation and provided an incentive for philanthropy while lightening the tax burdens on the poor and providing revenues to be redistributed downward. For example, in 1952 the tax for a single taxpayer on income of $1,000 was 9 percent, on $10,000 27 percent, on $100,000 70 percent, and on a million dollars 88 percent. This made very large incomes prohibitively expensive. A series of tax cuts begun in the 1960s and accelerated under the Reagan administration totally reversed this system, making taxes regressive. Under a regressive tax the poor, with their smaller incomes, pay disproportionately more and feel the burden more. By 1997 a $10,000 income was taxed at only 15 percent, and the top bracket was lowered to $278,450 and taxed at only 39.6 percent. This meant a savings of $484,000 for a millionaire income and of $1,200 for a $10,000 income. However, this caused an amazing upward redistribution of income. Applying the 1997 rates to the 1997 aggregate adjusted gross income of nearly $5 trillion predicts a potential tax reduction of $1.5 trillion from 1952 rates. More than $200 billion in savings would go to the 144,000 with millionaire incomes for an average savings of $1.4 million. The top 10 percent of taxpayers would receive over half of the benefit, and the top 25 percent of taxpayers about 75 percent. This was obviously not the only way that taxes could have been "reformed."

People with maintenance- and poor-level imperia are dependent on wage and salary incomes, which are subject to withholdings for Social Security. Furthermore, they are more burdened by regressive sales taxes because they must spend most of their income on basic needs.

Income tax reforms were accompanied by deep cuts in corporate taxes. This tax break made possible lavish executive compensation and produced higher profits and higher unearned income for shareholders, further amplifying the unearned income of those holding large financial assets. In 1952 corporations paid more than half of their net income in federal income taxes. Corporate income taxes represented one-third of federal revenues and equaled nearly 75 percent of the volume of all individual income taxes. By 1997 this had changed completely. Corporate taxes had dropped to a mere 16 percent of corporate income and they represented less than 12 percent of federal revenue and equaled less than 25 percent of income tax revenues. Corporations spent more on advertising in 1997 than on income taxes. They also spent about the same amount on executive compensation.

Figure 8.4 uses Census Bureau figures to illustrate the income effects of this great redistribution of social power, showing the proportional distribution of family income by decade from 1929 to 1998. In this graph the bottom 20 percent of families, ranked by income, represent "poor" household imperia; the middle 20 percent represent "maintenance"-level imperia; the upper 20 percent "elite" imperia and the top 5 percent "super-elite" imperia. Personal income grew during this period by approximately one order of magnitude in constant 1996 dollars from $793 billion in 1929 to $7.4 trillion in 1998, and per capita income increased by a similar magnitude from $6,511 in 1929 to $27,293 in 1999. However, from an income inequality peak in 1929 through approximately 1970, when the "natural" inequality effects of growth were restrained by progressivist tax policies, regulations on business, and downward income redistribution programs, the proportional income share of the elites and super-elites declined steeply, whereas maintenance- and poor-level households realized modest improvements in their share. These trajectories were dramatically reversed after 1980, when conservative political policies became dominant, until by 1998 the income distributions had begun to approach the gross inequities of 1929. These rapid transformations demonstrate that natural scale effects of growth can be moderated by social policies or they can be allowed to follow their "natural" course to disempower large numbers of people.

Percentage shares are of course important, but what really matters is how proportional distributions interacted with growth to produce huge order-of-magnitude income differences by imperia. Although percentage inequalities were not as extreme in 1998 as in 1929, nevertheless, because of the scale

Figure 8.4 **Percentage Distribution of U.S. Income by Imperia Ranking, 1929–1998**

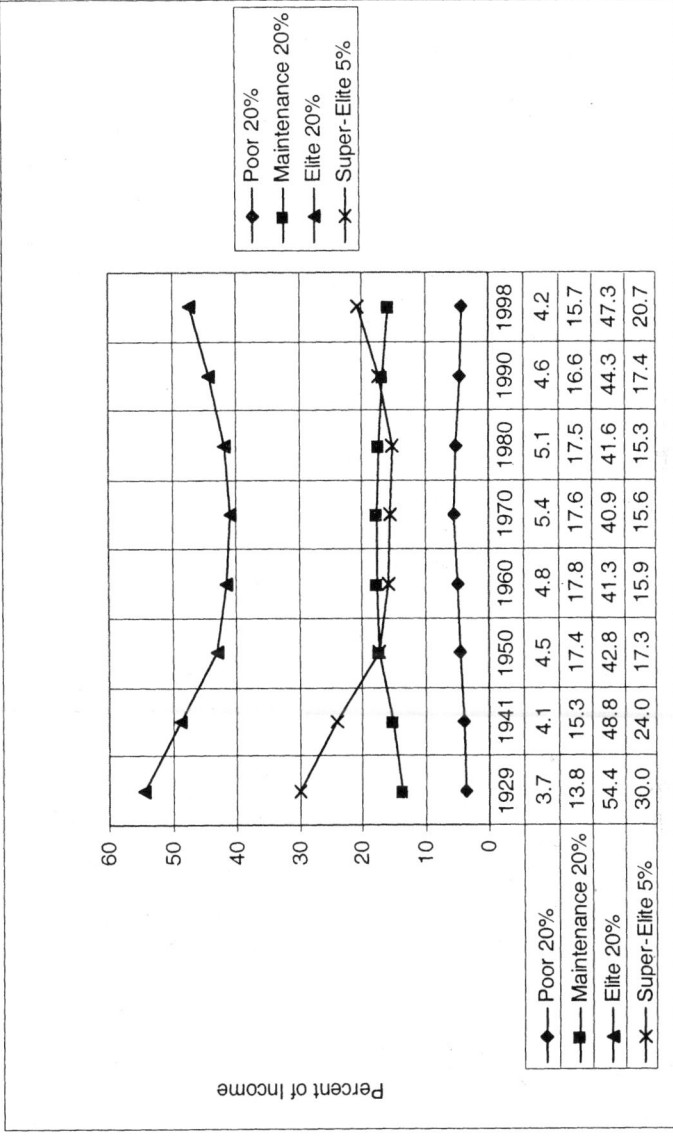

	1929	1941	1950	1960	1970	1980	1990	1998
Poor 20%	3.7	4.1	4.5	4.8	5.4	5.1	4.6	4.2
Maintenance 20%	13.8	15.3	17.4	17.8	17.6	17.5	16.6	15.7
Elite 20%	54.4	48.8	42.8	41.3	40.9	41.6	44.3	47.3
Super-Elite 5%	30.0	24.0	17.3	15.9	15.6	15.3	17.4	20.7

Source: U.S. Bureau of the Census 2001, Table 670.

effects of growth in total income at upper income levels, the actual gap in constant dollars between elites and nonelites increased by a power of ten. Unequal income trajectories were amplified by the particular political and economic circumstances during the last quarter of the twentieth century. Elite-directed changes in production techniques and in the organization of business suddenly opened new opportunities at the top for people with financial resources and specific technical skills, but also caused repeated crises that worked against people with limited financial resources and few skills.

It seems unlikely that the ruthlessly disadvantaged majority would have chosen these changes if given the chance. Just as in the original Industrial Revolution, automation and increased rationalization of production eliminated jobs, imposed more rigid controls on workers, and shifted many functions to consumers (Ritzer 2000) without producing real improvements in the quality of life for most workers or consumers. These changes were accompanied by a new frenzy of corporate consolidations—"downsizing," and "deindustrialization" that eliminated many well-paid jobs when production was moved overseas (Bluestone and Harrison 1982; Harrison and Bluestone 1988; Bartlett and Steele 1992). Even as insecurity increased in the work place, and wages stagnated or declined at the middle and lower levels, both employers and state and federal governments reduced social supports such as retirement, medical, and unemployment benefits in a process that paralleled the "structural adjustments" imposed by the IMF on governments in the "developing" world. Other politically conservative "reforms" shifted millions of people off public welfare programs into low-paying jobs or back onto the streets and into homeless shelters. Government policies suddenly became less humane.

The neoliberal economic globalization agenda was contested in 1971 by a coalition in the U.S. House and Senate who proposed legislation to tax and regulate overseas investment and profits of American-based multinational corporations while reducing tax advantages and subsidies that encouraged overseas expansion. They hoped to protect workers and restrict imports, but their efforts were viewed as a threat to business and were defeated by a coalition of business associations lead by David Rockefeller's Emergency Committee for Foreign Trade, the National Association of Manufacturers (NAM), and the national Chamber of Commerce.

Between 1981 and 1992, some 10.6 million American adults lost their jobs due to corporate reorganization, experiencing what anthropologist Katherine Newman (1988, 1993) called "declining fortunes." Newman collected detailed life histories of hundreds of people during this period and found that most accepted their fate as a personal failure. Her findings were echoed by June Nash's (1989, 1994) research on General Electric's closure of its Massachusetts plant in 1986 that eliminated 5,000 jobs. Nash attributed the GE workers' passivity to the ideological hegemony of the corporate elite that made it seem natural for corporate profits to be more important than the fate of individual employees. By the mid-1990s American investors and corporate CEOs were being richly rewarded by the transformations associated with the revolution in information technology and the related processes of corporate restructuring and economic globalization. After-tax profits soared from 4.7 percent in 1973 to 7 percent in 1995 and CEO compensation quadrupled, while the stock market reached unprecedented heights. At the same time, most working households needed two incomes to stay even, as worker wages declined.

Elite Power in the Global Market Society

The radical transformation of the world in the last quarter of the twentieth century can be understood as the cumulative effect of the exercise of social power by a relatively small, self-interested elite. The global super-elite of corporate executives, wealthy investors, and political officials, who with their households represented only about 0.5 percent of global population, were able to effectively employ all the instruments of social power to shape the world in ways beyond the reach of most of humanity. A careful inventory of American elites conducted in the early 1980s suggests that as few as 5,778 individuals controlled the major corporations, the federal government, the news media, and the most important cultural institutions (Dye 1983). These dominant few could command other people by dispensing liberal financial rewards as well as severe economic punishments. They could also define what was natural, inevitable, and proper in the world order by means of the funding that they could direct into giant media corporations, universities, foundations, and private think thanks. Such use of social power to influence what other people believe is perhaps the most efficient and effective form of command (Russell 1938, 136).

Ultimately this was not a broadly democratic transformation process. It depended on financial support from a handful of wealthy donors. Those who commanded wealthy imperia exercised power over American public policy by influencing how political candidates were selected and elected, by serving as unelected advisors and commissioners, and by indirect control through the private foundations that they funded. Their foundations in turn funded a network of private policy-planning and political lobbying organizations whose work the donors implicitly approved. A few elite planners in the most influential policy networks then defined the limits of "responsible" public policy debate, formulated legitimizing economic theory and political ideology, and applauded the "correct" decisions. Similar power was exercised by the Special Studies Project discussed above; however, by the 1970s some elites began to direct their funding toward removing all limits on private power, and defining taxes and government regulations as obstacles to growth. Significantly, what characterized the new conservative policy network was the religious fervor of its leaders, the absolute certainty of their beliefs, and their explicit determination to gain political power.

The possibility that wealthy benefactors could use private foundations and trust funds to shape American public policy and culture was first examined by Eduard C. Lindeman in the 1930s (1936, 1988). He saw the existence of foundations as evidence that more wealth was accumulating in private hands than individuals could profitably reinvest without producing overproduction and unemployment. During the 1921–30 decade, Lindeman estimated that there were some 300 foundations, giving out $135 million a year ($1.3 billion in constant 1996 dollars). He concluded that elites used foundations to redistribute these surpluses in a conservative way to maintain the social status quo. However, it is clear that some of the largest foundations were already being used to transform the world. For example, John D. Sr. created the Rockefeller Foundation in 1913 with an initial endowment of $100 million "to promote the well-being of mankind throughout the world." By the year 2001 the foundation's endowment had grown to $3.5 billion, making it the twelfth largest in the country. Between 1913 and 2001 the foundation gave out more than $11 billion (in constant 2000 dollars). In 2001 the foundation's objective was to help deal with "the root causes of the world's complex ills." Likewise, the Rockefeller Brothers' Foundation, formed in 1940, had given out a total of some $525 million for "promoting the well-being of all people in the transition to global interdependence." By 2001 there were some 10,000 foundations giving out $21 billion annually, but their power remained highly concentrated. The 500 largest were distributing approximately half of all foundation grants (Foundation Center 2001, xiv).

A few individuals in a network of interconnected personal imperia and corporate institutions were at the center of the neoliberal economic transformation movement. Strategically placed foundation money and a few private donors had a measurable impact on the neoliberal revolution, especially after 1970. For example, twelve private foundations provided $64 million to ten influential politically conservative policy research institutions from 1977 to 1986, and 120 other major foundations provided an additional $25 million (Allen 1992). The top three of these policy "think thanks"—the Hoover Institution, the American Enterprise Institute, and the Heritage Foundation—received nearly 70 percent of the foundation funds distributed to these groups. Two of the top three were particularly influential with formulating policy during the Reagan and Bush administrations. A single donor, billionaire Richard Mellon Scaife, donated some $620 million to these conservative policy organizations over four decades (Judis 2000, 158). In 1981 the American Enterprise Institute (AEI) received 40 percent of its support from some 600 corporations as well as the Scaife Foundation. The most influential book on supply-side economics, *The Way the World Works,* written by *Wall Street Journal* editor and AEI fellow Jude Wanniski (1978), popularized the neoliberal argument for aggressive tax cuts and became the ideological centerpiece of President Reagan's economic policies. Reviewers on the back cover of the fourth edition (1998) praised the book as "an absolute revelation" and "utter truth." Their conservative political ideology gained a tremendous boost with the sudden collapse of the Soviet empire in 1991, which was immediately trumpeted as marking the "end of history" (Fukuyama 1992).

Early business associations and think tanks like the Council on Foreign Relations, the National Association of Manufacturers (NAM), and the Committee on Economic Development (CED) were originally moderate, nonpartisan associations drawing on what they believed was objective social science applied in the broad national interest. They did not think of themselves as representatives of a particular party or social class, although they were elites, and they did share a general belief in growth. The creation of the Business Roundtable in 1971 changed all that. It was specifically designed as a political lobby representing the largest corporations in the country (Judis 2000). The new organizations and the think tanks that they supported were partisan, narrowly self-interested groups. The prominent Heritage Foundation was founded in 1973 "to formulate and promote conservative public policies based on the principles of free enterprise, limited government, individual freedom, traditional American values, and strong national defense" (Johnson, Holmes, and Kirkpatrick 1998). In 2000 it claimed to be "America's most broadly supported think tank," yet it had only 200,000 members and received more than one-fourth of its $28 million income from foundations and corporations. Its board contained three members of billionaire families, including Richard Scaife, and several multimillionaires.

The Trilateral Commission and the World Economic Forum (WEF) were logical global-level extensions of business-centered planning networks developed by American economic elites. These self-selected world leaders openly and unabashedly set about the task of running the world. The Trilateral Commission was created in 1973 by David Rockefeller, then chair of Chase Manhattan Bank, and Zbigniew Brzezinski, President Carter's national security advisor working with other "private citizens" from Japan, North America, and Europe (Sklar 1980b). Its membership consists of some 400 business leaders, academics, and political professionals, as well as labor leaders, but they cannot be active government officials. The results of their private meetings are published as task force reports. For example, one of their books reflects "on the challenges, over the next ten years or so, of managing the international system and of democratic industrialized societies in that system" (Emmott, Watanabe, and Wolfowitz 1997). The World Economic Forum (WEF) is a similar global business think tank whose members are the CEOs of the thousand largest corporations in the world. It originated with a Swiss foundation established in 1970 by business professor Klaus Schwab. The forum held its first meeting of world economic leaders in Davos, Switzerland in 1982, and has held meetings annually since then. The Forum in 2000 brought together 800 corporate CEOs, 200 government leaders, and some 300 specialists. Its global mission is to act "in the spirit of entrepreneurship in the global public interest to further economic growth and social progress . . . by creating partnerships between and among business, political, intellectual and other leaders of society to define, discuss and advance key issues on the global agenda." Global governance was prominent on the WEF agenda during its 2002 meeting in New York.

Wriston, Citicorp, and the Globalization of Finance Capital

In 1970 New York was the center of the global money market and Citibank, soon renamed Citicorp, was the city's largest bank with assets of $26 billion (Leinsdorf and Etra 1973). One man, Walter Bigelow Wriston, who headed Citicorp from 1967 to 1984, has been credited with using his great financial power and personal political influence to initiate the large-scale expansion of private commercial banks into overseas lending, the expansion of consumer credit in the United States, the deregulation of American financial markets, and the leveraged buyout mania (Zweig 1995). These changes rank alongside the creation of the World Bank and the IMF as the key factors giving the global capitalist economy its specific character. These transformations in the financial world reflected Wriston's strong ideological commitment to free market, neoliberal economic ideology. Unfortunately, these changes also contributed to the collapse of 163 Savings and Loan banks in the United States between 1983 and 1988, and the subsequent bailout by the federal government, which may ultimately cost taxpayers more than $1 trillion (Simon 1999, 27–29, 51–58; Waldman 1990). Financial liberalization also helped produce the international debt crises experienced by many countries such as Russia, Thailand, Mexico, Brazil, and Argentina since 1982.

His biographer considered Wriston "the world's most influential banker." He ranks with J.P. Morgan and A.P. Giannini, founder of Bank of America, as the top three twentieth-century bankers for his role in dismantling the regulatory safeguards that Congress had imposed on American financial markets following the great collapse of 1929. Zweig (1995, 1–2) declared, "Using Citicorp as an assault weapon for promulgating free market principles, he blew away many of the archaic rules that prohibited banks from operating across state lines, from competing with Wall Street investment banking houses . . . and built a money machine for Citicorp in the process." Using the language of power, Zweig described Wriston's "combative personality, unchallenged reputation, hardheaded views, force of intellect, hobnail boots, financial muscle," and so forth. Wriston turned Citicorp into a constant state of "turmoil and chaos," even pitting Citicorp bankers against each other. Under his direction Citicorp promoted giant corporate mergers, the automated teller revolution, and the lending to developing countries that helped to create the vast backlog of debt leading the IMF to promote socially destructive structural adjustments around the world. By 1980 Citicorp had become the largest bank in the country.

Wriston was especially well positioned to influence American economic policy. He knew personally all the U.S. secretaries of state from FDR's administration on and was a close friend of George Shultz under Reagan (1982–89). He was also well acquainted with economist Milton Friedman and admired his neoliberal theories. Wriston served on Reagan's Economic Policy Advisory Board and helped design the dramatic tax cuts of the "Reagan Revolution." This supply-side approach, dubbed "Reaganomics," was legitimized by the "Laffer curve" theory that lower taxes would increase federal revenues because the wealthy would invest their tax savings in more growth and benefits would trickle-down to everyone else.

Under Wriston, Citibank began an agressive overseas expansion in 1969. By 1977 overseas activities produced 82 percent of Citibank's profits, and one-third of these profits came from developing countries. The bank's overseas lending program was guided by its assessment of the political risks of social unrest or expropriation that might threaten loan payback. Thus, loans to overseas subsidiaries of American multinationals were preferred. This caused "development" lending to increase dependency on imported capital, imported goods, and imported oil. When oil price increases made loan repayments difficult, banks were forced to renegotiate loans and in the process obtained concessions from the local governments that sometimes carried severe social costs. For example, in 1978, before agreeing to renegotiate loans to the Southern Peru Copper Corporation, which was more than 50 percent owned by an American mining company, the lenders waited until the Peruvian government eliminated an export tax that was used to subsidize food imports for the poor (Mintz and Schwartz 1985, 118, 120–121). Often lenders demanded internal economic changes to increase export production in ways that undermine local self-sufficiency, increasing dependency and lowering living standards for many people. Eventually all of these events constrained the U.S. government's foreign and domestic policies.

Implicit in the elite globalization project Wriston championed was a reduction in the role of national governments in global affairs. The new business-dominated world order envisioned a world system in which "global governance" decisions would increasingly be made by "regimes" operating within "civil society" rather than by governments (Young 1997). This approach to global affairs has the potential of further marginalizing the mass of humanity and further expanding the power of individuals who already play commanding roles in the world of big business. The concept of civil society formally recognizes the decision-making role that elites like Wriston have long quietly assumed as private citizens. Elite planners draw a distinction between international and transnational. International refers to the existing political society of world politics where governments are presumed to be the actors. Transnational refers to the new world of global "civil society" where private citizens, giant corporations, and nonprofit, nongovernmental organizations are the actors. This is the world of transnational business; it is a logical continuation of aggressive reductions in the role of governments under the influence of laissez-faire, neoliberal capitalism. In theory, global *governance* over environmental issues, resources, finance capital, and property rights does not require government. A regime can be any institution such as the World Bank or the WTO, or any set of rules applied to particular issues. However, effective participation in such regimes may be open to only a few. If most citizens already have difficulty influencing the actions of their governments in national and international political society, they will have even greater difficulty being heard in a global civil society where giant corporations are larger than most countries. For example, in 2001, the fourteen largest global corporations received $2 trillion in revenues, which exceeded the U.S. federal budget in 2000 and represented 5 percent of global GDP. The $3 trillion revenues of the twenty-five largest corporations exceeded the GDP of every country in the world except the United States. Those speaking for giant global corporations will be the strongest voices.

9

Beyond 2000: An Optimal-Scale Commercial World

Previous chapters presented abundant evidence that throughout history growth was an elite-driven process that primarily benefited the elite and super-elite few, while the increasing mass of humanity became disempowered in poor and maintenance-level households. This trend only began to be locally and sporadically reversed after about 1950 as a result of political reforms, when liberal democracies in Europe and the United States began to institute policies that redistributed social power to poor and maintenance-level households. This process was facilitated by continued economic globalization that sustained growth and capital accumulation but shifted many of the costs to the rest of the world. This redistribution process also proved reversible when elites were able to reassert conservative political ideologies in combination with neoliberal economic policies. The present chapter assumes that in an optimal-scale commercial world the power of scale would be democratically managed for the maximum human benefit, and it considers what scale limits might be at work as growth thresholds are approached. The concepts of maximum growth thresholds and *optimum* scale for societies, markets, and business enterprises in a commercially organized world are also explored using the United States as an example. The objective is to contrast the globalization strategy that currently dominates policy making with less prominent but more promising policy initiatives that seek to diffuse power and stabilize growth at optimum levels to maximize human well-being. The larger question is the feasibility of implementing smaller-scale alternative cultural designs to diffuse power, strengthen democracy, and improve the quality of life for the maximum number of people.

Scale Thresholds and the Good Life

A society that combined the advantages of small, domestic-scale societies with the benefits of industrial production and commerce to produce a just, sustainable, and rewarding life for the majority would direct growth and development toward a humanly defined optimum scale on all dimensions and would seek to diffuse social power and decision making as widely as possible. Following the lead of political scientist Leopold Kohr (1977), Table 9.1 explores a range of population optimums for such a society in which individuals could satisfy the important goals of humanization, sociability, prosperity, security, and a satisfying cultural life. These are the conditions that allow people to be fully human. They also represent an ideal living standard that people might collectively define as "the good life," the *summum bonum*. When households, neighborhoods, towns, cities, governments, businesses, and markets are at their optimum size, there is no necessary conflict between what is good for individuals and what is good for society. When any of these social structures become either too large or too small, their functionality declines and conflicts of interest between individual and social objectives may emerge. It is important that social units at each scale retain their independence and functionality as growth in total social scale occurs. The danger is that as growth occurs, the power of scale will concentrate too much power in too few hands at higher levels, allowing a few to direct growth in ways that disempower the majority. Lower-level units must combine in loose federations of equally powerful units to form larger social structures rather than being submerged in a larger, centrally controlled whole (Bookchin 1991). For example, a regional economic community centered on a market town could be formed in which the members of independent villages or local communities organized to gain the scale efficiencies of economic specialization and exchange from their own factories and markets. Such small economic communities could then agree to tax themselves to support full-time political specialists such as police, judges, and defense forces in a "national-scale" total society. The larger total society would be large enough to support the additional cultural functions supplied by poets, musicians, artists, and scholars. An optimum-scale society would necessarily be characterized by freedom and democracy, and the effects of social rank and hierarchy would presumably not prevent anyone from enjoying the good life.

Assuming preindustrial technology and renewable solar energy, Kohr's scale ranking of social subsets yields an order-of-magnitude sequence of

Table 9.1

Social Scale and the *Summum Bonum*

Individual objectives	Organization, institutions	Optimum population scale	Post optimum socialized objectives
Humanization reproduction, maintenance	Household	5–25 household	Social health
Sociability companionship	Village clubs, taverns	500 village, community	Social welfare
Prosperity leisure and wealth	Town factories, markets	5,000, town, region	Economic growth GNP
Security security, peace, justice, defense	City courts, city hall, armories	10,000–200,000 city, nation, absolute extended maximum 15 million	Military power Empire
Expressive culture	Metropolis, State theaters, churches, museums, galleries, universities	100,000–200,000 metropolis, nation, technological maximum 15 million	National glory

Source: Data from Kohr 1977.

social units from 5,500, 5,000, 10,000, to 100,000 people. This scale model predicts that under ideal conditions an optimum total society might be attained within a range of 100,000–200,000 people. This sequence corresponds to settlement rankings by powers of ten of household, village, town, city, and metropolis. Growth beyond optimum scale would not add to human happiness and would soon begin to subtract from it as the social costs of increasing scale began to rise. Rather than growing larger under central control, societies can grow and still remain optimally sized by means of segmentation and colonization when territory and resources are available, otherwise growth would stop.

Kohr suggests that costly *size commodities* such as telecommunication devices, computers, cars, and airplanes can stretch the limits of the optimum total society to an absolute optimum of over 10 million people (12 to 15 million), but this would presumably add little to the sum of human happiness. Size commodities simply use technology to provide amenities that would otherwise be easily available face to face, in a smaller society. Kohr observes that the effective mass and social impact of population, like money, is increased by its velocity. The greater movement made possible by technological innovations such as the automobile greatly increases the apparent population problem. This is a scale problem because larger scale produces greater distance between work and home, administrative center and home, producer and consumer. These become *technological distances,* that must be spanned by increasingly expensive technology. With a more pedestrian way of life people would live where they worked, thereby reducing the velocity expenditures of commuting.

The concept of optimum social scale and the folly of using technology to continually raise the growth threshold were anticipated by economist Ralph Borsodi (1929a, 1929b). Writing on the eve of the Great Depression, Borsodi argued that capital-intensive production and distribution systems made it more difficult for most people to obtain "the essentials of normal living," which corresponded to the classical definition of the *summum bonum.* He maintained that most people who worked in factories, earning wages to purchase manufactured goods, experienced a reduced quality of life, but this was a scale problem. Borsodi (1929b, 39) called it a "natural law" that as economic scale increased, otherwise unnecessary scale costs for management, finance, marketing, and transportation would increase faster than the costs of labor and materials. He showed that for many basic subsistence products these unnecessary scale costs actually exceeded primary production costs and consequently left workers far behind. Borsodi thought that many mass-produced goods were nonessential luxuries and argued that it would be more efficient to manufacture labor-saving devices such as sewing machines, washing machines, home refrigerators, pressure-cookers, food grinders, and mixers to support domestic production for household consumption and local markets. Like Kohr, Borsodi's argument focused on the problem of scale and he made the needs of households primary.

Whenever societies grow beyond the social optimum they become *post optimum* societies and begin to experience the negative problems of vulnerability, or criticality, when sudden collapse might occur. In post optimum societies, the humanization, sociability, economic, political, and expressive social functions that individuals need will begin to be compromised, and human freedom and democracy will decline. Criticality sets in motion the crucial transition from societies designed to serve individual needs to those that seem designed to serve the collective needs of society as a whole, with features such as institutionalized social welfare, militarization and warfare, economic growth, and national glory. This transition takes place in ways that may actually undermine individual well-being for the majority. When this happens, benefits will shift disproportionately to the elites who direct the system, and costs will be paid by the majority. When the criticality threshold is crossed the maintenance of society becomes an apparent end in itself, superior to the needs of individuals. Humanization will no longer be the dominant goal of culture, except perhaps for an elite subset of society who use their growing imperia to direct cultural development and enjoy its full benefits. This means that the costs of growth will have been socialized, or collectivized, whereas the rewards will have been narrowly individualized. Perhaps more importantly, it will no longer be possible to define optimum size for social units mobilized to meet collective social goals. National glory has no natural limits, and it is not surprising that national leaders may be viewed as gods.

Kohr's social optimum has seldom if ever been realized except in the tribal world, but this was not because there is anything wrong with Kohr's scale theory. When scale theory is combined with the conceptual tool of the *imperium* it appears that the organization of social power is as important in defining criticality, or the limits of growth, as scale itself. The anthropological and historical record suggests that until now in the history and prehistory of human cultural development only people living in domestically organized tribal societies have managed to stabilize their societies at the optimum to achieve the *summum bonum*. Tribals did so by limiting the scale of society to a maximum tribal world of a few thousand people who could provide each other with economic security at a modest subsistence level. Tribals satisfied their individual needs for sociability, prosperity, security, and expressive culture largely within the sociability unit of 500 people, but more important, they refused to allow politically and economically based imperia to dominate the direction of cultural development. In the real worlds of history, growth in social scale to larger social units was directed by individuals seeking to build ever larger personal imperia. This growth probably did not occur as a result of popular demand, and this made it difficult, if not impossible for the theoretical social optimum to be realized.

Crossing into the political-scale imperial world, where political imperia came to dominate, necessarily required the shift from societies defined by the individualistic optimums of humanization, sociability, prosperity, security, and expressive culture to the collectivist objectives of social welfare, warfare, economic growth, and national glory. This did not occur simply because social growth superseded the theoretical optima. Collectivist social goals such as imperial conquest, nationalism, growth in GNP, and global economic competitiveness were created by the elites who most benefited from these activities. Everyone else needed to be persuaded that these collective goals were in everyone's interests, but this was an expensive proposition. A similar process occurred when giant corporations appeared to become the agents and objectives of growth.

The common explanation for why there should be no cultural limits to the wealth accumulation that created ever larger imperia was that the wealthiest create jobs and are the most beneficial members of society. In his "Wealth and Poverty" mandate for uninhibited capitalism written at the beginning of the longest run of uninterrupted economic growth in American history, George Gilder argued that capitalism was really about gift-giving. He was impressed by "The unending offerings of entrepreneurs, investing capital, creating products, building businesses, inventing jobs, accumulating inventories. . . ." He took this to be "the vital impulse and moral center of capitalism" (Gilder 1982, 30). This led him to conclude that "Entrepreneurs must be allowed to retain wealth for the practical reason that only they, collectively, can possibly know where it should go, to whom it should be given." Sociologist Thorstein Veblen, writing in 1899 from a different perspective, concluded that wealth accumulation was driven by competitive pecuniary emulation between individuals seeking superior distinction, or esteem (Veblen 1994). Veblen argued that wealth had to be displayed by conspicuous leisure and conspicuous consumption. As he explained, "In order to gain and hold the esteem of men it is not sufficient merely to possess wealth or power. The wealth or power must be put in evidence, for esteem is awarded only on evidence" (Veblen 1994, 36–37). This is surely not a morally superior motivation, and those driven exclusively by such objectives may not be the best directors of cultural development. However, the particular motivation of individual elites is irrelevant. What matters are the human consequences of elite-directed growth.

Elites used fossil fuel–based technologies to lift scale thresholds, but this was a dangerous and costly choice. It was not a law of nature that per capita energy consumption would increase by orders of magnitude, or that a few giant corporations would monopolize energy resources. It was also not inevitable that petroleum would be used in a capital- and energy-intensive way to distribute food and basic necessities in a global-scale market. Economic growth based on the fossil fuel revolution cannot continue indefinitely because fossil fuels are being consumed faster than nature produces them. Given known reserves, continued production at the 1997 rate would totally exhaust the world supply of petroleum by 2039, even earlier than previously predicted (Hubbert 1969; Barney 1977). Finding more reserves will not change the order of magnitude of these projections. Even using an endless supply of petroleum resources would be problematic because it would accelerate global warming from the greenhouse effect. Even with no global warming, an infinite source of energy would only temporarily lift the technological limits to growth, because at a 5 percent annual increase in global energy use, world energy production would produce waste heat equal to solar warming, effectively cooking the earth within 200 years (Luten 1974). In any event, the present leaders of the world's great petroleum corporations are already anticipating another transformation, as indicated by the remarks of Mike Bowlin, CEO of ARCO, in 1999: "We've embarked on the beginning of the Last Days of the Age of Oil" (Brown 2000, 12).

Small Scale in Colonial New England

The social power significance of scale in a commercially organized society, and the appeal of growth, can be illustrated by a brief look at the very first New England colonies. In spite of their idealized image in American folklore, the puritan settlers transplanted a highly stratified social structure to America, but it was such a small society, and so democratic, and the total income was so low that even the most successful families could accumulate relatively little wealth and property within a single lifetime. The entire population of Massachusetts colony contained fewer than 100,000 people until after 1720, and most people lived in relatively small, rather isolated, and highly self-provisioning agrarian settlements. The small size of the Puritan society and total wealth meant that the differences in absolute power between the rich and poor were not as great as among their contemporaries in Stuart England. There was pervasive inequality, as shown by property inventories recorded in Plymouth in 1652, where the range from poorest to richest was £3 to £375 (Demos 1970, 37). The poorest would still have ranked as paupers in England, but the richest would have reached only the lower gentry elite. A census conducted in the Massachusetts town of Bristol in the year 1689 showed a proportional distribution of household well-being closely resembling the modern situation three centuries later (Demos 1970, 194). However, in comparison with Stuart England there was proportionately far less poverty and a much larger maintenance-level population in Bristol than in England. There was also a larger elite. Clearly, many people were significantly better off in America than in England at the same time, even though social inequality remained strong. The difference was scale—in the total size of society, the absence of large cities, the small absolute size of the economy, and the strength of democratic, local self-government. It is also significant that in a small-scale society such as Bristol in 1689, the poor were not destitute. They were either living independently in their own households or they were incorporated as dependents within more prosperous households.

A close look at the demography of people living in the colonial township of Andover, a few miles north of Boston, shows that where land distribution was equitable and urban growth was minimized, prosperity could be widely diffused (Greven 1970). The forty original Andover household heads received house lots according to their social status, but the size range was narrow. The minimum allotment was set at four acres and the maximum at twenty. Over the four generations of Andover residents covered by town records from 1650 to 1800, people prospered. Growth occurred, but it was limited. The town's population grew from 435 in 1680 to a peak of just under 3,000 in 1776. The first three generations proved to be healthier, longer-lived, and produced larger, more stable families than their counterparts in England at the same time. There were clearly human advantages to life in small-scale societies.

The Growth-Maximizing Nation: How America Overshot the Optimum

In 1790, a small group of national elites led by President George Washington, Secretary of State Thomas Jefferson, Treasury Secretary Alexander Hamilton, and the 128 senators and representatives in the federal legislature began to frame the growth policies that would determine the future of the newly independent United States of America. As national goals, the elites might have chosen any of four future American nations: (1) small-scale agrarian; (2) small-scale industrial; (3) large-scale agrarian; or (4) large-scale industrial (Figure 9.1). The small-scale agrarian alternative was the actual 1790 population of 4 million people with a per capita income of $1,163 and a $5 billion national income in 1990 dollars. The small-scale industrial alternative would raise per capita income to 1990 values of $18,695, producing an order-of-magnitude increase in national income to $75 million. The large-scale agrarian alternative would increase population to the 1990 population of 250 million. Per capita income would remain constant, but national income would again increase to $290 million. The large-scale industrial alternative would require scale increases in population to 250 million and in national income to $5 trillion, while per capita income would remain at $18,695. The total economy would have increased under each option by scale ranks from a baseline of $5 billion in 1790, to $75 billion, $290 billion, and $5 trillion. The difference in per capita income between the agrarian and industrial economy from thousands of dollars to more than ten thousand dollars represents a significant material improvement in living standards above the 1790 level, but it is a modest mathematical average improvement compared to the gains enjoyed by the top elites. Furthermore, under a "natural" lognormal income distribution only a few would enjoy the benefits of such growth

The growth alternative chosen by the nation's leaders was, of course, the large scale industrial option. This gave maximum legal and political advantage to the largest, most capital and energy intensive, corporately organized business enterprises, mass production, and mass distribution. Such a course

Figure 9.1 **Outcomes of American Growth Options, 1790–1990**

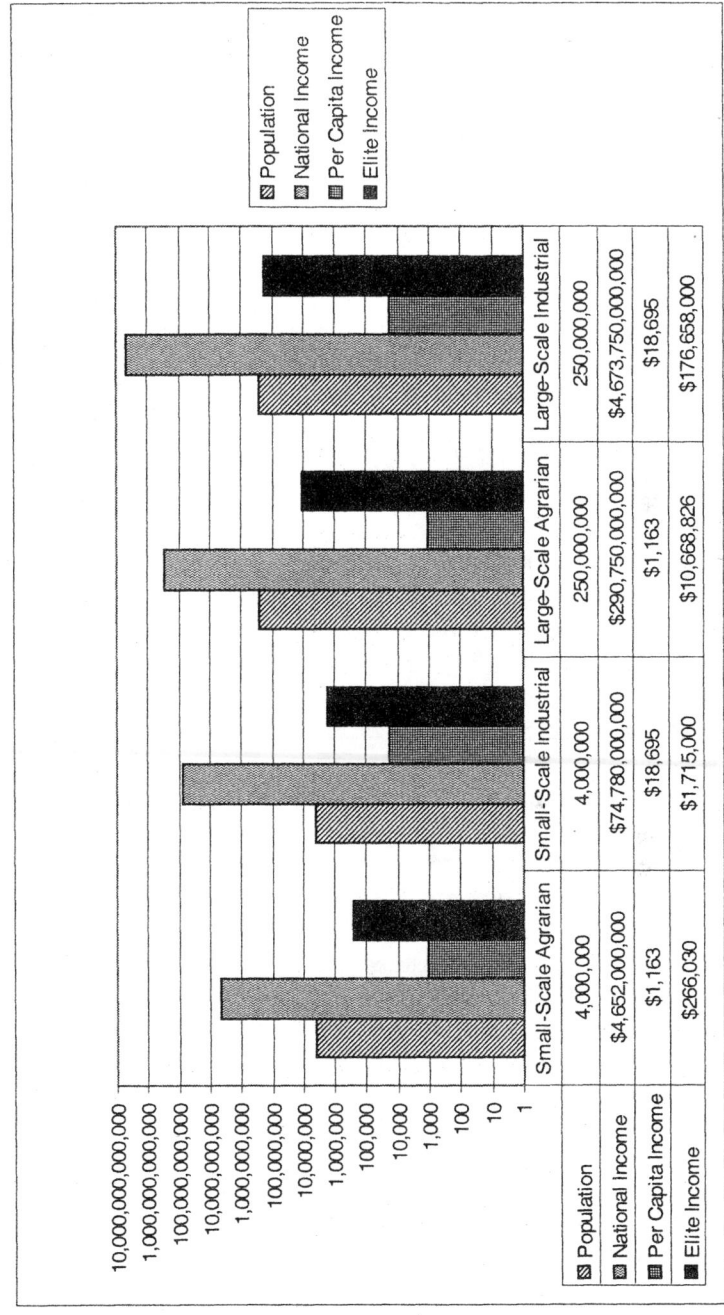

maximized total wealth and wealth concentration, but did not necessarily "promote the general welfare," which, according to its Preamble, was the objective of the U.S. Constitution. The evidence presented in Chapter 6 shows that the maximum growth alternative did not just happen as a natural, evolutionary unfolding; it was deliberately legislated and adjudicated, and required the intentional exercise of political and financial power. It seems likely that America's political and commercial leaders chose this growth path, not because it was inevitable, and not because everyone wanted it, but because maximum growth produced the largest total economy and from the very beginning brought the highest return to the top decision-makers and for those who would share the top positions in the future.

If we assume a constant 1990 distribution of power, each growth alternative would show order-of-magnitude improvements in the average income for the top 2,000 households from $266,030 to $176,658,000. This would have resulted from the mathematical effects of a top elite of 2,000 receiving a constant share of an increasing volume of total national income. The small-scale industrial nation would have been more beneficial for the average American than the large-scale industrial option because more people could have been independent business owner-managers. The very best alternative would have been an intentionally more equitable distribution pattern of social power, rather than "natural" inequity, but this would not have brought extraordinary benefits to the decision makers. In fact, American society was transformed from a modestly prosperous collection of small-scale, rural, agrarian, and largely self-provisioning local and regional societies, operating as an appendage of a London-based global political economy, into a maximum-scale, urban, industrial, nationally organized society at the very center of the global commercial economy. Along the way, the elite had to totally transform America's institutional structures of law, politics, property, business, and finance, as well as the transportation infrastructure, the energy base, productive technology, food system, and the social support system. What did not change was the power structure or the distribution of social power to households. By 1998 there were many more, very wealthy people at the very top of society, but a great many more who were poor. As noted in Chapter 2, there were some 3.5 million American millionaires by 1998, but 35 million people were officially considered poor. Thirty-five million was the entire population of the United States in 1865.

Imperia and the Scale of Business: When Is Big Too Big?

Throughout the political reforms of the Roosevelt era and during the immediate postwar period while progressivist thinking still predominated in the

U.S. government, there was a broad consensus that business could become too big and that monopoly power was a threat to both democracy and small businesses. Several federal investigations of economic concentration undertaken during this period, such as by the "Study of Monopoly Power" Subcommittee of the House Judiciary Committee begun in 1949, assumed that the objective of business activity was to keep markets competitive and maximize benefits for communities and small business people in local and regional markets. This view contrasted sharply with the beliefs of many in the big business community, such as business analyst John Moody, who opposed antitrust regulation. Moody declared in 1904 that Morgan and Rockefeller were not responsible for monopoly power. Monopolies were products of a "natural law" and were essential to progress. Furthermore, he believed economic concentration was unstoppable. In striking contrast to such apologists for big business, on the first day of the House Judiciary Committee hearings on monopoly power in 1949, Attorney General Tom C. Clark stated emphatically: "Monopoly handcuffs the individual and enchains democracy. It is a tool of totalitarianism" (United States, House Committee on the Judiciary 1949, 93). Clark was also certain that monopoly was not natural, stating that "Monopolies and cartels don't just happen. They are carefully conceived and nourished by those who would substitute private control for competition" (1949, 93).

President Truman reiterated his endorsement of the findings of the Temporary National Economic Committee in 1938–1941, declaring that "one of the gravest threats to our welfare lay in the increasing concentration of power in the hands of a small number of giant organizations" (United States, House Committee on the Judiciary 1949, 68–69). Truman expressed great concern that economic concentration had been encouraged by the war effort, and he specifically advocated decentralization of industry, emphasizing: "We must assure small business the freedom and opportunity to grow and prosper. To this purpose, we should strengthen our antitrust laws by closing those loopholes that permit monopolistic mergers and consolidations" (1949, 69). The 1949 committee considered the case of Safeway Stores, which between 1940 and 1947 had grown by downward vertical expansion into its suppliers, acquiring twelve meatpacking companies, fifteen cheese companies, eight butter firms, a bakery company, and a gelatin company. Horizontally it bought three supermarket chains operating 966 smaller groceries. Likewise, General Foods acquired forty-three other packaged food manufacturers between 1925 and 1946. All of these acquisitions took economic power away from local communities.

During the war the Special Senate Committee to Study Problems of American Small Business commissioned an in-depth ethnographic study of the effects of big business on civic welfare in six American cities with populations from 30,000 to 150,000 people (Mills and Ulmer 1946). The big-business cities were dominated by a few large manufacturing corporations, each with thousands of employees working in a few industries, whereas small-business cities had numerous small businesses, each with fewer than 200 employees working in diverse areas of the economy. Employment conditions were more stable in the small-business cities, there was less labor conflict, the economy was overall more balanced and stable, the middle class was larger, more were self-employed, and the gap between very rich and poor was smaller. Big-business cities experienced more boom-and-bust real estate cycles. Retail sales per capita were higher in small-business cities, because more locally produced goods and services were available, and local people were better able to buy. Furthermore, civic welfare, measured by public health and sanitation, infant mortality, and public expenditures on libraries, education, parks, and recreation, was substantially higher in small business cities. Housing was also less crowded in small-business cities, there was more home ownership, and there were more telephones and electricity and fewer slums.

The researchers attributed the superior civic welfare of small-business cities to the presence of a stronger middle class of independent business people who derived social status from the local community and wanted it to prosper. The problem with big-business cities was that they were politically and economically dominated by the officials of externally owned corporations who had no long-term interest in the local community. They could exert control by threatening to close down the factory, refusing to support civic projects they disapproved of, or by gaining personal influence over local business leaders. Perhaps most telling, the report concluded that "in big-business cities, dominated by large absentee-owned firms, money in large quantities is siphoned out to other parts of the country" (Mills and Ulmer 1946, 13).

Antitrust hearings continued in the Senate from 1957 to 1963 under the direction of Senator Estes Kefauver (1965), who sought relentlessly to expose the social costs of economic concentration and the advantages of fostering small business and genuinely "free" enterprise. However, by the mid-1960s, the pro–small business climate was beginning to weaken. Significantly, the 1964 Senate Judiciary Subcommittee on Antitrust and Monopoly held hearings on the Concentration of Economic Power, rather than "Monopoly Power." Senator Philip A. Hart opened the hearings with his observation that many small- and medium-sized business people were complaining that increasing economic concentration was making it more difficult for them to compete in the marketplace. Paradoxically, he was careful to note that *economic concentration,* not "bigness," was the issue. Nevertheless, the legitimacy of holding any hearings on economic power was immediately challenged by Senator Hruska, who thought that such hearings were a "wild goose chase" because economic concentration was a complex and confusing topic. He also suggested that such hearings might weaken public confidence in the "private" enterprise system, causing doubt and suspicion (United States, Senate Committee on the Judiciary 1964, 1–6). These hearings did not lead to legislation to halt the trend toward greater concentration.

In 1972 Ralph Nader's "Study Group Report on Antitrust Enforcement" (Green, Moore, and Wasserstein 1972) referred to the U.S. economy as a "closed-enterprise system," describing it as monopoly capitalism and corporate socialism, meaning that an elite few were managing the economy as a collective. Citing government figures, they reported that by 1967 the hundred largest manufacturing corporations already controlled nearly half of all corporate manufacturing assets, which was more than 200 corporations controlled in 1950. This trend continued until by 1993 the 100 largest industrial corporations had 69 percent of assets. The Nader report concluded that "a veritable revolution against citizens had occurred that was costing people billions of dollars from antitrust violations, price-fixing, and 'price-leadership' exercised by large corporations." Entry costs into markets already dominated by such concentrated power were so high that meaningful competition was virtually excluded. The report also noted that joint ventures between already giant corporations, the presence of interlocking management and directors, and connections between the largest banks and other large corporations made it even easier for economic concentration to be turned into control over the market. Government regulators in the Justice and Commerce Departments were also easily swayed to favor big business. The report did not suggest that this was a conspiracy to set prices and control the market, but rather that "an elaborate cue system for prices and interest rates which do not require meetings . . . condition[s] response, with only occasional explicit coordination required" (Green, Moore, and Wasserstein 1972, viii). The Nader report estimated that monopoly power cost Americans $60 billion, but by 1996 the cost may have grown to $2.6 trillion (Estes 1996).

In spite of the obvious political triumph of American big business after 1950, there was little evidence that the large conglomerate firms that had aggregated thousands of small factories and service industries from all over the country under a few directors had actually improved overall productivity. Jewkes (1960) found that after 150 years of industrial expansion, most factories, but not the corporate businesses that owned and directed them, still remained small, suggesting that economies of scale in productive units had already been reached. Between 1914 and 1939 there was very little change in the size of factories. Most industrial production could be efficiently conducted with firms of "quite moderate size" (Robinson 1960, xvii).

Before market globalization became a dominant ideology after 1980, there was also considerable doubt that larger-scale markets were actually better. An international conference held in 1957 to consider the potential of expanded international common markets concluded that that the argument for greater economic integration between nations was "not overwhelmingly conclusive" (Robinson 1960). Even as markets expanded, governments would still be needed to continue independently regulating national monetary policy, employment, and social welfare. It was argued that countries with populations as small as 10 to 15 million people could sustain all but a few heavy transportation industries, and that a nation of 50 million could gain market efficiencies to support all forms of production. However, these heavy industries would be needed primarily to produce the "size commodities" that Kohr referred to, and thus there would not be obvious human advantages. Gains in larger markets were more likely due to monopoly power.

A crucial problem that neoliberal economic theory overlooked was the way personal imperia allowed individuals to combine power from different domains, creating unique power-building opportunities for super-elites. This power accumulation process involves what earlier reformers identified as the problem of interlocking directories. Power networks of this sort necessarily involved a conflict of interest for the person playing multiple roles, and offered many opportunities for corruption and abuse of power that were magnified when the regulatory role of government was reduced under the influence of neoliberal theory. Interlocking directories, where the same individual sits on the boards of multiple corporations, afford individuals an opportunity to coordinate the activities of several businesses and thereby manage markets. Board members representing banks and other large institutional investors such as insurance companies or retirement funds may play crucial roles in directing the flow of finance capital between giant corporations (Ussem 1984; Mintz and Schwartz 1985).

In their comprehensive survey of director interlocks among *Fortune* 500 companies, Mintz and Schwartz (1985) found that in 1962, 998 out of 1,131 companies were joined together within a single vast network that connected most members within three links. Banking companies averaged 25 interlocks, whereas industrial companies averaged only 8.8. Because financial companies had so many interlocks and because they both sent and received so many top executives, Mintz and Schwartz concluded that the interlock system "reflects and consolidates financial hegemony" (1985, 151). Big banks are very attractive boards to serve on, because they are quite literally the center of the financial action, the source of the major flows of capital. The network "allows banks to appropriate the firsthand knowledge, information, and expertise of the chief executive officers of major corporations" (1985, 152–153). The role of outside directors is so important that they call them "business diplomats." Companies gain other advantages through joint ventures and mergers. The bigger the company, or the greater its assets, the more interlocks it is likely to have. "These results reveal that a handful of centrally placed financial institutions have dominated capital-investment decision making for decades. They directly control a significant proportion of all stock that changes hands; they lead a majority of lending consortia; and they are involved in almost half of all large financial holdings in major nonfinancial firms." Banks are the primary hubs, the central institutions at the center of several linked companies. Insurance companies tend to form bridges between different hubs.

Mintz and Schwartz believe that the power structure of American business is only loosely coordinated but serves the interests of the largest financial institutions. They conclude that the tendency is toward cooperation and coordination rather than competition among leaders of the dominant financial companies. The power of the large banks comes from their ability to alter the capital flows that influence corporate decision making.

In a few cases enormous economic and political power have been combined in a single family imperium. The Rockefeller family empire received careful public scrutiny in 1974 when Nelson Rockefeller was appointed by President Ford to serve as his vice president after the resignation of President Nixon. The issue considered by House and Senate hearings was whether his great personal wealth and his family's complex interconnection with the nation's largest corporations, foundations, and political interests would constitute a conflict of interest. In his public disclosure statement Rockefeller declared that he and his wife were worth $229 million (Kutz 1974) but the family's total interests were in the billions of dollars. Part of the family wealth was managed jointly as Rockefeller Family and Associates. Rockefeller family office manager J. Richardson Dilworth explained that the phrase "Rockefeller Family and Associates" was a name for the 84 descendants of John D. Jr. and the 154 staff people and miscellaneous other employees who worked for the family on three floors of the RCA building at 30 Rockefeller Plaza in New York City. This office provided family members with investment, tax, public relations, travel, messenger, and legal services, and maintained a library and cafeteria. The financial management section of the office had separate divisions for standard investments, venture capital, and real estate. The specialists working in these divisions referred to the family members as "clients," but Dilworth explained that they were actually their employers. Dilworth argued that the family members were simply "investors." They were not interested in "controlling" anything, and did not act in concert on financial matters. As he explained, "Our aim is to obtain satisfactory investment results for our clients over time."

At that time Rockefeller family interests cross-cut all major areas of the economy. Fifteen members of the family office held 118 directorships on ninety-seven major corporate boards, including ten with assets of more than $1 billion. More troubling was the blending of public and private interests. Nelson gave large interest-free loans, which often turned into gifts, to a number of people who moved back and forth between public offices and positions in the family office or other family-supported enterprises. Such gifts may have been legal, but their ambiguous nature made the recipient a client. Nelson used tax-exempt foundations in ways that benefited his political campaigns. He provided much of the funding for the New York Republican party, and served as party head while he ran for office. Nelson's imperium was such a web of personal and private activities that it was virtually impossible to monitor effectively. Under close questioning by the congressional committee, Nelson insisted that he was a good person who took the oath of office seriously and therefore "so far as I am concerned, there would be no conflict of interest" (U.S. Congress 1974, 65–66). To affirm his lack of self-interest, he mentioned that while representing the president on a recent tour of Latin America, protestors firebombed all eighteen of his family-owned IBEC supermarkets in Argentina and sixteen were totally destroyed, but this did not deter him from "holding the American flag high." When pressed further that great concentrations of personal wealth might threaten democracy, Nelson declared that Congress could pass laws to protect the people, but if he became president he would have had veto power. This highlights the human problem whereby a personal imperium that can harness the power of scale can frustrate controls that rely on personal trust and good intentions.

The collapse of the energy giant Enron corporation in 2002 revealed a similar tangled web of overlapping personal imperia connecting numerous individual donors, political party officials, lobbyists, government officials, corporate officials, shareholders, and members of conservative policy organizations. Some individuals played multiple roles. Enron was the seventh largest American *Fortune* 500 corporation, with stated revenues of $100 billion. Enron corporate officers had lavished political donations on 71 senators and 187 representatives and given abundantly to both political parties. Enron officials had previously cultivated close relationships with the Clinton administration (Allison 2002). Enron CEO Kenneth Lay personally donated $166,500 toward George W. Bush's Texas gubernatorial and presidential campaigns and was one of his top fund raisers. Lay was also on the American Enterprise Institute board. Employees of Arthur Andersen, the accounting firm that worked for Enron, had contributed over $200,000 to Bush since 1998, and spent $25,000 on his inaugural as Texas governor (Dunbar and Heller 2002). Officials in the Bush administration with connections to Enron included Secretary of the Army Thomas White, a former Enron vice chairman; U.S. Trade Representative Robert Zoellick, who served on Enron's Advisory Council and held Enron stock; and National Economic Council Director Lawrence Lindsey, who was a paid consultant for Enron. Fourteen of the top 100 Bush officials owned Enron stock, including Bush's top advisor, Karl Rove, who owned more than $100,000 in Enron stock (Wetherell 2002a). U.S. Senator Phil Gramm's wife, Wendy Gramm, was an Enron director. She was also a director of Archer Daniels Midland, "supermarket to the world," and IBP, perhaps the world's largest meat processor, and was previously a member of the Commodities Futures Trading Commission and of the Regulatory Affairs Committee of the White House Office of Management and Budget (Krebs 2002). Wendy Gramm also directed the Regulatory Studies Program at the George Mason University Mercatus Center and chaired the Texas Public Policy Foundation, a Texas version of the Heritage Foundation, which was also closely linked with President Bush Jr., who was a member of its advisory board. Texas multimillionaire James Leininger, who founded Texas Public Policy, was also an important Bush donor. The chairman of the Republican National Committee was simultaneously a professional lobbyist with a Texas law firm and personally represented Enron (Lewis 2001). At the same time, twenty-two top White House officials were significant shareholders of thirty-three separate corporations that were lobbying the government for special benefits (Wetherell 2002b).

President Bush, Vice President Cheney, and the cabinet secretaries were all global super-elite multimillionaires, with average net worths ranging from $9.3 to $27.3 million (Wetherell 2002b). Bush himself was worth more than $27 million, and the wealthiest cabinet member, Deputy Commerce Secretary Samuel Bodman, was worth anywhere from $49 to $164 million based on his public disclosure statement. The cumulative net worth of these sixteen top officials was between $149 and $434 million, which was an order of magnitude greater than that of former President Clinton and his cabinet, some of whom may not have been millionaires and whose cumulative net worth was between $14.5 and $45.9 million. Most cabinet members had left companies, or still owned stock in companies, that were either actively lobbying the government for special interests or already held important government contracts.

In a curious twist on capitalist ideology, some theorists cite Hayek (1960), Berle and Means (1933), and other well-credentialed capitalists to argue that giant limited liability corporations weaken the core capitalist values of private property, individualism, and personal freedom and responsibility because they evade social responsibility, separate ownership from control, diffuse ownership into tiny shares among dispersed owners, and concentrate too much power (van Eeghen 1997). The assumption of corporate personality is the basis for these anticapitalist features of corporations because it allows both shareholders and managers to escape responsibility for corporate actions, separating self-interest from social interest and reducing competition. This makes it difficult for the "invisible hand" of the market to operate in ways that actually benefit society. Furthermore, because the state protects corporations and often provides them with large subsidies—whereas society at large bears the costs—a political economy dominated by giant corporations could legitimately be called "corporate socialism."

Market Scale and Social Power in American Urban Places

A careful look at how growth in the scale of American markets and businesses influences the distribution of social power demonstrates dramatically that elite-directed growth did not benefit the majority of society and helps explain why not. In 2000 there were more than 19,000 incorporated urban places in the United States, but marketers considered only about a thousand business centers to be worthy of rating by their market power (Rand McNally 2002). Marketers calculated the scale, or power, of a market as a weighted proportion of total American disposable income (.5), retail sales (.3), and population (.2). For example, Montpelier, Vermont, with 8,000 people and only $158 million in disposable income, was one of the smallest business centers in the country, with a market power rating of 3.3. New York City, with 8 million people and $172 billion in disposable income, was at the top, with a market power rating of 2,658. In a commercial society such as the United States, where growth is a supreme value, it might be expected that increases in the scale of important measures of growth, as reflected in a city's market power, would significantly elevate income and wealth for the majority of households. However, the opposite seems to have been the case because by itself market power is not concerned with the human effects of the distribution of disposable income among households and is thus a poor measure of how well a given society does at providing for human needs. Very high market power can exist along with very low quality of life for most citizens.

Figure 9.2 arranges five American business center cities by order-of-magnitude differences in their market power from Montpelier (3) to New York (2,658), showing scale increases in population, total disposable income, and retail sales all paralleling scale increases in the market. These parallel increases are to be expected because market power is a product of these variables. Significantly, however, both per capita income and median household income vary only slightly and erratically across all scales, remaining basically flat. Aggregate income growth keeps pace with population expansion, but no dramatic improvement occurs in median or per capita income. A stagnant median income means that even as the total economy expands with increases in market scale, the *majority* receive little if any income benefit. This income pattern cross-cutting market scales also holds true for median income in the country as a whole across more than two decades of market globalization between 1970 and 1998, when median income in constant 1998 dollars fluctuated up and down between $34,471 and $38,885, ending up slightly, but showing no clear upward trend. The possibility that this absence of any broad sharing of the benefits of growth either over time, or by growth concentrated in particular places, is a sampling error is dispelled by Figure 9.3, which plots market power and median income for 138 business centers in 2000. The absence of improvement in median income is strikingly obvious across all of these market centers of different scale. Like other forms of social power, median household income is lognormally distributed by place. Over half of the median incomes are below the average median value of $31,735, whereas only one center, Bellevue, Washington, with a market power of only 69, had a median exceeding $50,000. This conspicuous concentration of income was primarily associated with the nearby presence of Microsoft, and the benefits were not widely diffused.

At the national level growth in per capita income did occur between 1970 and 1998, but the average mathematically available to households was significantly higher than the median household income because the real beneficiaries of growth were found in the upper end of the power distribution. Figure 9.4 graphs the net worth of the wealthiest individuals (Berentson 2002) by market scale in ninety-eight market centers. At this level in the social power hierarchy there are striking order-of-magnitude increases in net worth that do correspond to increases in the scale of market power. Clearly there is a growth trend here, but again, it was not widely shared. Looking at these charts, it is difficult to see why the majority would apparently believe so strongly in the beneficial effects of growth.

Growth benefits are unlikely to be widely shared because larger markets necessarily focus on the needs of larger businesses. In order for markets to increase in scale they must shift from serving the domestic needs of people to serving the needs of commerce itself. For example, marketers viewed the United States as 47 major market areas and 487 basic market areas, and distinguished more than one thousand principle urban and suburban business centers (Rand McNally 2002). The major markets were large tributary areas of different size centered on one or more national or regional principle

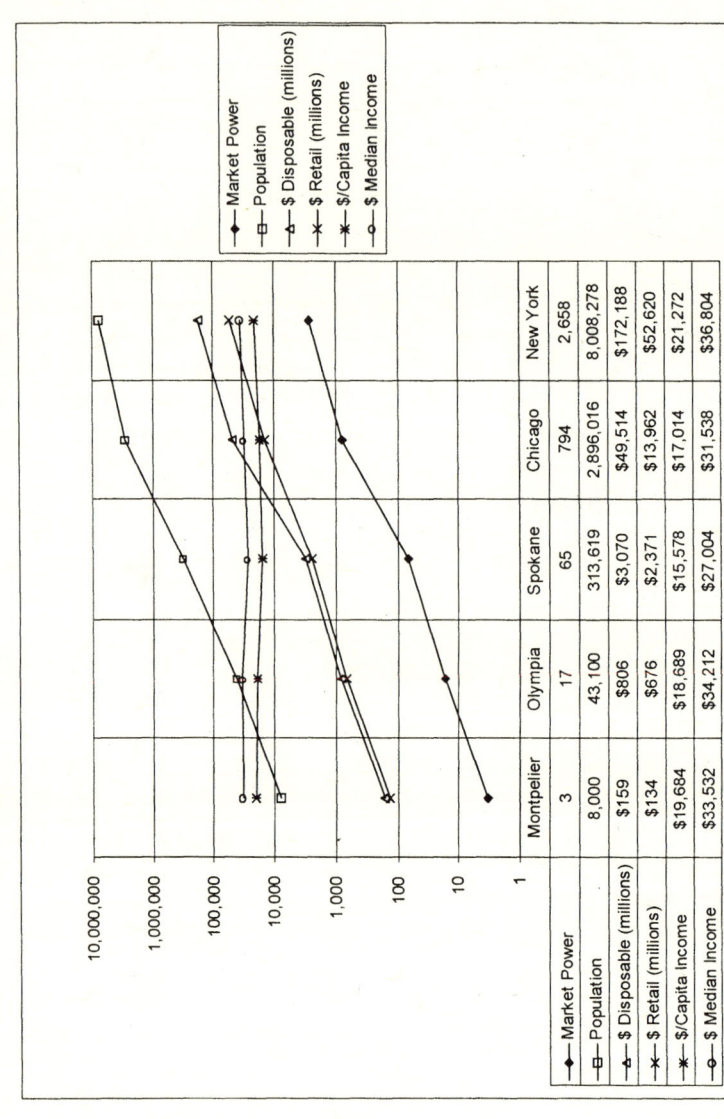

Figure 9.2 Correlates of Market Power in Sample American Business Centers, 2000

Source: Rand McNally 2002.

Figure 9.3 **Median Income and Market Power in Principle American Business Centers, 2000**

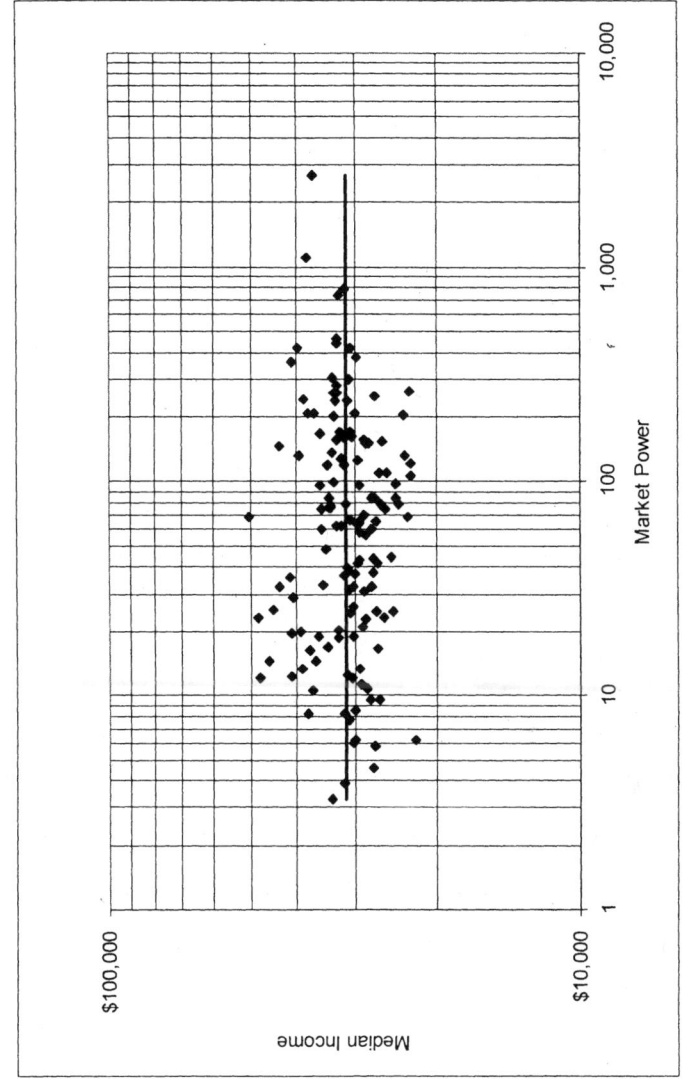

Source: Rand McNally 2002.

256

Figure 9.4 **Market Power and Net Worth of the Wealthiest Person in Principle Market Centers, 2000**

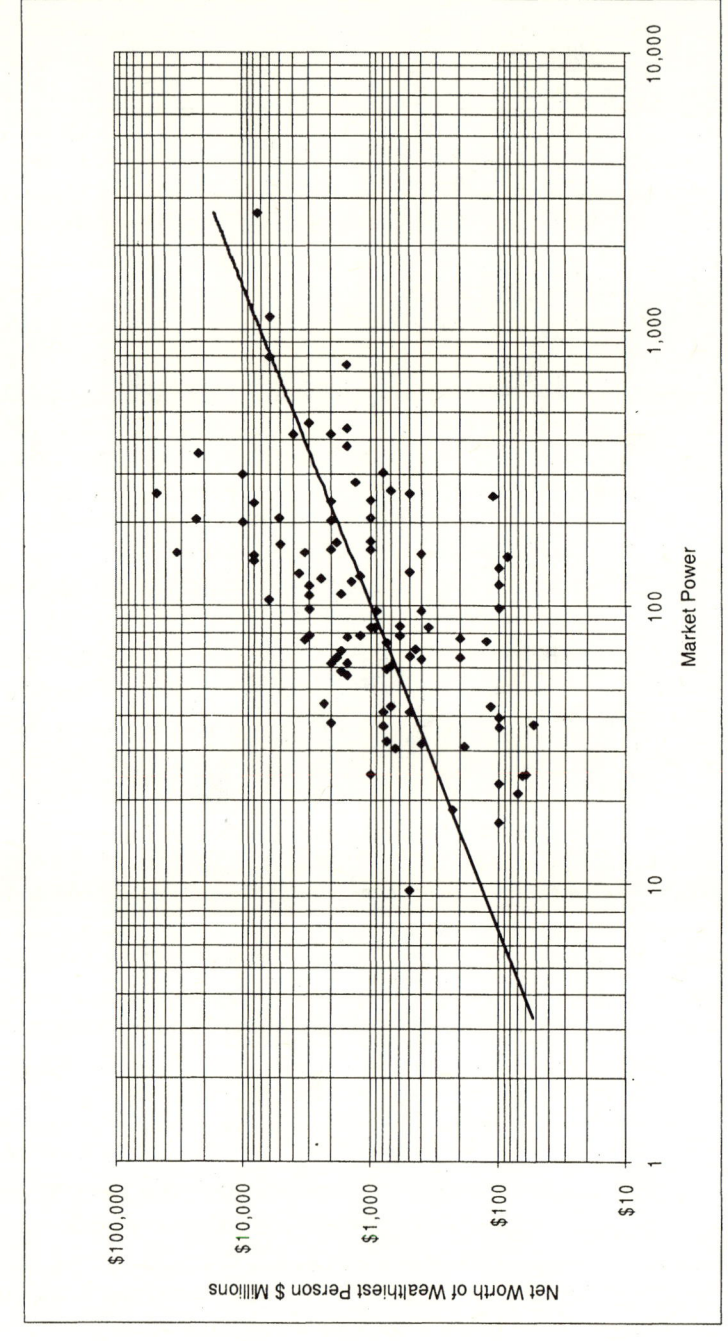

Sources: Berentson 2002; Rand McNally 2002.

business centers engaged in large-scale wholesaling, retailing, banking, and advertising activities, whereas the basic market areas were smaller retail shopping markets. Increases in market power correspond to profound changes in the geographic reach of the largest businesses located in the largest centers. Significantly, in 2001 overall market power was skewed in a typical lognormal distribution such that the five most powerful major market areas (New York, Los Angeles–San Diego, Dallas–Fort Worth, San Francisco–Oakland–San Jose, and Chicago) had about one-third of the national population, disposable income, retail sales, and overall market power. At the national level the economic power of New York City and its immediate suburbs was overwhelming. New York controlled the largest major market area, the largest basic trading area, and was the largest urban business center. There were eighty headquarters of *Fortune* 500 corporations in New York City and its immediate vicinity. In 2001 the eighty largest *Fortune* 500 companies accounted for approximately $3.7 trillion in business revenues, which was 20 percent of the $18 trillion in total business revenues in the country in 1997. This immense economic power was directed by a few major corporate executives, who of course received a disproportionate benefit.

The human advantages of small-scale markets and small businesses can be demonstrated by the distribution of social power in urban places in the state of Washington. Washington became a state in 1889 when its population was about 350,000 people, and it grew rapidly to nearly 6 million people by 2000. Washington is well known as a global center for high-tech industries and is home to some of the world's wealthiest individuals. Washington's growth produced a hierarchy of urban places with five cities of over 100,000 people and clearly shows scale trends toward great concentrations of personal wealth and commercial power, accompanied by only small declines in the number officially considered poor. Official poverty levels are significantly lower than the "maintenance level" used in the present analysis. In 1980 there were 538,000 official poor and 512,000 in 1998, mostly concentrated in the largest urban centers. These growth trends are also reflected in a decline in home ownership rates, more concentrated property ownership and business power in larger urban places, as well as unusual aggregations of elite households in a few select places (Bodley 1999b, 2001b).

Careful comparisons of the number of households at poor, maintenance, and elite levels of well-being in urban places of increasing scale in 1990 showed that the number of poor households increased at a faster rate than elites. This parallels the general trend in the distribution of social power at national and global levels examined in Chapter 8. It is likely that an important cause of these trends was the concentration of social power that accompanied growth in scale. In one region, the largest individual property owner in an urban metropolis of over 100,000 people owned nearly as much property as 10,200 people in twenty local villages. In 1998 the eleven multimillionaires and billionaires in Washington were worth $102 billion. At a 10 percent return on net worth they could have received personal income equal to more than 6 percent of all personal income in the state in 1998. As larger businesses emerged in larger urban places, they captured a progressively disproportionate share of total sales volume. In the largest places, fewer than 3 percent of businesses received more than 80 percent of revenues. Larger businesses in larger places were also more likely to be externally owned. Scale itself was the dominant *natural* determinant of such economic concentration. Fewer than ten giant corporations with revenues in the billion-dollar range accounted for nearly half of all business revenues in the largest urban places, whereas in cities ranging in size from 10,000 to under 100,000, an average of fewer than ten businesses with revenues of $100 million and over dominated nearly half of all business revenues. In towns and villages of under 10,000 people the few dominant businesses had revenues of $10 million and over. It was only in Washington's few villages that did not experience rapid growth that small businesses with revenues of under $500 thousand predominated. In these small business villages, property and income were most equitably distributed and home ownership rates were the highest in the state. Unlimited growth may not be a desirable policy anywhere if growth within a single American state disproportionately benefits a few cities, businesses, and households.

The Indigenous People Challenge

The persistence of no-growth tribal peoples into the twenty-first century with their relatively egalitarian social systems still intact demonstrates that perpetual growth is not inevitable, and offers a model of successful small-scale corporate communities operating democratically in support of the humanization process. Many contemporary tribal peoples self-identify as "indigenous peoples" to call attention to their connection with their ancestral territory, language, and culture. They have a self-consciousness of themselves as a distinct people with a distinct way of life that sets them apart from dominant national societies and the global commercial culture. Indigenous peoples are not merely ethnic groups; they are corporate groups with a strong sense of self-identity who occupy a common territory and seek to maximize their political autonomy and economic self-sufficiency. They typically manage their natural resources as a common property, making decisions by consensus. Virtually all indigenous people live at the nonmonetary equivalent of a maintenance level, even though many have minimal cash incomes. Tribals are not poor as long as they remain in control of their territory and its natural resources. These people offer a clear challenge to the commercial superelites who would prefer to run global civil society as a single company town.

In 1987 there were an estimated 200 million indigenous people living in some 400,000 distinct, low-density communities scattered worldwide on the fringes of the global commercial economy in the rural areas of North and South America, Africa, Asia, and the Pacific. Throughout the twentieth century indigenous people worldwide managed to struggle back from the brink of almost certain total annihilation and were able to gain widespread recognition of their legitimate right to exist as autonomous societies and cultures. This was a very slow process against continuous opposition and often brutal oppression. Indigenous people themselves were often bystanders while others spoke for them and acted on their behalf during the initial stages of creating a global human rights ideology that recognized the unique rights of indigenous people. For example, in 1514, at the beginning of the European colonization of the Western Hemisphere, a prominent Catholic missionary priest, Bartolomé de las Casas (1474–1566), began a campaign for humane treatment of the "Indians," arguing persuasively that were in fact human beings with souls. Killing and enslaving them was therefore immoral, but they could be converted to Christianity. Such humanitarian thinking was contrary to the prevailing ideology that native Americans were not fully human and could be legally killed or enslaved by colonists. Over the following centuries many later authorities on international law declared that native peoples were legally and morally entitled to possession of their lands and deserved to be treated as sovereign nations (Snow 1921). Most Western governments followed these rules in principle, but often violated them in practice. However, this meant that tribal lands could still be taken and their political autonomy extinguished by "legal" wars of conquest, or indigenous peoples could still "consent" to sign away their legal claims to land and sovereignty in formal treaties. Such legal loopholes were used to legitimize a continuous conquest of tribal territories, but early international legal opinion did provide a precedent for the indigenous claims that followed.

In the absence of effective human rights protections, the survival of indigenous people up to 1945 depended primarily on their relative isolation from urban centers and their ability to use force to maintain their independence. As shown in Chapter 7, most government policies were based on the assumption that independent tribal peoples were inevitably doomed to extinction or assimilation into dominant commercial societies. However, after 1945 the "principle of equal rights and self determination of peoples" proclaimed in Article 1 of the UN Charter provided an opening for treating tribal survival as a question of human rights. The crucial issue was that tribals needed to gain recognition as indigenous *peoples* in order to claim rights as corporate communities. Under Articles 73 and 76 many tribal territories were included under the heading of "nonself-governing territories," subject to "constructive development" by outside agents. However Article 22 of the 1948 Universal Declaration of Human Rights stated that everyone could claim "cultural rights," and this was reaffirmed by the International Covenant of Human Rights adopted by the UN General Assembly in 1966 (see Chapter 7).

In addition to the general humanitarian guidelines laid down by the United Nations, the first set of international guidelines written specifically to apply to indigenous peoples was the International Labour Organization's (ILO) Convention 107. The ILO is a UN affiliate that was originally created in 1919 by the Versailles Treaty as part of the League of Nations to deal with labor issues. The agents who drafted Convention 107 represented governments and businesses, and included expert anthropologists, but not indigenous people. They debated how fast indigenous peoples would be integrated into national societies, but did not consider the possibility of their continued autonomy. The experts wanted to protect the human rights of tribals as individuals, but did not affirm their group rights as members of indigenous communities. They considered tribals to be "impoverished" and in need of "development," which would require their incorporation into the market economy as individuals. Ideally, tribal ways of life were to be respected, and tribes were to be left in possession of their land unless it became necessary to resettle them for development purposes. Protections were seen as temporary measures until tribals could be educated "to identify themselves with the values of technologically advanced societies" (ILR 1954, 422–424). The experts considered the integration process to be inevitable. As anthropologist Horace Miner piously declared: "The realist recognizes the inevitability of increasing encroachment of civilization on the remaining outposts of preliterate culture" (Miner 1955, 441). This was a self-fulfilling prophecy.

The "inevitability" that tribals would lose their autonomy was facilitated by loan decisions made by a handful of officials at the newly created World Bank in Washington, D.C. The World Bank was one of the principle funding agents behind the massive development projects that displaced tribal peoples throughout the world and especially in the Amazon, the Philippines, and New Guinea, where bank-funded dams, highways, and colonization projects intruded on scores of still autonomous tribes in the 1970s and 1980s. Bank officials legitimized these actions using the self-fulfilling ideology incorporated earlier in ILO Convention 107 and called on development agents to "minimize the imposition of different social or economic systems until such time as the tribal society is sufficiently robust and resilient to tolerate the effects of change" (Goodland 1982, 28).

The development context began to change dramatically in 1968 when it became public that agents of Brazil's Indian Protectorate Service had conspired with local landowners to kill thousands of still autonomous tribals with machine guns, explosives, poison, and deliberately introduced disease in order to clear their lands for development. Shocked by these revelations, a small group of Scandinavian anthropologists led by Helge Kleivan immediately formed the International Work Group for Indigenous Affairs (IWGIA) to defend the human rights of indigenous peoples. Headquartered in Copenhagen and funded in part by development aid money from various Scandinavian governments, the IWGIA worked to publicize abuses, lobbied governments to respect indigenous rights, and helped mobilize indigenous leaders to form their own political organizations. As indigenous peoples established a forum, it become much more difficult for outside interests to invade their territories with impunity and their forced integration and absorption into the global commercial system suddenly seemed less inevitable.

All over the world indigenous people demanded the right to maintain their independent existence and shape their own futures by controlling their own natural and cultural resources. The Sami peoples in northern Norway, Sweden, and Finland had already formed a transnational organization in 1953 and provided a model for the First Circumpolar People's Conference (held in Copenhagen in 1973) that brought together sixteen indigenous groups from Alaska, Canada, Greenland, Norway, Finland, and Sweden. The World Council of Indigenous Peoples held its first assembly on Vancouver Island, British Columbia, in 1975, bringing together fifty-two representatives of indigenous groups from nineteen countries. Soon indigenous organizations were recognized by the United Nations as official nongovernmental organizations (NGOs) and were able to participate in certain UN activities. In 1981, 130 representatives of indigenous NGOs met in Geneva to begin drafting a UN Declaration on the Rights of Indigenous Peoples. Indigenous leaders hoped for General Assembly approval of such a declaration by 1992 to commemorate the European invasion of the Western Hemisphere, but the UN Commission on Human Rights did not approve the draft resolution until 1994, and by 2002 the declaration had still not been approved by the General Assembly. Nevertheless, the UN declared 1995–2004 to be the International Decade of the World's Indigenous Peoples for "the promotion and protection of the rights of indigenous people and their empowerment to make choices which enable them to retain their cultural identity while participating in political, economic and social life, with full respect for their cultural values, languages, traditions and forms of social organization." In 2000 a Permanent Forum on Indigenous Issues was established to serve as an advisory body to the UN Economic and Social Council on indigenous issues.

The reluctance of the UN General Assembly to approve the Declaration on the Rights of Indigenous People is understandable because the document implies that 500 years of European colonialism and the more recent push for economic globalization were a gross violation of the rights of tribal people. It would also be an admission that small-scale self-sufficient cultures were destroyed not by nature but by fundamentally immoral human decision making as an exercise of social power. Returning power to indigenous communities is a vital step toward guaranteeing their existence. However, it is a hopeful sign that special recognition of indigenous peoples, their resources, and cultures is incorporated in the ongoing Earth Charter Initiative, which is a broadly based social movement designing a new ethic for a social and economic justice in a sustainable global system based on human values. Achieving such an objective will necessarily require a diffusion of social power to smaller-scale social entities.

Conclusion

Self-interested elites have made some bad choices for humanity, but democratic decision making by the majority at local, national, and global levels can solve the problems of scale and create a world that will be more equitable, stable, and secure—for everyone. The power of scale is a tool that is too important to be left to a self-interested few. Theoretically, sustainable forms of growth may need to continue in certain disadvantaged areas, but at a global scale continued growth is neither socially nor environmentally sustainable, and has objectively left too many people too far behind. Further increasing the scale of global commerce to further maximize economic growth will merely continue the power-concentrating trends of the past and is unlikely to solve the human problems of poverty, social disorder, and environmental deterioration.

References

Adas, Michael. 1981. "From Avoidance to Confrontation: Peasant Protest in Precolonial and Colonial Southeast Asia." *Comparative Studies in Society and History* 23(2): 217–247.
Alföldy, Géza. 1985. *Römische Sozialgeschichte. The Social History of Rome.* Beckenham, Kent: Croom Helm.
Allen, Michael Patrick. 1992. "Elite Social Movement Organizations and the State: The Rise of the Conservative Policy-Planning Network." *Politics and Society* 4: 87–109.
Allison, Bill. 2002. "Enron, Integrity, Reader Feedback, and Clearing Up a Few Misconceptions." Investigative Report, *The Public I*, January 25. Washington, DC: Center for Public Integrity.
Ashton, Thomas Southcliffe. 1968. *Iron and Steel in the Industrial Revolution.* New York: Augustus M. Kelley.
Baltzell, E. Digby. 1958. *Philadelphia Gentlemen: The Making of a National Upper Class.* Glencoe, IL: Free Press.
Barlett, Donald L., and James B. Steele. 1992. *America: What Went Wrong?* Kansas City, MO: Andrews and McMeel.
Barney, Gerald O., ed. 1977–80. *The Global 2000 Report to the President of the United States.* 3 vols. New York: Pergamon.
Bateman, John. 1883. *The Great Landowners of Great Britain and Ireland.* 4th ed. London: Harrison.
Baxter, R.D. 1868. *The National Income.* London.
Beach, William W., and Gareth Davis. 1998. "The Institutional Setting of Economic Growth." In *1998 Index of Economic Freedom*, ed. Bryan T. Johnson, Kim R. Holmes, and Melanie Kirkpatrick, pp. 4–10. New York and Washington, DC: Dow Jones and Heritage Foundation.
Beard, Charles A. 1913. *An Economic Interpretation of the Constitution of the United States.* New York: Macmillan.
Beard, Charles A., and Mary R. Beard. 1934. *The Rise of American Civilization.* New York: Macmillan.

Beebe, Lucius. 1966. *The Big Spenders*. Garden City, NY: Doubleday.
Beloch, K.J. 1886. *Die bevölkerung der Griechisch-Römischen welt. Leipzig.* [n.p.]
Berentson, Jane, ed. 2002. "The Richest Person in Town: A Special Tenth Anniversary Report on the Influence of Wealth in 100 American Cities." *Worth* 11(2): 70–130.
Beresford, Maurice. 1967. *New Towns of the Middle Ages: Town Plantation in England, Wales, and Gascony*. New York: Praeger.
Beresford, Philip. 1990. *The Sunday Times Book of the Rich*. London: Penguin.
Berg, Maxine. 1980. *The Machinery Question and the Making of Political Economy, 1815–1848*. Cambridge: Cambridge University Press.
Berle, Adolf A., Jr., and Gardiner C. Means. 1933. *The Modern Business Corporation and Private Property*. New York: Macmillan.
Berreman, Gerald. 1978a. "Scale and Social Relations: Thoughts and Three Examples." In *Scale and Social Organization*, ed. Fredrik Barth, pp. 41–77. Oslo: Universitetsforlaget.
———. 1978b. "Scale and Social Relations." *Current Anthropology* 19(2): 225–245.
Betzig, Laura L. 1986. *Despotism and Differential Reproduction: A Darwinian View of History*. New York: Aldine.
———. 1992. "Roman Polygyny." *Ethology and Sociobiology* 13: 309–349.
———. 1993. "Sex, Succession, and Stratification in the First Six Civilizations: How Powerful Men Reproduced, Passed Power on to Their Sons, and Used Power to Defend Their Wealth, Women, and Children." In *Social Stratification and Socioeconomic Inequality*, ed. Lee Ellis, pp. 37–74. Westport, CT: Praeger.
———. 1997a. "Introduction: People Are Animals." In *Human Nature: A Critical Reader*, ed. Laura Betzig, pp. 1–17. New York: Oxford University Press.
———. 1997b. "Why a Despot?" In *Human Nature: A Critical Reader*, ed. Laura Betzig, pp. 399–401. New York: Oxford University Press.
"Billionaires 2001." *Forbes*, July 9.
Birdsell, Joseph. B. 1957. "Some Population Problems Involving Pleistocene Man." *Cold Spring Harbor Symposium on Quantitative Biology* 22: 47–70.
———. 1971. "Ecology, Spacing Mechanisms, and Adaptive Behavior in Aboriginal Land Tenure." In *Land Tenure in the Pacific*, ed. Ron Crocombe, pp. 334–361. Melbourne: Oxford University Press.
———. 1973. "A Basic Demographic Unit." *Current Anthropology* 14(4): 337–350.
———. 1979. "Ecological Influences on Australian Aboriginal Social Organization." In *Primate Ecology and Human Origins: Ecological Influences on Social Organization*, ed. Irwin S. Bernstein and Euclid O. Smith, pp. 117–151. New York: Garland STPM.
Bluestone, Barry, and Bennett Harrison. 1982. *The Deindustrialization of America*. New York: Basic.
Bodley, John H. 1969. "The Actual Situation of the Gran Pajonal Campa (The Last Independent Campa)." *Peruvian Times*, September 5, pp. 8–10.
———. 1970. "Campa Socio-Economic Adaptation." Ph. D. diss., University of Oregon, University Microfilms, Ann Arbor, Michigan.
———. 1972a. *Tribal Survival in the Amazon: The Campa Case*. Document No. 5 IWGIA (International Work Group for Indigenous Affairs), Copenhagen.
———. 1972b. "A Transformative Movement Among the Campa of Eastern Peru." *Anthropos* 67: 220–228.
———. 1973. "Deferred Exchange Among the Campa Indians." *Anthropos* 68: 589–596.

———. 1981. "Deferred Exchange Among the Campa: A Reconsideration." In *Networks of the Past: Regional Interaction in Archaeology*, ed. Peter Francis, F.J. Kense, and P.G. Duke, pp. 49–59. Calgary: University of Calgary Archaeological Association.

———. 1988. *Tribal Peoples and Development Issues*. Mountain View, CA: Mayfield.

———. 1992. "Anthropologist at Work: Inequality and Exploitation in the Peruvian Amazon." In *Discovering Anthropology*, ed. Daniel R. Gross, p. 483. Mountain View, CA: Mayfield.

———. 1993. "Human Rights, Development and the Environment in the Peruvian Amazon: The Ashaninka Case." In *Who Pays the Price? Examining the Sociocultural Context of Environmental Crisis*, ed. Barbara Rose Johnston, pp. 31–36. Washington, DC: Island Press.

———. 1994. "A Cultural Scale Perspective on Human Ecology and Development." In *Advances in Human Ecology*, ed. Lee Freese, vol. 3, pp. 93–112. Greenwich, CT: JAI Press.

———. 1995. "Indigenous Peoples vs. The State: A Cultural Scale Approach." In *Indigenous Peoples in Remote Regions: Comparative Perspectives*, ed. Ken Coates and John Taylor, pp. 6–29. Centre for Northern Studies, Lakehead University, Occasional Paper 17.

———. 1999a. *Victims of Progress*. 4th ed. Mountain View, CA: Mayfield.

———. 1999b. "Socio-Economic Growth, Culture Scale, and Household Well-Being: A Test of the Power-Elite Hypothesis." *Current Anthropology* 40(5): 595–620.

———. 2000. *Cultural Anthropology: Tribes, States, and the Global System*. 3rd ed. Mountain View, CA: Mayfield.

———. 2001a. *Anthropology and Contemporary Human Problems*. 4th ed. Mountain View, CA: Mayfield.

———. 2001b. "Growth, Scale, and Power in Washington State." *Human Organization* 60(4): 367–379.

Bogucki, Peter. 1999. *The Origins of Human Society*. Oxford: Blackwell.

Bookchin, Murray. 1991. *The Ecology of Freedom: The Emergence and Dissolution of Hierarchy*. Montreal: Black Rose.

Booth, Charles. 1892–1903. *Life and Labour of the People in London*. London: Macmillan.

Borsodi, Ralph. 1929a. *This Ugly Civilization*. New York: Simon and Schuster.

———. 1929b. *The Distribution Age: A Study of the Economy of Modern Distribution*. New York: Appleton.

Brewer, John. 1989. *The Sinews of Power: War, Money and the English State, 1688–1783*. New York: Knopf.

Broehl, Jr., Wayne G. 1968. *The International Basic Economy Corporation*. United States Business Performance Abroad Series. Washington, DC: National Planning Association.

Bowen, H.V. 1989. "Investment and Empire in the Later Eighteenth Century: East India Stockholding, 1756–1791." *Economic History Review* 42: 186–206.

Brown, J.H., and B.A. Maurer. 1986. "Body Size, Ecological Dominance, and Cope's Rule." *Nature* 324: 248–250.

Brown, Lester R. 2000. "Challenges of the New Century." In *State of the World 2000: A Worldwatch Institute Report on Progress Toward a Sustainable Society*, ed. Lester R. Brown et al., pp. 177–197. New York: Norton.

Burke, Peter. 1994. *Venice and Amsterdam: A Study of Seventeenth-Century Elites.* 2d ed. Cambridge: Polity.
Cain, P.J., and A.G. Hopkins. 1993. *British Imperialism: Innovation and Expansion, 1688–1914.* London: Longman.
Califano, Dave. 1998. "The Battle for Assets." *Worth* 7(11): 106.
Cantillon, Richard. 1959. *Essai sur la nature du commerce en général,* ed. and (English) trans. Henry Higgs. London: Frank Cass.
Caplow, Theodore. 1964. *Principles of Organization.* New York: Harcourt.
Carcopino, Jérôme. 1940. *Daily Life in Ancient Rome: The People and the City at the Height of the Empire.* New Haven, CT: Yale University Press.
Carneiro, Robert L. 1967. "On the Relationship Between Size of Population and Complexity of Social Organization." *Southwestern Journal of Anthropology* 23(3): 234–243.
———. 1970. "A Theory of the Origin of the State." *Science* 169: 733–738.
———. 1988. "The Circumscription Theory: Challenge and Response." *American Behavioral Scientist* 31: 497–511.
Caro, Robert A. 1974. *The Power Broker: Robert Moses and the Fall of New York.* New York: Knopf.
Carroll, Sean B. 2001. "Chance and Necessity: The Evolution of Morphological Complexity and Diversity." *Nature* 409: 1102–1109.
Carosso, Vincent P. 1970. *Investment Banking in America: A History.* Cambridge, MA: Harvard University Press.
———. 1987. *The Morgans: Private International Bankers, 1854–1913.* Cambridge, MA: Harvard University Press.
Carruthers, Bruce G. 1996. *City of Capital: Politics and Markets in the English Financial Revolution.* Princeton, NJ: Princeton University Press.
Castells, Manuel. 1998. *The Information Age: Economy, Society and Culture.* Vol. 3, *End of Millennium.* Malden, MA: Blackwell.
Cateau, Heather, and S.H.H. Carrington, eds. 2000. *Capitalism and Slavery Fifty Years Later: Eric Eustace Williams—A Reassessment of the Man and His Work.* New York: Lang.
Chadwick, Sir Edwin. [1842] 1965. *Report on the Sanitary Condition of the Labouring Population of England.* Edinburgh: Edinburgh University Press.
Chandler, Alfred D., Jr. 1977. *The Visible Hand: The Managerial Revolution in American Business.* Cambridge, MA: Harvard University Press, Belknap Press.
Chandler, David G. 1966. *The Campaigns of Napoleon.* New York: Macmillan.
Chandler, Tertius. 1987. *Four Thousand Years of Urban Growth.* Lewiston, NY: St. David's University Press.
Chernow, Ron. 1990. *The House of Morgan: An American Banking Dynasty and the Rise of Modern Finance.* New York: Atlantic Monthly.
Christaller, W. 1933. *Die zentralen Orte in Süddeutschland.* Jena: Fischer.
Claeys, Gregory, ed. 1991. *Robert Owen: A New View of Society and Other Writings.* London: Penguin.
Clark, Grover. 1936. *The Balance Sheets of Imperialism: Facts and Figures on Colonies.* New York: Columbia University Press.
Collier, Christopher, and James Lincoln Collier. 1986. *Decision in Philadelphia: The Constitutional Convention of 1787.* New York: Random House.
Collier, Peter, and David Horowitz. 1976. *The Rockefellers: An American Dynasty.* New York: Holt.

Colquhoun, Patrick. 1815. *A Treatise on the Wealth, Power, and Resources of the British Empire*. London: Joseph Mawman.
Cook, Earl. 1971. "The Flow of Energy in an Industrial Society." *Scientific American* 224(3): 134–44.
Cornford, Francis MacDonald. 1945. *The Republic of Plato*. London: Oxford University Press.
Dahl, Robert. 1958. "A Critique of the Ruling Elite Model." *American Political Science Review* 52: 463–469.
———. 1961. *Who Governs?* New Haven, CT: Yale University Press.
D'Altroy, Terence N., and Timothy K. Earle. 1985. "Staple Finance, Wealth Finance, and Storage in the Inka Political Economy." *Current Anthropology* 26(2): 187–206.
Dalzell, Robert F., Jr. 1987. *Enterprising Elite: The Boston Associates and the World They Made*. Cambridge, MA: Harvard University Press.
Davis, Joseph S. 1917. *Essays in the Earlier History of American Corporations*. Cambridge, MA: Harvard University Press.
Davis, Lance E., and Robert A. Huttenback. 1986. *Mammon and the Pursuit of Empire: The Political Economy of British Imperialism, 1860–1912*. Cambridge: Cambridge University Press.
Day, Dent C. 1982. "Ciudadelas: Their Form and Function." In *Chan Chan: Andean Desert City*, ed. Michael E. Moseley and Kent C. Day, pp. 55–66. Albuquerque: University of New Mexico Press.
DeForest, Robert W., and Lawrence Veiller, eds. 1903. *The Tenement House Problem: Including the Report of the New York State Tenement House Commission of 1900*. 2 vols. New York: Macmillan.
Demos, John. 1970. *A Little Commonwealth: Family Life in Plymouth Colony*. New York: Oxford University Press.
De Vries, Jan. 1993. "Between Purchasing Power and the World of Goods: Understanding the Household Economy in Early Modern Europe." In *Consumption and the World of Goods*, ed. John Brewer and Roy Porter, pp. 85–132. London: Routledge.
Dewhurst, J. Frederic, ed. 1947. *America's Needs and Resources: A Twentieth Century Fund Survey Which Includes Estimates for 1950 and 1960*. New York: Twentieth Century Fund.
———. 1955. *America's Needs and Resources: A New Survey*. New York: Twentieth Century Fund.
Dickson, P.G.M. 1967. *The Financial Revolution in England: A Study in the Development of Public Credit 1688–1756*. London: Macmillan.
Dolan, Kerry A., and Luisa Kroll, eds. 2001. "The World's Richest People." *Forbes* 168(1): 110–124.
Dollar, David, and Aart Kraay. 2000. "Growth Is Good for the Poor." Preliminary paper, Development Research Group. Washington, DC: World Bank.
Domhoff, G. William. 1983. *Who Rules America Now? A View for the '80s*. Englewood Cliffs, NJ: Prentice-Hall.
———. 1990. *The Power Elite and the State*. Hawthorne, NY: Aldine de Gruyter.
———. 1996. *State Autonomy or Class Dominance?: Case Studies on Policy Making in America*. Hawthorne, NY: Aldine de Gruyter.
Douglas, David. 1964. *William the Conqueror*. Berkeley: University of California Press.

Drewnoski, Adam, and Barry M. Popkin. 1997. "The Nutrition Transition: New Trends in the Global Diet." *Nutrition Review* 55(2): 31–43.

Dublin, Thomas. 1979. *Women at Work: The Transformation of Work and Community in Lowell, Massachusetts, 1826–1860.* New York: Columbia University Press.

DuBois, Josiah E., Jr. 1952. *The Devil's Chemists: 24 Conspirators of the International Farben Cartel Who Manufacture Wars.* Boston: Beacon.

Dunbar, John, and Nathaniel Heller. 2002. "Administration Ties to Arthur Andersen Nearly as Tight as Those to Enron." Special Report, *The Public I*, January 16. Washington, DC: Center for Public Integrity.

Duncan-Jones, Richard. 1980. "Demographic Change and Economic Progress in the Roman Empire." In *Technologia, economia e società nel mondo romano*, Como 1979 (Como), pp. 67–80.

———. 1990. *Structure and Scale in the Roman Economy.* Cambridge: Cambridge University Press.

Dunlop, Ian. 1985. *Royal Palaces of France.* New York: Norton.

Dupuy, T.N. 1979. *Numbers, Predictions and War: Using History to Evaluate Combat Factors and Predict the Outcome of Battles.* New York: Bobbs-Merrill.

Dye, Thomas R. 1983. *Who's Running America?: The Reagan Years.* Englewood Cliffs, NJ: Prentice-Hall.

Earle, Peter. 1989. *The Making of the English Middle Class: Business, Society and Family Life in London 1660–1730.* Berkeley: University of California Press.

Earle, Timothy. 1987. "Specialization and Social Organization of Wealth: Hawaiian Chiefdoms and the Inka Empire." In *Specialization, Exchange, and Complex Societies*, ed. Elizabeth Brumfiel and Timothy Earle, pp. 64–75. Cambridge: Cambridge University Press.

Easterlin, Richard A. 1996. *Growth Triumphant: The Twenty-First Century in Historical Perspective.* Ann Arbor: University of Michigan Press.

Emmott, Bill, Koji Watanabe, and Paul Wolfowitz. 1997. "Managing the International System over the Next Ten Years: Three Essays." *Task Force Report #50.* The Trilateral Commission.

Encyclopaedia Britannica. 1975. "Slavery, Serfdom, and Forced Labour." *Encyclopaedia Britannica*, 15th ed., Macropaedia, vol. 16, pp. 853–866. Chicago: Author.

Estes, Ralph. 1996. *Tyranny of the Bottom Line: Why Corporations Make Good People Do Bad Things.* San Francisco: Berrett-Kohler.

Feinstein, Charles H. 1998. "Pessimism Perpetuated: Real Wages and the Standard of Living in Britain During and After the Industrial Revolution." *Journal of Economic History* 58(3): 625–658.

Feinstein, Charles H., and Sidney Pollard. 1988. *Studies in Capital Formation in the United Kingdom 1750–1920.* Oxford: Clarendon.

Ferguson, Niall. 1998. *The House of Rothschild: Money's Prophets 1798–1848.* New York: Viking, Penguin.

Finn, R. Welldon. 1973. *Domesday Book: A Guide.* London: Phillimore.

Fischer, David Hackett. 1996. *The Great Wave: Price Revolutions and the Rhythm of History.* New York: Oxford University Press.

Fletcher, Roland. 1995. *The Limits of Settlement Growth: A Theoretical Outline.* Cambridge: Cambridge University Press.

Flynn, Dennis O., and Arturo Giráldez. 1995. "Born with a 'Silver Spoon': The Origin of World Trade in 1571." *Journal of World History* 6(2): 201–221.

Fogel, Robert William. 1964. *Railroads and American Economic Growth: Essays in Econometric History.* Baltimore: Johns Hopkins University Press.
Foundation Center. 2001. *The Foundation Directory 2001 Edition.* New York: The Foundation Center.
Friedman, Milton. 1970. "The Social Responsibility of Business." *New York Times Magazine* (September 13) 33: 122–126.
Fukuyama, Francis. 1992. *The End of History and the Last Man.* New York: Free Press.
Galbraith, John Kenneth. 1952. *American Capitalism: The Concept of Countervailing Power.* Boston: Houghton Mifflin.
———. 1955. *The Great Crash, 1929.* Boston: Houghton Mifflin.
———. 1958. *The Affluent Society.* Boston: Houghton Mifflin.
———. 1967. *The New Industrial State.* Boston: Houghton Mifflin.
Gardner, Gary, and Brian Halweil. 2000. "Nourishing the Underfed and Overfed." In *State of the World 2000: A Worldwatch Institute Report on Progress Toward a Sustainable Society*, ed. Lester R. Brown, Christopher Flavin, Hilary French, and Linda Starke, pp. 59–78. New York: Norton.
Gates, Bill, with Nathan Myhrvold and Peter Rinearson. 1996. *The Road Ahead.* 2nd ed. New York: Penguin.
Geertz, Clifford. 1980. *Negara: The Theatre State in Nineteenth-Century Bali.* Princeton, NJ: Princeton University Press.
Geertz, Hildred, and Clifford Geertz. 1975. *Kinship in Bali.* Chicago: University of Chicago Press.
Gemini Consulting. 1998. *World Wealth Report 1998.* New York: Cap Gemini.
———. 2001. *World Wealth Report 2001.* New York: Cap Gemini.
George, Susan. 1992. *The Debt Boomerang: How Third World Debt Harms Us All.* Boulder, CO: Westview.
———. 1999. "A Short History of Neo-Liberalism: Twenty Years of Elite Economics and Emerging Opportunities for Structural Change." Paper presented at Conference on Economic Sovereignty in a Globalizing World, Bangkok, March.
Gies, Frances. 1994. *Cathedral, Forge, and Waterwheel: Technology and Invention in the Middle Ages.* New York: HarperCollins.
Gilder, George. 1982. *Wealth and Poverty.* New York: Bantam.
Gleick, James 1987. *Chaos: Making a New Science.* New York: Penguin.
Goddard, Stephen G. 1994. *Getting There: The Epic Struggle Between Road and Rail in the American Century.* New York: Basic.
Goldschmidt, Walter. 1978. *As You Sow: Three Studies in the Social Consequences of Agribusiness.* Montclair, NJ: Allanheld, Osmum.
Goldstein, Joshua S. 1988. *Long Cycles: Prosperity and War in the Modern Age.* New Haven, CT: Yale University Press.
Goldthwaite, Richard A. 1980. *The Building of Renaissance Florence: An Economic and Social History.* Baltimore: Johns Hopkins University Press.
———. 1993. *Wealth and the Demand for Art in Italy 1300–1600.* Baltimore : Johns Hopkins University Press.
Goodland, Robert. 1982. *Tribal Peoples and Economic Development: Human Ecologic Considerations.* Washington, DC: World Bank.
Goodrich, Carter. 1960. *Government Promotion of American Canals and Railroads, 1800–1890.* New York: Columbia University Press.

Gould, Stephen Jay. 1996. *Full House: The Spread of Excellence from Plato to Darwin.* New York: Harmony.

Grant, James. 1992. *Money of the Mind: Borrowing and Lending in America from the Civil War to Michael Milken.* New York: Farrar Straus.

Gras, Norman S.B. 1915. *The Evolution of the English Corn Market: From the Twelfth to the Eighteenth Century.* Cambridge, MA: Harvard University Press.

Green, Mark J., Beverly C. Moore, Jr., and Bruce Wasserstein. 1972. *The Closed Enterprise System: Ralph Nader's Study Group Report on Antitrust Enforcement.* New York: Bantam.

Greven, Philip J., Jr. 1970. *Four Generations: Population, Land, and Family in Colonial Andover, Massachusetts.* Ithaca, NY: Cornell University Press.

Griswold, A.B., and Prasert na Nagara. 1977. "Epigraphic and Historical Studies, No. 17: The 'Judgments of King Man Ray.'" *Journal of the Siam Society* 65(1): 137–160.

Gross, Daniel R., and Barbara A. Underwood. 1971. "Technological Change and Caloric Costs: Sisal Agriculture." *American Anthropologist* 73(2): 725–740.

Hadfield, Charles. 1969. *The Canal Age.* New York: Praeger.

Haeger, John Denis. 1991. *John Jacob Astor: Business and Finance in the Early Republic.* Detroit: Wayne State University Press.

Hagesteijn, Renée. 1989. *Circles of Kings: Political Dynamics in Early Continental Southeast Asia.* Verhandelingen van het Koninklijk Institut Voor Taal-, Land- en Volkenkunde No. 138. Dordrecht, Holland: Foris.

Hall, Peter Dobkin. 1982. *The Organization of American Culture, 1700–1900: Private Institutions, Elites, and the Origins of American Nationality.* New York: New York University Press.

Hammack, David C. 1982. *Power and Society: Greater New York at the Turn of the Century.* New York: Russell Sage Foundation.

Hancock, David. 1995. *Citizens of the World: London Merchants and the Integration of the British Atlantic Community, 1735–1785.* Cambridge: Cambridge University Press.

Hanks, Lucien M. 1972. *Rice and Man: Agricultural Ecology in Southeast Asia.* Chicago: Aldine.

———. 1975. "The Thai Social Order as Entourage and Circle." In *Change and Persistence in Thai Society*, ed. G. William Skinner and A. Thomas Kirsch, pp. 197–218. Ithaca, NY: Cornell University Press.

Hannay, David. 1926. "Navy and Navies." *Encyclopaedia Britannica.* 13th ed., vol. 19, pp. 299–317. London: Encyclopaedia Britannica.

Harrison, Bennett, and Barry Bluestone. 1988. *The Great U-Turn: Corporate Restructuring and the Polarizing of America.* New York: Basic.

Hayek, Friedrich A. [1944] 1960. *The Road to Serfdom.* Chicago: University of Chicago Press.

Hayes, Peter. 2001. *Industry and Ideology: IG Farben in the Nazi Era.* Cambridge: Cambridge University Press.

Hoberman, Louisa Schell. 1991. *Mexico's Merchant Elite, 1590–1660.* Durham: Duke University Press.

Homer-Dixon, Thomas F. 1991. "On the Threshold: Environmental Changes as Causes of Acute Conflict." *International Security* 16(2): 6–116.

Hopkins, Keith. 1978a. "Economic Growth and Towns in Classical Antiquity." In *Towns in Societies: Essays in Economic History and Historical Sociology*, ed.

Philip Abrams and E.A. Wrigley, pp. 35–77. Cambridge: Cambridge University Press.

———. 1978b. *Conquerors and Slaves*. Sociological Studies in Roman History. Vol. 1. Cambridge: Cambridge University Press.

Hopkins, M.K. 1966. "On the Probable Age-Structure of the Roman Population." *Population Studies* 20: 245–264.

Hubbert, M. King. 1969. "Energy Resources." In *Resources and Man*, ed. National Academy of Sciences, pp. 157–242. San Francisco: Freeman.

Hummel, Ralph P. 1987. *The Bureaucratic Experience*. New York: St. Martin's Press.

International Labour Review (ILR). 1954. "Reports and Inquiries: The Second Session of the ILO Committee of Experts on Indigenous Labour." *International Labour Review* 70(5): 418–441.

Jaher, Frederic Cople. 1972. "Nineteenth-Century Elites in Boston and New York." *Journal of Social History* 6(1): 32–77.

———. 1982. *The Urban Establishment: Upper Strata in Boston, New York, Charleston, Chicago, and Los Angeles*. Urbana: University of Illinois Press.

Jewkes, J. 1960. "Are the Economies of Scale Unlimited?" In *Economic Consequences of the Size of Nations: Proceedings of a Conference Held by the International Economic Association*, ed. E.A.G. Robinson, pp. 95–116. New York: St. Martin's.

Johnson, Allen. 1975. "Time Allocation in a Machiguenga Community." *Ethnology* 14: 301–310.

———. 1983. "Machiguenga Gardens." In *Adaptive Responses of Native Amazonians*, ed. Raymond B. Hames and William T. Vickers, pp. 29–63. New York: Academic.

———. 1985. "In Search of the Affluent Society." In *Anthropology: Contemporary Perspectives*, ed. David E.K. Hunter and Phillip Whitten, pp. 201–206. Boston: Little, Brown.

Johnson, Allen, and Clifford A. Behrens. 1982. "Nutritional Criteria in Machiguenga Food Production Decisions: A Linear-Programming Analysis." *Human Ecology* 10(2): 167–189.

Johnson, Bryan T., Kim R. Holmes, and Melanie Kirkpatrick. 1998. *1998 Index of Economic Freedom*. New York and Washington, DC: Dow Jones and Heritage Foundation.

Johnson, Charles. 1950. *Dialogus de Scaccario, The Course of the Exchequer and Constitutio Domus Regis, The King's Household*. London: Thomas Nelson.

Johnson, Gregory A. 1973. *Local Exchange and Early State Development in Southwestern Iran*. Anthropological Papers No. 51. Ann Arbor: Museum of Anthropology, University of Michigan.

———. 1982. "Organizational Structure and Scalar Stress." In *Theory and Explanation in Archaeology: Beyond Subsistence and Dating*, ed. C.E. Redman et al., pp. 87–112. New York: Academic.

Jones, A.H.M. 1974. *The Roman Economy: Studies in Ancient Economic and Administrative History*. Totowa, NJ: Rowman and Littlefield.

———. 1977. *American Colonial Wealth: Documents and Methods*. 3 vols. New York: Arno.

———. 1980. *Wealth of a Nation to Be: The American Colonies on the Eve of the Revolution*. New York: Columbia University Press.

Jonge, Alex de. 1977. *Napoleon's Last Will and Testament*. New York: Paddington.

Judis, John B. 2000. *The Paradox of American Democracy: Elites, Special Interests, and the Betrayal of Public Trust.* New York: Pantheon.
Jumsai, Sumet. 1988. *Naga: Cultural Origins in Siam and the West Pacific.* Oxford: Oxford University Press.
Kahn, Herman, and Anthony J. Wiener. 1967. *The Year 2000: A Framework for Speculation on the Next Thirty-Three Years.* New York: Macmillan.
Kefauver, Estes. 1965. *In a Few Hands: Monopoly Power in America.* New York: Pantheon.
Kennickell, Arthur B. 2000. "Recent Changes in U.S. Family Finances." *Federal Reserve Bulletin* 86: 1–29.
Keynes, John Maynard. 1936. *The General Theory of Employment, Interest and Money.* London: Macmillan.
King, Gregory. [1696] 1936. *Two Tracts*, ed. Jacob H. Hollander. Baltimore: Johns Hopkins University Press.
King, Leslie J. 1984. *Central Place Theory.* Beverly Hills, CA: Sage.
Kirsch, A. Thomas. 1973. *Feasting and Social Oscillation: Religion and Society in Upland Southeast Asia.* Data Paper No. 92, Southeast Asia Program, Department of Asian Studies, Cornell University, Ithaca, New York.
Kissinger, Henry A. 1957. *Nuclear Weapons and Foreign Policy.* New York: Harper.
Kohr, Leopold 1977. *The Overdeveloped Nations: The Diseconomies of Scale.* New York: Schocken.
Komlos, John. 1998. "Shrinking in a Growing Economy? The Mystery of Physical Stature During the Industrial Revolution." *Journal of Economic History* 58(3): 779–802.
Kondratieff, Nikolai. 1984. *The Long Wave Cycle.* New York: Richardson and Snyder.
Kosse, Krisztina. 1990. "Group Size and Societal Complexity: Thresholds in the Long-Term Memory." *Journal of Anthropological Archaeology* 9: 275–303.
Krebs, A.V. 1992. *The Corporate Reapers: The Book of Agribusiness.* Washington, DC: Essential.
———. 2002. "Commentary: Greed and Corruption Blatant as Growing ENRON Scandal Unfolds." *The Agribusiness Examiner*, no. 140. Special edition.
Kroeber, Alfred L. 1915. "The Eighteen Professions." *American Anthropologist* 17: 283–289.
———. 1917. "The Superorganic." *American Anthropologist* 19: 162–213.
Kutz, Myer. 1974. *Rockefeller Power.* New York: Pinnacle.
Lachmann, Richard. 2000. *Capitalists in Spite of Themselves: Elite Conflict and Economic Transitions in Early Modern Europe.* New York: Oxford University Press.
Lamoreaux, Naomi R. 1986. "Banks, Kinship, and Economic Development: The New England Case." *Journal of Economic History* 46(3): 647–667.
Landon, Margaret. 1944. *Anna and the King of Siam.* Garden City, NY: Garden City Publishing.
Langford, Paul. 1989. *A Polite and Commercial People: England 1727–1783.* Oxford: Clarendon.
Lansing, Carol. 1991. *The Florentine Magnates: Lineage and Faction in a Medieval Commune.* Princeton, NJ: Princeton University Press.
Leach, Edmund. 1964. *Political Systems of Highland Burma: A Study of Kachin Social Structure.* London School of Economics Monographs on Social Anthropology No. 44. London: The Athlone Press, University of London.
Leinsdorf, David, and Donald Etra. 1973. *Citibank: Ralph Nader's Study Group Report on First National City Bank.* New York: Grossman.

Leonowens, Anna Harriette. 1870. *The English Governess at the Siamese Court: Being Recollections of Six Years in the Royal Palace at Bangkok.* Boston: Fields, Osgood.
———. 1953. *Siamese Harem Life.* New York: Dutton.
Levi-Strauss, Claude. 1966. *The Savage Mind.* Chicago: University of Chicago Press.
Lewis, Charles. 2001. "New GOP Chairman Marc Racicot Mixes Politics and Profits." Center Report. *The Public I*, December 20. Washington, DC: Center for Public Integrity.
Lindeman, Eduard C. 1936, 1988. *Wealth and Culture: A Study of One Hundred Foundations and Community Trusts and Their Operations During the Decade.* New Brunswick, NJ: Transaction.
Lindert, Peter H., and Jeffrey G. Williamson. 1982. "Revising England's Social Tables 1688–1812." *Explorations in Economic History* 19: 385–408.
———. 1983. "Reinterpreting Britain's Social Tables, 1688–1913." *Explorations in Economic History* 20: 94–109.
Lloyd, Howard Demarest. 1894. *Wealth Against Commonwealth.* New York: Harper.
———. 1910. *Lords of Industry.* New York: Putnam.
Lundberg, Ferdinand. 1937. *America's 60 Families.* New York: Vanguard.
Luten, Daniel B. 1974. "United States Requirements." In *Energy, the Environment, and Human Health*, ed. A. Finkel, pp. 17–33. Acton, MA: Publishing Sciences Group.
McConnell, Grant. 1953. *The Decline of Agrarian Democracy.* Berkeley: University of California Press.
McCurdy, Charles W. 1978. "American Law and the Marketing Structure of the Large Corporation, 1875–1890." *Journal of Economic History* 38(3): 631–649.
McDonald, Forrest. 1958. *We the People: The Economic Origins of the Constitution.* Chicago: University of Chicago Press.
———. 1979. *E Pluribus Unum: The Formation of the American Republic.* 2d ed. Indianapolis, IN: Liberty.
McKendrick, N. 1959. "Josiah Wedgwood: An Eighteenth-Century Entrepreneur in Salesmanship and Marketing Techniques." *Economic History Review* 12: 408–433.
———. 1982. "The Consumer Revolution of Eighteenth-Century England." In *The Birth of a Consumer Society: The Commercialization of Eighteenth-Century England*, ed. Neil McKendrick, John Brewer, and J.H. Plumb, pp. 9–33. Bloomington: Indiana University Press.
McKendrick, Neil, John Brewer, and J.H. Plumb, eds. 1982. *The Birth of a Consumer Society: The Commercialization of Eighteenth-Century England.* Bloomington: Indiana University Press.
McNeill, William H. 1982. *The Pursuit of Power: Technology, Armed Force, and Society Since A.D. 100.* Chicago: University of Chicago Press.
MacDonald, William Lloyd, and John A. Pinto. 1995. *Hadrian's Villa and Its Legacy.* New Haven, CT: Yale University Press.
Madden, J. Patrick. 1967. *Economics of Size in Farming: Theory, Analytic Procedures, and a Review of Selected Studies.* Agricultural Economic Report No. 10, Economic Research Service, USDA.
Mager, Nathan H. 1987. *The Kondratieff Waves.* New York: Praeger.
Maisels, Charles Keith. 1990. *The Emergence of Civilization: From Hunting and Gathering to Agriculture, Cities, and the State in the Near East.* London: Routledge.

Majewski, John. 1996. "Who Financed the Transportation Revolution? Regional Divergence and Internal Improvements in Antebellum Pennsylvania and Virginia." *Journal of Economic History* 56(4): 763–788.

Malthus, Thomas R. [1798] 1895. *An Essay on the Principle of Population.* New York: Macmillan.

Manchester, William. 1964. *The Arms of Krupp 1587–1968.* Boston: Little, Brown.

Mandelbrot, Benoit B. 1977. *Fractals: Form, Chance, and Dimension.* San Francisco: Freeman.

Mann, Michael. 1986. *The Sources of Social Power.* Vol. 1, *A History of Power from the Beginning to A.D. 1760.* Cambridge: Cambridge University Press.

Mansel, Philip. 1987. *The Eagle in Splendor: Napoleon I and His Court.* London: George Philip.

Marchand, Roland. 1998. *Creating the Corporate Soul: The Rise of Public Relations and Corporate Imagery in American Big Business.* Berkeley: University of California Press.

Marquet, Pablo A. 2000. "Invariants, Scaling Laws, and Ecological Complexity." *Science* 289: 1487–1488.

Marshall, Peter, ed. 1986. *The Anarchist Writings of William Godwin.* London: Freedom.

Marx, Karl, and Friedrich Engels. 1967. *The Communist Manifesto.* [1888 English translation based on first German edition of 1848.] London: Penguin.

Mather, F.C. 1970. *After the Canal Duke: A Study of the Industrial Estates Administered by the Trustees of the Third Duke of Bridgewater in the Age of Railway Building, 1825–1872.* Oxford: Clarendon.

Mathias, Peter, and Patrick K. O'Brien. 1976. "Taxation in Britain and France, 1715–1810." *Journal of European Economic History* 5: 601–650.

Mayhew, Bruce H. 1973. "System Size and Ruling Elites." *American Sociological Review* 38: 468–475.

Mayhew, Bruce H., and Paul T. Schollaert. 1980a. "Social Morphology of Pareto's Economic Elite." *Social Forces* 59: 25–43.

———. 1980b. "The Concentration of Wealth: A Sociological Model." *Sociological Focus* 13: 1–35.

Mayhew, Henry. 1861–62. *London Labour and the London Poor.* 4 vols. London: Griffin, Bohn.

Mercer, Lloyd J. 1982. *Railroads and Land Grant Policy: A Study in Government Intervention.* New York: Academic.

Mills, C. Wright. 1956. *The Power Elite.* New York: Oxford University Press.

Mills, C. Wright, and Melville J. Ulmer. 1946. *Small Business and Civic Welfare: Report of the Smaller War Plants Corporation to the Special Committee to Study Problems of American Small Business.* U.S. Senate, Document No. 135, Seventy-Ninth Congress. Washington, DC: Government Printing Office.

Miner, Horace M. 1955. "Planning for the Acculturation of Isolated Tribes." *Proceedings of the Thirty-First International Congress of Americanists* 1: 441–446.

Mintz, Beth, and Michael Schwartz. 1985. *The Power Structure of American Business.* Chicago: University of Chicago Press.

Moody, John. 1904. *The Truth About the Trusts: A Description and Analysis of the American Trust Movement.* New York: Moody.

Morgan, Dan. 1979. *Merchants of Grain.* New York: Viking.

Morgan, Lewis Henry. 1877. *Ancient Society.* New York: Holt.

Morris, Ian. 1994. "The Community Against the Market in Classical Athens." In *From Political Economy to Anthropology*, ed. Colin A.M. Duncan and David W. Tandy, pp. 52–79. Montreal: Black Rose.
Morton, Frederic. 1961. *The Rothschilds*. Greenwich, CT: Fawcett.
Moseley, Michael E., and Kent C. Day. 1982. *Chan Chan: Andean Desert City*. School of American Research. Albuquerque: University of New Mexico Press.
Moses, Robert. 1970. *Public Works: A Dangerous Trade*. New York: McGraw-Hill.
Namier, Sir Lewis, and John Brooke. 1964. *The History of Parliament: The House of Commons 1754–1790*. Vol. III. New York: Oxford University Press.
Naroll, Raoul. 1962. "Floor Area and Settlement Population." *American Antiquity* 27(4): 587–589.
Nash, June. 1989. *From Tank Town to High Tech: The Clash of Community and Industrial Cycles*. Albany: State University of New York.
———. 1994. "Global Integration and Subsistence Insecurity." *American Anthropologist* 96(1): 7–30.
Newman, Katherine S. 1988. *Falling from Grace: The Experience of Downward Mobility in the American Middle Class*. New York: Free Press.
———. 1993. *Declining Fortunes: The Withering of the American Dream*. New York: Basic.
Newmyer, R. Kent. 1987. "Harvard Law School, New England Legal Culture, and the Antebellum Origins of American Jurisprudence." *Journal of American History* 74(3): 814–835.
News Tribune. 2001. "Some of Seattle's Wealthiest Residents Are Red-Faced over Exorbitant Power Use." *News Tribune*, March 19, p. B2.
Noble, David F. 1977. *America by Design: Science, Technology, and the Rise of Corporate Capitalism*. New York: Knopf.
———. 1984. *Forces of Production: A Social History of Industrial Automation*. New York: Knopf.
———. 1993. *Progress Without People: In Defense of Luddism*. Chicago: Kerr.
Nolan, Joseph R., and M.J. Connolly. 1979. *Black's Law Dictionary*. 5th ed. St. Paul, MN: West.
O'Brien, Patrick K. 1988. "The Political Economy of British Taxation, 1660–1815." *Economic History Review* 41(1): 1–32.
Odum, Eugene P. 1997. *Ecology: A Bridge Between Science and Society*. Sunderland, MA: Sinauer.
Odum, Howard T. 1971. *Environment, Power, and Society*. New York: Wiley, Inter-Science.
Offner, Avner. 1981. *Property and Politics 1870–1914: Landownership, Law, Ideology and Urban Development in England*. Cambridge: Cambridge University Press.
Olmstead, Alan L., and Paul W. Rhode. 1995. "Beyond the Threshold: An Analysis of the Characteristics and Behavior of Early Reaper Adopters." *Journal of Economic History* 55(1): 27–57.
Olson, Alison Gilbert. 1992. *Making the Empire Work: London and American Interest Groups 1690–1790*. Cambridge, MA: Harvard University Press.
Padgett, John F., and Christopher K. Ansell. 1993. "Robust Action and the Rise of the Medici, 1400–1434." *American Journal of Sociology* 98(6): 1259–1319.
Paine, Thomas. [1792] 1961. *The Rights of Man*. Garden City, NY: Dolphin Books, Doubleday.
Pareto, Vilfredo 1896–1897. *Cours d'économie politique*. 2 vols. Lausanne: Rouge.

Pessen, Edward. 1973. *Riches, Class, and Power Before the Civil War.* Lexington, MA: Heath.
Phillips, Kevin. 1990. *The Politics of Rich and Poor: Wealth and the American Electorate in the Reagan Aftermath.* New York: Random House.
Pocock, J.G.A. 1980. *Three British Revolutions: 1641, 1688, 1776.* Princeton, NJ: Princeton University Press.
———. 1982. "The Political Economy of Burke's Analysis of the French Revolution." *History Journal* [Great Britain] 25(2): 331–349.
Polanyi, Karl. 1944, 1957. *The Great Transformation: The Political and Economic Origins of Our Time.* Boston: Beacon.
———. 1968. *Primitive, Archaic, and Modern Economies: Essays of Karl Polanyi,* ed. George Dalton. Garden City, NY: Anchor.
Popkin, Barry M. 1998. "The Nutrition Transition and Its Health Implications in Lower-Income Countries." *Public Health Nutrition* 1(1): 5–21.
Porter, Kenneth Wiggins. 1931. *John Jacob Astor, Business Man.* 2 vols. Cambridge, MA: Harvard University Press.
Post, Emily. 1927. *Etiquette: The Blue Book of Social Usage.* New York: Funk and Wagnalls.
Poster, Mark. 1971. *Harmonian Man: Selected Writings of Charles Fourier.* Garden City, NY: Anchor Books, Doubleday.
Poumisak, Jit (pseudonymn Somsamai Srisudravarna). 1987. "The Real Face of Thai Saktina Today." In *Thai Radical Discourse: The Real Face of Thai Feudalism Today*, ed. and trans. Craig J. Reynolds, pp. 43–148. Studies on Southeast Asia, Cornell University, Ithaca, New York.
Quesnay, François. [1758] 1972. *Tableau économique,* ed. and trans. Marguerite Kuczynski and Ronald L. Meek. London: Macmillan.
Rabb, Theodore K. 1967. *Enterprise and Empire: Merchant and Gentry Investment in the Expansion of England, 1575–1630.* Cambridge, MA: Harvard University Press.
Rabibhadana, Akin. 1969. *The Organization of Thai Society in the Early Bangkok Period, 1782–1873.* Data Paper No. 74, South East Asia Program, Department of Asian Studies, Cornell University, Ithaca, New York.
Radin, Paul. 1971. *The World of Primitive Man.* New York: Dutton.
Rand McNally. 2002. *Commercial Atlas and Marketing Guide.* 133rd ed. Chicago: Rand McNally.
Randall, Monica. 1987. *The Mansions of Long Island's Gold Coast.* New York: Rizzoli.
Redfield, Robert 1947. "The Folk Society." *American Journal of Sociology* 52: 293–308.
Reid, Anthony. 1992. "Economic and Social Change, c 1400–1800." In *The Cambridge History of Southeast Asia, Volume 1, From Early Times to c. 1800*, ed. Nicholas Tarling, pp. 460–507. Cambridge: Cambridge University Press.
Riis, Jacob A. 1904. *How the Other Half Lives: Studies Among the Tenements of New York.* New York: Scribner.
Ritzer, George. 2000. *The McDonaldization of Society.* Thousand Oaks, CA: Pine Forge.
Roberts, Clayton, and David Roberts. 1980. *A History of England: Prehistory to 1714.* Vol. 1. Englewood Cliffs, NJ: Prentice-Hall.
Robinson, E.A.G. 1960. *Economic Consequences of the Size of Nations: Proceedings of a Conference Held by the International Economic Association.* New York: St. Martin's.

Rochester, Anna. 1936. *Rulers of America: A Study of Finance Capital.* New York: International.
Rockefeller Panel. 1961. *Prospect for America: The Rockefeller Panel Reports.* Garden City, NY: Doubleday.
Roover, Raymond de. 1963. *The Rise and Decline of the Medici Bank 1397–1494.* Cambridge, MA: Harvard University Press.
Rostow, W.W. 1960. *The Stages of Economic Growth: A Non-Communist Manifesto.* London: Cambridge University Press.
Roy, William G. 1997. *Socializing Capital: The Rise of the Large Industrial Corporation in America.* Princeton, NJ: Princeton University Press.
Rubinstein, W.D. 1981. *Men of Property: The Very Wealthy in Britain Since the Industrial Revolution.* New Brunswick, NJ: Rutgers University Press.
Rummel, R.J. 1997. *Death by Government.* New Brunswick, NJ: Transaction.
Russell, Bertrand. 1938. *Power: A New Social Analysis.* New York: Norton.
Russell, Josiah Cox. 1972. *Medieval Regions and Their Cities.* Bloomington: Indiana University Press.
Sahlins, Marshall. 1992. *Historical Ethnography.* Vol. 1. *Anahulu: The Anthropology of History in the Kingdom of Hawaii,* ed. Patrick V. Kirch and Marshall Sahlins. Chicago: University of Chicago Press.
Sahlins, Marshall, and Elman Service. 1960. *Evolution and Culture.* Ann Arbor: University of Michigan Press.
Scheper-Hughes, Nancy. 1992. *Death Without Weeping: The Violence of Everyday Life in Brazil.* Berkeley: University of California Press.
Schlosser, Eric. 2001. *Fast Food Nation: The Dark Side of the All-American Meal.* Boston: Houghton Mifflin.
Schulte-Nordholt, Henk. 1996. *The Spell of Power: A History of Balinese Politics 1650–1940.* Verhandelingen van het Ko Leiden: KITLV.
Schumpeter, Joseph A. 1942. *Capitalism, Socialism and Democracy.* New York: Harper.
Schweitzer, Arthur. 1964. *Big Business in the Third Reich.* Bloomington: Indiana University Press.
Sen, Amartya. 1981. *Poverty and Famines: An Essay on Entitlement and Deprivation.* Oxford: Clarendon.
Service, Elman. 1975. *Origins of the State and Civilization: The Process of Cultural Evolution.* New York: Random House.
Seward, Desmond. 1986. *Napoleon's Family.* New York: Viking.
Sewell, Tom. 1992. *The World Grain Trade.* New York: Woodhead-Faulkner.
Shapiro, Martin M., ed. 1972. *The Pentagon Papers and the Courts: A Study in Foreign Policy-Making and Freedom of the Press.* San Francisco: Chandler.
Shoup, Laurence H., and William Minter. 1980. "Shaping a New World Order: The Council on Foreign Relations' Blueprint for World Hegemony." In *Trilateralism: The Trilateral Commission and Elite Planning for World Management,* ed. Holly Sklar, pp. 135–156. Boston: South End.
Simon, David R. 1999. *Elite Deviance.* 6th ed. Boston: Allyn and Bacon.
Skinner, G. William. 1964. "Marketing and Social Structure in Rural China" (Part 1). *Journal of Asian Studies* 24(1): 3–43.
———. 1977. "Cities and the Hierarchy of Local Systems." In *The City in Late Imperial China,* ed. G. William Skinner, pp. 275–351. Stanford, CA: Stanford University Press.
Sklar, Holly, ed. 1980a. *Trilateralism: The Trilateral Commission and Elite Planning for World Management.* Boston: South End.

———. 1980b. "Trilateralism: Managing Dependence and Democracy—An Overview." In *Trilateralism: The Trilateral Commission and Elite Planning for World Management*, ed. Holly Sklar, pp. 1–57. Boston: South End.
Smith, Adam. [1776] 1994. *An Inquiry into the Nature and Causes of the Wealth of Nations*. New York: Modern Library.
Snooks, Graeme Donald. 1993. *Economics Without Time: A Science Blind to the Forces of Historical Change*. London: Macmillan.
Snow, Alpheus Henry. 1921. *The Question of Aborigines: In the Law and Practice of Nations*. New York: Putnam.
Solow, Barbara L., and Stanley L. Engerman, eds. 1987. *British Capitalism and Caribbean Slavery: The Legacy of Eric Williams*. Cambridge: Cambridge University Press.
Soltow, Lee. 1975. *Men and Wealth in the United States 1850–1870*. New Haven, CT: Yale University Press.
———. 1981. "Wealth Distribution in England and Wales in 1798." *Economic History Review* 34(1): 60–70.
———. 1983. "Long-Run Wealth Inequality in Malaysia." *Singapore Economic Review* 28(2): 79–97.
———. 1989. *Distribution of Wealth and Income in the United States in 1798*. Pittsburgh: University of Pittsburgh Press.
Sorokin, Pitirim. 1925a. "Monarchs and Rulers: A Comparative Statistical Study." *Journal of Social Forces* 3(1): 22–35.
———. 1925b. "American Millionaires and Multi-Millionaires: A Comparative Statistical Study." *The Journal of Social Forces* 3(4): 627–644.
———. 1926. "Monarchs and Rulers: A Comparative Statistical Study." *Journal of Social Forces* 4(3): 523–533.
———. 1962. *Social and Cultural Dynamics*. Vol. 3. *Fluctuation of Social Relationships, War, and Revolution*. New York: Bedminister.
Spencer, Herbert. 1866. *Principles of Biology*. New York: Appleton.
Staley, Edgcumbe. [1906] 1967. *The Guilds of Florence*. New York: Benjamin Blom.
Stambaugh, John E. 1988. *The Ancient Roman City*. Baltimore: Johns Hopkins University Press.
Stanley, Thomas J., and William D. Danko. 1996. *The Millionaire Next Door*. Atlanta: Longstreet.
Stannard, David E. 1989. *Before the Horror: The Population of Hawai'i on the Eve of Western Contact*. Honolulu: Social Science Research Institute, University of Hawaii.
Steinhart, John S., and Carol E. Steinhart. 1974. "Energy Use in the U.S. Food System." *Science* 184(4134): 307–316.
Sternstein, Larry. 1966. "The Distribution of Thai Centres at Mid-Nineteenth Century." *Journal of Southeast Asian History* 7(1): 66–72.
Steward, Julian. 1936. "The Economic and Social Basis of Primitive Bands." In *Essays in Anthropology Presented to A.L. Kroeber*, ed. Robert Lowie, pp. 331–345. Berkeley: University of California Press.
Stone, Lawrence. 1965. *The Crisis of the Aristocracy 1558–1641*. London: Oxford University Press.
Sutherland, Douglas. 1968. *The Landowners*. London: Anthony Blond.
Sutton, Antony C. 1976. *Wall Street and the Rise of Hitler*. Sudbury, Suffolk: Bloomfield.
Tambiah, S.J. 1976. *World Conqueror and World Renouncer: A Study of Buddhism and Polity in Thailand Against a Historical Background*. Cambridge: Cambridge University Press.

———. 1985. *Culture, Thought, and Social Action*. Cambridge, MA: Harvard University Press.

Taylor, Frederick Winslow. 1911. *The Principles of Scientific Management*. New York: Harper.

Thompson, Dorothy. 1984. *The Chartists: Popular Politics in the Industrial Revolution*. New York: Pantheon.

Thompson, E.P. 1963. *The Making of the English Working Class*. London: Gollancz.

Thornton, Russell. 1987. *American Indian Holocaust and Survival: A Population History Since 1492*. Norman: University of Oklahoma Press.

Tilly, Charles. 1995. *Popular Contention in Great Britain 1758–1834*. Cambridge, MA: Harvard University Press.

Tocqueville, Alexis de. 1961. *Democracy in America*. [*De la démocratie*], trans. Henry Reeve. New York: Schocken.

Tönnies (Toennies), Ferdinand. 1957. *Community and Society*, trans. Charles P. Loomis of *Gemeinschaft und Gesellschaft*. East Lansing: Michigan State University Press.

Tuchman, Barbara W. 1978. *A Distant Mirror: The Calamitous Fourteenth Century*. New York: Knopf.

Turner, Henry Ashby, Jr. 1985. *German Big Business and the Rise of Hitler*. New York: Oxford University Press.

United Nations, Department of Economic and Social Affairs. 1963. *Report on the World Situation*. New York: United Nations.

———, Department of Social Affairs. 1952. *Preliminary Report on the World Situation: with Special Reference to Standards of Living*. E/CN.5/26/267/rev.1. New York: United Nations.

U.S. Bureau of the Census. 1960. *Historical Statistics of the United States, Colonial Times to 1957*. Washington, DC: U.S. Government Printing Office.

———. 2000. *Statistical Abstract of the United States*. Washington, DC: U.S. Government Printing Office.

———. 2001. *Statistical Abstract of the United States*. Washington, DC: U.S. Government Printing Office.

U.S. Congress. 1974. *Nomination of Nelson A. Rockefeller to Be Vice President of the United States. Hearings Before the Committee on the Judiciary, House of Representatives, Ninety-Third Congress*. Serial No. 45. Washington, DC: U.S. Government Printing Office.

U.S. Federal Register Division, National Archives and Record Service, General Services Administration. 1949a. *Public Papers of the Presidents of the United States: Harry S. Truman, January 1, 1949 to December 31, 1949*. Washington, DC: U.S. Government Printing Office.

———. 1949b. *Public Papers of the Presidents of the United States: Dwight D. Eisenhower, January 1, 1960 to December 31, 1960*. Washington, DC: U.S. Government Printing Office.

U.S. House Committee on the Judiciary. 1949. *Study of Monopoly Power. Hearings Before the Subcommittee on Study of Monopoly Power of the Committee on the Judiciary, House of Representatives, Eighty-First Congress*. First Session. Serial No. 14, Pt. 1. Washington, DC: U.S. Government Printing Office.

U.S. Senate Committee on the Judiciary. 1964. *Economic Concentration. Hearings Before the Subcommittee on Antitrust and Monopoly of the Committee on the Judiciary. United States Senate, Eighty-Eighth Congress*. Second Session. Part 1. Overall and Conglomerate Aspects. Washington, DC: U.S. Government Printing Office.

van Eeghen, Piet-Hein. 1997. "The Capitalist Case Against the Corporation." *Review of Social Economy* 55(1): 85–113.
Useem, Michael. 1984. *The Inner Circle: Large Corporations and the Rise of Business Political Activity in the U.S. and U.K.* New York: Oxford University Press.
Veblen, Thorstein. 1899, 1994. *The Theory of the Leisure Class: An Economic Study in the Evolution of Institutions.* New York: Penguin.
Ver Steeg, Clarence L. 1954. *Robert Morris Revolutionary Financier.* Philadelphia: University of Philadelphia Press.
Vitousek, P.M., P.R. Ehrlich, A.H. Ehrlich, and P.A. Matson. 1986. "Human Appropriation of the Products of Photosynthesis." *BioScience* 36: 368–373.
Waldman, Michael. 1990. *Who Robbed America? A Citizen's Guide to the S&L Scandal.* New York: Random House.
Wales, H.G. Quaritch. 1934. *Ancient Siamese Government and Administration.* London: Bernard Quaritch.
Wallerstein, Immanuel. 1976. *The Modern World-System: Capitalist Agriculture and the Origins of the European World-Economy in the Sixteenth Century.* New York: Academic.
Wanniski, Jude. 1978. *The Way the World Works: How Economies Fail—and Succeed.* New York: Basic Books.
Weaver, Richard M. 1948. *Ideas Have Consequences.* Chicago: University of Chicago Press.
Weber, Max. 1930. *The Protestant Ethic and the Spirit of Capitalism*, trans. Talcott Parsons. London: Allen and Unwin.
———. 1968. *Economy and Society: An Outline of Interpretive Sociology*, ed. Guenther Roth and Claus Wittich. 3 vols. New York: Bedminster.
Wetherell, Derrick. 2002a. "Fourteen Top Bush Officials Owned Stock in Enron." Special Report, *The Public I*, January 11. Washington, DC: Center for Public Integrity.
———. 2002b. "Snapshot of Professional and Economic Interests Reveals Close Ties Between Government, Business." Investigative Report, *The Public I*, January 16. Washington, DC: Center for Public Integrity.
Whitaker, Joseph. 1900. *An Almanack for the Year of Our Lord 1900.* Vol. 32. London: Whitaker.
White, Leslie A. 1949. *The Science of Culture.* New York: Grove.
Wilkinson, David. 1992. "Cities, Civilizations, and Oikumenes: I." *Comparative Civilizations Review* 27: 51–87.
———. 1993. "Cities, Civilizations, and Oikumenes: II." *Comparative Civilizations Review* 28: 41–72.
Williams, Eric. 1944. *Capitalism and Slavery.* Chapel Hill: University of North Carolina Press.
Williams, Gwyn A. 1963. *Medieval London: From Commune to Capital.* University of London: Athlone.
Williams, William A. 1961. *The Contours of American History.* Cleveland: World.
Williams, William A., and David J. Horowitz. 1975. "International Relations (1945–c. 1970)." *Encyclopaedia Britannica, Macropaedia*, vol. 9, pp. 751–778. Chicago. Encyclopaedia Britannica.
Wittfogel, Karl A. 1957. *Oriental Despotism: A Comparative Study of Total Power.* New Haven, CT: Yale University Press.
Woloch, Isser. 2001. *Napoleon and His Collaborators: The Making of a Dictatorship.* New York: Norton.

Wootton, David. 1986. *Divine Right and Democracy: An Anthology of Political Writing in Stuart England.* London: Penguin.
World Almanac. 1900. *The World Almanac and Encyclopedia 1900.* Vol. 7. New York: The Press.
World Bank. 2001. *World Development Indicators.* New York: Oxford University Press.
World Trade Organization (WTO). 2001. *World Trade Organization Annual Report, 2001.* Geneva: WTO.
Wright, Henry T. 1969. *The Administration of Rural Production in an Early Mesopotamian Town.* Anthropological Papers No. 38. Ann Arbor: Museum of Anthropology, University of Michigan.
Wright, Robin. 2000. *Nonzero: the Logic of Human Destiny.* New York: Pantheon.
Wrigley, E.A. 1967. "A Simple Model of London's Importance in Changing English Society and Economy 1650–1750." *Past and Present* 37: 44–70.
Wyatt, David K. 1968. "Family Politics in Nineteenth Century Thailand." *Journal of Southeast Asian History* 9(2): 208–228.
Yergin, Daniel. 1991. *The Prize: The Epic Quest for Oil, Money, and Power.* New York: Touchstone, Simon and Schuster.
Young, Oran R., ed. 1997. *Global Governance: Drawing Insights from the Environmental Experience*, ed. Oran R. Young. Cambridge, MA: MIT Press.
Zeitland, Maurice. 1989. *The Large Corporation and Contemporary Classes.* New Brunswick, NJ: Rutgers University Press.
Zipf, George Kingsley 1949. *Human Behavior and the Principle of Least Effort.* Cambridge, MA: Addison-Wesley.
Zweig, Philip L. 1995. *Wriston: Walter Wriston, Citibank, and the Rise and Fall of American Financial Supremacy.* New York: Crown.

Index

A

acculturation, 173
Adas, M., 34, 36
affluent society, 212
Agency for International Development (AID), 209
Agricultural Adjustment Act, 159
Alföldy, G., 94
Allen, M., 230
Alliance for Progress, 209
Allison, B., 250
allometric growth, 77
American Association of State Highway Officials (AASHO), 162
American Enterprise Institute, 230, 232
American Fur Company, 151
American Revolution, 139, 179, 182
Amish, 188
anarchy, 13, 32, 185–186
Ansell, C., 109
Appleton family, Boston, 147
arbitrage, 25

Archer Daniels Midland, 251
Argentina, British investments, 122–123
  Tehuelche Indians, 172
armaments, 100, 125
armies
  World War I, 158
  World War II, 76, 158
arms race, 208
Arthur Anderson, 250–251
Ashaninka, 28–33, 70–71, 173, 174
Ashton, T., 126
Asiatic mode of production, 34
Astor, J., 150–152
Australian aborigines, 67–70
autarky, 13, 32
automobiles, 160–164
autonomy, 32

B

bacteria, 65
Bali, 44–45, 96, 97
Baltzell, E., 150
bands, size, 68

283

Bangladesh famines, 219
Bank of England, 116–117, 120
Bank of North America, 140
Barney, G., 240
Bartlett, D., 228
Barton, B., advertising, 148
Bateman, J. 123, 130
Battle of Yorktown, 140
Baxter, R., 123
Beach, W., 223
Beard, C., 140, 142
Beard, C. & M., 138, 139
Beebe, L., 167
Beggars' democracy, 92
Behrens, C., 28
Beloch, K., 102
beneficial owners, 145
Berentson, J., 252, 256
Beresford, M., 107, 108
Beresford, P., 131
Berg, M., 180
Berle, A. Jr., 196–197, 251
Berreman, G., 66
Betzig, L., 95
big man, 30
biological success, 95
Birdsell, J., 69
Bluestone, B., 228
Bodley, J., 29, 117, 171, 213, 220, 257
Bodman, S., 251
Bogucki, P., 83
Bonaparte, Louis-Napoleon, 135
Bonaparte, Napoleon, 134–135, 187
 Grand Army, 76
Bookchin, M., 236
Booth, C., 191
Borsodi, R., 238
Boston Associates, 147, 186
Boston Manufacturing Company, 147, 154

Boston Tea Party, 139
bourgeoisie, 192–193
Bowlin, M., 241
Boyd, Augustus, 119
Brazil
 tribals, 173
 Indian Protectorate Service, 261
Bretton Woods Conference, 203, 222
Brewer, J., 124, 126
Bridgewater, Duke of, 125
British East India Company, 116, 120–122, 139
British Empire, 124
Broehl, W., 219–220
Brown, J., 63
Brown, L., 241
Brzezinski, Z., 231
Buckley, W., 222
Buddhism, 33, 86
bureaucracy, 74–76
Burke, E., 179, 185
Burke, P., 81
Burma, 84–86
Bush, G., President, 250–251
Business Roundtable, 231

C

Cain, P., 122, 124
cakravartin, 44
Califano, D., 49
Cambacérès, J., 135
Cantillon, R., 106
capital, 23, 26
capitalism, 22–27
Caplow, T. 67
Carcopino, J., 94
Carnegie Foundation, 202
Carneiro, R., 83, 88
Caro, C., 163, 168
Carosso, V., 157

Carrington, S., 120
Carroll, S., 64
Carruthers, B., 116, 124
Castallane, Count B., 167
Castells, M., 221
Cateau, H., 120
central place theory, 73
ceramics, commercial development, 125–126
Chadwick, Sir Edwin, 190
Chakri dynasty, 37–44
Chan Chan, 95
Chandler, A., 145, 153, 154
Chandler, D., 76, 135
Chandler, T., 90
Chartist Land Company, 182
Chartists, 181–182, 187
Chase Manhattan Bank, 231
Cheney, R., Vice President, 251
Chernow, R., 156
Chicago, population, 148
chiefdoms, 84–86
China
  Manchu dynasty, 93
  imperial palace, 96, 97
  silver demand, Ming China, 118
  urban places, 73
chrematisike, 19
Christaller, W., 71–73
circles of kings, 34
circumscription, 83
Citibank, 232–233
city-state, 99–100
civil society, 234
Civil War
  U.S., 155
  English, 79
civilization, origins, 91
Claeys, G., 186
Clark, G., 128
Clark, T.C., Attorney General, 245

class struggle, 193
Clay, H., 151
Clinton, D., Governor, 151
Clinton, W., President, 251
Cold War, 207, 209
Collier, C. & J., 141
Collier, P., 204
colonialism, 117–123
Colquhoun, P., 117, 119, 122, 127, 129
commercialization, 24–25
Committee for Economic Development (CED), 204, 231
commodification, 24
Communist Manifesto, 192–194
competitive exclusion, 63
concubines, 95
Connoly, M., 91
contest states, 34
Continental Congress, 138, 139
Cook, E., 58
Cooperative Extension Service, U.S. Department of Agriculture, 159
Cornford, F., 175
corporate socialism, 252
corporations
  global, 234
  U.S., 145–148
corporatization, 26–27
cosmic scale, 58
Council on Foreign Relations (CFR), 202–203, 231
Crimean War, 133
crisis of feudalism, 111
cui bono, 91
cultural selection, 65
culture, superorganic, 81

D

Dahl, R., 81
Dalzell, R., 147

Danko, W., 47
Darwin, C., 62, 190
Davis, G., 223
Davis, J., 144
Davis, L., 122, 123, 185
Day, E., 95
DeForest, R., 169
demand side economics, 198, 224
Demos, J., 241
despotism, 92–93
de Tocqueville, A., 148
De Vries, J., 192
Dewhurst, J., 204
Dickson, P., 116, 117, 12 , 188
diggers, 179
Dilworth, J., 249–250
Diocletian, Emperor, 103
distributive justice, 211
divine kings, 99
divine right of king, 178
Dolan, K., 134
Dollar, D., 214, 216
domestic space, 95–96, 97
Domhoff, G., 81, 159, 203, 204
domination, 74, 96–10
Drewnowski, A, 220
Dublin, T., 147
Dubois, J., 194
Dunbar, J., 251
Duncan-Jones, R., 92
Dunlop, I., 168
Dupuy, T., 100
Dye, T., 229
D'Altroy, T., 100

E

Earle, P., 188, 189
Earle, T., 100
Earth Charter Initiative, 262
East India Company, 116, 120–122, 139
Easterlin, R., 191
ecocide, 171
Edward I, King, 108
Egerton, F., 125
elites, definition, 81
Elizabeth I, Queen, 115, 118
Emergency Committee for Foreign Trade, 228
Emmott, B., 232
emperors, biological success, 95
empires of domination, 99
Encyclopaedia Britannica, 117
energy consumption, and social scale, 58
Engels, F., 187, 192–194
Engel's law, 52
Engerman, A., 120
England
  canal development, 125–126
  commercialization, 110–115
  grain merchants, 112
  land distribution, 130–131
  poor-rates, 188
  poor relief, 183
  poverty, 190
    London, 191
  primogeniture, 184
  property ownership, 130
  public health, 190
  taxation, 183–184
Enron Corporation, 250–251
Estes, R., 27, 247
ethnocide, 171
eunochs, 21
European Economic Community (EEC), 210
evolution, progressive, 61–64
exchange value, 25

exemplary centers, 34
externality, 27
externalization process, 26–27

F

factory breaking, 180–181
factory farms, 158–160
Federal Reserve, 198
Federal Reserve Act, 155
Federalists, 141
Feinstein, C., 128, 190
Ferguson, N., 133
financial revolution, 115–117
financialization process, 25
First Circumpolar People's Conference, 261
fiscal-military state, 123–125
Fischer, D., 111
Flagler, H., 167
Fletcher, R., 88, 89–91
Florence, Italy, 108–110, 112–114
Flynn, D., 118
Fogel, R., 153
Forbes 400, 224
Ford, H., 160
Formosan hill tribes, 172
Fortune 500 corporations, 49, 248, 250, 257
fossil fuels, 55, 90–91, 129, 133, 157–158, 159, 160, 240
Foundation Center, 230
foundations, 230
Fourier, C., 188
Fortune 500 corporations, 49
fractal geometry, 58–61
Franco–Prussian War, 133
Franklin, B., 182
Friedman, M., 223, 233
fur trade, 150–152

G

G-7 nations, 209
galactic polities, 34
Galbraith, J., 201, 212
Gallatin, A., Treasury Secretary, 151
Gardner, G., 219, 220
Gates, B., 62, 211
Geertz, C., 34, 35
Geertz, C. & H., 44–45
gemeinschaft, 66–67, 82, 88
Gemini, 13, 213, 216
General Agreement on Tariffs and Trade (GATT), 210
General Education Board, 159
General Electric, 228–229
General Foods, 245
General Motors, 148, 163–164, 194
genocide, 22, 171
George II, King, 132
George III, King, 120, 132
George, S., 220, 222, 223
Germany, urban places, 71–73
gesellschaft, 66–67, 82, 88
Giannini, A., 232
Gies, F., 96
Gilder, G., 240
Giráldez, A., 118
Gleick, J., 58
global
  governance, 232, 234
  hunger, 218–221
  income, 212
  population, 12
  poverty, 208–209
  warming, 240
Glorious Revolution, 116, 179
Goddard, S., 161–163, 196
Godfrey, Michael, 116
Godwin, W., 185–186
Gold Coast, Long Island, 167–168

gold bullion, European imports, 119
gold standard, 221–222
Gold Standard Act, 155
Goldschmidt, W., 158
Goldstein, J., 125
Goldthwaite, R., 110
good life, 236
Goodland, R., 260
Goodrich, C., 154
Gould, A., 167
Gould, S., 64, 65
grain merchants
  England, 112
  U.S., 160, 195
Gramm, W., 251
Grange movement, 195
Grant, A., 119–120
Grant, J., 155
Gras, N., 112
Great Britain
  capital growth, 128
  Colonial Office, 122
  Georgian income distribution, 127–129
  Parliament, 138, 117, 181, 182
Great Chain of Being, 178
Green, M., 247
Green Revolution, 220
greenhouse effect, 240
Greven, P., 241
Griswold, A., 44
Gross, D., 219
Grosvenor family, 131–132
Grosvenor Group Holdings, 132
growth thresholds, 238

H

Hadfield, C., 125
Hadrian, Emperor, 95
Hadrian's Villa, 95
Haeger, J., 151
Hagesteijn, R., 34
Hall, P., 144
Halweil, B., 219, 220
Hamilton, A., 141, 242
Hammack, D., 166
Hancock, D., 119
Hanks, L., 39, 44
Hannay, D., 126
Hansen, A., 203
Harrison, B., 228
Hart, G., Senator, 246–247
Hawaii, sandalwood trade, 152
Hayek, F., 222–223, 251
Hayes, P., 194
hegemonic empires, 99
Heller, N., 251
Henry VIII, King, 115, 176, 178
Herero, 172
Heritage Foundation, 230, 231
High Net Worth Individuals (HNWI), 216, 218
Hill, J., 196
Hinduism, 33, 86
Hoberman, L., 118
Holmes, K., 231
Homer-Dixon, T., 211
Hoover Institution, 230
Hopkins, A., 122, 124
Hopkins, K., 94, 102
Horowitz, D., 204
House of Morgan, 156–157
Hruska, ?., Senator, 247
Hubbert, M., 240
human rights, 15–16, 21, 173, 259
Hummel, R., 75
Hundred Years War, 108
Huntington, H., 161–162
Huttenback, R., 122, 123, 185
Hutterites, 188

hydraulic civilizations, 34

I

IBP, 251
imperia rankings
   American, 48, 226–227
   Chakri dynasty, 42
   Florentine, 114
   Georgian Great Britain, 129
   global, 212–215, 217–218
   Norman England, 98
   Roman, 94
   Stuart England, 128
imperialism, 63
imperium, definition, 4
Inca bureaucracy, 76
Indian Protectiorate Service, Brazil, 261
Indians, U.S. legal status, 143
indigenous people, 171–174, 258–262
Industrial Revolution, 180
   England, 188–192
   Great Britain, 125–127
   United States, 147
interlocking directories, 119, 248, 250
International Basic Economy Corporation (IBEC), 219–220
International Covenant of Human Rights, 173–174
International Harvester, 159
International Labour Organization (ILO), 260
International Monetary Fund (IMF), 202, 210, 221, 228
International Work Group for Indigenous Affairs (IWGIA), 261
Interstate Commerce Commission, 196

investors
   British, 122–123
   London, 118–119
   English canals, 126
   U.S. railroads, 146–147
invisible hand, 189–190, 252
iron manufacturing, 126–127
irreducible minimum, 15–16

J

Jaher, F., 150
James II, King, 116
Jay's Treaty, 151
Jefferson, T., 140, 151, 182, 242
Jewkes, J., 247
Johnson, A., 28
Johnson, B., 231
Johnson, C., 96
Johnson, G., 88, 90
Jones, A.H., 76, 139
Jonge, A., 135
J.P. Morgan and Co., 203
Judis, J., 222, 231
Jumsai, S., 37, 39

K

Kachin, 84–86
Kahn, H., 211
Kamehameha III, King, 152
Kefauver, ?., Senator, 246
Kelley, O., 195
Kennedy, J.F., President, 209
Kennickell, A., 49
Keynes, J., 197–198
Keynesian economic theory, 222
King, G., 127–128, 189
King, L., 71
Kirkpatrick, M., 231
Kirsch, A., 85

Kissinger, H., 206
Kohr, L., 236–237, 239
Komlos, J., 190
Kondratieff, N., 125
Kondratieff waves (K-waves), 125
Kosse, K., 67
Kraay, A., 214, 216
Krebs, A., 159
Kroeber, A., 81
Kroll, L., 134
Krupp Corporation, 194
Kutz, M., 249

L

Lachman, R., 108, 115
Lafayette, Marquis, 182
Laffer curve, 233
laissez-faire economics, 23, 222, 234, 197–198
Lamoreaux, N., 155
Landon, M., 37
Langford, P., 188
Lansing, C., 108
Las Casas, B., 259
law of the small number, 74
Lay, K., 250
læsa majestas, 37
Leach, E., 84–86
legionary economy, 101–103
Leininger, J., 251
Leonowens, A., 37
Levi-Strauss, C., 82
Lewis and Clark Expedition, 151
life chances, 93–95
life expectancy, 209
  England, 190
  Roman, 91–92
Lindeman, E., 230
Lindert, P., 190

Lindsey, L., National Economic Council, 251
Lloyd, H., 194–195
Locke, J., 179
lognormal distribution, definition, 57
London
  entrepreneurs, 188
  financial revolution, 115–117
  investors, 118–119
  population, 111
  poverty, 191
  real estate values, 130
Los Angeles, trolley lines, 161–162
Louis XIV, Versailles, 95
Louisiana Purchase, 151
Ludd, Ned, 180
Luddites, 180–181
Lundberg, F., 164, 165
Luten, D., 240–241

M

MacDonald, H., U.S. Bureau of Public Roads, 162–163
MacDonald, W., 95
macroparasites, 100
Madden, J., 158
Madison, J., 140
Mager, N., 125
Maisels, C., 99
Majewski, J., 153
malnutrition, 219
Malthus, T., 190, 218
Manchester, W., 194
Mandelbrot, B., 58–61
Mann, M., 4, 83, 99, 102
Mansel, P., 134
Manu, Hindu Code, 41–42
Marchand, R., 148
market scale, 252–258

market towns, 71–73
Marquet, P., 58
Marshall, J., U.S. Supreme Court Justice, 144
Marshall, P., 185
Marx, K., 25, 26, 34, 192–194
Mather, F., 125
Mathias, P., 124
Maurer, B., 63
Mayhew, B., 61
Mayhew, H., 191
McConnell, G., 159, 196
McCormick harvesters, 159
McCurdy, C., 145
McDonald, F., 140, 142
McKendrick, N., 125
McNeill, W., 100
Means, G., 196–197, 251
means of production, 26
Medici, Cosimo d,' 109, 112–114
Medici Bank, 112, 113
Medici imperium, 108–110, 112
Mencius, 18
Mercer, L., 154
merchants, London, 119–121
Mesopotamia, urbanism, 90
military contractors, 120
military technology, 100, 194
millionaires
  Great Britain, 130
  U.S., 47, 150, 164–169
Mills, C., 81, 206, 246
Miner, H., 260
Mintz, B, 233, 248–249
Mongkut, King, 37, 38, 40
monopoly power, 245, 246
Monroe, J., 151, 152
Montagu, Charles, 116
Moody, J., 156, 195, 245
Moore, B., 247
Moore, Sir Thomas, 176

Morgan, D., 160
Morgan, J.P., 156, 195, 232
Morgan, J.P. Jr., 156, 157, 167
Morgan, L., 62
Mormons, 188
Morris, I., 176
Morris, R., 139–140
Morrison, C., 122–123
Morton, F., 132, 133, 134
Moses, R., 163, 168
Mu Tsung, Emperor, 118
muckrackers, 194
multiplier effect, 99

N

Nader, R., 247
Nagara, N., 44
Napoleonic wars, 134–135, 151
  armaments, 126
Naroll, R., 95
Nash, J., 228–229
National Association of Manufacturers (NAM), 228, 231
National City Lines, 163
Native Americans, legal status, 143
natural selection, 65, 190
Nazis
  gas chambers, 194
  genocide, 173
Nazism, 222
neoliberal economic theory, 221–229
Neolithic paradox, 82
network law, 88
New Domesday survey, 130
New England, commercialization, 144
new growth economics, 222
New Guinea, tribals, 173
New Lanark, 186

New York City
  elites, 166–169
  market power, 252
  population, 148
Newman, K., 228
Newmyer, R., 144
News Tribune, 58
Nixon, R., President, 221
Noble, D., 145, 180, 224–225
noble savage myth, 14
Nolan, J., 91
Norman England
  aristocracy, 96, 98
  social class, 96, 98
North American Free Trade Agreement (NAFTA), 210
North Atlantic Treaty Organization (NATO), 207
nutrition transition, 220

O

O'Brien, P., 124
Odum, E., 58
Odum, H., 159
Offner, A., 130, 131
oikonomia, 19
Olmstead, A., 159
Olson, A., 138
optimum scale, 237
Organization of American States (OAS), 207
Organization of Petroleum Exporting Countries (OPEC), 221
organizational theory, 67
organizational traits, settlement size, 89
oriental despotism, 34
Oswald, R., 119–121
overpopulation, 211, 218
Owen, R., 186–187

P

Pacific Fur Company, 151
Padgett, J., 109
Paine, T., 182–185
Pareto, V., 57, 61
Pareto's law, 57
Paterson, William, 116
Peace Corps, 209
peaceful pacification, 173
Pennsylvania RR, 154
Pentagon Papers, 221
People's Charter, 181
Pessen, E., 149, 150
petroleum development, 133–134
Philadelphia, population, 148
Phillips, K., 224
Phillips Petroleum, 163
physiocrats, 106
Pinto, J. 95
Plato, 19
  Republic, 174–176
plutocracy, 176
Plymouth Colony, 241–242
Pocock, J., 179
Point Four Program, 209
Polanyi, K., 19, 197–198
politicization, definition, 18
polities, number of, 65
Pollard, S., 128
Poor Law, 181
Popkin, B., 220
population pressure, 111
populists, 195
Porter, K., 152
Post, E., 168
post optimum society, 238
Poster, M., 188
Poumisak, J., 37–39, 43
power, definition, 4
power elite, 81

power law, 55–61
price revolution, 111
price-fixing, 247
progressivists, 201, 222, 244–245
proletarians, 192–193
Protestant Reformation, 110, 115
Proudhon, P., 186

Q

Quesnay, F., 22

R

Rabb, T., 118
Rabibhadana, A., 37, 43
Radin, P., 15
Rand McNally, 252–256
Randall, M., 167, 168
Rational Society, 187
Reagonomics, 233
Redfield, R., 66–67
Reid, A. 35
Renaissance, 110
residential space, 95–96, 97
Rhode, P., 159
Riss, J., 169
Ritzer, G., 228
Roberts, C. & D., 98, 115
Robinson, E., 248
Rochester, A., 156
Rockefeller family, 157–158, 164, 204, 205, 249–250
  Rockefeller, J.D., 156, 157, 167, 195, 228, 230, 231, 249
  Rockefeller, J.D. Jr., 164, 204
  Rockefeller, N., 167, 204, 219, 249–250
Rockefeller Foundation, 202, 219, 230
Rockefeller Panel Reports, 204–208, 211
Rockefeller philanthropies, 159
Roman Empire
  army 76
  economy, 101–103
  human benefits, 91–92, 93
  slavery, 101–103
Rome
  health conditions, 92,
  population, 90
Roosevelt, T., 156
Roover, R., 109, 110, 112–114
Rostow, W., 211–212
Rothschild family, 132–134
Rove, K., 251
Roy, W., 145, 147, 153, 154
Rubinstein, W., 123, 130, 131, 134
ruling elite, 81
Rummel, R., 21–22, 173, 194
Rusk, D., 206
Russell, B., 229
Russell, J., 106
Russian Revolution, 192

S

Safeway Stores, 245
Sahlins, M., 63, 152
Santa Clara Co. vs. Southern Pacific Railroad, 148
Sargent II, John, 119
Savings and Loan bank collapses, 232
Scaife, R., 231
scalar stress, 88
scale, definition, 5
scale theory, assumptions, 80
Scheper-Hughes, N., 219
Schlosser, E., 220

294 INDEX

Schollaert, P., 61
Schulte-Nordholt, H., 44
Schumpeter, J., 197–198
Schwartz, M., 233, 248–249
Schweitzer, A., 194
scientific management, 198, 224–225
Sen, A., 219
Service, E., 63, 91
settlement size, organizational traits, 89
Seven Years War, 120
Seward, D., 134
Sewell, T., 160
sexual access, 95
Shapiro, M., 221
Sherman Antitrust Act, 157, 196
shrinking effect, 190–191
Shultz, G., 233
silver exports
  Manila, 118
  Mexico City, 118
Simon, D., 232
Singer Sewing Machine Company, 145
size commodities, 237–238
Skinner, G., 73
Sklar, H., 231
slave trade, 120
Small Business Senate Committee, 246
Smith, Adam, 22, 189–190
Snooks, G., 98, 127
Snow, A., 259
social caging, 83
social Darwinism, 190, 223
socialism, 187, 222
Solow, B., 120
Soltow, L., 39, 130, 149
Sorokim, P., 134, 165–165
South Sea Company bubble, 124

Southeast Asia, kingdoms, 33–36, 84–87
Southern Pacific Railroad, 148, 161–162
Southern Peru Copper Corporation, 233
Soviet communism, 222
Soviet Union, atrocities, 173
space, domestic, 95–96, 97
Special Studies Project, 204–208, 211
Spencer, H., 62
Staley, E., 108
Standard Oil Company, 157, 159, 163, 194, 195, 205
Stanley, T., 47
Stannard, D., 152
Steele, J., 228
Steinhart, J. & C., 159
Sternstein, L., 38
Steward, J., 68
Stone, L., 111, 128
Storey, J., U.S. Supreme Court Justice, 144
Stuart England, income distribution, 127–128
Suez Canal, 133
summum bonum, 236–238
sumptuary regulations, 93
superorganic, culture, 81
supply side economics, 198, 222
supralocalization, 26–27
survival of the fittest, 62, 190
Sutherland, D., 131
Sutton, A., 194

T

Tambiah, S., 34
taxes, corporate, 226
Taylor, F., 178, 224–225
technological distances, 238

Tehuelche, 122, 172
Teller, E., 206
Temporary National Economic Committee, 245
Tenement House Commission, New York, 169
territorial empire, 99
textile manufacturing, 180, 186
  U.S., 147
Thai kingdom, 37–44
  royal palace, 96, 97
Thatcher, M., 223
Thompson, D., 181, 182
Thompson, E., 182
Thornton, R., 142
Tilly, C., 180–181
Tönnies, F., 66–67, 82
Too Big to Fail, 139
totalitarianism, 192–194, 222, 245
transnational business, 234
tribal peoples, depopulation, 117
  versus commercial societies, 171–174
Trilateral Commission, 231–232
Truman, H., President, 209, 245
Tuchman, B., 111
Tudor England, commercialization, 112–115
Turner, H., 194
Tuscany, 108–110
Twentieth Century Fund, 204
tyranny, 176

U

U.S.
  Articles of Confederation, 141
  Bureau of the Census, 51, 138, 155, 156

U.S. *(continued)*
  Chamber of Commerce, 228
  Congress, 250
  Constitution, 140–142
    First Amendment, 145
    Preamble, 244
  Federal Register Division, 208, 209
  Federal Road Act, 161
  Homestead Act, 143
  House Committee on the Judiciary, 245
  Legal Tender Acts, 155
  National Bank Act, 155
  Senate Committee on Small Business, 246
  Senate Judiciary Subcommittee on Antitrust, 246, 247
U.S. Steel, 194
Ulmer, M., 246
Underwood, B., 219
United Nations, 202
  Commission on Human Rights, 261
  Declaration of Human Rights, 173
  Declaration of Independence, 139, 182
  Department of Economic and Social Affairs, 211
  Department of Social Affairs, 208
  Declaration on the Rights of Indigenous Peoples, 262
  Food and Agriculture Organization, 219
  International Covenant of Human Rights, 173–174
  International Fund for Agricultural Development, 219
  Universal Declaration of Human Rights, 15–16, 21
  World Food Council, 219
  World Food Program, 219

296 INDEX

United States
  Big Business, 143–148
  financial imperia, 155–157
  financiers, 154
  Fourteenth Constitutional
    Convention, 141–142
  growth alternatives, 242–244
  highway system, 162–163
  imperia, 45–53
  income tax, 225, 164
  Indian Wars, 143
  population, 142
  property distribution, 149
  railroads, U.S., 152–154,
    195–196
    investors, 146–147
  Social Security, 198
  streetcars, 161
  trolley lines, 161
  wealthy, 149–150
urbanization, 71–73, 88–91,
  105–108, 143–144
use value, 25
Useem, M., 248
utopia, 174
Utopia (Sir Thomas Moore),
  176–178

V

van Eeghen, P., 252
Veblen, T., 167, 240
Veiller, L., 169
Ver Steeg, C., 140
Versailles, 95
village-state, 99–100
Viner, J., 203
violence, 21–22
Vitousek, P., 66

W

Waldman, M., 232
Wales, H., 37, 43
Waleys, Sir Henry le, 107–108
Wall Street, investment firms, 49
Wallerstein, I., 110, 115
Wanniski, J., 231
War of 1812, 151
Washington, G., 139, 182, 242
Washington State
  billionaires, 58
  imperia, 47
  social power, 257–258
  wheat production, 160
Wasserstein, B., 247
Watanabe, K., 232
Watergate, 221
Watt, J., 126–127
Weaver, R., 222
Weber, M., 25–26, 74–75
Wedgwood, J., 125–126, 127
Westminster, Duke of, 131–132
Wetherell, D., 251
Whitaker, J., 130
White, L., 62–63, 81
White, T, Army Secretary, 251
Wiener, A., 211–212
Wilkinson, D., 90
Wilkinson, J., 126
William, Duke of Hanau, 132,
  133
Williams, E., 120
Williams, W., 202
Williamson, J., 190
Wittfogel, K., 34, 92–93
Wolfowitz, P., 232
Woloch, I., 135
Woolworth, F., 167–168

Wootton, D., 179
World Almanac, 118
World Bank, 31, 202, 210, 212–218, 221, 234, 260
World Economic Forum (WEF), 231–232
World Trade Organization (WTO), 210–211, 234
Wright, H., 90
Wright, R., 63–64
Wrigley, E., 111
Wriston, W., 232–233
Wyatt, D., 41

Y

Yergin, D., 134

Z

Zeitland, M., 145
Zipf, G., 57
Zoellick, R., U.S. Trade Representative, 251
Zweig, P., 232–233
Zyklon B gas, 194

John H. Bodley is Edward R. Meyer Distinguished Professor of Anthropology at Washington State University, where he has taught since 1970. His Ph.D. is from the University of Oregon (1970). He conducted anthropological fieldwork in eastern Peru, supported by the National Science Foundation in 1966, 1968–69, and 1976–77. He was a visiting researcher at the International Work Group for Indigenous Affairs in Copenhagen (1980) and a visiting lecturer in cultural anthropology at the University of Uppsala, Sweden (1985), at the University of Alaska-Fairbanks (1986), and at the University of Vermont (2000). He served as a member of the Human Rights Subcommittee of the American Association for the Advancement of Science Committee on Scientific Freedom and Responsibility (1991–94).